Demagogue for President

Demagogue
for President

The Rhetorical Genius of Donald Trump

JENNIFER MERCIECA

TEXAS A&M UNIVERSITY PRESS | COLLEGE STATION

Library of Congress Cataloging-in-Publication Data

Names: Mercieca, Jennifer R., author.
Title: Demagogue for president: the rhetorical genius of
Donald Trump / Jennifer R. Mercieca.
Description: First edition. | College Station:
Texas A&M University Press, [2020] | Includes index.
Identifiers: LCCN 2019057727 | ISBN 9781623499068 (cloth)
| ISBN 9781623499075 (ebook)
Subjects: LCSH: Trump, Donald, 1946—Language. | Rhetoric—Political
aspects—United States—History—21st century. | Communication in
politics—United States—History—21st century. | Personality and
politics—United States—History—21st century. | Populism—
United States—History—21st century. | United States—
Politics and government—2017–
Classification: LCC E913.3 .M47 2020 | DDC 973.933092—dc23
LC record available at https://lccn.loc.gov/2019057727

In gratitude, I dedicate this book
to the journalists who did their best
to try to hold Trump accountable
for his words and actions.

〜

Contents

Preface

Warning! This book is going to make you angry. There is no way around it. You will get angry at me (your humble rhetoric scholar). You will get angry at Donald Trump (both the hero and the villain of this story). You will get angry at the media (both fake and real). And you will get angry at your fellow Americans. Trump does that to people: he makes them angry. And he's really good at it. Oh, there are some bad words in here too. Try to keep your wits about you.

~~~

When I received an email from Patrick Healy at the *New York Times* inviting me to participate in a week-long analysis of Donald Trump's campaign rhetoric in November 2015, I agreed enthusiastically. Since 2009 I had been trying to finish an essay on the history of demagogues, so I had done my share of research on them, and I had been—like everyone else—following Trump's campaign closely. At that moment in the campaign, Trump had already called Mexicans rapists, had already insisted that he saw Muslims celebrating in New Jersey on 9/11, had already mocked a reporter for the *New York Times* with a physical disability, and had already promised to build a wall along our southern border (and make Mexico pay for it). I learned from Healy that the *Times* was going to study Trump's language to see if it contained any demagoguery.[1] He wondered: What did I see in Trump's rhetoric that would signal demagoguery? And how did Trump compare to previous American demagogues like George Wallace, Huey Long, or Father Coughlin?

 I'm a rhetoric professor who teaches classes on argumentation, political communication, propaganda, social movements, and other things related to American history and democratic practice. I believe in the promise of American democracy. I believe that the tools of rhetoric and argument should help us solve problems and not be used for manipulation. I think that democracy should be the standard by which we judge our political leaders. I don't hate

Donald Trump. I recognize with begrudging admiration that he is very good at using rhetoric as a weapon, in fact. However, because I think that weaponized rhetoric is antidemocratic, I think that Trump's rhetoric is bad for American democracy.

I took my assignment from Healy seriously back in 2015. I watched all of Trump's speeches that week, listened to his interviews, read his tweets. When I was done, I had a list of six rhetorical tactics that Trump used repeatedly throughout the week to attract attention, attack his opponents, and prevent himself from being held accountable for his words and actions. I spoke with Healy about my observations; sent him my notes, as well as notes on rhetorical theorist Kenneth Burke's *Rhetoric of Motives* and his essay "The Rhetoric of Hitler's Battle"; and hoped that I had said something useful about how Trump's rhetoric worked.[2] The resulting story appeared on Sunday, December 6, 2015, on the front page of the *Times*, above the fold, under the headline "95,000 Words, Many of Them Ominous, from Donald Trump's Tongue."[3] Healy and Maggie Haberman used a few quotes from me to support their analysis, but they didn't use my six rhetorical terms. Still, I was pleased to be part of their excellent "deep dive" into Trump's language use. This was my first time being quoted in the *New York Times*. I didn't know that being quoted in the *Times* would be a life-changing event—and maybe it isn't always—but, for me, it was. Trump has a talent for attracting attention, which has a halo effect on researchers like me who study him.

Requests from reporters flooded my inbox, and I answered them. *The Conversation* invited me to write a piece on Trump and demagoguery. I agreed and typed up my research notes into a short article. That article was published under the headline "The Rhetorical Brilliance of Trump the Demagogue" and went on to be reproduced by at least twenty publishers; it was read worldwide and even translated into Japanese by *Newsweek*.[4] More reporters emailed. More article invitations followed. Over the course of the election, at least 250,000 people read my articles on Trump's rhetoric in *The Conversation*. And I have no idea how many people read quotes from me about him or heard me talk about him. I was invited on podcasts and radio programs. I was invited to be a panelist at high-profile public events like the Zócalo/Getty Villa conversation about demagoguery.[5] Famous reporters tweeted things I wrote. My explanation and definition of *paralipsis* ("I'm not saying; I'm just saying") was the word of the day (twice!). I was offered book contracts. And when Trump was inaugurated I was invited on NPR's *All Things Considered*, where I repeated (again) the same example of Trump using *paralipsis* from that week when I studied what Trump said for the *New York Times*.

It's been exhausting, terrifying, exhilarating, and humbling to be a part of the public conversation about Trump's demagoguery. The public response to my work—comments on articles, emails, tweets, phone calls, letters sent to my office (engagement, as they say)—was intense but mostly positive. I was criticized by Clinton supporters and by Trump supporters. Right-wing pundit Ann Coulter took the time to roll her eyes at me on Twitter when the *New York Times* article came out, which startled me, to be honest. Things got a little scary when a panel that I was on at the *Texas Tribune's* TribFest was ambushed by conspiracy theorist Alex Jones, who turned it into political theater for *InfoWars*.[6] But lots of people also encouraged me to keep writing and talking. Folks were kind enough to say that my explanations were useful.

I'm not a journalist, which means that I didn't interview anyone to write this book. I study texts and what has been said in public. This is a history book—a history of the present. To write this book, I've watched and rewatched every Trump rally. I've transcribed most of them. I've read Trump's books. I've watched all of his interviews and read his tweets. I've read as many articles as I could about what Trump was doing and why in traditional and nontraditional media. I've read white nationalists, conspiracy theorists, and the manosphere—all Trump's people—which helped me make sense out of Trump's more perplexing appeals. I've studied Trump relentlessly, in order to be able to explain his rhetorical strategies clearly. In October 2018 Jonathan Tilove of the *Austin-American Statesman* called me "probably the leading authority on Trump's rhetoric."[7] I maybe probably am. This is my take on how Trump used demagogic rhetoric to take advantage of preexisting distrust, polarization, and frustration to win the presidency in 2016.

Acknowledgments

I began writing about Trump's rhetoric in December 2015, and I've accrued a lot of debts since then. First, I'd like to thank the many journalists whose work I've quoted here. I couldn't have written this without the work of the dedicated professionals working in journalism today. I also learned a lot from the journalists with whom I talked while I was writing this book. Ostensibly they were interviewing me about Trump's rhetoric, but I benefited tremendously from being able to talk to them. I can't thank each person by name here, but I want to mention Maggie Haberman, Jonathan Tilove, and Matt Taibbi in particular for helping me understand different aspects of Trump's appeals. I also learned a lot from colleagues and audiences at the public talks that I gave about Trump's rhetoric. I'd like to thank Cara Finnegan and John Murphy at the University of Illinois, James Jasinski at the University of Puget Sound, and Meredith Johnson at the University of South Florida for their generous invitations to share my work in progress. I have several debts regarding the title of the book: Ashley Merryman helpfully told me that I had the parts of my book title backward, and Jonathan Tilove and Mike Pesca both helped me with the "genius" part of the title. Finally, I was incredibly fortunate in the fall of 2018 to have a Glasscock Humanities Center Internal Faculty Fellowship, which allowed me to complete this manuscript.

Since I wrote and thought and talked about Trump's rhetoric a lot in public between 2015 and 2019, many of the ideas, examples, and some of the writing have appeared elsewhere. As noted previously, I published several articles with *The Conversation*: "The Rhetorical Brilliance of Trump the Demagogue," "How Donald Trump Gets Away with Saying Things Other Candidates Can't," "Can America's Deep Political Divide Be Traced back to 1832?," "In Acceptance Speech, Trump Embraces Role as Hero of the Forgotten," "Donald Trump and the Dangerous Rhetoric of Portraying People as Objects," and "100 Days of Presidential Threats." I also published several articles with *Zócalo*: "When Paranoid Rhetoric and Falsehoods Prevail, Public Trust Crumbles," "The Greatest Story Ever Told about Hyperbole,

Humbug, and P. T. Barnum!," and "Preaching Civility Won't Save American Democracy." I wrote about dangerous demagogues and why we can think of Trump as an anarchist in two scholarly pieces: one in *Rhetoric Society Quarterly* (see the article "Dangerous Demagogues and Weaponized Communication") and another in Dr. Ryan Skinnell's 2018 *Faking the News: What Rhetoric Can Teach Us about Donald J. Trump* (see the chapter "Trump as Anarchist and Sun King"). I'm grateful to the three editors who helped me refine my ideas and writing as I was working on this book: Nick Lehr at *The Conversation*; Joe Matthews at *Zócalo Public Square*; and Ryan Skinnell, who edited my pieces for *RSQ* and *Faking the News*.

I'm especially grateful to my awesome editor at Texas A&M University Press, Jay Dew. When I started writing this book, I didn't think that Trump was going to win the election. The day after the election, I sent Jay a note asking him if I could really write a book calling the president of the United States a demagogue. Jay stood by me then ("Yes, it's academic freedom," he said), and he has stood by me and this project throughout. I know how lucky I am that Jay supported my choice to write this book in a way that I thought would best communicate how Trump's rhetoric works. I also have had the pleasure of working on this book with the world's best undergraduate editorial assistant, Maggie. I'm so grateful to Maggie for all of her help, but I'm especially glad that she loves to format endnotes (almost nine hundred!). She was the first one to read every draft and offered me great suggestions about how to make it better. And, finally, to D and V—you have my love, forever.

Demagogue for President

Introduction

Demagogue for President

The Announcement Spectacle

An hour before he was scheduled to announce his presidential campaign, members of Donald Trump's staff stood outside Trump Tower in New York City, inviting tourists to "come inside and make some memories."[1] Once inside the building's gleaming orange-and-pink marble and gold interior, staffers handed the tourists "Make America Great Again" T-shirts and signs reading "We Want Trump" and "Trump for Our Future," instructing them to stand near the Tower's famous escalators. The tourists joined hundreds of others—many were paid actors—also wearing staff-provided shirts and carrying signs.[2] The casting call had asked for actors willing to "help cheer him in support of his announcement," and so the tourists and the actors played their role. After his daughter Ivanka introduced him as "the opposite of politically correct," the tourists and actors could be seen enthusiastically waving their signs as Neil Young's "Rockin' in the Free World" blared out loudly from a sound system. Donald Trump and his wife Melania slowly descended from the upper reaches of the fifty-eight-story Trump Tower toward the stage below.[3] This was "some group of people, thousands," Trump enthused as he arrived at the podium to announce his plan to run for president and make America great again.[4] "It's great to be at Trump Tower," he said. "It's great to be in a wonderful city, New York. And it's an honor to have everybody here. This is beyond anybody's expectations. There's been no crowd like this."[5]

While members of the media gave credibility to Trump's presidential announcement event by reporting on it in large numbers, they did not report that they found Trump to be a credible candidate. "Donald J. Trump, the garrulous real estate developer whose name has adorned apartment buildings, hotels, Trump-brand neckties and Trump-brand steaks," Alexander Burns wrote drolly in the *New York Times*, "announced on Tuesday his entry into the 2016 presidential race, brandishing his wealth and fame as chief qualifications in an improbable quest for the Republican nomination."[6] Like the *Times*, most news reports of the event could barely contain their amused derision at "Trump's funhouse-mirror presidential campaign announcement."[7] Some news organizations did not even try. The conservative *National Review* described Trump's event as a "witless ape [riding an] escalator."[8] *Salon* announced, "The puckered sleazebag takes the plunge—America's least-respected reality TV star declares his 2016 intentions and makes life hell for the GOP."[9] *Rolling Stone* offered a bit more nuance when it explained that "Trump is widely considered to be an unserious candidate, a man who—despite an incredible amount of resources—is unlikely to secure the GOP nomination, and who is more interested in garnering attention."[10] *The Daily Beast* offered what turned out to be the most prescient take on Trump's campaign when it punned that it was "the best new reality TV show this season."[11]

While media reports derided the Trump presidential announcement spectacle, his speech specifically was ridiculed as "unending, utterly baffling, often-wrong" and a "rambling, hour-long stream-of-consciousness" that "strongly resembled performance art." Most news reports highlighted the controversial moments from Trump's speech, finding evidence that he was an arrogant, absurd, and racist charlatan, and arguing that the errors in judgment found in the content of the speech demonstrated that Trump was unelectable.[12] Reporters thought that Trump sounded hyperbolically arrogant when he said things like "I'm really rich" and "I will be the greatest jobs president that God ever created." Reporters thought that Trump sounded absurd when he said things like "[y]ou have to be hit by a tractor, literally, a tractor, to use [Obamacare], because the deductibles are so high; it's virtually useless." Reporters thought that Trump sounded racist when he said things like "when Mexico sends its people, they're not sending their best. . . . They're sending people that have lots of problems and they're bringing those problems with us. They're bringing drugs. They're bringing crime. They're rapists." And, finally, reporters thought that he sounded like a charlatan when he said, "I would build a great wall—nobody builds walls better than me. . . . And I would have Mexico paying for that wall."[13] And yet, despite all of the media disbelief that his "ludicrous" announcement meant that he would *really* launch an *actual* presidential campaign, Trump's spokesperson Hope Hicks sent out a press release claiming that indeed "today, Donald J. Trump announced his candidacy for President of the United States of America."[14]

Trump's speech drew more attention on social media than any other

Republican in the crowded primary field: many social media users joined in the chorus of derision found in traditional media outlets, but many others embraced Trump's campaign slogan, hoping that he could indeed make America great again. Several news stories reported that Trump's announcement prompted Twitter to have "the best day ever" and included roundups of celebrities, political pundits, and regular folks having a good time at Trump's expense: "If Donald wins the presidency he'll host another season of celebrity apprentice to fill his cabinet," quipped Hillsdale College student Thomas Novelly.[15] "Donald Trump sounds like America's drunk conservative uncle," observed Abby Johnston of the *Texas Monthly*.[16] Former Obama senior advisor Dan Pfieffer thought that "[t]he Trump candidacy is a *Veep* storyline that would have been discarded for being too absurd even for an HBO comedy."[17] And so on.[18]

But not all was fun and mocking on Twitter: Fox News took Trump's campaign more seriously than most, posting "Trump Delivers a Message Republicans Need," which included a video of news anchor Greta Van Susteren describing Trump's speech as "dazzling" and inviting viewers to tweet their responses to Trump's announcement to her.[19] In response, Saltwater Patricia said, "I love it. We need someone like him who's not afraid to tell it like it is" and included Trump's campaign slogan as a hashtag: "#MakeAmericaGreatAgain."[20] Another Fox viewer replied, "If anyone can Make America Great Again he can! If given the chance he will do great things for our country!"[21] Also using Trump's campaign slogan hashtag was Peter Enimil, who wrote that he supported Trump because he thought that he was a successful businessman: "Being a President is like owning a business. You need a way better CEO and who is better than Donald Trump? Let's Make America Great Again."[22] Proud Boy Nick thought that Trump alone could break the national gridlock: "Donald Trump WILL succeed where government has failed. This may be our ONLY opportunity to break through bureaucracy & get work done!" He also decried the media's treatment of Trump's announcement, fearing that "the media is not taking TRUMP seriously, they are all there talking about him & HE IS RIGHT!"[23] Sarah Carlson, like others, applauded Trump for being so honest and expressive, exclaiming that she loved "how Donald Trump speaks his mind regardless!"[24]

Facebook reported that 3.4 million users shared information about Trump 6.4 million times in the 24 hours after he announced his campaign; by comparison, that's nearly eight times more interest than Facebook reported

for Florida Governor Jeb Bush after his announcement just the day before—
users posted 849,000 messages about Bush. According to Google, Trump
was the most searched for Republican in every state the day of his announcement, and his "search interest"—the percentage of national queries for the
hour after he announced—was 87 percent.[25] We can say therefore at least that
Trump's announcement was successful in gaining him attention, if not universal respect, as a presidential candidate. And beyond this, we can say that
Trump's message of making America great again by protecting the nation's
borders, rejecting political correctness, and fighting corruption resonated
with some Americans on the day of his announcement. Eventually that message would win him the presidency, so why was it so difficult for political
pundits and reporters to take Trump's presidential campaign seriously on the
day of his announcement?

Well, for one reason, he didn't sound presidential. He didn't sound like
a typical presidential candidate and so political observers rejected his campaign as absurd. But perhaps the pundits simply did not understand Trump's
rhetorical strategy, which makes much more sense in retrospect. Trump's
unpresidential speech was designed to appeal to the distrusting, polarized,
and frustrated Americans who desired a change in leadership. Like 2008,
2016 was a "change election" year, and according to political science "fundamentals," any Republican should have defeated any Democrat in 2016.[26] But
of all the GOP hopefuls who ran, why did Republicans choose Trump? As
much as Barack Obama had *looked* different from every previous president
in 2008, Donald Trump *sounded* different from every previous president in
2016. For Trump's supporters, his aggressive and politically incorrect rhetoric toward the establishment was his best argument for why he should be
president. His absurd rhetoric was appropriately targeted to audiences who
thought that American politics was itself absurd.

One take on Trump's announcement event wondered if Trump might
be "America's most gifted political satirist," more akin to an entertainer like
Stephen Colbert than, say, a politician like Obama. Elspeth Reeve wrote in
The New Republic that as a satirist, "Trump's greatest genius is offering the
same political analysis we hear on sober Sunday talk shows, delivered in the
language of a vulgar oaf."[27] To be sure, Trump claimed to be a genius and he
used vulgar language. That vulgar language would have disqualified anyone
else from the presidency in a typical election year, but 2016 was not a typical election and Donald Trump was not a typical candidate. It was difficult

to understand at the moment in June 2015 that his vulgarity *was his appeal* because it enabled him to appear as an authentic truth teller—what the ancient Greeks might have called a *parrhesiastes*, "the one who speaks the truth"— which corroborated his claims of being able to put an end to widespread corruption in government if elected.[28] Ironically, when the establishment media mocked Trump, it only proved the validity of his outsider status—a tricky status to acquire for someone who claimed to be a billionaire real-estate mogul member of the ultra-elite.

Truth Teller or Demagogue?

Once political rivals, pundits, and reporters stopped laughing at Trump's campaign, they soon began to call him a demagogue—especially once he surged in the polls. On June 30, 2015, *Chicago Tribune* reporter Eric Zorn was one of the first (if not the first) to explain that you could laugh all that you wanted, but Trump's campaign wasn't a joke. In fact, after spending time with Trump during his interview with the *Tribune*'s editorial board shortly after his June 16 announcement, Zorn wrote that "in politics, simple sells. And Trump is a consummate salesman. I don't see him as a fearless truth-teller. I see him as a populist demagogue."[29] Not many seemed to notice Zorn's warning, but by July 11, 2015, Republican senator and GOP presidential hopeful Lindsey Graham appeared on CNN to denounce Trump's controversial remarks about immigrants: "What I think he's doing is being a demagogue," said Graham. "As a party, we should reject what he says because it's not true. And if we don't reject it we've lost the moral authority, in my view, to govern this country."[30] Graham's remarks received a great deal of attention in the media and resulted in the exchange of several insults between him and Trump. Trump ended the dispute by aggressively "doxxing" Graham, releasing his private cell phone number to a rally crowd in his home state of South Carolina on July 21, 2015.[31] Trump told CNN's Anderson Cooper that he was justified in releasing Graham's phone number: "Am I supposed to say that it's OK? I'm called a jackass. You have to fight back. And the country has to fight back."[32] Trump's aggressive tactics were praiseworthy, according to Trump, because in fighting for himself he was also fighting for America.

Zorn and Graham may have been the first to call Trump a "demagogue," but they were most certainly not the last. Throughout the presidential campaign he was called a demagogue: political opponents like Republican former

Texas governor Rick Perry, Republican Texas senator Ted Cruz, and Democratic Party nominee Hillary Clinton called Trump a demagogue; news organizations like the *New York Times, The Atlantic*, and Politico called Trump a demagogue; notable historians and political scientists like Garry Wills, H. W. Brands, Michael Singer, and Michael Kazin called Trump a demagogue.[33] Folks found many reasons to call Trump a demagogue. Politico's Jack Shafer called Trump a demagogue for "crimes against logic, his pandering to the uninformed, and his manipulative emotionalism."[34] Breitbart's Sydney Williams called Trump a demagogue for "spew[ing] vitriol rather than hope."[35] *USA Today* called Trump a "dangerous demagogue" for being "erratic," "ill-equipped to be commander in chief," trafficking in "prejudice," having a "checkered" business career, not "leveling with the American people," speaking "recklessly," coarsening the "national dialogue," and being a "serial liar."[36] Conservative columnist David Brooks called Trump "the kind of demagogue our Founders feared would upset the American experiment."[37] Even physicist Stephen Hawking called Trump "a demagogue who seems to appeal to the lowest common denominator."[38] According to Google Trends, search interest in "Trump demagogue" peaked between July 24 and July 30, 2016, during the Democratic National Convention in Philadelphia, where former New York mayor Michael Bloomberg called Trump a "dangerous demagogue" and President Barack Obama obliquely called Trump a "homegrown demagogue" in each of their convention addresses.[39]

So many called Trump a demagogue that some journalists began urging one another to stop referring to him using terms like "demagogue" and "fascist," and especially to stop comparing Trump to Hitler.[40] Someone even asked Trump how he felt about being compared to Hitler so frequently—George Stephanopoulos had the temerity to ask Trump the question directly on December 8, 2015, after the *Philadelphia Daily News* placed Trump on their cover with the headline "The New Furor" with his arm raised, seemingly making a Nazi salute.[41] Trump phoned in on *Good Morning America* to respond: "You are being compared to Hitler. Does that give you pause at all?" asked Stephanopoulos. Trump said that it did not "because what I'm doing is no different from what FDR [did]. . . . This is a president who was highly respected by all."[42] Trump "anchored" himself to FDR to dismiss the comparison to Hitler, thereby attempting to shift the audience's focus away from the point of the question.

When Rick Perry called Trump a demagogue in July 2015, Trump tweeted that Perry "doesn't understand what the word demagoguery means."[43] Perry might well have been confused. So what does the word "demagoguery" mean? First, let's note that technically both Trump and Perry are confused because there is a difference between a "demagogue" and "demagoguery." A demagogue (Greek: *dēmagōgos* from *dēmos* "the people" + agōgos "leading") is a person, a kind of leader. Although the word frequently has a negative connotation, it is technically understood more neutrally as "a leader of the people." Demagoguery is a way of communicating. It also has a negative connotation, but it is technically understood more neutrally as "demagogic practices and arts."[44]

What Trump a demagogue? Was Trump a demagogue because he inspired politically incorrect or hateful vitriol at his campaign rallies? Was Trump like Hitler? Was Trump like Hitler because he was shown on the cover of a tabloid making what appeared to be a Nazi salute? Or was Trump a *parrhesiastes*—a "fearless truth-teller"—like he claimed? Of course, it depends on who you ask. When we call Trump a "demagogue" or a "*parrhesiastes*," we use rhetoric to constitute him in particular ways.[45] Constitutive rhetoric can be thought of as similar to "framing" an issue—we use language to call attention to certain aspects of a person or thing, and in so doing we make those aspects the most meaningful or important for understanding it. If we constitute Trump as a truth teller, then we highlight very different things compared to if we constitute him as a demagogue. There is obviously a lot at stake in charging someone with being a demagogue, so we ought to tread carefully.

What is the technical difference between a truth teller (*parrhesiastes*) and a demagogue? Let's examine the notion of a "truth teller" first. The Ancient Greeks understood that a parrhesiastes "risks his life because he recognizes truth telling as a duty to improve or help other people."[46] There were five elements of fearless speech (*parrhesia*): frankness (saying all that you know); truth (speaking what you know to be true); danger (speaking the truth despite the risk to your safety); criticism (criticizing those in positions of power over you); and duty (feeling obligated to tell your truth to power, despite the risk). An authentic truth teller believed that it was his or her duty to speak their mind freely, holding back nothing that they believed to be true, even though criticism of those in power might put his or her life in jeopardy. The key elements of *parrhesia* were authenticity and risk: a *parrhesiastes* was a *parrhesiastes* because he or she risked life and limb to speak the truth, and this truth was understood to be *actually* true because of the risk involved in speaking it—no risk, no authentic truth. Based upon these criteria, was Trump a truth teller?

What would it mean for Trump to risk his life in the context of his presidential announcement or his presidential campaign? In his announcement speech and throughout his campaign, he practiced criticism by condemning politicians, media, other nations, immigrants, protestors, and numerous other people and groups. (A running list from the *New York Times* had Trump insulting 289 people over the course of his campaign with his Twitter feed alone.) Did those insults make Trump a *parrhesiastes*? Was it a dangerous thing to do? Was he risking his life by speaking truth to power? Perhaps not. Was "low-energy Jeb," for example, really going to harm Trump physically because of Trump's criticisms of him? It seems unlikely, particularly given Trump's aggressiveness compared to Bush's besweatered and mild-mannered habitus. Was Trump's life in danger for what he said about "Liddle Marco," "Lyin' Ted," the "Dishonest Media," or "Crooked Hillary"? No, his life was not literally in danger—at least not from the traditional politicians whom he insulted.

If Trump's life was not truly in danger for truth telling, could we say that he was still a *parrhesiastes* because he was authentically speaking the truth? Throughout his campaign, his statements became the subject of scrutiny by nonpartisan fact-checkers like FactCheck.org and Politifact, who routinely rated his statements as false. By December 2016, Politifact had rated 342 of his statements: Only 14 (4 percent) were rated "true." The overwhelming majority of his statements, 290 (85 percent), were rated either "half-true," "mostly false," "false," or "pants on fire."[47] Trump just shrugged at these rebukes and called the fact-checkers liars. They wouldn't admit the truth, he said, because they were dishonest and corrupt. Perhaps Trump had a point. As *Rolling Stone*'s Matt Taibbi noted, Trump's critiques of the corruption of the "triumvirate of big media, big donors and big political parties" *was* true. "No one should be surprised" about Trump's success during the Republican primary, Taibbi wrote, "because everything he's saying about his GOP opponents is true. They really are all stooges on the take, unable to stand up to Trump because they're not even people, but are, like Jeb and Rubio, just robo-babbling representatives of unseen donors."[48] Trump may indeed have told some truths, but it is difficult to call him an authentic "truth teller" in the classical sense.

If we ignore the standards established for truth telling in Ancient Greece or by fact-checkers, then could we say that Trump was a truth teller because he claimed that he was one? Could we call him a truth teller because his supporters believed that he did, in fact, tell the truth? It's more accurate to describe Trump as a person who has successfully marketed himself as a truth teller than it is to describe him as an authentic truth teller. Trump had established his image as a truth teller through his years of starring on the reality television show *The Apprentice*, which portrayed Trump as "a pop-culture truth-teller, an evangelist for the American gospel of success, a decider who insisted on standards in a country that had somehow slipped into handing out trophies just for showing up."[49] The "Donald Trump" character on *The Apprentice* was a tough, fair enforcer of high standards and was always the most powerful person in the room. He looked and sounded like someone with the good judgment to be president someday. That version of Trump was a fiction—production editors on *The Apprentice* worked hard to make Trump seem like a decisive leader with good judgment.[50] For example, the "Donald Trump" character on *The Apprentice* relished the opportunity to tell an underperforming contestant "You're fired!" It was the show's signature line and the climactic ending of every episode. Yet many of Trump's supporters would be surprised to learn that Trump doesn't actually like to fire people. According to Politico's Michael Kruse, in reality Trump found the task extremely unpleasant and often found indirect ways of dismissing his staff. After interviewing Trump's employees, Kruse found that the real-life Trump "bears little resemblance to the man viewers saw on the show."[51]

Trump had also cultivated his image as a truth teller via appearances on traditional right-leaning media like *Fox & Friends* and on social media in the years leading up to his presidential announcement—even Trump's "birther" quest was conducted under the guise of finding out the real "truth" about the location of President Barack Obama's birth. Justin McConney, Trump's personal social media director who is credited with introducing Trump to Twitter in 2011, reported holding a daily social media briefing with Trump to plan the day's media posts, explaining that his strategy for Trump's media brand was to make it appear "authentic." That meant "no lighting, no professional camera, no backdrop." McConney wanted audiences to believe that the posts were "real, right from his desk and in your face." He reported that Trump "is a marketing and media genius," an opinion that is shared by many in the marketing profession.[52] Trump had spent years cultivating his authentic "truth teller" brand, which helped him appeal to the distrusting, polarized, and frustrated 2016 electorate. Trump's presidential campaign social media director Dan Scavino explained to Breitbart News that voters "were looking for someone who was human, not a scripted politician. They got that in Trump."[53]

And yet, as he explained in his best-selling book *The Art of the Deal*, "I play to people's fantasies. People may not always think big themselves, but they can still get very excited by those who do. That's why a little hyperbole never hurts. People want to believe that something is the biggest and the greatest and the most spectacular. I call it truthful hyperbole. It's an innocent form of exaggeration—and a very effective form of promotion." While Trump appeared to believe that "truthful hyperbole" was an innocent way to inspire people, Ancient Greeks like Aristotle took a dim view of the practice, believing that hyperboles "are adolescent, for they exhibit vehemence" and are mostly spoken by "those in anger."[54] There is no doubt that Trump used something like truthful hyperbole throughout his career to attract attention, yet the phrase itself was not Trump's, but written by his ghostwriter Tony Schwartz. "I wrote the *Art of the Deal*," claimed Schwartz. "Donald Trump read it."[55] According to a *New Yorker* interview, Schwartz invented the "artful euphemism" in order "to put an acceptable face on Trump's loose relationship with the truth." Trump reportedly loved the phrase, likely finding it useful because it allowed him to say two things at once. Schwartz explained that "'truthful hyperbole' acknowledged that "'it's a lie, but who cares?'"[56]

Therefore, part of Trump's rhetorical strategy was in crafting an image of himself as either an authentic "truth teller" or, if not that, then as someone who used "truthful hyperbole" for strategic advantage. One way to make this distinction is that Trump was either telling the truth or he was using "bullshit."[57] Another way to make the distinction is to say that "the press takes him literally, but not seriously; his supporters take him seriously, but not literally." According to reporter Salena Zito, when she suggested the literal/serious gap to Trump in an interview, he remarked, "Now that's interesting."[58] Our takeaway has to be that Trump is neither truth teller nor bullshitter; his words can be taken neither literally nor seriously. As rhetoric scholar Ryan Skinnell put it, "Trump lies because lying works, plain and simple."[59] Trump is probably a marketing genius; he is, essentially, whatever he can convince us to believe that he is. Some call him a con man, some call him a truth teller, and some call him a demagogue.

If we can reject Trump's claim of being an authentic truth teller while also acknowledging that his supporters believe that he did authentically tell the truth, then can we justly call him a "demagogue" like Rick Perry and others did? Who is a "demagogue" exactly? Throughout political history, we find a character who is labeled "demagogue" but who is also sometimes labeled "agitator," "mob master," or more recently, "troll." Accusing someone of being a demagogue is primarily a fear appeal coupled with a critique of *argumentum ad verecundiam* (Latin for "appeal to authority") that constitutes a person as an unfit leader of the people. How the demagogue is judged "unfit" has changed over time, within various political systems, because what may make a leader "fit" under one political system may disqualify her or him in another. The accusation of demagoguery rests primarily upon the fear of power resting in the wrong hands. The charge of being a demagogue is often class based and carries with it a fear of popular rule: the "right" leaders have been displaced by "unfit" others who dupe the people (mob) into supporting the demagogue's candidacy or policies.[60] Often when we accuse a political leader of being a demagogue, we are also implicitly or explicitly critiquing rhetoric and popular rule. Often the hatred and fear of demagogues and democracy go hand in hand because we don't trust the people to be able to discern an authentic truth teller from a demagogue. Calling Trump supporters "deplorables" is merely the most recent example of a long tradition of attacking the people who support undesirable leaders.[61]

Those factors make "demagogue" a difficult word to make sense of. If we turn to the *Oxford English Dictionary*, we learn that a demagogue has two contradictory definitions. The first definition is neutral or positive: "in ancient times, a leader of the people; a popular leader or orator who espoused the cause of the people against any other party in the state." The second definition is explicitly negative: "a leader of a popular faction, or of the mob; a political agitator who appeals to the passions and prejudices of the mob in order to obtain power or further his own interests; an unprincipled or factious popular orator."[62] In the *OED*'s first definition, the demagogue is a hero; in the *OED*'s second definition, the demagogue is a villain. Trump's supporters understood him to be a *heroic demagogue* in the positive sense of the word—as a political leader who would champion the cause of the people against the corrupt establishment. Trump's detractors understood him to be a *dangerous demagogue* in the negative sense of the word—as a villainous political agitator appealing to the passions and prejudices of the mob for his own benefit.

We're not used to thinking of a "demagogue" as a hero, but that might be because our understanding of demagogues has come primarily from the critics of Athenian democracy like Aristotle, who believed that it was at best a "government in the interest of the poor," and like Plato, who believed that it was a government in which "the poor, winning the victory, put to death some of the other party, drive out others, and grant the rest of the citizens an equal share in both citizenship and offices."[63] Classicist M. I. Finely explained that while "there is no more familiar theme in the Athenian picture (despite the rarity of the word) than the demagogue and his adjutant, the sycophant," our understanding of Greek political life has been unduly influenced by antidemocratic writers. After all, according to Finely, "there is no eternal law . . . why 'demagogue,' a 'leader of the people,'" must become a "mis-leader of the people."[64]

According to classicist Ernest Barker in ancient Athens "the 'demagogue' proper had no official position; he simply exercised, in a peculiar degree and with a permanent influence, the right of the private member of the assembly to take the initiative and propose a policy." Historians trace the rise of the "demagogue" to 429 BCE when Pericles died, opening up the space for these "unofficial" leaders of the people to rise to power. The danger, according to Barker, was that "such a leader—having no official executive position—could exercise initiative and determine policy without incurring political responsibility, since it was not his duty to execute the policy which he had induced the assembly to accept."[65] The dangerous demagogue of Athenian political culture urged for policies, but he could not be held accountable for those policy's subsequent success or failure—he (it was always a "he") was dangerous because he was unaccountable.

Political accountability is necessary because rhetoric and political power are so easily abused. Just leadership *requires* accountability and transparency—an unaccountable leader is dangerous in any political community. As Barker teaches us, the defining characteristic of a dangerous demagogue from Ancient Greece through to today is *a political leader who cannot be held accountable for his or her words and/or actions*. We know that unaccountable leaders are dangerous to democratic stability in particular, because as Steven Levitsky and Daniel Ziblatt explain in their book *How Democracies Die*, democratic governments historically have been overturned by authoritarian or unaccountable leaders like Adolf Hitler or Benito Mussolini. Those unaccountable leaders (1) rejected or showed a weak commitment to democratic rules; (2) denied the legitimacy of political opponents; (3) tolerated or encouraged violence; and (4) were ready to curtail the civil liberties of opponents and the media.[66] Accountable leaders of the people (heroic demagogues) would show a commitment to the democratic process, respect political opposition, discourage violence, and protect civil liberties. We should therefore judge all potential political leaders based upon whether or not they uphold these four democratic practices.

Dangerous demagogues potentially have many strategies for preventing themselves from being held accountable—including using actual physical violence like Hitler and Mussolini did to gain and maintain compliance. A dangerous demagogue need not go as far as physical violence to gain compliance, however. A dangerous demagogue could be successful by "appealing to the passions and prejudices" of their followers, by using rhetoric as a weapon to gain compliance. There's an important difference between persuasion and forced compliance. Persuasion is democratic; it requires consent. Compliance is authoritarian; it is a kind of force. Scholars of rhetoric, argument, and logic have well-developed tools for understanding how to persuade without manipulation. I think of rhetoric as Aristotle did—as a method of decision making leading to practical wisdom (the Greek word is *phronesis*), rather than leading to philosophical or eternal truth (the Greek word is *sophia*). Aristotle thought that "rhetoric is the counterpart of dialectic," meaning that rhetoric is a method for arriving at truth in the same way that dialectic is a method for arriving at truth—two methods for two different kinds of truth.[67] Rhetoric is addressed to the conscious, rational mind: rhetoric addresses people who know that they are being addressed. Rhetoric is a meeting of the minds that invites people to change their opinions. Attempting to change another person's mind without using rhetoric denies that person the opportunity to consent and is antidemocratic. Dangerous demagogues do not use rhetoric to persuade; they use rhetoric to gain compliance.

Weaponized rhetoric—using rhetoric as a kind of force and as a strategic tool to gain compliance—is what rhetorical scholar Joshua Gunn called "a perversion" of rhetoric. Weaponized rhetoric is "a deliberate and knowing deviation from assumed 'norms.'"[68] Rhetorical scholar Patricia Roberts-Miller explained that dangerous demagoguery is itself an "escape from the responsibilities of rhetoric" because it relies on polarization to simplify public debate into in-group/out-group decisions. We agree to something not because we are persuaded, but because our side agrees; we disagree because our side disagrees.[69] Weaponized rhetoric functions much like how philosopher Jason Stanley explained "undermining propaganda": it is "an argument that appeals to an ideal, to draw support, in the service of a goal that tends to erode the realization of that ideal."[70] Weaponized rhetoric appears to be rhetoric—it appears to be a method of deliberation with a goal of democratic decision making—but it, in fact, undermines both democratic decision making and democracy itself.

During his announcement speech, Trump said, "I watch the speeches of these people, and they say the sun will rise, the moon will set, all sorts of wonderful things will happen. And people are saying, 'What's going on? I just want a job. Just get me a job. I don't need the rhetoric. I want a job.'" In so doing, he positioned himself as someone who did not use rhetoric, but instead was a straight talker—*he used rhetoric to deny that he used rhetoric.*[71] Trump denied that he used rhetoric but also crowed that he was a master at assessing the right thing to say, in the right way, in any rhetorical situation—a real rhetorical "genius." He bragged that he was good at rhetoric quite often even: "I mean I change for different settings," he explained to Fox News' Megyn Kelly. "If I'm in a board room I'm not going to be shouting and ranting and raving and doing it the same way that I would, you know, if I'm talking to 12 people, than if I'm talking to 25,000 people in a major arena someplace."[72] He also told us repeatedly not to pay attention to the way that he said things— he trivialized people's concerns about his rhetorical strategies by calling those concerns mere "political correctness," or complaining that people were polic- ing his "tone," or that women were trying to control how real men talk, or that such criticisms were just a part of the rigged system that was trying to destroy his campaign. In these ways Trump tried to have it both ways—he claimed to be a rhetorical genius and also told us that his rhetoric didn't matter. His rhetoric did matter.

The way that Trump used language tells you everything that you need to know about Trump as "a leader of the people." He used rhetoric like a weapon to gain compliance, and he used rhetoric to prevent people from holding him accountable for weaponizing rhetoric. Specifically, Trump used six rhetorical strategies as weapons during his campaign. His genius was in using these strategies to avoid accountability but also in using them to ingrati- ate himself with his supporters, while separating himself and his supporters from his opponents. Three of the strategies would unify Trump with his tar- get audience; three of the strategies would divide Trump from his opponents. The sum total of these six strategies was to unify his followers against his opponents.

Trump's Unifying Strategies

Argumentum ad populum (Latin for "appeal to the crowd"). Used by a demagogue to praise his or her supporters as wise, good, and knowledgeable. *Ad
populum* appeals can work in three different ways: first, *ad populum* appeals
can be used as an *argument ad verecundiam* (an appeal to authority), in which
demagogues try to persuade that some disputed thing is a "fact" because it is
commonly believed to be fact, or believed to be a fact by a select subset of the
population who supports the demagogue's argument.[73] Second, demagogues
can use the presence of a large crowd of people as evidence of widespread
support, claiming that the size of the crowd is evidence that the demagogue
speaks the truth and represents the true voice of the people. While appealing
to the size of a crowd may seem persuasive, large crowds can be unreliable
indicators of either truth or support. Third, demagogues can use large crowds
of people to heighten the emotional responses of audiences, relying on "socio-
psychological factors that play a part in meetings of large groups of people"
to manipulate "the emotions of those present" in order to "to get his way."
According to argument scholars Frans van Eemeren and Rob Grootendorst,
"the true demagogue knows how to play on both positive and negative emotions and how to touch both the group as a whole and the individuals com-
posing it. The positive emotions that may be exploited include, for example,
feelings of safety and loyalty; the negative ones, fear, greed, and shame."[74] *Ad
populum* appeals are fairly easy to recognize: any time an argument rests solely
on the popularity of some idea, person, fact, and so on, then it is likely to be
fallacious. Appeals to popular opinion are not always fallacious, of course,
but when "the crowd" is not representative of the whole (it consists of only
the demagogue's supporters or is manufactured through astroturfing), then
the appeal to the wisdom of the crowd is merely manipulation. Demagogues
use *ad populum* appeals to gain and maintain power because it is difficult to
challenge what is believed to be popular. Demagogues also use *ad populum*
appeals to prevent critical thinking by overwhelming people with the supposed authority of the crowd and *vox populi, vox dei* arguments (Latin for
"the voice of the people is the voice of God"). Indeed, the propagandistic
abuse of "the wisdom of the people" via arguments based upon *ad populum*
appeals is one of the more pernicious techniques of demagogues because it
erodes a society's trust in the wisdom of "the people" and in popular rule.
American exceptionalism (America's unique status among other nations in

the world). Used by a demagogue to motivate audiences to support the demagogue's policies. Alexis de Tocqueville first described America's exceptional situation relative to other nations in his 1835 *Democracy in America*. "The position of the Americans" being so far from Europe, de Tocqueville noted, "is therefore quite exceptional, and it may be believed that no democratic people will ever be placed in a similar one." He also noted that America's "strictly Puritanical" religion, "exclusively commercial habits," and the distractions of nature, "which seems to divert their minds from the pursuit of science, literature, and the arts" combined to create a distinctly American culture.[75] Political scientist Seymour Martin Lipset, like de Tocqueville, observed "America continues to be qualitatively different." Yet Lipset believes that this exceptionalism is "a two-edged phenomenon; it does not mean better. This country is an outlier. It is the most religious, optimistic, patriotic, rights-oriented, and individualistic."[76] While some take the word "exceptionalism" to mean "unequivocally good," Lipset explains that American exceptionalism has always been a technical distinction—America is simply different from other nations—in some good ways and some bad ways. Yet the "myth of American exceptionalism" elides America's "uniqueness" and substitutes instead America's "greatness." Appeals to American exceptionalism rely on Americans' pride and their desire to believe that their nation is the best among others, that it is chosen by God, and that it has a heroic destiny to spread democracy and enlightenment throughout the world. By using powerful appeals to American exceptionalism, demagogues may persuade audiences to support policies that they might not otherwise support. Because American exceptionalism techniques stir the patriotic emotions of pride, they can make critical thinking more difficult. We can easily recognize appeals to American exceptionalism when speakers invoke America's special status among other nations as the justification for policies, when speakers make appeals to uncritical nationalism, or when speakers appeal to audiences' patriotic pride as the reason for why their preferred policies ought to be adopted. American exceptionalism appeals are particularly pernicious because they take advantage of the nation's hope that it can be a beacon of freedom and liberty for others and turns what could be a positive approach to understanding the nation's obligations toward other nations into hubris and, potentially, to violence.

Paralipsis (Greek for "to leave to the side," or more colloquially, "I'm not saying; I'm just saying"). Used by a demagogue to circulate rumors and accusations, to ironically say two things at once, and to build a relationship with supporters. Rhetoric scholar Jeanne Fahnestock has explained that *paralipsis* "involves mentioning something in the act of denying the mention of it." One of the oldest rhetoric texts *Rhetoric Ad Herennium* explains that "it is of greater advantage to create a suspicion by *paralipsis* than to insist directly on a statement that is refutable."[77] Because *paralipsis* offers accusations without explanations or evidence, it often prevents critical thinking and gives a speaker "plausible deniability." For this reason, it has often been "used as a tool for damaging opponents." But, more than this, since *paralipsis* is a form of irony, it allows a speaker to say two things at once—denying while at the same time affirming. This form of irony connects audiences to demagogues by allowing audiences to believe that they see "the behind the scenes" or the "backstage" or the "real" thoughts of the demagogue—the thoughts that the demagogue can't or won't acknowledge that they have. This can cultivate an "us" versus "them" polarization between in-group audiences and out-group audiences and helps create a faux intimacy between demagogues and audiences because it allows audiences to believe that they know the "insider only" real and true thoughts of the demagogue. Furthermore, not only does *paralipsis* reward audiences by making them believe that they know the demagogue's real thoughts, but *paralipsis* is also rewarding because it is often funny. The ironic twist of the demagogue saying the thing that they say that they aren't saying is so obvious that it often elicits laughter from audiences, thus rewarding the speaker once again because audiences enjoy being entertained, especially at the expense of some abhorred outgroup other.

Trump's Dividing Strategies

Argument ad hominem (Latin for "appeal to the person," attacking the person instead of their argument). Used by a demagogue to misdirect the audience's attention and attack the character of their opponents. *Ad hominem* is a technique that shifts attention away from the issue by refocusing our attention on the person who raised the issue, or at a secondary level, on the demagogue's attack on the person. If successful, *ad hominem* attacks prevent critical thinking, as our attention is no longer on the debated question and is instead on the person. According to argumentation scholars Frans van Eemeren and Rob Grootendorst there are three variations of *ad hominem* attacks: first, "direct personal attack," which "consists of cutting down one's opponent by casting doubt on his expertise, intelligence, character, or good faith."

Second, "circumstantial" *ad hominem* attacks cast doubt on the "motives of one's opponent for his standpoint" by making them appear self-interested or biased. And, third, *ad hominem* attacks can be based on the charge of *tu quoque* (appeal to hypocrisy), in which "an attempt is made to find a contradiction in one's opponent's words or between his words and his deeds."[78] While there are certainly times when arguments about a person's qualifications or character would be relevant to consider, demagogues use these kinds of arguments typically to "appeal to our stereotypes or prejudices about people" and as distraction, diverting attention away from legitimate issues.[79] *Ad hominem* attacks undermine democracy by denying the legitimacy of political opposition. Furthermore, *ad hominem* attacks may help demagogues increase polarization by creating or reinforcing in-groups and out-groups by mocking or disparaging "others."

Argument *ad baculum* (Latin for "appeal to the stick," or threats of force or intimidation). Used by a demagogue to attack and overwhelm opponents. Like other "*ad*" appeals, demagogues use argument *ad baculum* to shift attention away from the argument. In this case, the demagogue's victim and the audience's attention is distracted by the threat of force.[80] Rhetoric scholar James Jasinski explains that *ad baculum* appeals involve some kind of threat but involve ambiguity because it's sometimes difficult to distinguish between a threat and a warning. *Ad baculum* tactics might include threats of physical violence but could also be things like overwhelming opponents or audiences with information so that it is difficult to track the arguments or have time to refute them, or could be things like threatening to release private or embarrassing information about an opponent. In all of these ways, and more, demagogues can use *ad baculum* attacks to put "pressure on [opponents] to refrain from taking up a position." Totalitarian demagogues may use more than threats of force to shut down resistance: for example, according to rhetoric scholar Kenneth Burke, "Hitler also tells of his technique in speaking, once the Nazi party had become effectively organized, and had its army of guards or bouncers, to maltreat hecklers and throw them from the hall. He would, he recounts, fill his speech with provocative remarks, whereat his bouncers would promptly swoop down in flying formation, with swinging fists, upon anyone whom these provocative remarks provoked to answer."[81] Obviously not all demagogues are willing to use physical force to prevent dissent and gain compliance; however, all *ad baculum* attacks—whether or not they contain actual physical violence—have the same end: to use coercion and intimidation to gain compliance. Ad baculum attacks are therefore designed to prevent critical thinking by putting pressure on opponents and making it difficult to question demagogues or make arguments against them.

Reification (from the Latin "*rēs*" for "thing"—thingification, treating people as objects). Used by a demagogue to signal that a demagogue's designated enemies are unworthy of fair treatment.[82] "All reification is a forgetting," wrote Max Horkheimer and Theodor W. Adorno, because reifying rhetoric allows speakers to "forget" that people are not things, that people have immanent value (that they have value *qua* people as opposed to value *qua* utility or capitalism).[83] According to philosopher Axel Honneth, reification "violates moral or ethical principles by not treating other subjects in accordance with their characteristics as human beings, but instead as numb and lifeless objects—as 'things' or 'commodities.'"[84] Political philosopher Martha Nussbaum explains that treating people as things is a power move, made to take advantage of people. She argues that reification treats people as instruments or tools; denies autonomy; denies agency; makes people interchangeable with other objects; treats people as violable, as lacking boundaries; treats people as things that can be owned by people; and, finally, denies the feelings and experiences of people. All of these factors have the consequence of empowering the demagogue at the expense of others.[85] In each of these ways, the demagogue who uses the technique of reification places himself or herself above the people who are designated as "objects." Demagogues use objects as a means to an end (or treat the objects as if they have no value at all). Demagogues seek to control people as objects, denying people their own free will and autonomy. Demagogues deny the value of individual people by treating them as objects that can be exchanged easily for other people who are also treated as objects. Demagogues violate bodies and deny the experiences and opinions of people. Furthermore, reification is a polarizing rhetorical strategy that demagogues use to divide people into the categories of "real people" and "objects," which allows demagogues to deny the perspectives of those who the demagogue treats as objects. Since objects cannot speak, they can neither consent nor criticize. Reification prevents critical thinking by delegitimizing the voices of the "objects" and in so doing denies critics the opportunity to question the demagogue or speak of their concerns. We can easily recognize the rhetoric of reification when demagogues use "that" rather than "who" to refer to people (refusing to use the pronoun for subjects); when demagogues refer to entire groups of people as "the," as in "the blacks" or "the gays"; when demagogues use polarizing words to deny the rationality or opinions of people by treating them as irrational objects of derision; when demagogues use exterminationist or infestation rhetoric to position people as objects of disgust or as animals; or when demagogues use strategies to deny the immanent value of people, treating them as a means to an end.

Did Donald Trump campaign as a heroic demagogue (a defender of the people's rights) or as a dangerous demagogue (a manipulator of the people)? He campaigned as both, depending on how you perceive his campaign. Trump is simultaneously America's hero and America's villain. Trump's supporters heard that he would act as a heroic demagogue, refusing to be controlled by a corrupted system and using his power to restore their rights and privileges. Trump's detractors heard that he would act as a dangerous demagogue, refusing to be controlled by decency, the constitution, tradition, or anything or anyone else.

About This Book/Argument/Overview

This is the story about how Trump used language as a weapon to win the 2016 election. Trump used language strategically to attack the American public sphere and the political process, and to prevent himself from being held accountable for his words and actions. Trump's rhetoric was so successful that the nation found itself in a position in which no one was powerful enough to control him—not the media who covered him, not established political leaders who tried to stop him, not newspaper editorial boards who refused to endorse him, not the political parties who tried to game the system against him, certainly not political correctness and commonly accepted standards of decency—not even Pope Francis was powerful enough to control Trump.

I explain how Trump used language strategically to support what he called his "counterpunching" campaign strategy.[86] I focus on how he weaponized rhetoric to captivate our interest, excite our emotions, and distract our attention. In so doing, Trump correctly guessed that dangerously high levels of distrust, polarization, and frustration could be exploited with a little (or perhaps a lot of) showmanship. My narrative of the 2016 campaign unfolds episode by episode, following Trump as he moved between the six different rhetorical strategies described above and the different contexts of a distrusting electorate, a polarized electorate, and a frustrated electorate.

In these stories we see Trump formulating arguments, attacks, and positions, all while testing and refining them. Trump bumbles through at times. He's led by white nationalists, he's led by conspiracy theorists, and he's led by his rally crowds. But, fundamentally, what we see is that Trump uses language in a strategic way, as a means toward a clearly defined goal. We see his rhetorical genius at work—whether he's an evil genius or not would be answered differently if you see him as a hero or a villain. From a rhetorical analyst's perspective, Trump's rhetoric was instrumentally successful, but because he used it to undermine public deliberation and democracy, it is morally repugnant. Most of the strategies that Trump relied upon are technically fallacies—errors of argumentation and rhetoric that would typically disqualify a speaker, denying them the standing to continue in a debate. Trump used these strategies defiantly to take advantage of distrust, polarization, and frustration—all negative qualities in an electorate—to win.

This book analyzes Trump's strategic use of rhetoric because, as I've shown already, Trump is a strategic speaker. This is a somewhat traditional analysis of figures of speech and fallacies, and how Trump used them to win. There are certainly other ways to think about rhetoric and to do rhetorical analyses. I'm not focusing on, for example, Trump's eloquence. I'm not focusing on how beautiful his prose was, or how he constructed an argument, used evidence, or led his audience to reason through difficult concepts. To do so would be an exercise in tedium—for Trump's rhetoric is neither beautiful nor well argued. And yet Trump's use of language was far more controlled and consistent than it would appear without careful scrutiny.

My hope is that readers of this book will learn how to recognize Trump's rhetorical strategies and understand why he uses them. Recognition and understanding are necessary for controlling the uncontrollable leader. Taken together, these six rhetorical strategies violated the norms of democratic political discourse—a problem that I address in the book's conclusion. Because of the danger of Trump's rhetorical strategies, I hope that this book will be of interest to a broad audience, not merely to rhetoric scholars. Scholars of authoritarianism, propaganda, and democratic erosion will find many troubling examples in the stories I tell about Trump's rhetoric, which will confirm their worst suspicions. I'll address those concerns in the book's conclusion.

Whether we think of Trump as a hero or villain, he is probably the most successful demagogue in American history. Let's take a closer look at how he attacked America to win the presidency.

PART ONE
Trump and the Distrusting Electorate

A mixture of gullibility and cynicism had been an outstanding characteristic of mob mentality before it became an everyday phenomenon of the masses. In an ever-changing, incomprehensible world the masses had reached the point where they would, at the same time, believe everything and nothing, think that everything was possible and that nothing was true. . . . Mass propaganda discovered that its audience was ready at all times to believe the worst, no matter how absurd, and did not particularly object to being deceived because it held every statement to be a lie anyhow. The totalitarian mass leaders based their propaganda on the correct psychological assumption that, under such conditions, one could make people believe the most fantastic statements one day, and trust that if the next day they were given irrefutable proof of their falsehood, they would take refuge in cynicism; instead of deserting the leaders who had lied to them, they would protest that they had known all along that the statement was a lie and would admire the leaders for their superior tactical cleverness.

Hannah Arendt, *The Origins of Totalitarianism*

ONE WAY TO DESCRIBE the 2016 electorate is that it had a historic and dangerous crisis in public trust.[1] According to a 2015 Pew Research poll, "only 19% of Americans today say they can trust the government in Washington to do what is right." The nation's distrust didn't start with the 2016 election, though. Pew reported that Americans' trust in their government had been declining since 2007.[2] This widespread distrust represented "the longest period of low trust in government in more than 50 years." Americans didn't just distrust their government; they also distrusted traditional leaders in all kinds of institutions. A 2016 Gallup poll found that the nation had historically low trust for clergy (44 percent of Americans had a very high or high opinion, down from well above 60 percent in the 1970s and 1980s), journalists (23 percent of Americans had a very high or high opinion), and lawyers (18 percent of Americans had a very high or high opinion).[3] Perhaps worse of all, according to a November 2015 Pew survey, "both parties have lost confidence and trust in [the] public's political wisdom." Pew found that since 2007 the amount of trust for the public declined from 61 percent to 36 percent for Republicans and from 57 percent to 37 percent for Democrats.[4] A democracy without trust is vulnerable.

We've known since Aristotle wrote about government "decay" in Ancient Greece that government stability is fragile and that established governments are always at risk for erosion or backsliding. It's accurate to describe the nation's terrible state of trust during the election as a "crisis" because the stability of any government, as political philosopher Jürgen Habermas explained, rests on trust and legitimacy.[5] According to Harvard political scientist Robert Putnam, Americans had become more suspicious of one another and their government for generations. Americans grew more distrustful of one another and their government because we had less "bridging social capital" and more "bonding social capital" than previous generations of Americans. That is, we spent more time with people like us and less time interacting with others, including government organizations and schools. For generations, we had failed to join public organizations like the PTA or the bowling league, and instead we had cocooned ourselves in our private-sphere lives or in our media bubbles. Our lack of participation negatively influenced our trust in one another and in the decisions made by the government because, in this case, unfamiliarity bred contempt.

Our lack of participation in our communities and our lack of trust in our government and for traditional leaders had left the nation vulnerable to attack. Within this crisis of public trust in which the very viability of democracy was at risk, Donald Trump ran a campaign that was *designed* to increase distrust for government and traditional leadership. As you'll see, Trump's rhetorical strategy sought to increase suspicion between his followers and the rest of the nation. Trump's *ad populum* (appealing to the wisdom of the crowd) appeal against "political correctness" told his followers that they had been lied to by poll-tested political stooges. Trump's *ad baculum* threats (threats of force or intimidation) against the press told his followers that the nation's watchdog over the government was too rigged and dishonest to believe. Trump's *reification* (treating people as objects) of Muslim refugees told his followers that they were a dangerous threat and not to trust the leaders who said otherwise. Trump's *ad hominem* attack (attacking the person instead of their argument) on a reporter for the *New York Times* with a physical disability told his followers to be suspicious of anyone who contradicted Trump's version of reality. Trump's *paralipsis* ("I'm not saying; I'm just saying") told his followers to be suspicious of other Republican candidates. Trump's *American exceptionalism* (America's unique status among other nations in the world) told his followers to distrust the corrupt politicians who would never put them and America first. Altogether, Trump took advantage of his followers' cynicism and gullibility; he told his followers to be suspicious of everyone and to trust no one but him.

CHAPTER 1

"I don't, frankly, have time for total political correctness."

Ad Populum

Cleveland, Ohio, August 6, 2015
Favorable: 26.4 percent; Unfavorable: 61 percent[1]

"They said 'his tone, t-o-n-e, tone,'" whined Trump, mocking his critics for complaining about his lack of political correctness at a rally in Boone, Iowa, on September 12, 2015. "And I said, you know, we need that tone today. We need energy. We need strength [Trump's rally crowd began nodding and applauding], and we can't be low key and nice and beautiful." Trump then told his crowd about a woman who supposedly told Trump that maybe he wasn't "nice enough to be president." In Trump's telling, he told the woman, "I don't think it matters this time. I think today we're looking for real super competence. We're tired with this nice stuff. We need people that are really, really smart and competent and can get things done. We need people—we need people with an *aggressive* tone. And we need people with tremendous energy. And I'm your candidate, OK?"[2] Trump's rally crowd cheered enthusiastically for their candidate. For Trump's supporters, his aggressive tone and politically incorrect rhetoric toward the establishment were exactly why they supported him for president.

Ivanka Trump had introduced her father at his June 16, 2015, presidential campaign announcement event as the "opposite of politically correct," and by February 23, 2016, right-wing Breitbart News Editor Milo Yiannopoulos called Trump "an icon of irreverent resistance to political correctness."[3]

Trump became that icon by arguing repeatedly over the course of his campaign that the twin scourges of corruption and political correctness were destroying America—that politically correct language was the outward or visible sign of corrupt political leaders who had prevented the "good" American citizens from controlling the government and prevented their problems from being solved. By that logic, politically *incorrect* language was the outward or visible sign of a just leader who would enable the good American citizens to control the government and solve their problems. Trump's campaign-long attack on political correctness was essentially one long *ad populum* appeal—it was one continuous appeal to the "wisdom of the crowd" against established leadership—and it both relied upon preexisting distrust and attempted to increase distrust between the people and their elected officials.

Attacking political correctness was a savvy campaign strategy because political correctness was decidedly unpopular. An October 30, 2015, Fairleigh Dickinson University Public Mind survey found that 68 percent of all Americans and 81 percent of Republicans agreed that "being politically correct" was "a big problem in this country."[4] Not only was political correctness unpopular, but polls found that Trump's supporters, in particular, were alienated from the politically correct mainstream. An April 5, 2016, a Quinnipiac University poll found that 90 percent of Trump supporters agreed that "public officials don't care much what people like me think"; 80 percent of Trump supporters agreed that "the government has gone too far in assisting minority groups"; 83 percent of Trump supporters agreed that "the old way of doing things no longer works and we need radical change"; and, perhaps most ominously, 84 percent of Trump supporters agreed that "what we need is a leader who is willing to say or do anything to solve America's problems."[5] Quinnipiac University Poll Director Douglas Schwartz interpreted these results to mean that while there was general dissatisfaction and alienation throughout the Republican Party, Trump supporters in particular "strongly feel that they themselves and the country are under attack."[6] Trump's attack on political correctness was designed to appeal to an alienated American population who saw themselves as under attack from, and blamed the nation's problems upon, politically correct politicians and media.

Trump's *ad populum* appeal worked well within a context in which average citizens distrusted party elites.[7] For example, Republican political consultant Frank Luntz was surprised to learn from a focus group in August 2015 that the rise of "Donald Trump is punishment to a Republican elite that wasn't listening to their grassroots." He found that Trump supporters believed that Trump had their "best interests in mind, while other Republicans" were "looking out for themselves." One panelist told Luntz that Republican politicians "treat us like crap and they lie to us and promise us things and then they expect us to vote again. That's why we want Trump."[8] For these voters, "political correctness" was a lie. Poll-tested, teleprompted, consultant-approved political doublespeak was both a form and sign of political corruption. As an anonymous Trump supporter wrote in *The Atlantic*, "we know that every politician we have to choose from is a liar and a flip-flopper. . . . Politicians pay lip service to the middle class but spend no time helping them."[9]

Trump took advantage of his followers' alienation and distrust of elites by arguing that politically correct politicians didn't care about Trump's people. First, he used political correctness as an *ad populum* appeal to divide his people from the establishment by arguing that when the elite used political correctness, they put public relations above Trump's people's safety. For example, at his February 22, 2016, rally in Las Vegas, Nevada, Trump warned his crowd that political correctness had made Americans weak and victims of terrorism. ISIS, he said, was "drowning people in steel cages," they were "chopping off people's heads," and all the while saying, "Can you believe how weak and pathetic the Americans are?" Americans were humiliated by ISIS because of political correctness. Trump recounted that at a recent debate, someone asked Texas senator Ted Cruz what he thought about water boarding. "I, well, I, uh. What do I say? I want to be politically correct," stammered Trump as he impersonated Cruz. "'Water boarding is so terrible,'" Trump mocked, "even though they're chopping off heads!" Trump said that when they asked him the question, he said, "It's great, but I don't think it goes far enough!" Trump's rally crowd chanted "USA! USA! USA!" in enthusiastic response to Trump's rejection of political correctness and defense of their safety.[10]

Second, Trump used political correctness as an *ad populum* appeal to heighten distrust and alienation by arguing that politically correct language took too long and prevented political leaders from solving the nation's (and Trump's people's) problems. For example, on August 30, 2015, Trump gave a speech to the National Federation of Republican Assemblies in Nashville, Tennessee, in which he praised members of his crowd and railed against political correctness. "I love the Tea Party people," Trump said. But Trump thought that his people had "not been treated fairly." Their concerns had been misrepresented and dismissed by the media. Trump told his audience that they were a powerful force, but that the other candidates didn't get it. He explained that he didn't understand why all the other candidates paid so much money to pollsters. Trump thought pollsters were "arrogant guys. They think they're hot stuff, and they tell the candidate what to say. 'You gotta say *this*. You have to be politically correct!'—no way, no way. I don't have time to be politically correct!"[11] Trump was a doer. He didn't have time to listen to arrogant pollsters who tried to tell him what to say. With these kinds of *ad populum* appeals, it's easy to understand why when Trump said something politically incorrect it only increased his supporters' appreciation for him. Trump's use of politically incorrect language was itself the shorthand for an argument—whenever he used it, he affirmed that he was against corruption and for his people.

Trump's supporters could participate in the pleasure of violating the norms of political correctness and fighting corruption by championing their hero and using language like he did. Spreading Trump's messages and attending Trump rallies allowed Trump's fans to be politically incorrect without repercussion. Trump campaign rallies became "safe spaces" for Trump supporters to say whatever they had been suppressing due to the scourge of political correctness.[12] News reporters described hearing violent and sexist slurs against Hillary Clinton and chants of "TRUMP THAT BITCH!" (and worse) at Trump rallies. Reporters described hearing obscene, racist, and homophobic slurs regularly, in fact. On August 3, 2016, the *New York Times* posted a video showing the "very inflammatory, and often just plain vile, things that many people showing up to support Mr. Trump's campaign were saying out loud—often very loudly—or wearing on their T-shirts and hats."[13] The video began with Trump declaring, "You know, the safest place in the world to be is at a Trump rally," to which the crowd responded, "Build the wall! Build the wall!" while someone shouted, "Fuck those dirty Beaners." In another clip, Trump said, "Our president has divided this country so bad," to which someone in the crowd responded, "Yeah, fuck that nigger!" And in yet another clip, a rally attendee wearing a "Trump for President 2016" shirt left the rally as he shouted "Fuck political correctness! Build that wall! Mexico is going to pay for it!" and grabbed his crotch while whooping. His fellow rally goers cheered for him in return. With politically correct speech banished, the rallies provided an outlet for distrustful and alienated Americans to find solace in a like-minded community and celebrate Trump as their hero. "When I talk to Trump supporters, they'll tell me that they don't consider him a thinker or a policy person," explained *Reason* editor Robby Soave. "He's a cultural hero to them the way that Beyoncé is to people on the left. They see him as an icon of resistance to people they don't like."[14]

The problem of political correctness created rhetorical opportunities for Trump: it enabled Trump supporters to identify with one another and created safe spaces for vitriol at his rallies, fueled outrage on the left, and glee on the right.[15] Political correctness served as a carrier for all of Trump's other messages. Trump used it to link to all sorts of things that his followers found odious—illegal immigration, terrorist attacks, racial unrest, globalization, lack of good jobs, and so on. But, more than this, by linking political correctness to corruption, Trump was able to say whatever he wanted to say, without accountability. Whoever opposed Trump's political incorrectness was corrupt. On August 6, 2015, during the first Republican primary debate, Fox News' Megyn Kelly observed, "One of the things people love about you is you speak your mind and you don't use a politician's filter." Kelly listed several examples of Trump making disparaging comments about women and asked, "[Is that] the temperament of a man we should elect as president?"

Trump didn't answer the question. Instead, he shifted the discussion away from whether or not what he had said about women was presidential and instead focused on the problem of political correctness: "I think the big problem this country has is being politically correct," said Trump. "I've been challenged by so many people, and I don't, frankly, have time for total political correctness. And to be honest with you, this country doesn't have time, either."[16] The debate audience in the room burst into applause, but political pundits declared his campaign all but over due to what they perceived as a horrific gaffe. Two days after the debate, Trump tweeted, "So many 'politically correct' fools in our country. We have to all get back to work and stop wasting time and energy on nonsense!"[17] Trump's supporters agreed. They heard him stand up to a "gotcha" question from a politically correct and corrupt reporter; others heard him refuse to deny or apologize for making sexist, demeaning, and derogatory comments about women, which they believed were so patently unpresidential as to merit disqualification from the presidency altogether.[18] Trump strategically used his attack on political correctness to claim the moral high ground while avoiding the question about his misogynistic use of language—a fascinating turn, given the circumstances.

Appearing to be a brave and authentic truth teller who rejected political correctness to speak the truth was crucial for Trump's campaign strategy,

but he had some difficulty appearing to be truthful. Early in his campaign—
and throughout—there was a lot of skepticism about whether or not Trump
was telling the truth about the "problem at the border," for example. Since
Trump's presidential announcement speech, he had been on the wrong side
of public opinion on the question. Only 7 percent of Americans thought
that immigration was the most important problem facing the nation, according to a July 20, 2015, Gallup survey.[19] Trump also faced a lot of backlash
for the things he said about immigrants. He had been condemned by other
Republican Party presidential hopefuls like Florida senator Marco Rubio,
who thought that "Trump's comments are not just offensive and inaccurate,
but also divisive."[20] Trump had lost business contracts.[21] His attacks against
immigrants had received four "Pinocchios" from the *Washington Post* fact-
checker.[22] "Mexican immigrants, as with all immigrants, have much lower
crime rates than native born," tweeted Rupert Murdoch, executive chairman
of News Corp and owner of Fox News, on July 12, 2015. "Eg El Paso safest
city in U. S. Trump wrong."[23] Murdoch wasn't the only one to find Trump
wrong on immigration.

Breaking the norms of political correctness was only politically expedi-
ent if Trump was seen as bravely speaking the truth and battling corruption.
Without that perception, Trump appeared to be a crackpot conspiracy theorist—or worse. On July 23, 2015, he staged an event on the US/Mexico border in Laredo, Texas, to demonstrate just how dangerous the border was, how
truthful he had been in his condemnation of immigrants, and how brave he
had been to speak the truth to the politically correct politicians who refused
to acknowledge the problems on the border like he had done.

In the days leading up to his border trip, he had received a great deal
of negative media attention for claiming that Arizona senator John McCain
was "not a 'war hero,'" despite having been captured and tortured during
the war in Vietnam. "I like people who weren't captured, let me tell you," he
had said at an event in Iowa—and so the trip to investigate the "trouble" at
the border gave Trump the opportunity to change the media narrative while
he debuted his soon to be ubiquitous "Make America Great Again" hat.[24]
Throughout the media event in Laredo, Trump commented on how risky it
was for him to travel to such a dangerous place. (Media reports showed that
Laredo was not at all dangerous and safer than Trump's hometown of New
York City.) "They say it's a great danger," Trump said to reporters in Laredo
about his border investigation, "but I have to do it. I love the country. There's

nothing more important than what I'm doing."[25] When asked by reporters to clarify "What danger are you talking about?," Trump responded with vague circularity: "There's great danger with the illegals, and we were just discussing that. But we have a tremendous danger along the border, with the illegals coming in." Reporters present at the event did not see any danger, though they did see a few protestors carrying signs. When asked about the protestors, Trump claimed not to have seen them. Jonathan Tilove of the *Austin-American Statesman* estimated that the whole investigation of the border, including Trump's two press conferences and a speech opportunity, didn't last longer than two and a half hours—more of a public relations stunt than a real "investigation."[26] As Tilove quipped, Trump's narrative of the "dangerous" events in Laredo forced "the large contingent of attendant press to choose whether to believe the blustery man of the hour or their own lying eyes."[27] While the press didn't trust the blustery man of the hour, his fans did.

Trump may have been incorrect about the dangers in Laredo, but he was correct when he told his rally crowd in Boone, Iowa, that he used the right tone for the toxic public discourse of the 2016 election. We can think of tone as word choices, delivery, and other elements of the speaker's performance of their speech. But more than that, tone also refers to the relationship between the speaker and his or her audience as expressed in the word choices made, the examples used, and the topics addressed in a speech.[28] As political communication scholars Roderick Hart, Jay Childers, and Colene Lind explain, "tone affects people's perceptions of others."[29] Speakers use tone to build relationships with audiences through their speeches; they also use their tone to reaffirm and validate existing relationships. Likewise, speakers use the tone of their speeches to divide themselves from audiences. Indeed, any time a speaker seeks to unify with one group, he or she is also dividing from other groups.[30] Presidential candidates typically seek to use their tone to indicate that they are serious people, that they embody the nation's values and its historical legacy, and that they possess the gravitas to lead the nation.

Trump's politically incorrect tone sought to identify him with the alienated and angry members of the electorate against the "spin" of corrupt elected officials. Trump's tone was also intended to unify him with the apparently large segment of the American electorate who rejected "political correctness" and who had taken to expressing their political beliefs in harassing and disrespectful ways via conservative talk radio, social media, and right-wing news organizations like Breitbart News.[31] His tone was meant to signal that he was an outsider, that he was in agreement with the right wing, and that he was aggressive about pursuing their shared policy plans. Many of the supportive comments on Twitter and other social media sites understood Trump in just this way, remarking that Trump spoke the truth, that he said what they were thinking, and that he was refreshingly blunt. For example, "Finally somebody's coming in that has the *cojones* to say something and to do something," said Trump supporter Ray Henry in April 2016. "I think he's saying what a lot of what America's feeling right now . . . enough's enough."[32]

One way to think about Trump's political correctness and corruption arguments was that they were strategically successful in tone for the 2016 presidential election because they gained and kept the nation's attention, sowed distrust and suspicion between Trump supporters and the mainstream, and allowed Trump to say whatever he wanted, without repercussion. Another way to think about those arguments is that they were very effective in silencing and subverting any and all opposition against him. When reporters like Megyn Kelly attempted to hold Trump accountable for commonly accepted standards of decency in language use or when they reported negatively on him or his policies, they played into the Trump corruption narrative, becoming targets of vitriol as well.[33] His opponents couldn't complain about his lack of political correctness, because it made them sound like they were just another corrupt politician saying whatever their arrogant pollsters told them to say. When Trump's opponents also tried to use politically incorrect attacks against Trump, they appeared inauthentic and desperate. For example, when Marco Rubio attacked Trump for his "small hands" and "spray tan" in the final weeks of his campaign, it fell flat, and he regretted it.[34]

Trump used *ad populum* to attempt to persuade the nation that the corrupt establishment used political correctness to hide its agenda, but that he, speaking for the wise crowd, saw through the corruption and the politically correct doublespeak. He was *their* candidate, as he said. Within Trump's narrative, the crowd was justified in not only distrusting existing leaders, but also rejecting all norms of "political correctness," including respect, politeness, and decorum. This allowed Trump and his followers to say whatever they wanted to say, without being held accountable for saying it. Counterintuitively, perhaps, the more outrageous Trump's language became, the more "truthful" and less "corrupt" he appeared to be to his supporters. Ultimately, for Trump's loyal supporters, his *ad populum* strategy was a success. They believed that since Trump wasn't politically correct, he also wasn't politically corrupt. As one supporter put it, "Mr. Trump is truthful. Good or bad, the truthfulness of his words are as clear as a breath of fresh air spoken from a foundation of experience and wisdom with a dash of enthusiasm. Lies are out; unrehearsed truth is in."[35]

CHAPTER 2

"It's going to be like this. . . . I'm going to continue to attack the press."

Ad Baculum

New York, New York, May 31, 2016
Favorable: 35.4 percent; Unfavorable: 58 percent[1]

"They say that [Russian president Vladimir Putin] killed reporters. I don't like that. I'm totally against that," Trump told his rally crowd in Grand Rapids, Michigan, on December 21, 2015. "By the way, I hate some of these people [Trump pointed at the press], but I would never kill them. I hate them. No, these people? I'll be honest. I'll be honest. I would never kill them; I would never do that. Ah, let's see . . . ?" Trump joked while his audience laughed and cheered. "No, I wouldn't. I would never kill them, but I do hate them. And some of them are such lying, disgusting people. It's true [the crowd cheered]. It's true, but I would never kill them and anybody who does, I think would be despicable."[2] Trump also explained to his rally crowd in Michigan that he didn't believe that Putin had actually killed or ordered reporters to be killed in Russia, so the issue was irrelevant.[3] Throughout his campaign, Trump used *ad baculum* (threats of force or intimidation) to exploit the nation's distrust for the media in an attempt to intimidate reporters into providing him with better coverage.

Trump found a lot of ways of exerting "force" on journalists and media corporations.[4] Not only did he verbally threaten and intimidate reporters in interviews, press conferences, and in his rallies,[5] but he also sued (and threatened to sue) reporters for writing stories that he didn't like;[6] forced news organizations to interview him at Trump Tower instead of at their studios so that he was guaranteed free advertising and a "home court advantage";[7] had reporters thrown out of press conferences and rallies;[8] led his rally crowds in jeering, harassing, and intimidating reporters;[9] blacklisted individual reporters and news organizations from attending campaign events or press briefings;[10] limited access to himself and to his rally crowds;[11] boycotted specific media organizations and asked his supporters to boycott them too;[12] overwhelmed the news cycle so that reporters couldn't keep up with him;[13] threatened to break up media corporations once he was elected;[14] fed reporters bad information and then attacked them for reporting it;[15] and repeatedly declared that once he became president, he would expand libel laws to punish journalists for writing stories that he didn't like.[16] There's no evidence that Trump crossed the line from threats of violence to using *actual* violence—he didn't have anyone killed—but he did encourage his followers to despise and intimidate what Trump often called "the dishonest media."[17] Trump expertly used *ad baculum* threats of force to turn his supporters against the media, even while using the media to garner more airtime—the equivalent of nearly five billion dollars in free media—than any other candidate.[18] As journalism critic and professor Jay Rosen explained, Trump tried to "break the press."[19]

Trump demanded that reporters write positive news stories about him and preferred to interact with reporters and news organizations that portrayed him positively, didn't ask tough questions, and didn't try too hard to hold him accountable.[20] When reporters asked questions that Trump judged "unfair," he used force to regain the upper hand. For example, on July 22, 2015, CNN's Anderson Cooper asked Trump about a just-released Quinnipiac University poll showing that Americans had a negative view of him.[21] Trump claimed not to know about the poll and attacked Cooper for failing to mention the polls that were more favorable to Trump (when in fact Cooper had mentioned the favorable polls). When Cooper continued to press the point, Trump lashed out, arguing that his popularity was evidence of the nation's distrust in the media: "All I know is I have a very large group of support, and I think one of the reasons is that people don't trust you and people don't trust the media. And I understand why. . . . I find that 60–70 percent of the political media is really dishonest."[22] Claiming the power to speak for an ambiguous "very large group," Trump denied the credibility of the negative news about him and in the process turned a negative poll about himself into an attack on the trustworthiness of the media. Trump's attack not only invoked the nation's distrust of media to discredit Cooper's question, but it

signaled to his followers that Cooper belonged in the 60–70 percent of politi
cal media who were "really dishonest."[23] It's an aggressive debate trick, and
Trump was a master of it.

On the rare occasion when the press succeeded in shaming Trump for
his actions, he lashed out in a violent defense of his honor.[24] One of the most
dramatic showdowns between Trump and the press occurred when reporters attempted to hold Trump accountable for his January 28, 2016, promise
to raise money for veterans. Trump had decided not to attend a Republican
primary debate because he thought he had been treated "unfairly" by Fox
News' Megyn Kelly at a previous debate. Instead, he chose to deliver a speech
in Des Moines, Iowa, to show that he would "stick up for his rights" and as
a fundraiser for veterans' groups. Trump claimed that night to have raised
more than six million dollars to support various veterans' organizations, but
when the *Washington Post's* David Fahrenthold and other reporters questioned whether veterans' groups had received all the money, they were unable
to confirm the receipts.

More than merely a matter of hypocrisy, the story of Trump's charitable
giving was about how he wielded his wealth and power. According to one of
Fahrenthold's Pulitzer Prize–winning reports about Trump's charitable giving, "Trump's fundraiser Jan. 28 was an indelible moment, a one-night show-
case of the GOP front-runner's boldness and charm. In a single evening in
Des Moines, Trump showed Fox News—the host of that night's Trump-less
debate—that he was powerful enough to spurn the Fox network. At the same
time, he showed a national audience that he could conjure a multi-million-
dollar benefit out of nothing, using connections, showmanship and his own
wealth."[25] But did he? In particular, Fahrenthold wondered about Trump's
pledge to donate one million dollars of his personal fortune to the veterans.
Where had that money gone?

The speech in Des Moines had been a triumph of Trump bravado: he
stood his ground in his showdown with Fox News, thereby denying the
conservative news organization's power over him; he refused to apologize
to Megyn Kelly over his "politically incorrect" comments, thereby refusing
to be shamed for his misogyny; and he positioned himself as the generous
and heroic champion of American veterans, thereby reaffirming his commitment to defend the rights of Trump's people against the corruption of elites.[26]
There was so much winning for Trump, in fact, that the mere implication
that he had not legitimately donated the money to the veterans' charities like

he had promised sent him into a rage. "Trump and his campaign repeatedly declined to give new details about how much they have given away," reported Fahrenthold. "'Why should I give you records?' Trump said in an interview with the *Post*. 'I don't have to give you records.'"[27] As media scrutiny intensified, Trump lost control of the news cycle: reports questioning his donations circulated and a group of veterans protested outside of Trump Tower, holding signs that said, "Trumpty Dumpty Didn't Serve; Trumpty Dumpty Broke His Word."[28]

Trump quickly gave away all of the promised money, and on May 31, 2016, he responded to the pressure from negative news reports with a press conference at Trump Tower.[29] Trump rejected the media's attempt to shame him by shaming them. "The press should be ashamed of themselves," Trump scolded, "instead of being like 'Thank you very much, Mr. Trump,' or 'Trump did a good job,' everyone's saying, 'Who got it, who got it, who got it?' And you make me look very bad." During his twenty-one-minute press briefing, Trump expressed his displeasure with journalists by calling them "not good people," "really disgusting" (twice), "dishonest and so unfair," and "the most dishonest people that I've ever met." When reporters asked him questions, Trump berated one as "real beauty," another as "a sleaze," and another as "a fool" with "no credibility." When asked if he agreed that he should be "completely accountable to people," Trump responded, "Oh, I'm totally accountable"; he just didn't want to be questioned. He called journalists' stories about his charitable contributions "probably libelous," implying and vaguely threatening that he could potentially sue over them. Finally, Trump ended the press conference by threatening to continue his attacks against the press: "It's going to be like this. . . . I'm going to continue to attack the press. Look, I find the press to be extremely dishonest. I find the political press to be unbelievably dishonest. I will say that."[30]

Trump's attack on the media received a lot of media attention. All three cable news networks—CNN, Fox News, and MSNBC—covered Trump's press event live. Headlines about his press conference predictably highlighted Trump's attacks: according to CNN, "Trump Launches All-Out Attack on the Press"; according to ABC, "Trump Attacks Media in Fiery News Conference"; according to the *Washington Post*, "Trump's Crazy, Insane, Nonsensical, Bonkers and Anti-democratic Press Conference"; and more.[31] Many of the comments on Twitter and traditional news sites showed that people didn't exactly see things from Trump's perspective. For example, when Trump's account tweeted, "So many veterans groups are beyond happy with all of the money I raised/gave! It was my great honor—they do an amazing job," a Twitter user named Gabiz responded, "Wimp trump can't handle transparency & accountability questions of public service."[32]

Conservative media had a different take, however: "Sleaze! Donald Trump Busts the Press," headlined Breitbart, while radio host Rush Limbaugh called it "the press conference Republican voters have wanted to see for years. . . . That's what you've all wanted. That's what everybody's been asking for I don't know how long. That was a press conference." Specifically, Limbaugh liked that Trump "took 'em all on," and that finally a Republican politician "ripped into [the media] here for the way they're going about their business."[33] Conservative news site Gateway Pundit republished Limbaugh's take on Trump's press conference to the approval of commenters: "He is right, we were all watching, laughing and cheering Trump on," wrote top commenter Deplorable Destiny Storm. "He owned them!"[34] Similarly supportive comments could be found across conservative media and on Twitter. "In watching the entire Presser, there was not one point of Trump's that I did not agree with," said India Maria in the top comment on the Breitbart story about the press conference. "The ClintonMedia is scum, and has been for decades. After watching Bush '41, Dole, Dubya, McCain and Romney cower in fear with each DriveByMedia shenanigan, it is DELIGHTFUL, appropriate and important to see our next POTUS show courage, leadership and AMERICAN fighting spirit against the slithering enemy of the AMERICAN people, i.e. the DemocratMedia."[35] Trump took to Twitter to declare, "I am getting great credit for my press conference today. Crooked Hillary should be admonished for not having a press conference in 179 days."[36] Trump's tweet was liked 21,000 times.

Trump's relationship with the press can be explained best by two Trump bon mots: first, he (or perhaps his ghostwriters) wrote in his campaign-related magnum opus *Crippled America: How to Make America Great Again*, "I have a mutually profitable two-way relationship with the media—we give each other what we need."[37] And, second, as Trump explained when asked about Megyn Kelly's "unfair" treatment of him at the first presidential debate on August 6, 2015, "When people treat me unfairly, I don't let them forget it."[38] Trump viewed his relationship with the press as "mutually profitable"—when he and the media cooperated to "give each other what we need"—but when the press treated him in ways that he judged "unfair," then he didn't "let them forget it." Trump also claimed in *Crippled America* that he didn't "mind being attacked. I use the media the way that the media uses me—to attract attention."[39] Trump was well-known for demanding loyalty of those around him, even threatening *Art of the Deal* "coauthor" Tony Schwartz for being disloyal when Schwartz revealed that he had actually authored the best-selling book and that he wouldn't be voting for Trump for president.[40] That Trump believed the political press corps would be loyal to him indicates, in part, that he expected favorable coverage in return for the ratings boon he gave them for running for office (as quid pro quo).[41]

In the broad sweep of his campaign, attacking and threatening the media was a winning strategy because it enabled him to frame them as part of the corrupt system, impeached their credibility whenever they wrote negative stories about him, reaffirmed "good" media sources over "bad" ones for his supporters, intimidated journalists and media corporations, and (importantly) made it more difficult for media to hold him accountable. Using threats of force may have appealed to the distrusting electorate in particular because such threats positioned Trump as the authoritarian leader who could and would drive out corruption. If no one could be trusted but Trump, then his forceful threats would seem to be warranted and he would appear to be a heroic demagogue defending the cause of the people.

Trump succeeded in using *ad baculum* threats of force to dictate the terms of interaction between his campaign and the press during the 2016 election. Of course, the majority of press coverage about Trump and his campaign was not favorable, but that hardly mattered when Trump (largely, but not always) controlled the tempo of the news cycle, drove the media's agenda, and framed the election for his supporters.[42] And yet Trump's threats of force were not successful on their own; they only succeeded because of larger forces at work. First, Trump was so good for ratings that the media could not ignore him, thus preventing them from retaliating against him by withholding coverage; and second, once Trump became the GOP frontrunner, presumptive nominee, and then the official party candidate, the media had no choice but to cover him. Due to the constraints of pecuniary interest and partisan control of the political process, the press was weakened and vulnerable to Trump's *ad baculum* threats. In the end, the press was largely unable to hold Trump accountable for his words, policies, or behavior.[43] What's worse, the press ended the election with less public trust than it had before the election: according to Gallup, the percentage of the public who said that they trusted the media "a great deal" or a "fair amount" fell from 40 percent to an all-time low of 32 percent over the course of the election.[44] Trump had apparently succeeded in using *ad baculum* threats of force to increase suspicion between his supporters and the media.

> On October 22, 2016, Trump told his rally crowd in Cleveland, Ohio: The system is rigged by the media. WikiLeaks shows . . . [Trump was interrupted by his audience booing loudly] WikiLeaks shows the media conspiring and colluding directly with the Clinton campaign. Emails even show the Clintons boasting gleefully about very friendly and malleable reporters who shower the Clintons with praise. I know the people they are talking about. To us they're very dishonest. For instance, those cameras back there [Trump pointed at the reporters in the "press pen" at the back of the room] will never show these crowds. They'll never show these crowds. It is all rigged. On November 8 we're going show them, and we are going to beat the system! [The crowd cheered enthusiastically.][45]

Trump's followers didn't just boo the press and cheer for their destruction; they also adopted Trump's *ad baculum* threats. Buzzfeed reporter Rosie Gray tweeted a video from Trump's rally in Cleveland with the caption, "Friendly interaction outside the press pen. 'Lügenpresse!'—a Nazi-era term for 'lying press.'"[46] Two Trump supporters are shown on the video staring menacingly at the reporters in the "press pen" while they shout, "Lügenpresse! That's what you are, Lügenpresse!"

CHAPTER 3

"You could have a Trojan horse situation. You could—this could be the ultimate Trojan horse."

Reification

Franklin, Tennessee, October 3, 2015
Favorable: 35 percent; Unfavorable: 58 percent[1]

On September 2, 2015, Americans awoke to a gruesome photo of a three-year-old Syrian boy named Aylan Kurdi lying lifeless and facedown on a beach on Turkey's Bodrum Peninsula.[2] News reports explained that the boy and most of his refugee family had drowned when their boat capsized while attempting to make the journey from Turkey to Greece. The heartbreaking image of the young boy served to draw "public attention to a crisis that ha[d] been building for years" and led to political leaders around the world pledging to take more refugees into their country.[3] Responding to "increasing pressure" from the international community, Pres. Barack Obama agreed to accept 10,000 Syrian refugees in 2016, up from 1,293 in 2015. Despite the outpouring of concern for the plight of refugees and migrants in the United States, the move to accept more people was controversial. "Refugees go through the most robust security process of anybody who's contemplating travel to the United States," Obama's press secretary Josh Earnest assured Americans as he announced the president's decision. "Refugees have to be screened by the National Counter Terrorism Center, by the FBI Terrorist Screening Center. They go through databases that are maintained by DHS, the Department of Defense and the intelligence community. There is biographical and biometric information that is collected about these individuals."[4] Yet, despite so much scrutiny, some Americans worried that taking in so many refugees would disrupt American life. Others worried that the refugees represented a national security threat.

Many Americans were suspicious of the refugees, particularly on the right of the political spectrum. An anti-Muslim blog called *The Muslim Issue* wrote on September 4, 2015, that the tragic picture of Aylan Kurdi was "dead toddler pornography" that was a "dream-come-true PR campaign serving ISIS."[5] *The Muslim Issue* claimed that "4 million Muslims pretend to escape 30,000 ISIS fighters who are not even near their towns, cities and even countries." It was all a "mass-migration fraud" that was actually "a medieval war strategy . . . called Hijrah. It's part of jihad." A video began to circulate on right-leaning websites that purported to show male Syrian refugees on a European train ominously chanting "Allahu Akbar"—God is great—on September 7, 2015. Prison Planet and InfoWars editor Paul Joseph Watson featured the footage in a video that he posted online, claiming "the truth about the migrant crisis,"[6] and conservative website The Right Scoop explained that the video was particularly troubling because "it is really difficult to get a handle on this immigrant crisis that is streaming into Europe. On the one hand, you have offensive stuff like this video which appears to be Syrian 'refugees' chanting an epithet and 'Allah Akbar.' But if you look at the mainstream media coverage of the event, it's all happy families and grateful women and old men."[7]

The next day, September 8, 2015, Rush Limbaugh questioned the truthfulness of the refugee crisis in a lengthy segment on his radio program.[8] "This refugee crisis or this invasion, this migration, whatever you want to call it, this is not being brought about by famine. It's not being brought about by disease, war-torn strife or any of that," Limbaugh told his listeners. "This whole thing is a massive invasion. I mean, it's astounding to watch what's really happening here. . . . ISIS has predicted this. They have promised this. ISIS has said that this is their long-range objective."[9] On September 9, 2015, the conspiracy news website InfoWars devoted its program to the story of the migrant crisis, calling it a "Trojan Horse for ISIS invasion,"[10] and Fox News' *Fox & Friends* explained that the clip of the chanting men on a train highlighted "just how many of these refugees, who are fleeing violence in Iraq and Syria, are Muslim" and that they could be "potential terrorists."[11]

As the public debate raged, reporters asked Trump what he thought about the growing crisis. At first on September 4, 2015, Trump called in to

MSNBC's *Morning Joe* and explained that the crisis was "so horrible on a humanitarian basis" that while "we have so many problems" he would "possibly" agree to accept refugees because "we should help as much as possible."[12] But Trump was also suspicious of the refugees. He told Fox News' Bill O'Reilly on September 8, 2015, "I wonder, you know, where all of these people are coming from exactly and what are they representing, because do you have people from ISIS in that group—you know there are a lot of security risks with it—but something has to be done. It is an unbelievable humanitarian problem." The problem was so great that Trump said that even though he hated "the concept of it, on a humanitarian basis with what's happening you have to. . . . It's living in hell in Syria, there is no question about it; they are living in hell and something has to be done."[13]

Right-wing Breitbart—then edited by future Trump campaign chief executive Steve Bannon—wondered if it was "a policy Trump has thought completely through?" Breitbart observed that Trump's proposal to allow "Syrian refuges into our country" might make his supporters "alarmed."[14] Trump seemed to reconsider. By September 9, 2015, Trump explained to Fox News' Sean Hannity, "Frankly, you have ISIS, and if you look at a lot of the people I've been watching on television, most of them are men." What Trump saw on television seemed to change his mind about accepting refugees, because while he still believed that "from a humanitarian standpoint, I'd love to help," he now declined to help, explaining, "We have our own problems. We have so many problems that we have to solve. We have to straighten out our own problems."[15] Not only had Trump changed his mind, but antirefugee sentiment had coalesced on conservative and right-wing media and resonated with Trump voters.[16] By November 24, 2015, according to an ABC/*Washington Post* survey, "47% of GOP voters held pro-deportation and anti-refugee positions and of those, a majority (75%) were committed to voting for Trump."[17]

Since early September 2015, right-wing and conservative media and Trump had responded to a series of questions (or "*stases*," Latin for "points of stopping") about how to understand the unfolding crisis: Are they refugees, or are they migrants? Are they families, or are they strong, military-aged men? Are they innocent victims, or are they dangerous attackers? How should we think about them, and what should be our policy? While at first Trump repeatedly used the terms "refugees" and "humanitarian crisis"—benign terms that implied that the United States should offer its help to the innocent victims of war and reaffirmed the "humanness" (the humanity) of the refugees—he quickly began to describe the crisis differently. At his September 30, 2015, rally in Keene, New Hampshire, Trump expressed his suspicions about the refugees: "They could be ISIS; I don't know. Did you ever see a migration like this? They are all strong-looking guys. There are so many men, and there aren't that many women. I say to myself, 'Why aren't they fighting to save Syria? Why are they migrating all over Europe?'" Trump thought the plan to take in refugees was particularly suspicious because "Where they are from? We have no idea. There's no identification and there's no anything." To the sound of the thunderous applause of his New Hampshire crowd, he vowed, "If I win, if I win, they are going back. I'm telling you; they are going back." Trump would send the refugees back, he explained, because "this could be one of the great tactical flaws of all time. A 200,000-man army maybe. Or 50,000 or 80,000 or 100,000."[18]

By his October 3, 2015, rally in Franklin, Tennessee, Trump had rebranded the refugees. They were not, in fact, refugees or victims; they weren't even people. Rather, as InfoWars had explained nearly a month earlier, they were a "Trojan horse."[19] "We can't take them in the country," Trump explained. "You could have a Trojan horse situation. You could—this could be the ultimate Trojan horse." He realized that it might sound far-fetched—"I don't think it is, it probably isn't, but the word 'probably' is unacceptable, right?" Trump's claim that the refugees were a potential enemy object—a Trojan horse—was based upon nothing but suspicion. He urged his followers to be suspicious as well. After all, Trump argued, a cunning enemy combined with "how stupid our leaders are" could possibly cause disaster.[20]

George Stephanopoulos asked Trump what had changed between when he made his original promise to take in refugees and his controversial comments from the night before on ABC's *This Week*. "I saw the migration," Trump said, explaining how his suspicion was aroused. "The migration was strange to me, because it seems like so many men. There aren't that many women; there aren't that many children. It looked like mostly men, and they looked like strong men. These looked like physically strong people. And I'm saying, 'Where are all the women? Where are all the children?'" Stephanopoulos explained to Trump that half of the refugees were actually children, but Trump didn't buy it: "We don't know where they're coming from; we don't know who they are. They could be ISIS. It could be the great Trojan horse. I mean this could be one of the greatest Trojan horses ever since the original."[21] Trump was suspicious of those claiming to be refugees because, despite the promised careful vetting process outlined by the Obama administration, "they have no documentation. They have no paperwork. There's no way they can prove where they're coming from."[22]

Trump repeated the same points at his rallies and on television interviews throughout October and November 2015, each time invoking the "Trojan horse" metaphor. For example, on October 6, Trump told Fox News that since the refugees had "no documentation" and we couldn't be sure "where they come from" that "this is insane, not only militarily, not only from the standpoint of the Trojan horse, meaning they come in and they turn out to be the enemy, and we pay for it, right? That's a beauty. This would be greater than the example of the Trojan horse; this would blow the Trojan horse away."[23] On November 17, 2015, he told Hannity, "They are strong men. They are making up papers" and warned that the refugees "could be the ultimate Trojan horse."[24] And on November 19, 2015, he told his rally crowd in Newton, Iowa, "We can't take them. It could be a Trojan horse. I looked at the migration. I see these people coming by the hundreds of thousands and I say they're men. They're young men. They're strong men. They look like soldiers. I say where are the women? Now there are some, a little bit, but not much. And I say where are the soldiers? What's going on? Why aren't they back fighting? They're supposed to be fighting for their country. Why are they leaving?" Trump once again warned his followers to be suspicious because "we don't know who they are. They don't have paperwork. They don't have anything." And he vowed to prevent the Trojan horse invasion: "We're going to have a wall. We're going to have a border. We're going to have such a strong border."[25]

Trump had simplified the confusing refugee/migrant/innocent/terrorist story by using the rhetorical figure of reification (treating people as objects) to repeatedly ask his audiences to understand the refugees themselves and the policy of accepting refugees into the United States as a Trojan horse. In Greek mythology the Trojan horse, of course, was the deceptive tactic used by the ancient Spartans at the conclusion of their ten-year war with Troy in about 1200 BCE. As told by Virgil, the Spartans were unable to breach the walls of Troy, so they built a giant wooden horse, hid their warriors inside, and left the horse outside of Troy for the Trojans to find. Lulled into believing that the Spartans had abandoned their siege of the city, the Trojans themselves brought the wooden horse inside their city's protective wall and celebrated what they believed was the successful end of the long war. Once the Trojans had fallen into a drunken sleep, the Spartan soldiers emerged from their hiding place inside the horse and drove the Trojans out of their own city, winning the war.[26] As "Trojan horse" the refugees were dangerous: they were seemingly benign but were actually an enemy object set on destruction. As "Trojan horse" the refugees were not people but a plotline: a deceptive ambush that would lead to American ruin. Trump's use of reification allowed him to justify his change in policy: it was no longer a "humanitarian crisis" as he once thought, but instead it was the "ultimate Trojan horse." Denying the humanity of the refugees made it easier to deny them refuge. In fact, it made it quite easy to ban them entirely, which is precisely what Trump proposed doing on December 7, 2015.

Calling both the refugees and the policy of admitting more refugees into the United States a "Trojan horse" was a clever use of reification because, according to legend, the Trojan horse was an object filled with people—it was both people and object. As Trump had explained repeatedly, the weak and corrupt leaders cared about the wrong people; those people were not actual people but were objects and enemies. The use of reification answered the potential objections to Trump's policies because objects don't have rights—only people do. Trump's reification rested entirely on distrust and suspicion, which was the takeaway from Virgil's story of the Trojan horse: "Beware of Greeks bearing gifts," Virgil had written. Trump didn't know if the refugees were actually plotting terror, but since he didn't know that they *weren't* plotting terror, he believed that we shouldn't take additional risks. Not only did Trump's use of reification deny the humanity of the refugees; it also resonated with a distrusting nation and directed its distrust at a potential threat. Throughout November 2015, Trump had drawn controversy around his statements about Muslims, but he held firm. The November 13, 2015, terrorist attack in Paris, France, and the December 2, 2015, attack in San Bernardino, California, only intensified his belief that all Muslims were a dangerous threat—enemy objects that must be controlled. Trump's dehumanizing reification of Muslims enabled him to argue for all sorts of policies that would rob them of their human dignity: he would surveil mosques, he would register American Muslims in a database, he would institute a travel ban preventing Muslims from entering the United States, and he would send Muslim refugees out of the United States.

Trump announced his Muslim Ban policy on December 7, 2015, at a rowdy campaign rally in Mount Pleasant, South Carolina. "I wrote something that is very, very important and probably not politically correct. I don't care,"[27] Trump said to the cheers and applause of his rally crowd. "We are out of control and have no idea who is coming into our country and no idea if they love us or hate us or want to bomb us. We have no idea what's going on." He said that only he would tell his audience the truth about Muslims, because "mainstream media wants us to surrender the Constitution. They are so dishonest." More cheers and applause issued forth from his rally audience. "Shall I read you this statement?" Trump asked. His crowd roared as he began to read, "'Donald J. Trump is calling for a complete shutdown of Muslims entering the United States until our country's representatives can figure out what the hell is going on! Have no choice. We have no choice." Wild cheers and applause arose from his rally crowd.[28]

CNN said that Trump's proposal "raised a firestorm of outrage." Peter Bergen, CNN's national security analyst, said that Trump's proposal had all of the "traits of a proto-fascist."[29] The *New York Times* editorial board said that his proposal showed a tendency toward a "vicious treatment of the weak and outsiders."[30] The *Detroit Free Press* said, "Trump's indictment of Muslims en masse is nothing more than rank bigotry and racism, a reach back to the darkest chapters of America's history and a betrayal of the founding principles of our nation."[31] Yet his proposal was a huge hit with his rally crowd when he read it in South Carolina, and a December 9, 2015, Bloomberg Politics/Purple Strategies poll found that 37 percent of GOP voters were more likely to vote for Trump *because* of his Muslim Ban policy.[32] A December 14, 2015, ABC/*Washington Post* poll found that while only 36 percent of all Americans supported Trump's Muslim Ban, 59 percent of Republicans did.[33] Trump's use of reification was successful in helping his followers make sense of the confusing refugee story: it was not a humanitarian crisis but an enemy invasion. His use of reification took advantage of preexisting distrust and suspicion and denied the humanity of those who needed America's help. "When Trump read the Muslim Ban in South Carolina," recalled CBS News reporter Sopan Deb, "a lot of us assumed it would be a death knell to his candidacy. He had a lot of criticism coming at him from both parties. It was an unexpected proposal, and it received a lot of backlash, or so we thought. When he read it in South Carolina, he got a prolonged standing ovation."[34]

CHAPTER 4

"Now, the poor guy. You gotta see this guy."

Ad Hominem

Myrtle Beach, South Carolina, November 24, 2015
Favorable: 34.8 percent; Unfavorable: 55 percent[1]

"Hey," Trump told a rally crowd in Birmingham, Alabama, on November 21, 2015, "I watched when the World Trade Center came tumbling down. And I watched in Jersey City, New Jersey, where thousands and thousands of people were cheering as that building was coming down. Thousands of people were *cheering*. So something's going on." He then declared ominously, "We've got to find out what it is." Trump's fourteen-year-old recollection of the "cheering" thousands in New Jersey who had supposedly celebrated the September 11, 2001, attack on the World Trade Center was sufficient evidence, he believed, to warrant the suspicion of all Muslims currently living in the United States. Since he had begun his presidential campaign, Trump had warned of the need for stronger borders, increased surveillance, extreme vetting, and other controversial policies designed specifically to thwart what he believed were the threats of illegal immigration and Muslim terrorism. His proposals in his Birmingham rally speech were consistent with his well-known preferences, but they had taken on new relevance in the aftermath of the November 13, 2015, terrorist attack in Paris, France, that had killed 129 people. "I do want surveillance. I will absolutely take database of the people coming in from Syria if we can't stop it, but we're going to," he promised his crowd in Birmingham.[2] "If I win, they're going back," Trump assured the cheering crowd. "We can't have them. We can't have them."[3]

Trump called for the increased scrutiny of Muslims living in the United States. "Certain things will be done that we never thought would happen in this country in terms of information and learning about the enemy," he told Yahoo! News on November 17, 2015. His views on Muslims had already caused quite a bit of controversy by the time he held his November 2015 Birmingham rally. In fact, his claim about seeing the 9/11 celebrations was an attempt to mitigate the outrage that had already erupted over his controversial plans. Rather than end the issue, Trump's recollection led to more controversies. "It was not clear what Mr. Trump was referring to," reported Maggie Haberman in the *New York Times*. "There were cheers of support in some Middle Eastern countries that day, which were broadcast on television. But a persistent internet rumor of Muslims celebrating in Patterson, NJ, was discounted by police officials at the time. A search of news accounts from that period shows no reports of mass cheering in Jersey City."[4]

The day after his Birmingham rally, Trump called into ABC's *This Week*, where George Stephanopoulos asked him about the claim. "The police say that didn't happen and all those rumors have been on the internet for some time," explained Stephanopoulos. "Did you misspeak yesterday?" Trump's response was unequivocal: "It did happen. I saw it. It was on television. I saw it. George, it did happen. There were people that were cheering on the other side of New Jersey, where you have large Arab populations. They were cheering as the World Trade Center came down." Not only was Trump adamant; he defiantly attacked Stephanopoulos for questioning his recollection. "I know it might be not politically correct for you to talk about it, but there were people cheering as that building came down—as those buildings came down. And that tells you something. It was well covered at the time, George. Now, I know they don't like to talk about it, but it was well covered at the time. There were people over in New Jersey that were watching it, a heavy Arab population, that were cheering as the buildings came down. Not good."[5] Trump had seen it with his own eyes. He was a truth teller. Stephanopoulos couldn't admit that Trump was telling the truth because (predictably) he was a corrupt, politically correct member of the media. Trump used an *ad hominem* attack (attacking the person instead of their argument), rather than acknowledging Stephanopoulos's argument's validity.

Stories questioning Trump's recollection circulated quickly on November 22, 2015, with fact-checkers like Snopes explaining that Trump's "claim was long since debunked"[6] and news organizations like NPR attempting to confirm the story, but after searching "contemporaneous news reports," failing to "turn up any news accounts of American Muslims cheering or celebrating in the wake of Sept. 11."[7] When Trump's staff searched for corroborating evidence to support his recollection, they found only a single article. "The media was going crazy. They were having a field day," Trump told a rally crowd in Columbus, Ohio, on November 23, 2015. "The reporters are calling all day, all night. They want to find out: Did Trump made a mistake? And one of my people came in: 'Mr. Trump, I have a story in the *Washington Post.*'" That article, written by Serge Kovaleski and Fredrick Kunkle and published by the *Washington Post* on September 18, 2001, had indeed reported, "in Jersey City, within hours of two jetliners' plowing into the World Trade Center, law enforcement authorities detained and questioned a number of people who were allegedly seen celebrating the attacks and holding tailgate-style parties on rooftops while they watched the devastation on the other side of the river."[8] Vindicated by the *Post* story, Trump tweeted a link to it, read it to his rally crowd, and demanded apologies from the media skeptics.[9]

"Fortunately somebody at the *Washington Post* wrote that," Trump told his rally crowd in Columbus, Ohio. But he warned his audience not to be surprised if the corrupt media "try to deny it. They'll probably say, 'Well, we made a mistake.'" Trump said that if reporters tried to deny it, then "I could show you how dishonest they all are; I might like that better. Let them say that. But they'll find some reason to deny it. They'll call it a typo—it was about a . . . it was a very long and winding typo. They'll try to deny it, but I don't think they'll be able to."[10] As it turned out, neither of the authors of the *Post* article could substantiate Trump's story: Serge Kovaleski disputed the claim that there were ever "thousands" of people suspected of celebrating. "I certainly do not remember anyone saying that thousands or even hundreds of people were celebrating. That was not the case, as best as I can remember," recalled Kovaleski. And Fredrick Kunkle explained that he "specifically visited the Jersey City building and neighborhood where the celebrations were purported to have happened. But I could never verify that report."[11]

With his credibility on the line, Trump did as he promised he would: he tried to show his supporters "how dishonest [reporters] all are" for denying his story. Trump frequently used an *ad populum* appeal (appealing to the wisdom of the crowd) to support his recollection: "I received hundreds of phone calls over the couple of days since I said it from people saying, 'Mr. Trump, you're right. You're right. We saw it. We live in New Jersey; we saw it. You're right.'" Even more frequently, he used *ad hominem* attacks (attacking the person instead of their argument) against those who attempted to discredit his story. His *ad hominem* attacks were designed to trivialize the truth claims made by his opposition, as well as to divide his supporters from the media gatekeepers of truth and prevent himself from being held accountable for the veracity of his recollection. This strategy allowed Trump to succeed in changing the conversation from one about his proposed antiterrorism policies or whether or not it was true that "thousands and thousands of people were cheering" on 9/11 to Trump's preferred topic of whether or not he had been politically correct or appropriate in the way that he had refuted reporters' claims. It was a strategy that positioned Trump as the one and only source of truth.

With an already distrusting electorate, one way to discredit the media was to claim that Trump was right about his recollection of 9/11 celebrations; the media knew it, and they were suppressing the evidence that would prove him right. On November 24, 2015, Trump's campaign manager Corey Lewandowski made exactly these claims in an interview with Breitbart News: "For the mainstream media to go out and say that this didn't happen is just factually inaccurate. [Trump has] provided many opportunities for them to go and see it, but they have their own agenda; the media has their own agenda." The media's agenda was to "try and discredit" Trump so that an "establishment candidate" could win.[12] That night at his campaign rally in Myrtle Beach, South Carolina, Trump took a similar approach when he explained that while he had "very strongly and very correctly" said that "they were dancing in the street and they were dancing on rooftops" on 9/11, he was "taking heat because you know the liberal media they want to guard that; they didn't want that out because that's not good for them." Trump said that while "I could have said I misspoke, I'm not big on that, am I? I'm not big on apologies."

Trump then broke his composure, and with his eyes bulging, his voice strained, his arms locked at the elbows, and his hands flapping, he oscillated his body back and forth while he impersonated the "nice reporter" Serge Kovaleski, who cowrote the now-disputed *Washington Post* story: "Now, the poor guy. You gotta see this guy. 'I-I-I-I don't know what I said. I don't remember,'" Trump said mockingly. "He's going like, 'I don't remember; maybe that's what I said.' This was fourteen years ago, and still, they didn't do a retraction! Fourteen years ago. They did no retraction!"[13] While there were two authors of the *Washington Post* story in question and both authors refused to substantiate Trump's version of history, only Kovaleski suffers from arthrogryposis, a congenital condition which limits the movement of his joints. Instead of addressing Kovaleski's claim that police investigations had found the rumors of mass celebrations to be unfounded, Trump mocked the reporter with an *ad hominem* attack—attacking his person instead of refuting his argument. Trump's impersonation was itself an argument: his parallel case argument compared Kovaleski's impaired body to what Trump believed was his impaired recollection of the 9/11 celebrations. Just as Kovaleski's body was impaired, so was his recollection. The argument hinged on comparing two things: one visible and apparent, one not. Trump's mocking performance of how Kovaleski responded to questions about the supposed 9/11 celebrations was no accident; it was an argument.

Over the next several days as criticism over Trump's impersonation intensified, Trump lashed out on Twitter at the "failing @nytimes," a news organization that was "poorly run and managed" and filled with "dopes." The *New York Times* "made all bad decisions over the last decade" and was therefore "incompetent!" and "so dismal." Trump advised that the "failing @ nytimes should focus on fair and balanced reporting rather than constant hit jobs on me."[14] Trump was indeed very generous with his *ad hominem* attacks against the news media, tweeting that *Meet the Press* anchor "Chuck Todd is a moron," that CNN was so "totally one-sided and biased against me that it is becoming boring," and that "highly untalented Wash Post blogger, Jennifer Rubin, a real dummy, never writes fairly about me. Why does Wash Post have low IQ people?"[15] Trump also thought that "3rd rate $ losing @Politico" had "no credibility."[16] All of these *ad hominem* insults were designed to force his followers to choose between believing him or believing mainstream media organizations—the choice was clear, he thought.

Trump stubbornly defended his impersonation of Kovaleski: he was just showing "groveling," he said repeatedly; he didn't even know about Kovaleski's condition. Kovaleski reminded Trump that they had known each other since the 1980s, were on a first-name basis, that he'd interviewed Trump on many occasions in his office at Trump Tower, and that they'd even flown together on Trump's airplane.[17] Kovaleski told the *New York Times* that he hadn't changed his story or groveled—"nothing could be further from the truth"—and explained to the *Post* that "the sad part about it is, it didn't in the slightest bit jar or surprise me that Donald Trump would do something this low-rent, given his track record."[18]

Many Americans agreed that Trump's behavior toward Kovaleski was "low-rent." An August 2016 Bloomberg poll showed that 62 percent of

Americans were "bothered a lot" by the incident and thought that this was the worst thing he had done over the course of his presidential campaign to that date (his *Access Hollywood* "hot mic" tape leaked in October 2016).[19] Yet Trump's loyal supporters held firm. Trump's Twitter account retweeted @pthebnyc, "No need to explain, Sir. We've got your back," on November 26, 2015, for example.[20] The next day, Trump retweeted another follower who asked, "Should the reporter's dishonesty be shielded from ridicule?"[21] Trump retweeted another follower who advised him, "So like the media to make something out of nothing. Don't let them sidetrack from the message."[22] Trump seemingly agreed. By December 1, 2015, Trump was pleased to tell his rally crowd in Waterville Valley, New Hampshire, that he had "the most loyal people": "You know, others if they sneeze they will drop you. Me, I can sneeze. I can. I can say things that I think are right."[23] The next day, Quinnipiac University released a poll showing that Trump was the undisputed leader in the crowded GOP primary field and that his support had actually improved 3 percent from the month before, now standing at 27 percent. Tim Malloy, assistant director of the poll, explained: "It doesn't seem to matter what he says or who he offends, whether the facts are contested or the 'political correctness' is challenged. Donald Trump seems to be wearing Kevlar."[24]

On December 6, 2015, the *New York Times* published its examination of a week's worth of Trump's rhetoric and found that he "tends to attack a person rather than an idea or a situation, like calling political opponents 'stupid,' 'horrible,' 'weak' and other names, and criticizing foreign leaders, journalists and so-called anchor babies. Mr. Trump uses rhetoric to erode people's trust in facts, numbers, nuance, government and the news media."[25] Trump routinely attacked the credibility of his opponents rather than their arguments, especially when he was in trouble for something that he had said or done. In this case, his use of *ad hominem* attacks against reporter Serge Kovaleski allowed him to defend his credibility against the already distrusted media. Trump's recollection about thousands and thousands of people celebrating on 9/11 resonated with his followers—those who were already suspicious of immigrants and refugees and more likely to believe that the United States should deport undocumented immigrants and should not accept refugees.[26] His false recollection helped increase suspicion against Muslims living in the United States while also implicating journalists in a conspiracy to cover up and suppress evidence. His eyewitness account of the alleged 9/11 celebrations proved the wisdom of his truth telling and his plans to address terrorism. His followers were routinely told to be suspicious of Muslims and of anyone who would criticize him. Reporters like Kovaleski couldn't be trusted; they were the enemy. The enemy's ideas didn't need to be engaged—the only appropriate response was to attack and mock them.

Trump continued to attack Kovaleski personally.[27] At a November 28, 2015, rally in Sarasota, Florida, Trump took his *ad hominem* attacks a step further by impugning Kovaleski's credibility about whether or not Trump had knowingly mocked him. Trump told his rally crowd that Kovaleski was self-interested; he was taking advantage of the whole controversy merely to get attention for himself: "He is so happy; people have heard of him now. Nobody ever heard of the guy. Now people will be, so he's having a good time." Trump thought that Kovaleski was "using what he's got to such a horrible degree. I think it's disgraceful."[28]

CHAPTER 5

"I'm not saying that he conspired; I'm just saying that it was all over the place."

Paralipsis

On the phone, *Fox & Friends*, May 4, 2016
Favorable 31 percent; Unfavorable 62.3 percent[1]

"BOTH Cruz AND Rubio are ineligible to be POTUS! It's a SLAM DUNK CASE!! Check it!" retweeted Trump on February 20, 2016, on the morning of the South Carolina primary election—the third primary on the road to the GOP nomination.[2] The tweet included a link to a story from the Powdered Wig Society—part of the "Patriot Ad Network," a website "dedicated to the restoration of and the strict obedience to the Constitution"—that showed an unnamed lawyer explaining how Rubio and Cruz couldn't become president because they weren't "natural born citizens" of the United States.[3] Trump retweeted the accusation without comment but perhaps hoped that he might be able to sow doubt about his competitors' eligibility for office in order to help his chances in a competitive race.[4] Trump won that night in South Carolina and appeared the next morning on ABC News' *This Week*, where George Stephanopoulos asked Trump about his retweet. "You actually sent out a retweet yesterday," he said, "suggesting that Marco Rubio might be ineligible to be president—a tweet that said both Cruz and Rubio are ineligible to be President of the United States. Do you really believe that?" asked Stephanopoulos. "Well," Trump said by way of explanation, "it was a retweet"—as if to say that retweeting someone else's claim meant that he wasn't responsible for the content. When pressed, Trump continued: "I mean, let people make their own determination. I've never looked at it, George. I honestly have never looked at it. As somebody said, he's not [eligible]. And I retweeted it. I have 14 million people between Twitter and Facebook and Instagram, and I retweet things and we start dialogue and it's very interesting."

Trump's response to Stephanopoulos was a *paralipsis*: "I'm not saying it; I'm just saying it" (here in the form of "I'm not tweeting it; I'm just retweeting it"). It wasn't his fact—he'd never even looked into it. He was just retweeting someone else's accusation. Throughout his campaign, Trump used *paralipsis* to make accusations that he could later disavow without having to take responsibility for his words. *Paralipsis* was a powerful rhetorical device for Trump because it allowed Trump to say two things at once—to both say the thing and to not say the thing—and it helped him spread rumors while avoiding consequences. He routinely used *paralipsis* to recirculate innuendo and to distance himself from the things that he said. Using *paralipsis* gave Trump the "out" of plausible deniability. This helped him impeach the credibility of established political leaders while giving his followers a supposedly candid—and often non–politically correct—glimpse at what he supposedly really thought. Trump often used it to tell jokes at his rallies and to signal to his followers that he and they were on the same team, against the despised opposition. In this way, *paralipsis* was incredibly rewarding for both Trump and his audiences. For example, "I'm going to be nice today," Trump said at a rally in Birmingham, Alabama, on November 21, 2015. "I'm not going to call Jeb Bush 'low energy'; I'm not going to repeat it. I'm not going to say that 'Marco Rubio is a lightweight.' I said I'm not doing it! I will not do it. I will not say that 'Ben Carson had a bad week.' . . . I said that I'm not going to say it, so I'm not saying it! So, I'm not saying any of those things about any of those people."[5] His rally crowd laughed and cheered. For another example, on December 1, 2015, at a rally in Waterville Valley, New Hampshire, Trump said, "All of the other candidates are weak, and they're just weak. I think they're weak, generally. You want to know the truth. But I won't say that because I don't want to get myself—I don't want to have any controversy. Is that OK? No controversy—so I refuse to say that they're weak, generally, OK?"[6] Trump told his audience that he both wanted to say it and knew that he ought not to say it—and in the process, he had said that his competitors were "weak" four times, while never "actually" saying it at all.

Trump continued to use *paralipsis* throughout his campaign, even on the day that he would secure enough primary votes to win the GOP presidential nomination—May 3, 2016. On that day, Trump caused controversy over his use of *paralipsis* to discredit the father of his biggest Republican rival, Ted Cruz. Trump had called in to *Fox & Friends* to discuss that day's Indiana primary and was asked for his reaction to a video of Cruz's father (Rafael Cruz) asking voters to "vote for the candidate that stands on the word of God and on the Constitution of the United States of America." Rafael Cruz predicted that Trump's election "could be the destruction of America." Trump's response was to call Rafael Cruz's speech a "disgrace" and then to denounce him with an *ad hominem* attack on his credibility and patriotism. "You know, his father was with Lee Harvey Oswald prior to Oswald being, you know, shot," said Trump, implying that the elder Cruz lacked standing because he conspired somehow with Lee Harvey Oswald. "I mean, the whole thing is ridiculous. What is this? Right prior to his being shot and nobody even brings it up. They don't even talk about that. That was reported, and nobody talks about it. . . . What was he doing with Lee Harvey Oswald shortly before the death? Before the shooting? It's horrible."[7]

Trump was referring to an article published in the supermarket tabloid the *National Enquirer* that had recently bubbled up through right-of-center conspiracy sites. The story first originated on April 7, 2016, with InfoWars regular and "investigative journalist" Wayne Madsen posting a long analysis on the *Wayne Madsen Report*, asking, "Was the father of presidential hopeful Cruz involved in the JFK assassination?" On April 14, 2016, a short Reddit[8] thread opened up, with a link to Madsen's article reposted on a blog called *Milfuegos*.[9] On April 15, 2016, Madsen posted the story on InfoWars, and on April 18, 2016, he joined Alex Jones's program to discuss the story.[10] On April 20, 2016, the *National Enquirer* posted a press release online, teasing for its May 2, 2016, cover story: "Ted Cruz's Father Now Linked to JFK Assassination!" it exclaimed, promising that the "world exclusive bombshell *Enquirer* probe reveals the photos that will destroy Lyin' Ted."[11] In their story, the *Enquirer* quoted Madsen, "If it is [Rafael Cruz], it raises questions about what he knew about Oswald," to support its claim that the "troubling photos suggest Rafael worked directly with Oswald before he fired the fatal shots from the Texas School Book Depository in downtown Dallas that killed Kennedy on November 22, 1963."[12] Wayne Madsen was the only source for the Rafael Cruz–Oswald–JFK story; no other credible source for the story emerged, and many news organizations and fact-checkers discredited the story.[13] As many fact-checkers noted, the picture in question was taken in New Orleans in August 1963 and showed Oswald distributing pro-Castro literature with a person who the Warren Commission was never able to identify and who could not be identified based upon the photo. Even *if* the picture turned out to be Rafael Cruz, there was no evidence that the person in the photo had any knowledge of a plot to assassinate JFK—an event that would occur three months later in a different state. Nonetheless, the *National Enquirer* and Trump led their audiences to believe that the photo proved a connection between Cruz and Oswald and JFK's assassination.

Trump had a well-known friendly relationship with *National Enquirer* publisher David Pecker—the *Enquirer* had run spoon-fed positive stories about Trump for years, published his "writings," urged him to run for president in both 2012 and 2016, used "catch and kill" techniques to suppress negative stories about Trump, denounced his opponents, and issued its first-ever presidential endorsement all in support of Trump's bid to become president.[14] Of course, while it's to be expected that a tabloid claim would be based upon circumstantial evidence, it was unexpected that Trump would repeat the accusation. Trump used *paralipsis* to defend himself against charges that he had inappropriately spread a malicious and unfounded rumor. Trump called into Sean Hannity's radio program on May 3, 2016, the same day that he made the Rafael Cruz-Oswald accusation and explained that he wasn't responsible for the truthfulness of the accusation because the *Enquirer* "wouldn't put it in if they could be sued, that I can tell you. They are very big professionals. It was put in." Since he had shifted responsibility for the accusation to the *Enquirer*, he was able to assume its truthfulness and elaborate upon the possible consequences: "But if that were true, what was he doing having breakfast or whatever they were doing three months before the JFK assassination? Why are they doing that? Why is the father meeting with Lee Harvey Oswald?"[15] While the picture in question showed men standing on a sidewalk holding flyers, Trump always called what they were doing "eating breakfast or whatever," which implied a more intimate connection than merely standing next to one another in a public place. According to Trump's defense, he had made the accusation but wasn't responsible for the accuracy of its content. Trump's series of associations and questions introduced even more doubt and suspicion about Rafael Cruz, hoping to escalate the drama of his initial accusation.

"Do you owe Ted Cruz's father an apology for saying that he was with Lee Harvey Oswald before the JFK assassination?" asked George Stephanopoulos on May 4, 2016. "No," said Trump. "The fact is that it was a cover story on the *National Enquirer*. It was picked up by many other people and magazines and periodicals and newspapers, and all I did was refer to it. . . . I'm just referring to an article that appeared; it has nothing to do with me." It had nothing to do with Trump; he wasn't responsible for it. "So no apology?" asked Stephanopoulos. "I'm just referring to an article that appeared; I mean, it has nothing to do with me. . . . I just referred them to articles that were in various periodicals."[16] *The Today Show's* Savannah Guthrie asked Trump to explain his accusation, as there was "no evidence of this." He responded: "I just asked about stories that were appearing all over the place, not just the *National Enquirer*, that a picture was taken of him and Lee Harvey Oswald and they didn't deny that picture. [Cruz's campaign did deny that the picture was of Rafael Cruz.] And I just asked, what was that all about? So this was just in response to some very, very nasty—I mean, honestly, very, very, very nasty remarks that were made about me. . . . All I did was refer them to some articles that appeared about his picture."[17] Trump explicitly used a *paralipsis* in his self-defense on CNN that night with Wolf Blitzer: "I'm not saying that he conspired; I'm just saying that it was all over the place. I said, 'Well, why don't you talk about that?' I'm not saying that he did it, but I'm just saying that it was all over the place." When Blitzer asked Trump if he actually believed the story that he had been repeating, Trump said, "Of course I don't believe that. I didn't believe it, but I did say, 'Let people to read it.'"[18] It was a classic Trump evasion strategy: "I'm not saying; I'm just saying, and no one can hold me accountable for what I'm not saying."

Ted Cruz responded to Trump's accusation on the morning of May 3, 2016: "Donald Trump alleges that my dad was involved in assassinating JFK. Now, let's be clear, this is nuts, it's not a reasonable position, this is just kooky. And, while I'm at it," Cruz deadpanned, "I guess I should just admit that, yes, my dad killed JFK, he is secretly Elvis, and Jimmy Hoffa is buried in his backyard."[19] Ted Cruz lost the Indiana primary and dropped out of the presidential race that night. "Wow, Lyin' Ted Cruz really went wacko today. Made all sorts of crazy charges. Can't function under pressure—not very presidential. Sad!" Trump tweeted in response.[20]

The next day on InfoWars, Alex Jones and Wayne Madsen wondered, "Did Cruz drop out to cover up the Kennedy assassination connection?"[21] During the interview, Madsen revealed to Jones that "a good source inside the hierarchy of the Republican Party" had told Madsen that "Ted Cruz knows that his father worked for the CIA and there were more skeletons that were going to be paraded out of that party had he not dropped out, so he was basically told that it was time for you to leave the campaign."[22] Whether or not the CIA was involved in Cruz's decision to drop out has not been proven, but the question of Rafael Cruz's relationship to Lee Harvey Oswald largely dropped out of public discourse. Trump brought it up again on July 22, 2016, on the day after he accepted the Republican nomination for the presidency.

Ted Cruz had made news on July 20, 2016, when he declined to endorse Trump in his Republican National Convention speech, urging Republicans instead to "vote your conscience."[23] In response to this overt insult, Trump pretended to be baffled, "All I did is point out the fact that on the cover of the *National Enquirer* there was a picture of his dad and crazy Lee Harvey Oswald having breakfast," he told reporters at a press conference. Then Trump blamed the whole Cruz drama on the media taking his *paralipsis* literally, causing the misunderstanding: "The press takes that, and they say, 'Donald Trump and his conspiracy theories; he went out and said his father was with Lee Harvey Oswald, and he assassinated the president.' What did I do? I know nothing about his father. I know nothing about Lee Harvey Oswald." He was just saying; he wasn't saying. Then he took the opportunity to say it again: "But there was a picture on the front page of the *National Inquirer*, which does have credibility, and they're not going to do pictures like that because they get sued for a lot of money if things are wrong, OK—a lot of money."[24]

Trump's use of *paralipsis* allowed him to recirculate the rumor and gave him the out-of-plausible deniability, but it also allowed him to impeach the credibility of his opposition, increasing his followers' suspicion of those in power. Trump's use of *paralipsis* against Ted Cruz allowed Trump to invoke suspicions about Cruz's ability to serve as president and whether or not his father was involved in assassinating JFK. Trump continued to use *paralipsis* to circulate rumor and innuendo, which perhaps counterintuitively helped him appear to be a heroic demagogue. He told his followers the awful truth about his opposition, even when he knew that he could get into trouble for saying (or not saying) that truth. Trump's use of *paralipsis* also helped his followers believe that they understood the real Donald Trump—that he was saying exactly what he thought because he often walked them through his thought process. He wanted to say it, but knew he ought not to. Such an intimate, "insider" view into Trump's thoughts rewarded audiences because it made it appear as though Trump was on their side, against the opposition.

Trump used *paralipsis* to divide his supporters from establishment political leaders, which helped him avoid accountability because it allowed him to say it—to make up, recirculate, and/or embellish rumors—while still having the plausible deniability of not saying it. Fox News' Bill O'Reilly called Trump's Rafael Cruz accusation "beyond bizarre" on May 4, 2016, but suggested that Trump "puts that out there just to create mayhem, and creating mayhem has won the election for him, has it not?"[25]

CHAPTER 6

"I am 'America First.' So, I like the expression. I'm "America First."

American Exceptionalism

New York, New York, March 26, 2016
Favorable: 30.4 percent; Unfavorable: 63.2 percent[1]

"We are in a competition with the world," Trump bellowed at his big America First economic policy speech in Detroit, Michigan, on August 8, 2016, "and I want America to win. When I am president, we will!"[2] American exceptionalism (America's unique status among other nations in the world) was always a part of Trump's campaign, from his announcement speech on June 16, 2015, to his election night victory speech on November 8, 2016. American exceptionalism—presented as American greatness—was the underlying logic motivating his campaign theme, "Make America Great Again." American exceptionalism oozed out of Trump campaign merch like T-shirts and hats, as hashtags on social media, and in every rally speech Trump delivered. Trump's invocation of American exceptionalism functioned to unite his supporters behind a hopeful vision of Trump's America, and at the same time it functioned as a political jeremiad—a warning that Americans had abandoned the principles that had made the nation great in the first place. Trump acted as the Biblical Jeremiah, as a voice in the wilderness, apart from Washington society, when he repeatedly claimed that he was not a politician, not bought by the lobbyists, not politically correct, and not a part of the swamp that needed to be drained.[3] Rhetoric scholar Kurt Ritter explained that a candidate would ask "What made America great?" in a typical political jeremiad and offer supporters "a single ideal (or a cluster of values) from our past which is missing in the present and whose absence accounts for our difficulties."[4] For Trump, the single answer to the question of what once made America great was "winning." Winning was what was missing, and only winning would make America great again. Trump's use of American exceptionalism as a political jeremiad allowed him to question the credibility of establishment politicians who either didn't know how to win or were too corrupt to win. Either way, establishment politicians were part of the problem and certainly couldn't make America great again. Trump, of course, was the solution: he offered himself as American exceptionalism personified, as the apotheosis of American winning. Because Trump was such a winner, he would win for America. He would, by the sheer force of his own winningness, make America win again.[5] He said it could be done easily, in fact.

"Make America Great Again" might have sounded good to his followers, but his critics charged that it was vague or racist or nostalgic, or worse.[6] On March 26, 2016, the *New York Times* published an extended interview with Trump in which veteran foreign affairs reporter David Sanger suggested to Trump that his campaign theme sounded like Trump was really saying to put "America First" in its relationships with other nations. Trump liked the sound of it. "I am 'America First.' So, I like the expression. I'm 'America First,'" Trump agreed. "We have been disrespected, mocked, and ripped off for many, many years by people that were smarter, shrewder, tougher. We were the big bully, but we were not smartly led." Soon Trump began to append "America First" to his campaign slogan and to his policies: Make America Great Again: [by putting] America First. America First meant strong, winning. It meant making decisions only with American interests in mind (foreign policy) and rebuilding the American economy (domestic policy). "What I want to do is make America great again," Trump told Sean Hannity on May 18, 2016. "You know, the theme is such a great theme and I didn't even realize it was that good until I started really getting out there and I add to it and it's called America first. We're going to put America first. On trade deals. Like we make deals that are so bad, they're so inconceivably bad. And I said, no, no, we want you all to do well. America first."[7] America First presumed American exceptionalism (it was America's destiny to be great) as well as Trump's heroic jeremiad (the nation's political leaders had failed to keep America great because they had failed to put America First). Trump would be America's hero—only he would put America First.

As a real-estate developer, Trump saw himself as a maker—as a deal maker, as a building maker. As maker, he would remake America. His ideal for what had made America great in the past was also based on a view of man as *homo faber*—man making. America was "great" during the manufacturing boom of the late nineteenth and early twentieth centuries when "making" was central to the national economy. When *New York Times* reporter Maggie Haberman asked Trump when America had been at its greatest, he said it was this period of unfettered industrialism and robust commercial expansion: "If you look back, it really was; there was a period of time when we were developing at the turn of the century which was a pretty wild time for this country and pretty wild in terms of building that machine, that machine was really based on entrepreneurship etc., etc."[8] Likewise, as he toured the rusted-out rust-belt states that would eventually tip the election his way—cities like Detroit, Michigan, that industrial capitalism had built and abandoned—he invoked this image of America winning, of America making, like it once did. He promised to make America great again by reopening America's closed factories, among other things. "When we were governed by an America First policy, Detroit was booming," Trump said in Detroit, Michigan, on August 8, 2016. "Engineers, builders, laborers, shippers, and countless others went to work each day, provided for their families, and lived out the American Dream. But for many living in this city, that dream has long ago vanished." Trump promised that Americans would join together to remake America, and the national project of remaking America would once again restore American greatness: "It will be American hands that rebuild this country, and it will be American energy—mined from American sources—that powers this country. It will be American workers who are hired to do the job." Trump explained his America First policy with a simple aphorism based upon American exceptionalism: "Americanism, not globalism, will be our new credo."[9] Trump would once again separate America from the rest of the world.

Above all, appeals to a simple and uncritical American exceptionalism steeped in nostalgia for the industrial revolution was a useful rhetorical strategy for Trump. In a negative sense, Trump used his version of American exceptionalism to separate his followers from established political figures: whenever he promised to make America great again with "so much winning," he also dismissed the qualifications of the political leaders who had let America lose in the first place. For example, in his announcement speech on June 16, 2015, he explained, "Politicians are all talk, no action. Nothing's gonna get done. They will not bring us—believe me—to the promised land. They will not." Establishment political leaders could "never make America great again" because they were corrupt: "They don't even have a chance. They're controlled fully—they're controlled fully by the lobbyists, by the donors, and by the special interests, fully. We have losers."[10] Likewise, in Detroit, Trump had blamed the nation's decline on the "politicians" who "rigged the system": "We need to stop believing in politicians and start believing in America."[11] Over and over again, when Trump expressed his shock at America's decline from greatness, he also told his followers to distrust the "stupid" leaders and politicians who he claimed had allowed it to happen. "A Trump administration will never, ever put the interests of a foreign country before the interests of our country," Trump said to a rally crowd in Iowa City, Iowa, on November 6, 2016. "From now on, it's going to be America first. To all Americans, I say this: it's time for real leadership and it's time for change. We're going to change."[12] Repeatedly, Trump used American exceptionalism (as winning) as the standard by which his followers ought to judge the conduct of their political leaders, and he repeatedly argued that by that standard the nation's political leaders had failed.

Uncritical American exceptionalism steeped in nostalgia for the Industrial Revolution was a useful rhetorical strategy for Trump in a positive sense as well. Trump used his version of American exceptionalism to promise to restore Americans' pride in themselves and in their nation, and in so doing, he also used it to express a kind paternalism—to position himself as both a heroic demagogue and also as a protective father figure. For example, as Trump accepted the Republican Party nomination on July 21, 2016, he invoked his heroic qualification as the apotheosis of American exceptionalism and pledged to use his greatness to restore American greatness: "I have made billions of dollars in business making deals—now I'm going to make our country rich again. . . . To all Americans tonight, in all our cities and towns, I make this promise: we will make America strong again. We will make America proud again. We will make America safe again. And we will make America great again."[13] On August 12, 2016, in Erie, Pennsylvania, Trump promised his cheering crowd in another rusted-out rust-belt town, "We're going to win again and you're going to be proud of your country again. We're not going to be the people that are laughed at all over the world for not knowing what we're doing, for allowing others to come in and just strip us of what we have. We are going to win. We are going to be America first. We are going to make America great again. And it's going to happen quickly."[14]

While Trump was not well-known as an empathic speaker, he found empathy for the plight of the "75 percent of the American people" who "think our country is headed on the wrong track."[15] He not only promised that "we are going to fix it" but also assured his followers that the nation's decline was not their fault. On April 18, 2016, he said the following before a rally crowd in Buffalo, New York—yet another town nostalgic for its former role in American manufacturing:

> Do not get scared. It is not your fault. It is politicians representing all of us who have no clue. Totally incompetent. These are people that represent us at the highest level, including the president of the United States, and look at what has happened here. Listen to this: Do not get discouraged. I am telling you, we're bringing it back fast. You watch what happens. . . . We will win at every element, we will win with the military, we will win with everything. We will win so much that you will get tired of winning; you will say from Buffalo, "Please, we don't want any more business. We are making too much money. . . . We don't want to win anymore." I will say, "Sorry, we are going to keep winning." We will win, win, win, and we will make America great again. America first, folks. America first.[16]

Trump reminded his followers that they had an important role to play in restoring American greatness, because, as he told his rally crowd in West Palm Beach, Florida, on October 13, 2016, "The only thing that can stop this corrupt machine is you. The only force strong enough to save our country is us. The only people brave enough to vote out this corrupt establishment is you the American people. We are going to have a policy, America first." In response, his rally crowd chanted "USA! USA! USA!"

Trump's trademarked "Make America Great Again" was always his campaign theme; it was a heroic promise to his followers. He would defend their interests against all enemies, be they foreign or domestic.[17] "It actually inspired me," Trump said about his campaign slogan, "because to me, it meant jobs. It meant industry and meant military strength. It meant taking care of our veterans. It meant so much."[18] And yet Trump's version of American exceptionalism could only persuade those Americans who believed in celebrating an uncritical version of the nation's past. For those who looked back at American history and saw American exceptionalism as an excuse for the exploitation of Native Americas, of African Americans, of women, and of children—for those Americans who saw in the nation's history the exploitation of labor, of the less powerful, of the environment—Trump's pledge to Make America Great Again by putting America First was not only divisive but frighteningly reactionary. To some Americans, Trump's "America First" nationalism seemed like fascism.[19]

Trump's loyal followers didn't seem to be concerned about whether or not "America First" was fascist. They understood him simply as the heroic demagogue who promised to make America great again. When prompted to describe Trump in their own words in August 2015, Frank Luntz's focus group members said things like, "'Tough.' 'Businessman.' 'Great.' 'Successful.' 'Not afraid.' 'Leader.' 'Has guts.' 'Charismatic.' 'A true American.' 'Kicks ass and takes names.'"[20] Such a heroic figure not only represented American exceptionalism but was exactly the sort of person who should be elected president, his followers believed. "We know his goal is to make America great again," said a woman in Luntz's focus group. "It's on his hat."[21]

PART TWO
Trump and the Polarized Electorate

If potential demagogues were to be screened out, it would have to be done by the parties. If parties ceased to perform this function—whether through design, inattention, or decay—the potential of demagoguery in the final election would loom much larger.

James Ceaser, *Critical Review*, 2007

The demagogue does not recognize controversial attitudes. He declares his adversary a liar, a traitor to the only truth. Dissension is no longer a matter of opinion, but of heresy. The "party line" wins a sort of mystic holiness. Totalitarian governments and their leaders are "infallible." To question their policies is sin. As soon as complete power is obtained, the monopoly over all instrumentalities of communication gives unlimited propaganda possibilities to the totalitarian.

Sigmund Neumann, *American Sociological Review*, 1938

ONE WAY TO DESCRIBE the 2016 electorate is that it had a historic and dangerous crisis of polarization. A June 12, 2014, Pew Research Center report found that "Republicans and Democrats are more divided along ideological lines—and partisan antipathy is deeper and more extensive—than at any point in the last two decades." Their research also found that the nation had moved away from the center over the past twenty years: the average Republican was more conservative than 93 percent of Democrats and the average Democrat was more liberal than 94 percent of Republicans.[1] By November 2016, Gallup found that 77 percent of Americans—a record high—believed that the nation was "greatly divided when it comes to the most important values."[2] Americans believed that they lacked common values, not just common policies.

With little common ground and few shared values, it's no wonder that another Pew survey found that 45 percent of Republicans said that Democratic policies were *a threat to the nation* and 41 percent of Democrats said the same thing about Republican policies.[3] Thinking that your political opposition is a "threat to the nation" is very different from mere partisan disagreement—only a nation's enemies threaten the nation. When we think of the people who hold different policy views from us as "enemies," we think of them as evil, not merely people with good reasons for thinking differently. Enemies cannot be trusted. Enemies are irrational because if they were rational, then they would think like we do. It isn't prudent to negotiate with evil, untrustworthy, irrational enemies; it's more prudent to try to destroy them.[4] In 2016 political polarization was a crisis that threatened the stability of the nation—perhaps even a "cold civil war."[5]

America's political polarization had left the nation vulnerable to attack. Within this crisis in which Americans believed that they had little common ground with their political opposition, that they did not share the same values, and that their opposition was an enemy of the state, Trump ran a campaign that was *designed* to increase polarization. As you'll see, Trump's rhetorical strategy sought to increase polarization between his followers and the rest of the nation. Trump's *ad populum* (appealing to the wisdom of the crowd) appeal against the Republican political establishment told his followers to reject the Republican intellectual elite that had done them wrong. Trump's *ad hominem* (attacking the person instead of their argument) attack against the Republican political establishment told his followers to reject the Republican elected officials who had done them wrong. Trump's *paralipsis* ("I'm not saying; I'm just saying") allowed him to disavow knowledge of racist violence while praising his supporters for fighting against their shared enemies. Trump's *ad baculum* (threats of force or intimidation) threats against his supporters' gun rights told them that they had to reject Hillary Clinton if they wanted to be safe. Trump's reification (treating people as objects) of immigrants separated Trump's good Americans from the infestation of dangerous invaders. And Trump's American exceptionalism (America's unique status among other nations in the world) told his followers that all other politicians supported the conspiracy of corruption, which only he could fix. Altogether, Trump took advantage of his followers' political polarization; he told his followers that anyone who was not with Trump was their mortal enemy.

CHAPTER 7

"I could stand in the middle of Fifth Avenue and shoot somebody and I wouldn't lose voters."

Ad Populum

Sioux City, Iowa, January 23, 2016
Favorable: 34.4 percent; Unfavorable: 57.8 percent[1]

On August 6, 2015, Fox News moderator Bret Baier posed the initial question of the first Republican Primary debate: "Is there anyone onstage—and can I see hands—who is unwilling tonight to pledge your support to the eventual nominee of the Republican Party and pledge to not run an independent campaign against that person?" Trump looked over his fellow Republicans on the debate stage, cocked his head to the side, and with an exaggerated smirk on his face, he raised his hand and then shrugged as he signaled that he would not, unequivocally, agree to remain loyal to the Republican Party.[2] Some in the debate audience cheered, while others booed. Trump was asked to explain himself. "Do you know that a divided party will likely elect another Clinton?" Baier asked. "I understand," replied Trump. "But I cannot say that I have to respect the person, if it's not me, the person who wins. If I do win, and I'm leading by quite a bit, that's what I want to do. I can totally make the pledge that if I'm the nominee I will pledge that I will not run as an independent. And I am discussing it with everybody, but I'm talking about a lot of leverage."[3] While Trump had actively sought the Republican Party nomination since he announced his campaign in June 2015, there had been quite a bit of controversy about whether or not Trump would pledge to support the eventual

Republican Party nominee, should it not be him. At first, Trump would only pledge to support himself—Trump was for Trump, he said. Trump's answer to the debate question reflected the fact that he ran a polarizing campaign against the Washington establishment of both parties.[4] Even though Trump did eventually sign a loyalty pledge to the Republican Party, it was an uneasy alliance.[5]

Whether or not Trump would be loyal to the Republican Party remained an active question throughout the election. For example, on December 8, 2015, Trump's Twitter and Facebook accounts shared the news of a *USA Today* poll that found that "68% of Trump's supporters say they would vote for the blustery billionaire businessman if he ran as an independent rather than a Republican; just 18% say they wouldn't."[6] Trump's social media followers liked what they saw in the poll numbers. Jennifer Schmelzle, for example, wrote the top comment in response to Trump's Facebook post: "Count me as one of them," she said. "I'm voting Trump either as a republican, idependent or as a write in, doesnt matter to me. Screw to worthless GOP."[7] Trump's supporters "liked" Schmelzle's comment more than 1,500 times. Trump's celebrity, unusual campaign, and controversial positions had attracted to him a base of loyal supporters—his "fans," he called them—and had, in the process, fractured the Republican Party. Throughout the election, Trump wielded his loyal followers like a cudgel—they gave him a lot of "leverage" as he said—while at the same time he protected his base of support by using *ad populum* arguments (appealing to the wisdom of the crowd) to praise his followers as wise, good, and "beautiful" real Americans.

Since by December 2015 no votes had been cast in any primaries no one knew for sure, but with his supporters reporting that they would bolt from the Republican Party with Trump, it *appeared* as though Trump was more powerful than the Republican Party. It was within this context that Rich Lowry, editor at the conservative *National Review*, decided to take a stand against Trump's presidential campaign. He invited twenty-two leaders of the conservative movement to contribute to a special issue, aptly titled "Against Trump," which was published online January 21, 2016—nine days before caucus goers in Iowa would cast the first votes of the presidential primary. Conservative movement opinion columnists, politicians, and media personalities used the *National Review* forum to argue that Trump was not one of them: "our basic argument about Trump," Lowry explained to Politico, "is simple and unassailable: He is a populist, not a conservative. Conservatism has always had a populist element, but it has been tethered to conservatism's animating causes of liberty, limited government and the Constitution."[8] The issue featured contributors like *Weekly Standard* editor William Kristol, National Rifle Association (NRA) spokesperson and radio personality Dana Loesch, Club for Growth president David McIntosh, and former attorney general Edwin Meese, who all explained that Trump, as populist, couldn't be trusted to be a true conservative.

Lowry claimed that conservatives like him and his contributors were not the "establishment" that Trump had denounced since his presidential announcement speech in June 2015—those elites were elected "office holders, especially high office holders," he said. He and his contributors were "principled conservatives."[9] Principled conservatives believed in liberty, limited government, and the Constitution. Predictably, "Against Trump" made news: CNN called the *National Review* issue "a blistering editorial,"[10] while Fox News observed "*National Review* Disses Donald Trump."[11] *The Atlantic* thought that "the *Review* declared war on Donald Trump,"[12] but Jeet Heer at *The New Republic* declared, "*National Review* Fails to Kill Its Monster."[13] Indeed, Trump's supporters viewed the *National Review* as the voice of the abhorred establishment. For example, when the *National Review* tweeted about its forum on January 21, 2016, Floss replied, "Shame on you. Think we were mad before, you haven't seen anything yet. . . . All this does is push people closer to Trump. We stand with Trump."[14] Floss's comment was followed by many others, like Patrick, who wrote, "NRO = Elitist Cons who are severely out of touch with the real party base."[15]

It's interesting that the *National Review*'s argument strategy to appeal to Trump's voters was to distinguish itself and the conservative cause it hoped to advance from Trump and Trump's populism because, for Trump, popularity was itself the argument for why he had greater standing than the *National Review* conservatives. For Trump, being popular—leading the polls, high ratings, good sales, and so on—was the one and only sign of value. There was no value in conservatism itself; there was only value in conservatism if it had high ratings. Trump easily dismissed the criticisms of the *National Review* conservative elites as unpopular.

On the night that "Against Trump" posted online, Trump's Twitter account posted three attacks on the *National Review*, which he echoed in person at a press conference in Las Vegas, Nevada, that same night. Trump called the *National Review* "a failing publication that has lost its way," claiming that its "circulation is way down, with its influence being at an all-time low." In fact, Trump tweeted, "very few people read the *National Review* because it only knows how to criticize, but not how to lead." Its founder, William F. Buckley, "would be ashamed of what had happened to his prize, the dying *National Review*!"[16] When a reporter asked Trump to react to the "Against Trump" conservatives, he reiterated that the *National Review* was a "dying paper" and added that the issue was a publicity stunt to attract attention. He didn't think that it would work because he was so popular: "The polls have just come out, as you saw, in Iowa, where I'm up by eleven points. Another one came out where I'm up by ten points, and you look at New Hampshire, you look at South Carolina, you look at Florida, where I have forty-eight, forty-eight points. I'm way up. I'm way up in every poll."[17]

Trump embraced the *National Review*'s distinction between populism and conservatism, arguing that populism was right and conservatism was wrong. He supported his argument for populism with a polarizing *ad populum* argument strategy: the wise people were better, more sensible, more informed, and more American than the *National Review* elites; thus Trump's enemies were really enemies of the good people. Trump defended himself from attack while praising his followers, all the while separating Trump's fans from traditional conservative Republicans in an "us versus them" strategy.

On that same night, Trump tweeted another *ad populum* appeal: "A wonderful article by a writer who truly gets it. I am for the people and the people are for me. #Trump2016." He included a link to an article written by a Chicago attorney named Doug Ibendahl on his news blog *Republican News Watch*, with a headline that read, "*National Review* Just Handed Donald Trump the Election."[18] Trump liked Ibendahl's article so much that he used it to defend himself from the attacks of the "gang of twenty-two" by reading, and embellishing upon, Ibendahl's editorial at three rallies. Trump read Ibendahl's article in Sioux City and Pella, Iowa, on January 23, 2016, and in Farmington, New Hampshire, on January 25, 2016. In so doing, Trump summoned an authority figure—albeit a minor player in national politics—to defend himself from the *National Review* attack on the grounds of populism.[19]

"Somebody wrote something that was so great; it was so great and I have to read just a few of these paragraphs," Trump began at a rally in Sioux City, Iowa, on January 23, 2016. His stream of consciousness patter segued from attacking "Against Trump" contributors Glenn Beck and Bill Kristol

("They're going down the tubes!"), to explaining that television shows "only want you if you get good ratings" and "I get good ratings," to praising the military ("I love you people!"). Trump didn't like to read things, he said, but since "they did this stupid *National Review*" issue, he thought that his crowd would like to hear from "a very respected guy," Doug Ibendahl. "I don't know him," said Trump as he began to read. "'So clueless is the gang of twenty-two they can't even see how they've stumbled right into the narrative Trump's been communicating so successfully for months.'" Trump continued to read the majority of Ibendahl's article, interrupting to expand upon the written text. Throughout his self-defense, Trump used polarizing strategies to divide his friends at his rally from his enemies at the *National Review*.

Trump first emphasized that the *National Review* was a "dying magazine; it's dying. I don't think it's gonna be in business in a year from now" and that the "gang of twenty-two" were "always complaining [but] they don't do anything about it." They were self-interested members of the "conservative entertainment complex," who earned "their income by pandering to conservative anger while offering no real solutions." After establishing the *National Review* as a feckless enemy and part of the corrupt problem, Trump next offered himself as the solution. He first quoted Ibendahl, arguing that Trump was more influential than the corrupt *National Review* elites—"'in just seven months of campaigning, Trump already has more Americans listening to a Republican message than the entire gang of twenty-two could muster over decades.'" Second, Trump argued that his popularity was evidence of both his power and the righteousness of his campaign: "Look at, look at what we have. Look at this room. Look at upstairs. Look at the balcony. You can't see that balcony's packed. There are people standing in the back of this massive balcony." Trump's popularity, as evidenced by his rally crowd size, *proved* that he was right. It's a clear (and circular) *ad populum* argument: we know that Trump is right because the people support him, and the people support Trump because he is right.

With his enemy established and his heroic credentials defended, Trump constituted his audience as loyal members of his team—as the good guys in the us-versus-them polarization. "'Trump returns the respect by recognizing regular, hard-working Americans are a lot smarter than any of the ideological eunuchs in all of their pontificating glory.'" Trump loved the people who loved Trump:

> It's true. The people, my people, are so smart. And you know what
> else they say about my people? The polls—they say I have the most
> loyal people. Did you ever see that? Where I could stand in the
> middle of Fifth Avenue [Trump made a gesture with his hand in
> the shape of a gun, pointed his finger directly toward the camera,
> looked over the 'barrel,' and pulled the trigger] and shoot some-
> body and I wouldn't lose any voters, OK? It's like incredible. [The
> audience laughed.] No, they say . . . [Someone in the audience
> yelled 'We love you, Trump!'] We love you too, man.

Throughout his speech (and his campaign), Trump reaffirmed both the importance of his popularity and sought to perpetuate his popularity by prais-ing his followers who loved him and whom he loved in return. Trump was so popular that he could easily dismiss the criticisms of the *National Review* without *even addressing them*, on the grounds of his popularity alone.[20]

News reports shifted from the merits of the *National Review*'s criti-cisms of Trump to the controversy Trump caused when he declared that he could shoot folks on Fifth Avenue and wouldn't lose supporters. When Wolf Blitzer at CNN asked Trump to explain his controversial remark on January 25, 2016, Trump reaffirmed the polarization between Team Trump and the establishment when he noted that "the establishment actually is against me," but "of course I'm joking." And yet Trump said with an *ad populum* appeal, "The purpose of that is to say the people love me. You know, they want to stay with me. They're loyal. They're tired of seeing our country being pushed around and led by people that are stupid people. They're tired of that."[21] Once again, Trump's popularity was proof that he was right and the "stupid people" at *National Review* were wrong.[22] Likewise, Melissa Francis at Fox News thought "that the rebuke actually helps him . . . because it ups his rebel cred. He says that he's not part of what's been here before, he's different." She thought that the *National Review* attack would end up helping "him with the people that he's trying to win over."[23]

Why did Trump take his beef with the *National Review* to his rally crowd to adjudicate? Because Trump's rallies themselves were *ad populum* appeals to a polarized electorate—the good people, the smart people, the wise people were all at Trump rallies, everyone else was corrupt or enemies—or both. On May 11, 2016, Trump told the Associated Press that his entire campaign plan was centered around his large, sold-out, controversial rallies: "My best investment is my rallies. The people go home; they tell their friends they loved it. It's been good."[24] Over the course of his campaign, Trump generally avoided the intimate voter meetings typical of a traditional presidential campaign. You never saw Trump shaking hands at a local pizza joint in Iowa, for example. Instead, Trump held massive and chaotic rallies in stadiums and airport hangers, which were broadcast live on cable news shows.[25] In total, Trump held 324 rallies over the 512 days he campaigned between June 2015 and November 2016. His largest rally attracted 28,000 people in Mobile, Alabama.[26] Trump's rallies were for Trump's people.

Trump used similar *ad populum* appeals to praise his followers at his rallies throughout the campaign. For example, in Muscatine, Iowa, on January 24, 2016, Trump said, "The people in this room are smart. My people are the smartest people in my opinion because they get it. These are the smartest people. The most loyal and the smartest. The most loyal and the smartest."[27] In Wilkes-Barre, Pennsylvania, on April 26, 2016, Trump said, "We have the smartest and most loyal people. The Trump people are the smartest, and they are the most loyal. By far. [People nodded in agreement behind Trump at the podium while the crowd in front of him applauded loudly.] They are by far. Loyal. The most."[28] On August 10, 2016, in Abingdon, Virginia, Trump said, "I have the greatest supporters. We have the most loyal supporters and the smartest. You know, they always like to demean everything. They try and demean supporters. They're always trying to put a—little shots. Boom, boom, boom. We've got the smartest, we've got the most loyal. [People nodded in agreement behind Trump while the crowd applauded.] We've got the hardest working; we have the best people. They like to demean, but we have amazing, amazing people."[29] As these few examples show, Trump consistently took advantage of the rhetorical possibilities inherent in the polarized context of the campaign to reaffirm that the fight for the presidency was about "they" versus "we"—and "we" were the smart, loyal, amazing, best, hardworking Americans. They, of course, had none of those redeeming qualities, but were the elite who liked to "demean" the good folks who support Trump.

On September 9, 2016, Democratic Party presidential candidate Hillary Clinton proved that Trump was right about what "they" say about Trump's "best people" when she told a fund-raiser crowd that "you could put half of Trump's supporters into what I call the basket of deplorables." Clinton thought that half of Trump's supporters were "irredeemable" because they held anti-American values such as being "racist, sexist, homophobic, xenophobic, Islamaphobic—you name it."[30] "Wow," Trump tweeted in response on September 10, 2016, "Hillary Clinton was SO INSULTING to my supporters, millions of amazing, hard-working people. I think it will cost her at the polls!"[31] Trump's supporters gleefully embraced their "deplorable" status—changing their Twitter and Facebook user names to include the word, wearing "deplorable" T-shirts to Trump rallies, and posting and sharing "deplorable" memes all as a sign of their allegiance to Trump.[32] "You know what's deplorable?" a Trump campaign ad asked. "Hillary Clinton viciously demonizing hardworking people like you."[33]

CHAPTER 8

"Low-Energy Jeb!"

Ad Hominem

Trump Tower, New York, New York, August 18, 2015
Favorable: 26.4 percent; Unfavorable: 61.0 percent[1]

On June 14, 2015, in anticipation of his presidential announcement speech the next day, the Republican establishment candidate who was at the top of the polls, the candidate whose insurmountable pile of campaign cash and dynastic family name had already forced out other potential candidates, and the one who most people expected would eventually win the presidential nomination, released his campaign logo. "Jeb!" it said, quite simply and enthusiastically.[2] Born John Ellis Bush, but known to his family and friends by his acronym JEB, Bush's announcement speech on June 15 was full of center-right promises to reduce taxes, create school choice programs, eliminate corruption and unnecessary government restrictions, and rebuild our military. "Great things like that can really happen," Bush assured his announcement speech crowd at Miami Dade College in Miami, Florida. "In this country of ours, the most improbable things can happen."[3]

On the morning of June 15, 2015, before Bush had even made his candidacy official, Trump called into *Fox & Friends* to dismiss Bush's chances: "The last thing we need is another Bush," Trump declared. "He looks like a person that doesn't have lots of enthusiasm. This country needs a cheerleader." Trump would use that same "cheerleader" line the next day to attack President Obama in his own announcement speech. He told his friends at Fox that he thought Bush was yet another "weak, ineffective politician" and that "people are tired of these guys."[4] Bush's announcement speech both acknowledged his family's distinguished presidential history—Bush was "a guy who met his first president on the day he was born and his second on the day he was brought home from the hospital"—and also anticipated the objection that the GOP nomination was rigged, because he was already the presumptive nominee: "Not a one of us deserves the job by right of resume, party, seniority, family, or family narrative," said Bush. "It's nobody's turn. It's everybody's test, and it's wide open—exactly as a contest for president should be."[5] In so doing, Bush's announcement speech attempted to defend his campaign from the kind of attack that Trump had made against him just that morning on *Fox & Friends*. Bush's campaign, before it even started, was Trump's target.

"Everyone thought, because of his name, that he was supposed to be the odds on favorite," Trump told Jimmy Kimmel on December 17, 2015. But Trump proudly explained that Bush's distinguished name was no match for Trump's power to brand: "I defined him," he crowed.[6] Trump did indeed succeed in defining poor "low-energy" Jeb Bush. Trump has a knack for branding; he has a particular ability to polarize people by branding his and their shared enemies. In using *ad hominem* to brand his enemies, Trump attempts to delegitimize his political opposition. The month before his Kimmel interview, *Business Insider* reported that Trump had told them that "there was no backstory behind the tag—no moment where it 'clicked' that he should constantly use it in interviews and on the trail," but that version of the story isn't exactly true.[7] Trump actually had a little trouble finding just the right brand for his first campaign nemesis, Jeb Bush.[8]

Trump first tried to brand his enemy on the June 18, 2015, *Morning Joe*: "He's a man that doesn't want to be doing what he's doing. I call him 'the reluctant warrior,' and 'warrior's' probably not a good word. I think Bush is an unhappy person. I don't think he has any energy, and I don't see how he can win."[9] As Trump acknowledged, "reluctant warrior" wasn't quite the right way to capture Bush's essence. Bush didn't come across as a warrior—reluctant, unhappy, or otherwise. The branding attempt failed for its lack of resonance and sloganability. No one began calling Bush "the reluctant warrior."

Trump tried to brand Bush again with a tweet on June 24, 2015: "the highly respected Suffolk University poll just announced that I am alone in 2nd place in New Hampshire, with Jeb Bust (Bush) in first."[10] "Jeb Bust" had some merits: it was a funny play on words, it had a clear and succinct message, and it told the story of Bush's ultimate failure in the race. But it had one drawback: Trump deployed it too soon. The race had only just begun, and since no one thought that Trump would win in New Hampshire (except Trump), it was hard to know if the Suffolk poll was an outlier or if Bush's boom was really going bust, with Trump triumphant.[11] No one began calling Bush "Jeb Bust."

On August 14, 2015, Trump did an interview with *The Hollywood Reporter*, in which he refined his June 15 *Fox & Friends* claim that Bush "doesn't have lots of enthusiasm" and his June 18 claim that he didn't "think he has any energy" into a more pithy slogan: "Jeb is a very nice person," Trump said with a shrug, "but he is very low energy." Bush's low energy was a problem, Trump thought, because the nation faced such great problems, and "you need a person with great energy, enthusiasm and brainpower to straighten out our country. Our country is a mess in almost every way."[12] Trump effectively dismissed Bush in two ways: first, Bush was a "nice guy" and, of course, nice guys finish last; second, Bush was too low energy to solve the nation's great problems. That issue of the *Hollywood Reporter* wouldn't come out until August 20, but Trump must have liked his "is a nice person but he is very low energy" formulation, because it became his standard refrain on Bush thereafter.

On August 18, 2015, Trump successfully used the "low-energy" brand as a classic *ad hominem* attack (attacking the person instead of their argument): he used it to dismiss Bush's claim that Trump was unqualified to be president by changing the question from whether or not Trump was qualified to whether or not Bush had low energy. Trump used his power to brand his enemies to attack Bush's person, rather than his argument. The mini-drama began on August 16 when Trump told Chuck Todd on *Meet the Press* that he got his military advice from watching "the shows."[13] The next day, Bush seized on Trump's admission as evidence that Trump was unprepared to be president, revealing his own twenty-one-person, all-star foreign policy advisory team: "I'm not going to fall into the trap to say that I watch *Meet the Press* and I get my foreign policy from that," Bush told a crowd in South Carolina on August 17.[14] On August 18, Trump met with *Time*'s Nancy Gibbs, Michael Scherer, and Zeke Miller for an interview in Trump Tower. The interview photos featured Trump with a bald eagle, which landed Trump an August 31, 2015, *Time* cover that read "Deal with it."[15] Someone asked Trump to react to Bush's criticism that "it's not enough to watch television" to understand foreign policy, and Trump responded, "Well, Jeb is a very-low-energy person. So he can sit around a table all day long with one general and talk and talk, and you know."[16] Trump avoided the question about his qualifications for office by attacking his opponent personally, a distraction technique that easily allowed Trump to sidestep the question while insulting his opposition. Why didn't "low-energy" Jeb get his foreign policy advice from "the shows" like (presumably) high-energy Trump did? Not because that wasn't the best way to get foreign policy advice, but because Bush didn't have the energy to do more than sit around and talk all day long. Trump was an enviable doer, a man of action; he would act with great energy to make America great again, unlike pitiful low-energy Jeb. Trump's *ad hominem* attack was polarizing: it invited Trump's audience to see Bush as both illegitimate and as an object of ridicule.

Trump also used his brand for Bush as an *ad hominem* attack in an August 19 CNN interview. When Chris Cuomo asked Trump to respond to Bush's criticism about his qualifications for office, Trump said, "A very-low-energy person, Jeb Bush. Very low energy. It's good, if you want to lead a long life. But he is a low-energy person. Perhaps he sits down all day long with a particular general. But you know what? I can get a lot of information in a very short time."[17] Trump's *ad hominem* attack repeated his "low-energy" branding three times in as many sentences, making sure that his audience heard clearly that his response to Bush's criticism was that Bush was too "low energy" to do anything other than sit around. Trump, of course, by contrast, was high energy, a quick study, decisive, and able to lead. On that same day, Trump told reporters at his Derry, New Hampshire, town-hall campaign event, "I don't see how he's electable. Jeb Bush is a low-energy person. For him to get things done is hard. He's very low energy." Bush happened to be holding his own campaign event across town, which gave Trump the opportunity to use his branding to ridicule his competitor: "You know what is happening to Jeb's crowd right down the street?" Trump asked. Then, with perfect comedic timing, he responded: "They're sleeping. They're sleeping now!"[18] Reporters did indeed show a video of one woman sleeping at Bush's event across town, thus confirming Trump's joke and the "low-energy" brand.

From that point forward, Trump frequently repeated his *ad hominem* attack against Bush, calling him "a nice person" who "doesn't have the energy or the capacity to make America great again" because he was such a "very, very-low-energy person" in Mobile, Alabama, on August 21, 2015.[19] Trump folded his branding into his standard talking point against illegal immigration at a press conference on August 25: "He's a very-low-energy person. You need a lot of energy to get this country turned around, including immigration. . . . Jeb Bush doesn't have a clue, doesn't even have a clue. And if

I weren't in this campaign, Jeb Bush would not be talking about illegal immigration. If you remember, he said they come as an act of love. OK?"[20] Trump again used his *ad hominem* attack at an August 25, 2015, Iowa rally: "I think Jeb is a nice person. He's very low energy. I'm not used to that kind of a person. [laughter] I'm just not used to it. I'm used to dealing with killers."[21] At an August 28, 2015, rally in Norwood, Massachusetts, Trump playfully used his *ad hominem* branding with a *paralipsis*, telling the cheering crowd: "And we have some low-energy people. Some really loooooow. I'm not gonna say Jeb is low energy, but he's pretty low. How would you like him negotiating with Iran?"[22] Trump's assaults on Bush went on and on, relentlessly branding Bush "low-energy Jeb" and inviting his followers to ridicule Bush as boring, unmanly, and unable to lead.[23] This time Trump's branding worked.

Trump succeeded in defining Bush with his *ad hominem* attacks. People began to call Bush "low energy" on August 19, 2015, repeating the line from Trump's speech in New Hampshire, and it quickly took hold. Most early uses of "low-energy Jeb" on Twitter were from journalists and others live-tweeting Trump's rallies or television interviews, with little commentary, except to draw attention to the unusualness of Trump's insult and to speculate that it could be something like "a rhetorical knife in the craw that may do lingering damage," as the *New York Times*' Maggie Haberman put it on August 21, 2015.[24] However, even from Trump's first public use of the attack, some of his fans cheered him on. For example, on August 19, 2015, Thomas O tweeted, "'Jeb Bush is a low energy person.'—Donald Trump. Another townhall meeting, another epic take down of the establishment #Jeb2016 #Trump2016."[25] Likewise, on August 24, 2015, Red821 tweeted, "Mr. Trump defintely Jeb Bush is a low energy idiot,"[26] and on August 25, 2015, Robert Stevens tweeted, "Donald Trump just did an impression of a 'low energy' Jeb Bush. Please somebody make a GIF."[27] On September 8, 2015, Trump's campaign posted a short video on its Instagram and Facebook pages with the caption, "Wake up Jeb supporters!" that showed a woman sleeping at a Bush rally while Bush droned on about health care savings accounts. The voiceover said, "Having trouble sleeping at night? Too much energy? Need some low energy? Jeb, for all your sleeping needs." The post garnered 1.1 million views on Facebook, 43,000 reactions, 9,930 shares, and 7,800 comments. The top comments were "LOVE YA DONALD YOU GOT MY VOTE!!!!!!" and "Wake up America!!! We Need Trump!!!!"[28] Clearly, Trump's "low-energy" attack resonated with his followers. Throughout the campaign, Trump and his followers mocked Bush as "low energy"—it was never used as a compliment, a term of endearment, or a term of honor. Low-energy Jeb had been positioned as an enemy of Trump, his followers, and America.

"Here's the deal," Bush told a group gathered at an Orlando, Florida, community center on July 27, 2015. "I don't have anger in my heart." Bush was already defined by Trump's *ad hominem* attacks and struggled both to defend his approach to campaigning and to rebrand himself. "I'm not a grievance candidate," Bush explained. "I'm the tortoise in the race—but I'm a joyful tortoise."[29] Bush didn't directly deny that he was "low energy" and even attempted to acknowledge his slowness and turn it into a positive characteristic. "Jeb! The Joyful Tortoise" became Bush's brand. He tweeted a photo of a large tortoise with the caption "I met a fellow joyful tortoise on my way to the Reagan Library,"[30] and he carried toy turtles in his pocket and handed them out at events,[31] prompting comedian Stephen Colbert to ask, "Is that a toy turtle in your pocket, or are you just really bad at running for president?"[32] Not only did Bush attempt to turn Trump's *ad hominem* attack into a positive, but he also attacked Trump's negativity: Bush repeatedly accused Trump of "trying to insult his way to the presidency"[33] or trying to "get elected president by disparaging people, by attacking people all the time." Bush explained to Fox News, "That's not going to work. You lift people's spirits up to become president of the United States." But Bush was mistaken: attacking people all the time *was* a successful strategy for winning the presidency, at least in 2016.[34]

"At some point," Bush told CNN on September 9, 2015, "if you're being defined by a guy who can just make a phone call and just get on, get on the talk shows all the time, and all he does is disparage you, yeah, you've got to fight back."[35] Aware of the power of Trump's attacks being amplified throughout social and traditional media, Bush tried to fight back. At first he attacked Trump for his negativity and attempted to embrace Trump's branding by proclaiming himself a "joyful tortoise." Then Bush tried making fun of the name: he appeared on Stephen Colbert's September 8, 2015, inaugural show and explained, "I've been using 'Jeb!' since 1994," and then deadpanned, "It connotes excitement."[36] As his polling numbers slid, he tried a show of machismo: in a cringeworthy GOP debate performance on September 17, 2015, he responded that his Secret Service code name would be "Eveready" and then looked at Trump standing next to him and said, "It's very high energy, Donald," before participating in an awkward high five with Trump.[37]

He defended himself against Trump's attacks in Spanish.[38] He defended himself against Trump's attacks in English. He made speeches describing his hectic schedule to show just how much energy he really had.[39] In December 2015, he accused Trump of being a "false flag" candidate who was actually a covert Democrat working to get Hillary Clinton elected president.[40] None of these tactics enabled Bush to overcome what the *New York Times*' Ashley Parker described as "the damning four-syllable caricature Mr. Trump first lobbed at him."[41] After a string of primary losses, Bush dropped out of the presidential race on February 20, 2016.

Trump was proud of his *ad hominem* attack strategy—he explained to *Business Insider* on November 19, 2015, that he "hit him really hard, because I thought he was going to be the guy. You know, he's the establishment guy. So I hit him very hard."[42] And Trump explained to Jimmy Kimmel on December 17, 2015, that he "gave him this, this term 'low energy.' I said that he's a low-energy individual. We do not need in this country low energy. Do you agree?"[43] Bush went from being the presumed front-runner and the GOP establishment's preferred candidate to an also-ran, but did Trump's *ad hominem* attacks really destroy Bush's campaign, as Trump claimed? If they did, then why did they work? *Washington Post* columnist David Weigel explained on August 28, 2015, that "Trump's attack on Jeb! for being "low-energy" resonates bc a lot of the GOP base say their nominees went too easy on Obama in 08 and 12."[44] Perhaps the GOP base wanted more of a fighter than a "joyful tortoise." If so, then Bush's campaign was doomed. Frank Luntz reported that one of his GOP debate focus groups laughed when Bush tried to attack Trump at the December 15, 2015, Las Vegas primary debate, for example. Reportedly "the focus group started laughing hysterically and saying, 'Oh, there's the low-energy guy.'" Luntz tweeted, "My #GOPDebate focus group's words to describe Jeb Bush: 'weak,' 'desperate,' and 'whiny.'" Luntz told the *New York Times*' Ashley Parker that his focus group repeated "Trump's exact words. [Bush] is absolutely qualified and capable to be president, and yet no one respects his candidacy—and Donald Trump is the reason why."[45] By the time Bush withdrew from the election, his name circulated in the general cultural lexicon as synonymous with tired or slow, such as "I feel so Jeb Bush—I mean, low energy—today."[46]

Not only was Bush not a fighter, but Trump's attacks on Bush took advantage of the preexisting distrust of establishment Republican leadership and positioned Trump as the heroic leader of the opposition. His attacks took advantage of polarization within the Republican Party—the disconnect between an elite leadership that had already decided who would be its nominee and the electorate who nominally got to choose their party's nominee. Trump's *ad hominem* attacks made Bush an object of ridicule for a portion of a polarized party that wanted nothing more than to ridicule the establishment elite. *Ad hominem* attacks work particularly well in a highly polarized context like the 2016 presidential election, because within an environment like that it is easy to frame decisions as "us versus them." In such a context only enemies would make arguments in opposition to your side, and the arguments of the opposition/enemies would necessarily be suspect and not worth addressing. Such arguments would be easily dismissed by attacking the person who made them and exposing them to ridicule—just as Trump did. Yet, while such a strategy positioned Trump as a heroic demagogue, it was also authoritarian. Trump used his *ad hominem* attacks to delegitimize his political opposition, which is an antidemocratic strategy. Trump's *ad hominem* attacks took advantage of preexisting polarization to position Trump as a heroic demagogue and Bush as a low-energy, effete, establishment elite.

After "low-energy" Bush's campaign succumbed, Trump continued to brand his enemies—"attacking people all the time" to win the presidency— "Lyin' Ted," "Liddle Marco," and "Corrupt Hillary" each suffered from Trump's knack for branding and marketing via *ad hominem* attacks.[47] "I'm the writer," Trump explained to *New York Magazine*'s Gabriel Sherman. "Let me start with Little Marco. He just looked like Little Marco to me. And it's not 'Little.' It's 'Liddle.' L-I-D-D-L-E. And it's not L-Y-I-N-G Ted Cruz. It's L-Y-I-N apostrophe. Ted's a liar, so that was easy."[48] When Rubio and Cruz attempted to fight back against Trump's branding by calling him "a conman" at the February 25, 2016, GOP debate, Trump went on Fox News to dismiss their criticism with the ultimate insult in the polarized 2016 Republican primary: "They can say what they want; at the end of the day, they're just establishment guys."[49]

CHAPTER 9

"I didn't tweet; I retweeted somebody that was supposedly an expert. Am I gonna check every statistic? All it was is a retweet. And it wasn't from me."

Paralipsis

Trump Tower, New York, New York, November 23, 2015
Favorable 34.8 percent; Unfavorable 55 percent[1]

"We won, brothers. All of our work. It has paid off. Our Glorious Leader has ascended to God Emperor," Andrew Anglin wrote on his popular neo-Nazi website Daily Stormer on November 9, 2016. "Make no mistake about it: we did this. If it were not for us, it wouldn't have been possible. We flooded the tubes, we created the energy, we made this happen. We were with him every step of the way. And the great news is, we're going to be given credit for it," wrote Anglin. "Hail Victory."[2] Likewise, Kevin MacDonald, who the Southern Poverty Law Center described as "the neo-Nazi movement's favorite academic," celebrated Trump's election victory in the white nationalist *Occidental Observer* as "a victory of White Americans over the oligarchic, hostile elites what have run this country for decades."[3] Eleven days after Trump's election, it appeared as though the white nationalists had already conquered the nation's capital when "alt-right" leader Richard Spencer proclaimed, "Hail Trump, hail our people, hail victory!" while giving a Nazi salute to attendees at the National Policy Institute conference in Washington, DC.[4] The white nationalists returned Spencer's Nazi salute.

It is easy to imagine that Trump's campaign was meant to appeal to Americans who were polarized from establishment politics and politicians, but Trump's campaign also drew the attention of Americans who existed well outside of the mainstream of American political discourse: members of the so-called alt-right—"white nationalists" or white supremacists.[5] The alt-right gained the nation's attention over the course of the Trump campaign because Trump repeatedly pointed attention to them by discussing their issues or retweeting their content. Under pressure from reporters, Trump also repeatedly "disavowed" any association with his white nationalist supporters. Trump's embrace and disavowal of white nationalism confused those inside and outside of the movement. As Mark Potok of the Southern Poverty Law Center said, it wasn't clear "if Trump views himself as a white nationalist, but he has white nationalist positions."[6] Was Trump one of them? At first, white nationalists weren't sure.

Trump's ability to say two things at once via *paralipsis* ("I'm not saying; I'm just saying") allowed him to simultaneously embrace and disavow the white nationalists who supported him. *Paralipsis* allowed Trump to recirculate white nationalist racist sentiment without having to take responsibility for being a racist. Within the highly polarized environment of the 2016 campaign, this strategy worked particularly well for Trump because his double-talk signaled who were his enemies and who were his friends. Trump used *paralipsis* to embrace white nationalists as friends and nonwhite Americans and immigrants as enemies, but no one could tell for sure if he was really a racist or if, like Potok said, he just had white nationalist positions. Trump's use of *paralipsis* also gave plausible deniability for Americans who wanted to support his campaign but didn't see themselves as racist.

Americans were certainly polarized along party lines during the 2016 election, but white nationalists hoped to capitalize on the increased visibility directed toward their group to polarize the nation along racial lines as well. For example, white nationalist Andrew Anglin posted "A Normie's Guide to the Alt-Right" on the Daily Stormer to explain their philosophy to those newly interested in their movement: "the core concept of the movement, upon which all else is based, is that Whites are undergoing an extermination, via mass immigration into White countries which was enabled by a corrosive liberal ideology of White self-hatred, and that the Jews are at the center of this agenda."[7] White nationalists initially debated whether or not Trump was truly one of them, but most of them decided that because his campaign had moved "the Overton Window"—had changed what was permissible to debate in public about race relations—that they ought to use all of their energy to support and exploit his campaign. And support and exploit his campaign they did.[8] "Think of all the niggers, jews, and SJW [social justice warriors] that will be chimping in the streets protesting, rioting, etc. around the clock if Trump wins," said one poster on Vanguard News Network. "If anything it will push the polarization of Team White vs. Team jew/mud across the country."[9]

As Andrew Anglin said on election night, the white nationalists "were with him every step of the way." On June 28, 2015—only two weeks after Trump's campaign announcement—Anglin declared his (and Daily Stormer's) support for Trump by endorsing him as "the only candidate who is even talking about anything at all that matters."[10] On July 10, 2015, Kevin MacDonald wrote an approving story about Trump's announcement and endorsed his campaign in the *Occidental Observer*, which received a large number of enthusiastic comments.[11] For example, Mr. Curious wrote that the mainstream media's rejection of Trump's polarizing tone was evidence that Trump shared his values. It was "a simple rule of thumb," he wrote. "If the Zionist Media are constantly ridiculing and abusing a White Man, BACK HIM," he urged. "They are doing it because he threatens the PC feminist/marxist/zionist consensus of kosher power to practice White Genocide. God bless you, Donald. Keep up the good work."[12] By February 25, 2016, the nation's most prominent white supremacist—former Ku Klux Klan grand wizard David Duke—told his radio show listeners that "voting against Donald Trump at this point is really treason to your heritage."[13]

As white nationalists searched for evidence to support their hope that Trump was one of them, they posted news accounts of his racist past: the many times Trump had been accused of racist business practices; news accounts of his reputed white supremacist reading habits, alleging that Trump had once kept a copy of Hitler's speeches by his bedside; and news accounts of Trump's view of eugenics—especially videos of Trump explaining why he believed in genetic superiority and his "racehorse theory" of his own superior genes.[14] While all of this evidence helped white nationalists believe that Trump thought like they did, they primarily chose to support Trump's campaign because he was on the right side of what they called the "National Question."[15] White nationalists believe that "diversity" is code for "white genocide"—that a systematic program of increased immigration, political correctness, and "white self-hatred" over generations had made a once powerful race (and nation) weak. In Trump's campaign they heard their own concerns about the nation voiced, and they heard a tough-talking candidate promise to thwart political correctness, end illegal immigration, restrict legal immigration, reject refugees, and build a wall between the United States and Mexico to protect the white nation. Members of the white nationalist community had no trouble finding evidence to support their hope that Trump held the correct position on the National Question.[16] From the moment his campaign began on June 16, 2015, until his election on November 8, 2016, Trump consistently argued to protect the US border.[17] For example, "We, as a country, either have borders or we don't," Trump tweeted November 12, 2015. "IF WE DON'T HAVE BORDERS, WE DON'T HAVE A COUNTRY!"[18] He repeated these words (or similar) at rallies and in tweets throughout his campaign.

According to a Southern Poverty Law Center report, Trump's campaign caused white nationalist websites like Daily Stormer and Storm Front to surge in page views and postings, and according to the FBI, race-related hate crimes increased dramatically across the nation, especially just after Trump's election.[19] Trump's campaign was only two months old when two brothers from Boston—Scott and Steve Leader—viciously beat a sleeping homeless man with a metal pipe and urinated on him, sending him to the hospital. When police asked why they attacked the man, Scott Leader responded, "Donald Trump was right. All these illegals need to be deported." Incidents like the Leader brother attack made news, and reporters forced Trump to respond. "I haven't heard about that," Trump said on August 19, 2015, when asked by a reporter if he was worried that his campaign was inciting violent incidents like the one in Boston, as well as causing his supporters to send death threats to Fox News anchor Megyn Kelly. "It would be a shame, but I haven't heard about that." Trump then praised his supporters: "I will say the people that are following me are very passionate. They love this country; they want this country to be great again."[20] Trump's strategy was to deny any knowledge of violent and racist support, coupled with praise for his supporters. It was a polarizing strategy designed to disavow knowledge of racist violence while praising his supporters for fighting against their shared enemy. Trump used this pattern to disavow and embrace racists throughout his campaign, which made it very difficult to hold him accountable for inciting racist violence.

Whether or not Trump was a racist continued to be a question in the mainstream media throughout the campaign, and reporters frequently asked

Trump if he was a racist. Each time he was asked if he was a racist, he emphatically denied it: on November 24, 2015, he told Bill O'Reilly that he was "the least racist person on Earth"; on December 9, 2015, he told Don Lemon, "I'm the least racist person that you have ever met. I am the least racist person"; and on June 10, 2016, he told Marc Fisher, "I am not a racist. In fact, I am the least racist person that you've ever encountered."[21] While many news stories traced the history of Trump's racist past or highlighted the racism at his rallies, each time Trump was asked the question, news articles dutifully reported Trump's denials.[22] On August 26, 2015, Buzzfeed explained Trump's complicated relationship with white nationalists: "Top racists and neo-Nazis back Donald Trump; he might not want their endorsement, but white nationalists want him."[23] Likewise, on February 5, 2016, a CNN headline declared: "Trump's unwelcome support: White supremacists."[24] And on August 29, 2016, a *Vanity Fair* headline dismissed Trump's white nationalist support: "David Duke Missed the Memo That Trump Doesn't Want His Support: The Republican Nominee's KKK Problem Isn't Going Away."[25] These kinds of headlines took Trump's denials at face value and allowed for Trump's nonracist supporters to deny his racism. Yet if Trump claimed that he was not a racist and did not want the support of racists, then why did the racists believe that he was one of them and they were fighting together to get him elected? Why was *he* their Glorious Leader?

On August 26, 2015, Mark Halperin and John Heilemann asked Trump why white supremacists like David Duke supported his campaign and whether that support made him "wonder about his message." Trump shifted the terms of debate away from whether or not white supremacists endorsed him to whether or not he needs anyone's endorsement: "I don't need his endorsement; I certainly wouldn't want his endorsement." In fact, Trump said, "I don't need anyone's endorsement."[26] When asked about why white supremacists in particular liked him, Trump denied the premise of the question by responding, "A lot of people like me. Republicans like me; liberals like me. Everybody likes me." While mainstream news organizations reported that Trump "doesn't want David Duke's endorsement," white nationalists saw the exchange differently.[27] "The interviewer then asks specifically about David Duke supporting him," wrote Andrew Anglin on Daily Stormer, "and says 'would you repudiate David Duke?' The Donald, mocking the faggot, says 'sure. I would do that if it made you feel better. I don't know anything about him.'" According to Anglin, the general line of questioning was "these evil

ones support you, so you must be evil" and concluded that what he saw as
an attack on racism and white nationalists (good things, in his mind) "fell
pretty flat, Jews. Trump did not break stride. Not that he ever does."[28] The
white nationalist take on Trump's "repudiation" of Duke was that *it was all
for show*—that Trump was, in fact, mocking the question. In other words, it
was possible to read Trump's denial and repudiation of white nationalism as
an affirmation.

Throughout the campaign, Trump used *paralipsis* to cultivate ambiguity
about whether or not he was a racist. For example, on November 22, 2015,
Trump retweeted SeanSean252 with a graphic of homicide data delineated
by race that purported to show that "Blacks" were responsible for most of
the homicides in the United States.[29] The tweet was criticized for being both
racist and inaccurate—fact-checkers like FactCheck.org found that "almost
every figure in the graphic is wrong."[30] Trump responded to the criticism on
November 23, 2015, by denying responsibility for the content of the tweet: "I
didn't tweet; I retweeted somebody that was supposedly an expert," Trump
told Bill O'Reilly. "Am I gonna check every statistic? All it was is a retweet.
And it wasn't from me. It came out of a radio show and other places. This
was a retweet. And it comes from sources that are very credible. What can
I tell you?"[31] Since Trump had merely retweeted someone else, he argued
that he could not be held accountable for the content of the message. This, of
course, is the logic of *paralipsis*: "I'm not saying it; I'm just saying it" ("I'm
not tweeting it; I'm just retweeting it"). While Trump denied that his retweet
was an endorsement in *this* instance, back on August 25, 2015, a reporter
asked Trump, "Tell us [about] your retweet strategy—do you endorse what
you retweet?" At that time, Trump responded, "Well, I do retweets and, well,
to a certain extent, yeah, I think that's right. Do you want me to say no? I
retweet, you know. I retweet for a reason, right?"[32] Were Trump's retweets
meaningful or not? It was difficult to tell for certain, but white nationalists
were thrilled to see Trump amplify their content and to see the issue debated
in the mainstream media. A thread about Trump's retweet on Storm Front
had more than one hundred enthusiastic replies, including one poster who
said that he now understood "the thrill and elation people felt when they saw
the Führer speak in person. I understand how they would willingly take a bullet to protect him. Trump has the ability to inspire white men."[33]

Trump continued to thrill and elate white nationalists by retweeting their
content. He also continued to use *paralipsis* to deflect criticism that he was

courting white supremacists. According to an analysis by *Fortune* by March 2016, Trump had "retweeted at least 75 users who follow at least three of the top 50 #WhiteGenocide influencers. Moreover, a majority of these retweeted accounts are themselves followed by more than 100 #WhiteGenocide influencers."[34] Andrew Anglin understood Trump's retweets as a sign that "our Glorious Leader and ULTIMATE SAVIOR has gone full-wink-wink-wink to his most aggressive supporters. . . . Whereas the odd White genocide tweet could be a random occurrence, it isn't statistically possible that two of them back to back could be a random occurrence. It could only be deliberate. There is no way that this could be anything other than both a wink-wink-wink and a call for more publicity on his campaign."[35] While Trump continued to face criticism in the mainstream media for retweeting white nationalists, he simply shrugged it off. For example, when Jake Tapper asked him about his retweets on February 21, 2016, Trump said, "I don't know about retweeting. You retweet somebody and they turn out to be white supremacists. I know nothing about these groups that are supporting me."[36] Once again, Trump's defense took the form of a denial coupled with a *paralipsis*: I didn't tweet it; I just retweeted it.[37]

A few days later on February 25, 2016, David Duke urged his radio show listeners to vote for Trump and volunteer for his campaign, which caused the Anti-Defamation League (ADL) to call "on presidential candidate Donald Trump to distance himself from white nationalist and former KKK Grand Wizard David Duke, as well as other white supremacists, and publicly condemn their racism."[38] The next day a reporter asked Trump to react to Duke's endorsement. Trump replied, "I didn't even know he endorsed me. David Duke endorsed me? OK. All right. I disavow, OK?"[39] Yet, on February 28, 2016, when Jake Tapper asked Trump to disavow David Duke and the KKK in a CNN interview, Trump had some trouble doing so. "I don't know anything about what you're even talking about with white supremacy or white supremacists," Trump said. "So I don't know. I don't know—did he endorse me, or what's going on? Because I know nothing about David Duke; I know nothing about white supremacists."[40] The next day, Trump called in to the *Today Show* to explain that despite having no visible difficulty hearing during the Tapper interview, he fumbled the Duke disavowal because he had trouble "with a very bad earpiece that they gave me, and you could hardly hear what he was saying."[41]

"I love it when Trump plays dumb," said one Vanguard News Network

poster in response to Trump's comments on Duke.[42] The consensus interpretation across the white nationalist community was that Trump "owned"
Tapper and the rest of the reporters who asked him to disavow Duke. According to one poster on Storm Front, "Trump was reluctant to allow Tapper to
control the dialogue, and instead of jumping through the hoop the way he
wanted, to his credit, Trump didn't just automatically agree and give legitimacy to Tapper's vague accusations and attempts at guilt by association."[43]
Another white nationalist thought that "once again The Donald shows a
media whore who's the master and who's the boss."[44] When The Daily Beast
asked David Duke to respond to Trump's disavowal of him, Duke said, "If he
disavows me, fine. Let him do whatever he thinks he needs to do to become
president of the United States. It's good for him to be judicious."[45]

Duke had urged his radio show listeners to "get off your rear end. . . .
When this show's over, go out, call the Republican Party, but call Donald
Trump's headquarters. Volunteer."[46] Other white nationalists agreed. "We
need to go full-bore into the Trump campaign. We can't risk Trump becoming
another Reagan. If the GOP dies, fine. If the GOP survives, we need to have
influence over it," urged a poster on Vanguard News Network. He thought
white nationalists should make it clear that "Trump is a fascist icon. Trump
represents America's racism. Trump is the candidate of angry White men.
Push this line, fuck whatever Trump's actual positions are. Make it so a Trump
presidency is a symbolic victory for White racists."[47] Likewise, notorious
hacker and self-proclaimed "world's foremost internet troll" weev (Andrew
Auernheimer) urged readers of Daily Stormer (by now the most popular white
supremacist website in the United States) that "there is no method of ruin too
rude or personal to destroy these people. We bombard their employers with
hateposting. We show up at the doors of their homes to call them cucks and
traitors to their faces. We do whatever is necessary to run these people out of
town and make sure they never try to slink back."[48] White nationalists made
active efforts to support Trump with endorsements, Twitter troll armies, paid
robocalls, advertising, Twitter happy hours, coordinated hashtags, in-person
voter intimidation, hacking printers, and, of course, voting.[49] They sought
influence over Trump and the national dialogue by targeting Trump to try to
get him to retweet and spread their messages. They also targeted those who
attacked Trump or supported other candidates. "Have fun with the whole
thing; I know I am," one poster on Vanguard News Network said. "Verbally
battling the jewz & their SJW [social justice warrior] & #NeverTrump Muh

Constitution Cruz-monkeys on Twitter. I haven't enjoyed anything political this much since those old Bermuda shorts & black socks kikes accidentally knocked up chads for Buchanan in Florida."[50]

Daily Stormer users organized themselves into what they called the "Stormer Troll Army" in support of Trump's campaign and coordinated attacks against Trump's and their mutual enemies. For example, on April 27, 2016, *GQ* published Julia Ioffe's profile of Melania Trump, which told the story of Melania's childhood in Slovenia, her family, her modeling career, and how she met and married Donald Trump.[51] The Trumps were not happy that the story included information about Melania's secret half-brother or Melania's legal issues with her beauty brand, calling the story "yet another example of the dishonest media and their disingenuous reporting" on Melania's Facebook page.[52] In response, Andrew Anglin published a story on Daily Stormer under the headline, "Empress Melania Attacked by Filthy Russian Kike Julia Ioffe in *GQ*!" and called for fellow Stormers to "send her a tweet and let her know what you think of her dirty kike trickery. Make sure to identify her as a Jew working against White interests, or send her the picture with the Jude star from the top of this article. Gogoogogogoogogogo. Because I'd bet dollars to hot dogs she's a LOLCOW."[53] Stormers gleefully posted screenshots of their tweets to Ioffe in their comments on Anglin's article. Ioffe retweeted some of the anti-Semitic tweets, images, and phone calls that she received, filed a police report against the threats, and discussed the coordinated attack on television.[54] In response, Anglin posted, "Let it be known, Jews: if you go against us, you will end up with hurt feelings from mean words. . . . The Stormer Troll Army: We ride for the God Emperor, cleansing the galaxy of Necron filth in His Holy Name."[55]

A few days later on May 4, 2016, Trump became the GOP presumptive nominee. "Some of your supporters have viciously attacked this woman Julia Ioffe with anti-Semitic attacks, death threats," Wolf Blitzer said to Trump on CNN. "These people get so angry. What's your message to these people?" he asked. "I haven't read the article," Trump said, shifting the topic from what Trump would say to condemn the attackers to what Trump thought Ioffe had done to earn the attacks, "but I heard that it was a very inaccurate article and I heard it was a nasty article." Blitzer again asked Trump to comment on "the death threats that followed." Trump said, "I don't know about that. I don't know anything about that. Do you mean fans of mine? I know nothing about it. I don't have a message to the fans."[56] Trump denied any knowledge about the threats to Ioffe and called the white nationalists who threatened her his "fans," which white nationalists like Anglin read as an endorsement for the work of the Stormer Troll Army. "Asked by the disgusting and evil Jewish parasite Wolf Blitzer to denounce the Stormer Troll Army, The Glorious Leader declined," wrote Anglin. "The Jew Wolf was attempting to Stump the Trump, bringing up stormer attacks on Jew terrorist Julia Ioffe. Trump responded to the request with 'I have no message to the fans' which might as well have been 'Hail Victory, Comrades!'"[57] Trump's apparent denial was actually an embrace and a victory for white nationalists: "always remember: he looked straight at the camera and said 'I have no message for the fans.' Anything after that is just politics," Anglin wrote the next day.[58]

Trump routinely took advantage of the ironic wink-wink-wink of *paralipsis*—of saying the thing that he said that he wasn't saying—so that it was impossible to tell whether or not he condoned violent racist attacks or not. Trump's ironic double-speak was precisely the language of internet trolls like white nationalists. In fact, Anglin wrote early in Trump's campaign that if anyone thought that there was a difference between "trolling and flat-out racism," then "the joke is on you." According to Anglin, "What if I told you the whole 'well I can't tell if he's joking or not' thing is the most brilliant response to Jewish psychological warfare ever developed? And you haven't figured out what's happening here yet. The Jews have also failed to figure out what is happening with The Donald's refusal to condemn we trolls and/or actual Jew-hating racists. Yes, maybe The Donald is the new Hitler. Or . . . maybe he is just trolling you?"[59] White nationalists saw Trump as a fellow troll; they correctly read Trump's ambiguous denials and disavowals of them as encouragement to attack their shared enemies. Together they won the election. "This is the way the cucks end," wrote weev on Daily Stormer. "Not with a bang, But a shitpost."[60]

CHAPTER 10

"If she gets to pick her judges, nothing you can do, folks. Although the Second Amendment, people, maybe there is. I don't know."

Ad Baculum

Wilmington, North Carolina, August 9, 2016
Favorable: 33.4 percent; Unfavorable: 60.7 percent[1]

"In any Republican primary, everyone is going to say they support the Second Amendment," explained Texas senator Ted Cruz at the January 15, 2016, GOP primary debate. "Unless you are clinically insane," Cruz said to the laughter of the audience, "that's what you say in a primary."[2] Cruz wasn't wrong. In July 2016 against a backdrop of increased gun violence, terrorism, and Black Lives Matter protests, Pew asked Americans about their top issue priorities for the 2016 election. Gun policy was the fifth most important issue—selected by 74 percent of Clinton voters and 71 percent of Trump voters.[3] The next month, Pew asked Americans which gun policy would make America safer—controlling gun ownership or protecting gun rights. Ninety percent of Trump supporters thought that "protecting gun rights was more important than controlling gun ownership," and 89 percent thought that "gun ownership does more to protect than to put people's safety at risk." The Clinton supporters surveyed thought the opposite: 79 percent of Clinton supporters thought the nation should "prioritize controlling gun ownership over protecting gun rights" and 65 percent thought that "gun ownership does more to endanger personal safety than protect people from becoming victims of crime."[4] With gun policy being a top-five issue in the election and with 90 percent of Trump supporters and 89 percent of Clinton supporters holding the exact opposite view about gun ownership, it was easily among the most salient and polarizing, if not *the* most salient and polarizing, issue of the 2016 campaign.

Because gun policy was already an important issue upon which Republicans held strong opinions, there wasn't much room to persuade people to change their minds. Rather, when candidates talked about gun policy during the campaign, they sought to activate their partisans to act on their already strong opinions. One way to activate partisans is through fear appeals—threatening that whatever they hold most dear will be taken from them. That's precisely what Trump did during his campaign: he used *ad baculum* (threats of force or intimidation) *against* his followers, knowing that they were very committed to their gun rights and that such threats would motivate them to act.

When Trump launched his campaign on June 16, 2015, he didn't include much about gun rights in his speech. He promised to "fully support and back up the Second Amendment," but otherwise his speech focused more on corruption, illegal immigration, and trade policies.[5] On September 18, 2015, Trump released his second campaign position paper (his first position paper was on immigration), which explained what he would do to support the Second Amendment. Trump first argued unequivocally for a natural right of gun ownership: it was "a fundamental right that belongs to all law-abiding Americans. The Constitution doesn't create that right; it ensures that the government can't take it away."[6] Trump thought that the "Second Amendment's purpose is to guarantee our right to defend ourselves and our families. This is about self-defense, plain and simple." Trump sought to guarantee the self-defense rights of law-abiding Americans, first, by preventing bans on guns: "Law-abiding people should be allowed to own the firearm of their choice. The government has no business dictating what types of firearms good, honest people are allowed to own." Second, he would fix the background check system and "make it work as intended." Third, he would guarantee a national right to concealed carry, "which is a right, not a privilege." Fourth, he would end gun-free zones on military bases: "our current policies leave them defenseless." In his position paper, Trump reinforced the 'us versus them' polarization around gun rights when he framed the nation's gun issue as "good, honest" "law-abiding Americans" with guns against the "violent criminals," "drug dealers and gang members," and "deranged madmen" with guns. Trump explained that the "anti-gun politicians, gun control groups and the media" all threatened law-abiding Americans by wanting to take away their natural right of self-defense, leaving them vulnerable to violent criminals.[7] He would continue to take advantage of the rhetorical possibilities of framing the issue as us versus them, good guys versus bad guys, and life versus death when discussing gun rights throughout his campaign.

As Trump campaigned, he portrayed himself as a tough good guy with a gun, as he did in an interview with Barbara Walters in December 2015: "I'm a big believer in the Second Amendment," explained Trump. "The bad guys will always have guns, Barbara. So, Paris—boom, boom, boom. If you look at California, nobody had guns except the bad guys. If you had three or four people like me—I have the right to carry. I have a license to carry. If you had people like me in that room, and somebody started shooting, I guarantee you we're going down shooting."[8] Trump repeated a version of this same story in nearly every campaign appearance until election night: The world is divided into good guys and bad guys. The bad guys all have guns; we need to make sure that the good guys (like Trump and his followers) have guns too. It's a simple message that resonated well with the 90 percent of Trump supporters who agreed with him that they should be armed for self-defense.

Trump used highly descriptive and evocative language when he warned about the bad guys with the guns. For example, in Mount Pleasant, South Carolina, on December 7, 2015, Trump called the bad guys "dirty, rotten scum" to the cheers and applause of his rally crowd.[9] Likewise, in Clear Lake, Iowa, on January 9, 2016, Trump described the Paris terrorists as "these thugs, these dirty, rotten, very stupid demented people."[10] They were "these thugs, this scum, this garbage" in Valdosta, Georgia, on February 29, 2016, and "thugs, these thugs. The guy with the dirty white cap, the thugs" in Atlanta, Georgia, on June 15, 2016.[11] A thug, of course, is another word for a gangster—coded language that suggests that the bad guys were nonwhite.[12] Trump described these dangerous "thugs" as dirty, rotten, stupid, demented, scum, and garbage, which made them seem even more irrational and even more dangerous.

Trump routinely emphasized the personal danger his rally crowd faced from these dangerous thugs by dramatically telling the story of the November 13, 2015, Paris terrorist attack that killed 130 people. Trump used the story to compare the danger faced by unarmed Americans to the dangers faced by the unarmed victims in Paris, noting that "France has the toughest gun laws in the world. Only the bad guys have the guns."[13] To reinforce his point, Trump reenacted the scene from Paris, forming his fingers into a gun and shooting at his rally audience, heightening the sense of danger intended by his comparison. For example, in Clear Lake, Iowa, on January 9, 2016, Trump told the story of the Paris attack by playing the part of the bad guys who "walk in, and they say, 'Get over.' [Trump made his hand into a gun, shooting a member of the audience.] Boom! [He pointed toward another member of the audience.] 'Over.' [He motioned for the audience member to move over.] Boom! [He shot the audience member.] Not one gun in the room, except for the bad guys," Trump explained as he shook his head with pity.[14]

As Trump talked about gun rights, he reenacted this scene repeatedly. Trump shot members of his audience on February 29, 2016, in Valdosta, Georgia.[15] Trump shot members of his audience in Tuscan, Arizona, on March 19, 2016.[16] Trump shot members of his audience in Atlanta, Georgia, on June 15, 2016.[17] Trump shot and shot and shot, and each time when he stopped shooting, he said (some version of), "If some of the people in those places where there was absolute slaughter had guns, you wouldn't have the carnage that you had in Paris! [Trump's rally crowd cheered and applauded.] You wouldn't have had that carnage. So important the Second Amendment— we have to preserve it and cherish."[18] Trump would then frequently point at members of his audience and enlist them to be gun-carrying self-defenders, like he did in Milford, New Hampshire, on February 3, 2016:

> If we had a few people in this room, I can look at them. [Trump pointed at an audience member.] That guy right there; he's mean. If we had a few of the people, you, you, you. [Trump pointed at more audience members as hands went up for Trump to call them into battle.] Let me pick a woman. [Trump wiggled his finger around and around in a circle, then pointed at a woman.] You. And if somebody had a gun on their belt or somebody had a gun wrapped around her ankle, and those bullets started coming at you or you see they were going to, folks, you'd shoot them. That is our form of protection.[19]

Trump's rally crowd thundered its approval. Trump's message to his rally crowds was clear and simple: they were the good guys, their very lives were at stake, and they must use their guns to protect themselves and defeat their shared enemies.

Staunch gun rights advocate and Supreme Court justice Antonin Scalia died unexpectedly on February 13, 2016, which provided the opportunity for Trump to intensify his *ad baculum* appeals by threatening that Scalia's death made Americans' gun rights (and lives) even *less* secure. "Our country has been taken away from us," Trump threatened to his rally crowd in Walterboro, South Carolina, on February 17, 2016. "It's going so fast. The Second Amendment is under siege, you know that. . . . We lost a great Supreme Court justice, and nobody thought this was gonna be part of the equation. And all of a sudden, if somebody gets in and it's the wrong person, they'll take that Second Amendment away so fast your head will spin."[20] The scary "wrong person," of course, was Hillary Clinton. Throughout the campaign, Trump threatened that Hillary Clinton was determined to take away Americans' guns. Yet, according to fact-checkers, Trump repeatedly misrepresented Clinton's stance on gun rights. By May 10, 2016, his comments had attracted the attention of the nonpartisan FactCheck.org, which judged that Trump "distorts the facts." They called attention to his May 7, 2016, rally in Lynden, Washington, where he said, "Hillary Clinton wants to abolish the Second Amendment. She wants to abolish it. Hillary Clinton wants to take your guns away and she wants to abolish the Second Amendment. She wants to take the bullets away. She wants to take it."[21] After examining Clinton's public statements about gun rights, they found "Clinton's gun violence prevention proposal would impose restrictions, including a ban on semi-automatic 'assault weapons,' but it does not call for banning all guns."[22] Likewise, PolitiFact rated Trump's accusation "false."[23] Trump's hyperbolic description of Clinton's intention wasn't meant to pass fact-checkers, of course; it was meant as a threatening fear appeal, to scare voters.

On May 20, 2016, National Rifle Association (NRA) chief executive officer Wayne LaPierre endorsed Trump on behalf of the "patriots" of the NRA, imploring its members to unite against "the damage that will be done" to Second Amendment rights by a possible Hillary Clinton presidency. Trump's speech accepting the NRA endorsement was full of polarizing *ad baculum* fear appeals. "If she gets to appoint her judges," Trump threatened NRA members, using the same words that he used in his rallies, "she will, as part of it, abolish the Second Amendment." Trump warned that Clinton's explicit plan was to unleash "violent criminals from the jails, including drug dealers and those with gun crimes" many of whom were "illegal immigrants"—as well as "thousands of dangerous drug-trafficking felons and gang members who prey on civilians." Once Clinton had released these dangerous predators into the community, she planned to take away law-abiding Americans' guns to leave them "defenseless." According to Trump, Clinton's diabolical plan was "to take away any chance they have of survival." With their very lives on the line, Trump argued that NRA members should fear Clinton's "pledge to issue new antigun executive orders" as "the behavior of, you could say, a dictator." Figured as a possible dictator, Clinton could serve as a unifying symbolic threat for NRA members and all Trump supporters.

Trump continued to repeat his threats about Clinton, the Supreme Court, and the Second Amendment. Throughout his presidential campaign, he used the dangerous threat of the effects of a Clinton presidency as a cudgel—as an *ad baculum* threat against his own supporters. Such threats functioned as a polarizing fear appeal to motivate gun owners to unify behind his campaign against their shared enemies. But Trump didn't just use threats to scare his supporters. Trump used *ad baculum* threats as fear appeals in two directions: he used threats against his followers to scare them into voting for him, and he used threats against Clinton to rally his followers into voting for him in order to punish her.

On August 9, 2016, Trump brought several pages of notes with him to the podium. "I just wrote this down today," Trump said as he began a comparison between himself and Clinton. "Hillary wants to abolish, essentially abolish, the Second Amendment," Trump told his rally crowd in Wilmington, North Carolina, as they began to boo. "By the way, [more booing] and if she gets to pick [Trump was interrupted by the crowd booing]—if she gets to pick her judges, nothing you can do, folks. Although the Second Amendment, people, maybe there is. I don't know [crowd laughed and cheered]. But I will tell you what, that will be a horrible day, if, if Hillary gets to put her judges—right now, we are tied and you see what's going on.[24] Trump's talking point was the same as it had been—as was his *ad baculum* strategy of threatening his supporters' rights and safety. But Trump's embellishment that perhaps "Second Amendment people" could do something to stop Clinton was new and sounded especially dangerous. "The Secret Service is aware of the comments made this afternoon," it tweeted ominously.[25]

The response to Trump's "Second Amendment people" remark was swift: "Donald Trump suggests 'Second Amendment People' could act against Hillary Clinton," wrote the *New York Times*;[26] "Donald Trump hints at assassination of Hillary Clinton by gun rights supporters," wrote *The Guardian*;[27] "Trump's assassination dog whistle was even scarier than you think," wrote *Rolling Stone*; and so on.[28] The US Secret Service reportedly spoke to the Trump campaign "regarding his Second Amendment comments," and Hillary Clinton called Trump's comments "the latest in a long line of casual comments from Donald Trump that cross the line."[29] While some political commentators attempted to explain away Trump's statement as a clumsy joke, others thought that Trump's comment should be taken both literally and seriously. "Don't treat this as a political misstep," wrote Connecticut senator Chris Murphy. "It's an assassination threat, seriously upping the possibility of a national tragedy & crisis."[30]

Trump's campaign issued a statement deflecting the criticism by praising his supporters: "It's called the power of unification—2nd Amendment people have amazing spirit and are tremendously unified, which gives them great political power."[31] Trump appeared that night on Fox News, where he agreed with Sean Hannity that he had meant nothing more than "there is a strong political movement within the Second Amendment." "There can be no other interpretation," Trump said to Hannity. "I mean, give me a break."[32] As the debate raged about Trump's comments, it became clear that some of Trump's supporters were willing to be called into service to protect their Second Amendment rights, just as Trump had enlisted his supporters at his rallies. For example, on August 10, 2016, a Trump supporter named Greg called into C-SPAN to explain that "Mr. Trump was not threatening assassination of Hillary." Instead, Greg thought that Trump meant that "if Hillary got her way and did do away with Second Amendment rights, there are a lot of us who are gun owners who are going to object to that very strongly. And since we do have firearms, it might, if it comes down to it, be us having to defend our rights with those guns, just as the revolutionaries did in the Revolutionary War."[33] Greg had received Trump's *ad baculum* message well: he believed that Clinton was determined to take away his Second Amendment rights, and he was glad to be called into service to use his guns to defend his rights.

The NRA also approved of Trump's comments and used his *ad baculum* strategy to encourage gun rights advocates to vote for Trump. The NRA tweeted its support on August 9, 2016, "@RealDonaldTrump is right. If @HillaryClinton gets to pick her anti-#2A #SCOTUS judges, there's nothing we can do. #NeverHillary,"[34] followed by a new set of advertisements that used a threatening line from Trump's May 2016 NRA speech. (The NRA spent more than \$419 million on political ads and lobbying in 2016 alone.[35]) In that speech, Trump had used the issue of gun rights to threaten Clinton's safety directly. To the thunderous cheers of the NRA crowd, Trump explained that if Clinton didn't want good, law-abiding Americans like them to own guns, then her security detail "should immediately disarm. Let's see how good they do. Let's see how they feel walking around without their guns and bodyguards."[36] The NRA ad showed a Clinton look-alike moving with a security detail through city streets, parking, and entering a private jet where a video clip played showing Clinton saying, "I fully appreciate how hard life is for so many Americans today." The ad's voiceover said, "She's one of the wealthiest women in politics. Combined income: \$30 million. Tours the world in private jets. Protected by armed guards for thirty years. But she doesn't believe in your right to keep a gun at home for self-defense. She's an out-of-touch hypocrite. And she'd leave you defenseless."[37] Another NRA ad launched a few weeks later followed the same *ad baculum* strategy as Trump's campaign. It showed a woman sleeping when a noise woke her up as ominous music played. She reached for the phone to call for help, and she reached for her gun from a lockbox, which faded away before she could get her gun. The voiceover said, "She'll call 911. Average response time? 11 minutes. Too late. She keeps a firearm in a safe for protection, but Hillary Clinton would take away her right to self-defense. And with Supreme Court justices, Hillary can. Don't let Hillary leave you protected with nothing but a phone."[38]

CHAPTER 11

"'Oh, shut up, silly woman,' said the reptile with a grin. 'You knew damn well I was a snake before you took me in!'"

Reification

Cedar Falls, Iowa, January 12, 2016
Favorable: 34.0 percent; Unfavorable: 57.3 percent[1]

"These are the best and the finest," Trump pronounced as he pointed at members of the audience of tourists and paid actors at his June 16, 2015, presidential announcement speech in Trump Tower. "When Mexico sends its people, they're not sending their best. They're not sending you. [Trump pointed out at his audience.] They're not sending you. [Trump looked up and pointed to more audience members.] They're sending people that have lots of problems, and they're bringing those problems with us. They're bringing drugs. They're bringing crime. They're rapists. And some, I assume," Trump said with a shrug, "are good people." Trump's audience in Trump Tower was "the best and the finest": they and the nation they inhabited were pure and good, but they and the nation were in danger, according to Trump. The pure nation was being polluted, infested with "lots of problems," with dangerous drugs, crimes, and rapists. To mitigate the problem of dangerous Mexicans pouring into the United States, Trump promised in his announcement speech that he would "build a great, great wall on our southern border. And I will have Mexico pay for that wall. Mark my words." Trump's wall was central to his polarizing political campaign strategy: with it, he would separate the good Americans from the dangerous attackers.

The key to understanding how Trump used reification (treating people as objects) to polarize Americans around the issue of illegal immigration to is pay careful attention to how Trump portrayed the nation as inherently pure and illegal immigrants as a dangerous infestation. The word "infest" comes from the Latin *infestus,* or "hostile," and *infestare,* or "assail," and is commonly used to refer to insects or animals that appear in "large numbers, typically so as to cause damage or disease." Trump's rhetoric framed illegal immigrants as a hostile and damaging infestation of the pure nation. As Trump frequently said, "illegal immigration" was "killing our country." While infestation rhetoric is not new, it is a sophisticated strategy. As historian and political scientist Benedict Anderson explained, nations are "imagined communities"—they are constructed by our laws but also in our imaginations. We cannot see the entirety of our nation or its borders. We cannot know all the people of our nation. We accept that there is "a nation" on trust alone. It therefore takes an act of imagination to believe that a nation exists and another to believe that some people belong and others do not. It takes yet another act of imagination to decide that those who belong to the nation are pure and those who do not are a dangerous threat. Trump's use of infestation rhetoric helped him argue that illegal immigrants were a dangerous threat to the pure nation, which helped him polarize the nation. Because illegal immigrants were a dangerous threat, they were enemy objects that should be purged. Because the nation was pure, it should be protected. Therefore, according to Trump, any politician who treated these "objects" as people was either weak or dumb.

Trump's announcement speech caused outrage on both sides of the US-Mexico border. "Regarding the comments made by Donald Trump," said Mexican interior minister Miguel Angel Osorio Chong on June 17, 2015, "to me they seem prejudiced and absurd."[2] Trump's comments not only caused outrage, but also cost Trump business relationships. On June 25, 2015, Univision announced that it was "ending the Company's business relationship with the Miss Universe Organization, which is part-owned by Donald J. Trump, based on his recent, insulting remarks about Mexican immigrants," and on June 29, 2015, NBC announced that "due to the recent derogatory statements by Donald Trump regarding immigrants, NBC Universal is ending its business relationship with Mr. Trump."[3] Macy's ended its relationship with Trump two days later, saying, "We are disappointed and distressed by recent remarks about immigrants from Mexico."[4] Trump dismissed all of these rebukes. They were put up to it by the Mexican government, he said. He quit them first, he explained. They didn't know the facts about the infestation, or they knew the facts but wouldn't admit them. Although Trump acknowledged that there had been a lot of criticism of what he said at his announcement speech, he refused to apologize. "You have people coming in, and I'm not just saying Mexicans," Trump told Jake Tapper in a June 28, 2015, CNN interview. "I'm talking about people that are from all over, that are killers, and rapists, and I mean they're coming into this country." Tapper said that Trump was "painting eleven million" people with a "very broad brush" when he called them criminals and rapists, when it was "probably a very small percentage." "No, no," said Trump. "I don't think it's a small percentage. It's a lot."[5]

One reason that Trump's comments caused so much controversy was because American public opinion disagreed with him about immigration. An August 12, 2015, Gallup poll found that 65 percent of Americans favored "a plan to allow immigrants who are living illegally in the U.S. to remain in the country and become citizens if they meet certain requirements over time." However, Gallup's poll noted that there was a wide partisan gap between the 50 percent of Republicans and the 80 percent of Democrats who favored the "path to citizenship" plan.[6] Trump exploited that partisan gap. On the campaign trail, Trump used fear appeals to highlight the danger that illegal immigrants "pouring in" posed to the United States. Trump repeatedly described immigrants as "sick with hate," as "gang members" that committed "tremendous crime," warning that "drugs and criminal cartels are pouring into our country on an hourly basis" due to border weakness. Time and again, Trump used fear appeals to divide and polarize. For example, "We talk about the wrong people coming into our country and we can't allow it, we can't allow it," Trump told his rally crowd in Vienna, Ohio, on March 14, 2016, "and I love you. Look at this crowd—I love you."[7] Trump took advantage of "us versus them" polarization when he expressed his love for his rally crowds and for the people of the United States and his hatred for those "bad hombres" who came into the United States illegally and who he claimed were determined to commit terrible crimes.[8]

On August 16, 2015, Trump published his campaign's official "Immigration Reform That Will Make America Great Again" plan and went on *Meet the Press* to sell it to the nation. Trump's plan was based on three "core principles" that were meant to defend the pure nation: first, "a nation without borders is not a nation"; second, "a nation without laws is not a nation"; and third, "a nation that does not serve its own citizens is not a nation." Those three principles led Trump to argue that the nation ought to be purged of illegal immigrants (including removing an estimated eleven million currently residing undocumented immigrants and ending "birthright citizenship") and that the nation ought to be protected from the threat of further illegal immigrants "pouring" over the southern border by building a wall. "They have to go," Trump explained when Chuck Todd asked Trump to defend his policy of deporting the illegal immigrants currently living in the United States. "We either have a country or we don't have a country." Todd asked Trump a series of feasibility questions about his plan (How would you do it? How much would it cost? Would you separate families?), but Trump avoided giving specific answers. "Chuck, it'll work out so well. You will be so happy. In four years, you're going to be interviewing me, and you're going to say, 'What a great job you've done, President Trump.'" Todd appeared unpersuaded. But three days later, Rasmussen released a poll that indicated broad support among Republican likely voters for two parts of Trump's immigration plan: 92 percent agreed with Trump's plan to purge criminal illegal immigrants from the United States, and 70 percent agreed with Trump's plan to protect the nation from further illegal immigration by building a wall along the nation's southern border.[9] Trump's purge and protect plan wasn't popular with all Americans, but it resonated with the voters whose support he needed to win the Republican Party nomination.

Trump used his fear appeals to persuade his followers not only that illegal immigrants were a mortal threat to the nation, but that they ought to be purged via mass deportation. His fear appeals focused on the crimes committed by a small number of illegal immigrants. "People came into the country illegally and killed their children," Trump said somberly at a July 10, 2015, press conference as he stood in front of several families who had lost a family member to a crime committed by an illegal immigrant. Trump's press conference provided a platform for the families to tell their stories to the press, which Trump used as evidence to support his claims about the dangers of illegal immigration.[10] From then on, Trump told the stories of "beautiful Kate," who "was gunned down by an illegal immigrant"; of "Jamiel Shaw," who was "was viciously shot and killed by an illegal immigrant"; of the "sixty-four-year-old Air Force veteran," who was "who was raped and beaten and tortured by this animal"; and other victims whose stories functioned as proof of

Trump's claim about the dangers of illegal immigrants.[11] At his presidential announcement, Trump had called Mexicans "rapists," but as he clarified his strategy, Trump shifted from the general accusation "they're rapists" to specific examples of crimes, which he described in graphic and gruesome detail. The stories were a powerful *synecdoche* (the part that stood for the whole) of Trump's argument. Telling the gruesome stories provided Trump with a compelling accumulation of evidence.

His rally audiences could often be seen wincing at the graphic and tragic details of Trump's stories, but according to Politifact, Trump's claim that "thousands of Americans have been killed by illegal immigrants" was only "half-true." "At his rallies, Trump portrays a picture of undocumented immigrants as a strong force of violent crime," but, according to Politifact, "Trump puts no timeframe on his comment, leaving his audience to fill in the blanks. In reality, there is no solid data for homicides committed by people here illegally. His implicit suggestion is that people should fear illegal immigrants more than citizens, and we don't see evidence for that. Research shows immigrants are less likely to engage in criminal behavior than the native-born population."[12] While only half true, Trump's scary infestation rhetoric was still effective.[13] "There are more than two million criminal aliens in this country right now," Trump said as he finished describing several gruesome crimes at his rally in Prescott Valley, Arizona, on October 5, 2016. "When I am president, we are getting them out and getting them out fast! [The crowd roared with approval.]"[14]

Trump's infestation rhetoric was designed to appeal to his followers' fears but also to appeal their sense of disgust, because—on a very basic level—what causes us disgust should be purged. Trump said that the problem was so dire that he would end birthright citizenship, protected by the Fourteenth Amendment of the US Constitution, because it enticed illegal immigrants to come to the United States to deliver "anchor babies," or children born to noncitizen parents. ("Anchor" is another reification, obviously.) On September 15, 2015, at a rally at the USS *Iowa* in Los Angles, California, Trump explained (with a rare use of anaphora, the figure of repetition) that he and his campaign represented "the silent majority" who were

> disgusted with our incompetent politicians. They are disgusted
> with the people that are giving our country away. They are dis-
> gusted when they tell the border patrol agents who were good

people and can do the job. They are disgusted when they allow
people to walk right in front of them and standing there helpless
as people just pour into the country. They are disgusted when
a woman who is nine months pregnant walks across the border
and has a baby and you have to take care of that baby for the next
eighty-five years. They are disgusted by what's happening to our
country![15]

Trump bellowed as the crowd cheered enthusiastically. The nation was
infested and burdened with caring for the "anchor babies" of illegal immigrants, which disgusted Trump and his followers. Trump, therefore, was
justified in acting on that disgust by purging the nation of the natural-born
citizens of illegal immigrants and preventing more "disgusting" babies from
being born in the United States.

Not only would Trump purge the nation of scary "criminal illegals" and
disgusting "anchor babies," but Trump would protect the pure nation from
further infestation by building a wall of separation between the United States
and Mexico. Chants of "Build a wall! Build a wall! Build a wall" sent his campaign rallies into an ecstatic frenzy. Trump often led the chants, like he did at
his rally in Columbus, Ohio, on November 23, 2015. He was in the middle of
describing the November 13, 2015, Paris terrorist attacks—in which "people
were gunned down like sitting ducks, like sitting ducks. They were helpless,
couldn't do a thing"—when he began talking about his promise to build a
wall.

So what happens is we look at that, and I've been working very
hard on the borders. And I'm the only one, by the way, believe
me. I know all the guys. I've been working on the border. And all
of a sudden, the borders, because we will build a wall, believe me.
[Audience cheered.] We're gonna build a wall. We're gonna build
a wall. Build. A. Wall! [Trump lifted his index finger and like a
band leader keeping time, he raised and lowered his finger to the
beat to encourage the crowd to chant.] "BUILD A WALL! BUILD
A WALL! BUILD A WALL! BUILD A WALL!" [The audience
began chanting on its own while Trump spun away from the
podium and gave two thumbs up to the chanting audience members
behind him.] Incredible![16]

Trump promised that the wall would be "big" and "beautiful." Trump said that the wall would be a "strong wall," a "great wall," and, above all, a "real wall" that would prevent the infestation of dangerous criminals from "pouring across the border." Trump promised that the wall would have "a big door for the right people to come into our country legally." Sometimes Trump fantasized that the wall would be named after him—"The TRUMP Wall" or "The Great Wall of TRUMP," he said.[17]

Trump promised that Mexico would pay for the wall, even when Mexico assured Trump that it would not.[18] On September 1, 2016, Mexican president Enrique Peña Nieto tweeted, "Repito lo que le dije personalmente, Sr. Trump: México jamás pagaría por un muro."[19] ("I repeat what I said personally, Mr. Trump: Mexico would never pay for a wall.") Nieto was reiterating what former Mexican president Vicente Fox had told ABC News on February 26, 2016: "I am not going to pay for that fucking wall. He should pay for it. He's got the money."[20] Undeterred, Trump liked to lead a call and response with his rally crowds, insisting that Mexico really *would* pay for the wall: "Who's going to pay for it?" Trump asked on January 7, 2016, in Burlington, Vermont. "MEXICO!" his audience yelled in response. "I've never done that before. That's cute," said Trump.[21]

The first time Trump read "The Snake" on January 12, 2016, at a rally in Cedar Rapids, Iowa, he said that he "read this the other day and I said, 'Wow, that's really amazing!'"[22] Trump attributed it to Al Wilson, but according to the *Washington Post*, the "poem originated in the 1960s from a soul singer and social activist in Chicago, Oscar Brown Jr."[23] The short poem told the story of a snake, freezing and near death, that was rescued by the care of a "tender" woman. Once the snake was healthy again, it bit the woman, killing her with its poison. Trump loved to emphasize the poem's last lines, "'Oh, shut up, silly woman!' said the reptile with a grin. 'You knew damn well I was a snake before you took me in!'" After Trump finished his last line, typically to the thunderous applause of his rally crowds, he would explain what his fans should learn from the poem. "I read it and I just sort of put it together," said Trump in Iowa. "We have no idea what we're doing. We have no idea who we're taking in, and we better be careful, OK?"[24] He told his rally in Vienna, Ohio, on March 14, 2016, to "remember this poem. We talked about the wrong people coming into our country, right? We cannot allow it. I love you. Look at this crowd. I love you."[25] Trump explained to his rally crowd in Denver, Colorado, on July 29, 2016, that the poem was about the dangers of "people coming across the border and people coming in from Syria. That we have no idea who they are."[26] Trump said the United States was infested by dangerous "snakes," like in the poem, and he thought that the poem offered evidence to support his purge-and-protect policies. He told his rally in Erie, Pennsylvania, on August 12, 2016, "This is what is going on in our country. By the way, we are going to have a strong border. We will have a wall. It will be a strong wall, and Mexico is going to pay for. And we have no choice." Trump said that the poem "really pertains to what is happening to the United States. And it has to do with being fooled. It has to do with a lot of different things, but when you're listening to this, think of our border. Think of the people we are letting in by the thousands. [The rally crowd cheered enthusiastically.] Get ready, folks, get ready. We are led by stupid people."[27] Trump could see the infestation for what it was; he was no "silly woman" who would be fooled by "snakes" like illegal immigrants.

Trump was so convinced of the veracity of his immigration plan that he was immune to contradictory facts. "I'm talking about illegal immigration. And it has to be stopped," Trump explained to CNN's Don Lemon on July 1, 2015. "It's killing our country." Trump argued, as he had done since his announcement speech, that "people are pouring over the borders," which was scary to him because "we don't even know where they come from." Lemon challenged Trump about why he had called immigrants "rapists" in his announcement speech a few weeks before: "Why did you have to say that they're rapists, though, Donald?" Trump explained that if "you look at the statistics," like he had done, "look at the statistics on rape, on crime, on everything coming in illegally into this country, they're mind-boggling." Trump specifically told Lemon to read an investigation posted on Fusion that Trump said proved his claims. That article, "Is Rape the Price to Pay for Migrant Women Chasing the American Dream?," explained that "a staggering 80% of Central American girls and women crossing Mexico en route to the United States are raped along the way." The article further explained that the migrant women were abused by "coyotes, other migrants, bandits, or even government authorities."[28] Lemon told Trump that he *had* read the article and that it was actually about migrant "women *being* raped. It's not about criminals coming across the border or entering the country." Lemon thought that Trump was wrong to blame migrants, but Trump insisted he was correct. "Well, somebody's doing the raping, Don. Who's doing the raping? Who's doing the raping?" Trump wouldn't acknowledge the facts of the case, especially because the facts contradicted his goal of building a wall of separation to protect the nation from what he saw as an infestation of dangerous rapists: "The problem is you have to stop illegal immigration coming across the border. You have to create a strong border, Don. If you don't, we don't have a country."[29]

Throughout the campaign, Trump rejected evidence that proved him wrong about the border and the dangers of illegal immigrants. "What have I said that's wrong?" Trump asked Chuck Todd on the March 13, 2016, episode of *Meet the Press*. "I mean, I talk about illegal immigration. I talk about building a wall. I say Mexico's going to pay for the wall, which they will. And all of these things. I mean, what have I said that's wrong? You tell me."[30] It didn't matter to Trump that Mexico refused to pay for the wall; it didn't matter to Trump that the illegal immigrant crime statistics that he quoted were untrue; it didn't matter to Trump that the article he used to support his claim that Mexicans were "rapists" did not say what he claimed it said. No facts could permeate Trump's belief in his infestation rhetoric. For example, in a July 8, 2015, interview, Katy Tur pressed Trump to defend his claims by pointing out that "the murder rate in El Paso, Texas, on the border is the lowest for any of the big cities in the country." Trump's response was mocking: "Look, don't try and convince me that there's no crime. That it's wonderful. The people being forced in—and these just aren't Mexican people—they are forcing them into our country, and we're taking and putting them in our jails and hospitals, and we're paying them money through different sources. It is a disgrace. Don't tell me about safety. Are you trying to justify the safety of the border?" Tur explained that there is a "lower incarceration rate for Mexican immigrants and illegal immigrants than for US born citizens," but Trump mocked her again when he told her to "go check your numbers. It is a wrong statistic. Check your numbers. It sounds good. Check your numbers." Tur tried again: "Immigration is down. Why is this a big topic right now?" "Immigration is a big topic. Look at all the crime being committed," insisted Trump, despite the statistics just mentioned by Tur. She tried yet again: "The research says the crime does not match what you're saying." Trump retorted, "Don't be naive. You are a very naive person. You don't even know what you're talking about."[31] Despite evidence and research and fact-checks, Trump would not be convinced that illegal immigrants were not as dangerous as he claimed.[32]

No less an authority figure than Pope Francis tried to convince Trump to recognize immigrants as people, rather than as dangerous objects. "Perhaps it will not be easy for you to look into their souls," Pope Francis said in his September 23, 2015, speech before the US bishops. "Perhaps you will be challenged by their diversity. But know that they also possess resources meant to be shared, so do not be afraid to welcome them."[33] The next day, in a speech before Congress, Pope Francis urged US lawmakers to recognize the "thousands of persons" who were "in search of a better life for themselves and for their loved ones, in search of greater opportunities," and in recognizing the immigrants as "persons," to treat them "with the same passion and compassion with which we want to be treated." Immigrants should not be reified as an infestation according to Pope Francis, "but rather view them as persons, seeing their faces and listening to their stories, trying to respond as best we can to their situation. To respond in a way which is always humane, just, and fraternal."[34] When asked about Pope Francis's speeches on CNN later than night, Trump said, "I think his words are beautiful. I respect the pope and I like the pope very much. . . . [But] we have tremendous crime problems, as you know, [and] the illegal immigrants are coming in." The infestation was so dangerous, according to Trump, "we're having tremendous crime waves. We have a lot of problems coming in. Drugs pouring over the borders. We have to seal our borders. We have to do something about illegal immigration."[35] Pope Francis had not persuaded Trump to think of the immigrants as "persons"; they were only a dangerous infestation, and Trump would not agree to treat them in ways that were "humane, just, and fraternal."

February 11, 2016, Trump appeared on Fox Business's *Varney & Company* and called Pope Francis a "very political person" who "doesn't understand the problems our country has. I don't think he understands the danger of the open border that we have with Mexico."[36] Pope Francis gave a speech at the US-Mexican border on February 17, 2016, in which he argued that "we cannot deny the humanitarian crisis" at the border. He explained that "the human tragedy that is forced migration is a global phenomenon." He called it a "crisis which *can* be measured in numbers and statistics; we want *instead* to measure with names, stories, families. They are the brothers and sisters of those expelled by poverty and violence, by drug trafficking and criminal organizations."[37] That night as the pope traveled back to Rome, a reporter asked him what he thought of Trump calling him a "political person" and "whether a Catholic in the United States could vote [for Trump]." "Well, thank God he said that I am a political *person*," responded Pope Francis, "because Aristotle defined the human being as a 'political animal.' At least I am human!" He said that he would not comment on whether or not people should vote for Trump, but he added, "A person who thinks only of building walls, wherever it may be, and not of building bridges, is not Christian."[38]

Trump's response, posted on Facebook, on his campaign website, and tweeted out on February 18, 2016, began by threatening that ISIS was going to attack the Vatican, "which as everyone knows is ISIS's ultimate trophy." Trump's statement claimed that the pope didn't know what he was talking about with illegal immigration because "he didn't see the crime, the drug trafficking, and the negative economic impact the current policies have on the United States"—he didn't see the effects of the infestation, so he didn't know that immigrants were "snakes."[39] That night on CNN and on February 22, 2016, at a rally in Las Vegas, Nevada, Trump told the story of his disagreement with the pope.[40] "The pope is hitting me hard," said Trump, "and he said things about the border and you can't have a wall. And I said, 'Wow, but I've seen the Vatican. That's the biggest, strongest wall I've ever seen. I've never seen a wall like that.'"[41] Trump's response to Pope Francis asking him to see the immigrants as people rather than as an infestation of dangerous objects was to threaten, berate, condemn, and trivialize him. Trump used a *tu quoque* (an appeal to hypocrisy) to argue that the pope had no standing to make his claims because the Vatican was surrounded by a wall. Despite all evidence and appeals from humanitarian figures like Pope Francis, Trump would not modify his infestation rhetoric. Illegal immigrants were only a dangerous infestation on the pure nation—either you have a border or you don't have a country; either you have a wall or you don't have a country. Trump wanted to have a country with a strong border guarded by a Great Wall of Trump. And, as Trump said at a rally in Prescott Valley, Arizona, on October 5, 2016, "I am not running to be president of the world. I am running to be president of the United States of America."[42]

CHAPTER 12

"Drain the Swamp."

American Exceptionalism

Newtown, Pennsylvania, October 21, 2016
Favorable: 35 percent; Unfavorable: 61.1 percent[1]

"You see these phony statistics put out by politicians—basically, all talk and no action politicians?" Trump asked the National Federation of Republican Assemblies, on August 29, 2015. "They show those phony statistics where we are 5.4 percent unemployment. The real number? I saw a number that could be 42 percent, believe it or not." Trump certainly believed the high number that he claimed to have seen and not the phony official government numbers. As Trump continued, he argued that his supporters also saw through the government's phony statistics; they knew all about the politicians' lies. Trump's supporters believed him over them because "people in this country are smart. They don't believe a lot of what they see in the media." Trump's smart people knew that the same media that lied about phony unemployment statistics also lied about Trump. But he didn't think that any honest American would believe the negative things about him, "because if you believe these people, you know, why are they doing this? I mean, why are they even saying it?" In fact, Trump thought, his followers understood that there was a conspiracy to prevent Trump from saving the nation, as was his plan and his destiny. "You'd think that if somebody's good for the country—and I'll be great for the country, 'cause I'm going to make great deals for our country. We don't win anymore. Our country doesn't win any more. You'd think if somebody's even a liberal person or a Democrat liberal, and I mean really liberal—if somebody's going to make the country—why are they knocking it? Why are they knocking it? Why do they fight? You'd think they'd say, 'Let's do it; it's good for all of us. Because our country's in trouble.'"[2]

Trump's series of "why" questions implied that there was a hidden truth, a hidden agenda, a hidden conspiracy against him and America. The apparent was not the actual; the attacks against him were well-orchestrated lies in the service of a plot. Trump was wise to the conspiracy. He knew that *everyone* knew that the country was in trouble. Trump also knew that everyone knew that he could save it. Trump also knew the only people who would oppose him were those who were a part of the conspiracy against America. That there was a determined conspiracy against America was an overarching campaign theme that Trump returned to again and again. "You know what I don't understand?" Trump asked his rally crowd in Myrtle Beach a few months later, on November 24, 2015. "I want to make our country great again. For the liberals, for the Democrats, for the Republicans, for conservative Republicans. I want to make—OK? Why do people fight us? Why? Why? Because it's so obvious what's happening."[3]

Trump—who told *Playboy* magazine in 1990, "I'm a very untrusting guy. I study people all the time, automatically; it's my way of life"—was a connoisseur and purveyor of conspiracy theory.[4] Conspiracy theory was very good for Trump's political ambitions: in 2011, Trump transitioned from reality television figure to political figure because of conspiracy theory: He led the "birther" conspiracy over President Barack Obama's birth certificate, in which Trump accused Obama of not being American, of not being born in the United States, and of being a secret Muslim.[5] Trump's birther conspiracy coincided with a possible 2012 presidential election bid and led immediately to a weekly spot on Fox News' *Fox & Friends*, where he regularly gave his opinions about politics, developing a loyal following.[6] Trump saw corruption and conspiracy in all aspects of American life. He saw it in elected officials like Obama, in immigrant and refugee communities, in the media, in established political institutions, and in science like inoculations and climate change.[7] By May 2016, according to one count, Trump had advanced more than fifty different conspiracies within the year since he had launched his presidential campaign.[8]

Conspiracy theory creates suspicion and also polarizes: it divides the world into those who know the truth, those who are duped (wittingly or not) by the plot, and those who conspire and plot against the rest. As a genre of discourse, conspiracy theories are appealing because they reward believers by cynically positioning them as more knowledgeable and less gullible than those who are duped by the conspiracy. As historian Richard Hofstadter famously noted, conspiracy rhetoric is premised on the "paranoid style," which tells an apocalyptic story of a network of agents determined to infiltrate and undermine the nation. The paranoid style's "heated exaggeration, suspiciousness, and conspiratorial fantasy" creates a coherent narrative of a dangerous yet hidden plot. Conspiracy theories rely on the difference between appearance and reality: what is apparent is false and hides plotting and subterfuge.

Once the narrative of conspiracy and corruption takes hold within a political community, it is difficult to dispel. Conspiracy is "self-sealing," meaning that any holes in the story are quickly covered up by the logics of conspiracy as a narrative and as an epistemology—both as a story and as a way of knowing. Conspiracy theory is different from "fake news" or "propaganda" because its narrative can never be proven true or untrue. "No evidence is allowed to count against it."[9] Conflicting evidence is explained away by the conspiracy. Nonexistent confirmatory evidence is explained away by being suppressed by the conspiracy. Those who attempt to discredit the conspiracy are stooges or conspirators. In short, as argumentation scholar J. Anthony Blair explains, conspiracy theory is *metaphysical* rather than *empirical*—it deals with what could *possibly* be true, rather than what is true. Yet the conspiracy is presented as *the truth*. As such, it is a "conceptual framework which structures all experience and evidence, requiring it to fit the predetermined pattern, rigidly accepted, rejecting or reinterpreting all findings so as to reinforce that grid, or at least leave it unaltered."[10] By its inescapable narratives, logics, and rules for evidence, conspiracy theory structures reality.

Conspiracy rhetoric also creates a perverse and powerful legitimacy for anyone who uses it because whoever can name and expose the conspirators' plot isn't a stooge and can point suspicion in whichever direction they choose. This legitimacy is not dependent upon whether or not the plot exists or doesn't exist, because the plot can never be proven or disproven. The leader who wields conspiracy counts on distrusting audiences who are both gullible and cynical, who are prepared to believe everything and nothing. Trump argued repeatedly that there was a conspiracy to deprive him of the presidency and prevent him from making America great again.[11] Trump's campaign-long conspiracy narrative had an evolved plotline: First, there was a conspiracy against American exceptionalism (America's unique status among other nations in the world, here conveyed as American greatness).

The conspiracy was led by Obama and Clinton, who weren't even American (Obama) and were completely controlled by global interests (Clinton). The conspiracy was supported by journalists (purveyors of fake news and suppressors of the truth) and the FBI and DOJ (who covered up Clinton's email scandal) and the DNC (who rigged the Democratic primary for Clinton). The conspiracy's goal was to destroy America from within by erasing national borders, polluting the nation with dangerous immigrants, and destroying the American economy. The conspiracy was so powerful that it would rig the presidential election to make Clinton president (like it rigged the primary against Bernie Sanders). But Trump and his followers were more powerful than the conspirators, and because they could clearly see the conspiracy, they would elect Trump president so that he could drain the swamp of corruption. So doing would make America great again, which was Trump's and America's destiny. Trump's campaign-long conspiracy theory was motivated by American exceptionalism: Trump would make America great again, unless the conspirators' plot succeeded.

As a connoisseur and purveyor of conspiracy theory, Trump associated with other well-known conspiracy theorists. Most notably, Trump appeared with infamous conspiracy theorist Alex Jones—who the Anti-Defamation League called "the conspiracy king"—on his InfoWars program.[12] Trump's appearance on InfoWars was arranged by self-proclaimed "agent provocateur" and long-time Trump political advisor and InfoWars regular Roger Stone, who would later be found guilty on seven counts of "lying, obstruction, and witness tampering" to prevent or obscure the investigation into the DNC email hack and WikiLeaks.[13] Not only did Stone, Jones, and Trump share an interest in conspiracy; they also shared an interest in getting Trump elected, and Jones had a large audience of potential Trump voters. By January 2017 Jones had attracted nearly nine million monthly unique page visitors, who returned to his page nearly fifty million times each month. Jones's YouTube videos had accumulated more than 1.2 billion views before he was "deplatformed" in August 2018 for violating Facebook, YouTube, and Twitter's terms of service for his hate speech–filled conspiracy theories.[14] Jones believed, among many things, that the September 11, 2001, terrorist attacks on the World Trade Center and Washington, DC, were a "false flag" perpetrated by the US government. He denied that there was a mass shooting at Sandy Hook Elementary School in 2012 and believed that news stories about the tragedy featured crisis actors rather than murdered children and their grieving parents. In Jones's world, juice boxes made men infertile, tainted drinking water turned frogs gay, Bill Clinton caused the 1995 Oklahoma City bombing, a globalist conspiracy would send every American into FEMA camps, and so on.[15]

Most usefully to Trump, Jones believed that there was a "war for the soul of this country" and that Donald Trump's campaign was "George Washington level," or so he said when Trump appeared on InfoWars on December 2, 2015, amid controversies over Trump's Muslim Ban; his recollection of Muslims supposedly celebrating after the September 11, 2001, terrorist attack; his mocking of Serge Kovaleski; and his retweeting of white supremacists. "The December interview would reverberate into the general election," explained the *Washington Post*, "as Hillary Clinton tried to use it to paint Trump as an irresponsible crackpot associating with an irresponsible crackpot."[16]

Jones knew that Trump wanted "to have a free country for your children and grandchildren," and he knew that Trump was "smart." While Jones said that he didn't want to "get to inside baseball with [Trump]," he claimed that "I already know the inside baseball." And so, knowing what he knew, Jones asked Trump, "Are we at a crossroads to decide whether this country's done?" Trump agreed that the nation was indeed at a crossroads. Jones asked Trump to "tell people what's really happening" and, especially, to explain how "there are globalists that want to have a world government, a system run by select crony capitalists using socialism at the grassroots to make people dependent." Trump agreed about the threat of globalists but said that he believed that there was still time to turn the nation around and "make America great again." Trump warned that "this is the most important election our country's ever had. If we don't get it right . . . if we put another one of these people that, like Hillary—she she's so corrupt, she's so corrupt, and she shouldn't even be allowed to run."

"You're pure American," Jones told Trump. "I love Americana. Donald Trump, let me say this: my audience, I'd say 90 percent, support you." Trump liked hearing that. Trump returned the compliment by telling Jones that "your reputation is amazing. I will not let you down. You will be very, very impressed, I hope, and I think we'll be speaking a lot."[17] Trump did not go on InfoWars again during the campaign, but he often echoed their news stories. Trump echoed Jones about Muslim refugees being a "Trojan horse," he echoed Jones about Ted Cruz's dad being implicated with Lee Harvey Oswald, he echoed Jones that "Hillary is the founder of ISIS, along with

Obama," he echoed Jones that Obama was going to use "executive orders to go after our guns," he echoed Jones that "Hillary Clinton is a god-damned demon," he echoed Jones that Clinton would be on drugs during the debates, and that Clinton stole the primary and would try to steal the general election.[18] Trump echoed Jones so frequently that on August 11, 2016, Jones told his InfoWars audience that it was "surreal to talk about issues here on air and then word for word hear Trump say it two days later. It is amazing. And it just shows how dialed in this guy is and why they're so scared of him."[19]

Trump's conspiracy theories formed a central argument of his presidential campaign, especially in the month leading up to Election Day. "Hillary Clinton is the most corrupt person ever to run for the presidency of the United States," Trump began as he unveiled his new five-point plan for ethics reform at a rally event in Green Bay, Wisconsin, on October 17, 2016.[20] Trump's ethics reform plan was tied directly to the conspiracy that Trump claimed was destroying America. His ethics reform plan gave him the opportunity to indict Clinton for the part that he said that she played in the conspiracy against America and to promise that he would rid the nation of corruption and make America great again. Throughout the remainder of the campaign, Trump used the ethics reform plan talking point to weave together his narrative of conspiracy and corruption, with stolen information provided by the document-leaking organization WikiLeaks.[21]

"I don't know if you know this," Trump said at his rally in Green Bay as he began to unspool his conspiracy theory one thread after the next in what was billed as an "ethics" speech. His speech was punctuated with the language of conspiracy: "believe me," "this is so true," "can you believe it?," "what's going on here?," "you never hear this," "nobody even knows about it," and so on. Because Trump was wise to the conspiracy, he positioned himself as a credible truth teller. "Believe me," Trump said, "there's a lot going on. Do you ever hear these people? They say there's nothing going on." Conspirators would never reveal their plot, which was why Trump was the one and only credible source of information. "You don't read about this, right? They don't tell you about this. They don't want to tell you about this," Trump said knowingly.

In Trump's conspiracy narrative, Clinton was portrayed as a duplicitous conspirator: Clinton gave a "secret speech"; she took "secret meetings"; she had done things that were "illegal," "crimes," a "criminal act"; she was a part of a "conspiracy"; she was "crooked Hillary," who "lied under oath" and "pretended not to know"; she was "part of a quid pro quo," which was "totally corruption by any standards." The whole thing was "worse than Watergate" and "one of the great miscarriages of justice in the history of this country," and so on.

Trump positioned himself as the demagogic hero who represented American exceptionalism personified—he was "pure Americana," as Alex Jones had said. He claimed ominously that "if we let the Clinton cartel run this government, history will record that 2017 was the year America lost its independence." With the very viability of the nation at stake, Trump—who saw the conspiracy clearly—was the only hope that America had. "We figured it out," Trump assured his rally crowd. "We're not going to let that happen to us, OK?" Trump acknowledged with pride that as America's hero, fighting the conspiracy, he was "taking abuse the likes of which nobody has ever run for office has taken." But he was determined to destroy Clinton and end the conspiracy against American greatness. "I'm working for you, folks. I'm working for you, believe me," Trump told his rally crowd in Green Bay. But, he warned, echoing what he had told Jones the December before, the situation was urgent and dire: "Either we win this election, or we lose our country. I mean that. I really believe this is the last time. This is that, folks. This is it. I really believe this is the last shot we have."[22]

Trump's talk of conspiracy and corruption typically whipped his rally crowd into a frenzy of chants ("USA! USA! USA! LOCK HER UP! LOCK HER UP! LOCK HER UP!") and so it did on this occasion, but the first time that Trump half-heartedly read "drain the swamp" as he concluded his ethics speech in Green Bay on October 17, 2016, it fell flat—only receiving a smattering of applause. Trump tried again the next day in Colorado Springs, Colorado: "We're going to end the government corruption, and we're going to drain the swamp in Washington, DC," said Trump as he concluded the section of his rally speech on Clinton and corruption. The rally crowd merely applauded.[23]

Interest in the phrase "drain the swamp" picked up on October 19, 2016, after the second presidential debate in which moderator Chris Wallace asked Trump whether or not he would pledge to "absolutely accept the result of this election." Trump declined, to the surprise of Wallace and derision of Clinton: "I will tell you at the time. I'll keep you in suspense, OK?" The next day, on October 20, 2016, Trump told his rally crowd in Delaware, Ohio, that he would "totally accept the results of this great and historic presidential election—if I win," which landed him a thunderous round of applause from his fans. He explained that since the election was rigged, since Clinton was a criminal, and since there was a conspiracy to destroy America, he wouldn't concede the election unless he won—as he knew that he would—because the only way he could lose was if they cheated. As an American hero, Trump would stand his ground and fight. He ended his speech with "it's time to drain the swamp of corruption in Washington, DC, and we're going to do it." The rally crowd cheered enthusiastically.[24] By the next day, when Trump said, "drain the swamp," he had to pause his speech to allow his rally crowd to chant—"DRAIN THE SWAMP! DRAIN THE SWAMP!" It had taken four days for the phrase to join other three syllable phrases like "BUILD THE WALL!," "USA!," and "LOCK HER UP!" in the lexicon of potent Trump rally chants.

As a phrase, "drain the swamp" represented the conspiracy against America that Trump had been campaigning against since June 2015: the American government was a corrupt "swamp" and Trump was determined to "drain" it when he became president. "When I first heard that term," Trump told his rally crowd on October 29, 2016, in Phoenix, Arizona, "I hated it. I said, 'Oh, that's so hokey. That's so hokey.' But, I said, 'Look, let's give it a shot.'" Trump misremembered that he "tried it and the place went crazy," which it did not. "Then I said, maybe we will try it again. The place went crazy, and now I like it."[25] Trump liked the slogan because it was successful at getting his rally crowds excited about his conspiracy narrative. When his crowds chanted "DRAIN THE SWAMP!" they were acknowledging Trump's truth that there was a horrible and powerful conspiracy against American greatness. The success of the "drain the swamp" chant demonstrated that Trump had created a conspiracy narrative that was embraced by his followers, polarizing them from the rest of America. Trump's followers were wise to the conspiracy, and they were the heroes who would help end it. Voting for Trump would drain the swamp in Washington, DC, of corruption and ensure that Trump would once again make America great. It was his destiny, it was America's destiny, and it was Trump's supporters' destiny.

Without draining the swamp, Trump claimed, American exceptionalism was doomed. "It's time to drain the swamp in Washington, DC," said Trump in Newtown, Pennsylvania, on October 21, 2016. His rally crowd first began to cheer and then chanted "DRAIN THE SWAMP! DRAIN THE SWAMP!" Enthused by the crowd, Trump made the link between his conspiracy theory, himself, his election, and American greatness explicit when he stopped his speech and dramatically walked over to an American flag on the stage. Trump looked out to his crowd as he wrapped his arms around the flag in a long embrace. Trump clapped his hands while the rally crowd went wild, all the while chanting "DRAIN THE SWAMP!" After hugging the American flag, Trump returned to the podium and asked his crowd, "Is there any place more fun to be than a Trump rally?"

The next day, on October 22, 2016, in Gettysburg, Pennsylvania—site of the most gruesome battle on American soil in American history, consecrated as sacred in Abraham Lincoln's Gettysburg Address—Trump folded his conspiracy into one of the most powerful phrases of American exceptionalism. Because he was American exceptionalism personified, Trump was America's hero. He would drain the swamp and end corruption. Trump's election would lead to a new birth of freedom. Trump declared that "we will drain the swamp in Washington, DC, and replace it with a new government of, by, and for the people." He couldn't help himself but to punctuate his vow with the language of conspiracy: "Believe me."[26]

PART THREE
Trump and the Frustrated Electorate

Trump makes brash and uncompromising statements about issues many people feel very passionate about. When he spoke about illegal immigration he made statements that many people agree with and are afraid to state. A lot of that fear is a fear of being labeled a racist or a fear of violating constantly changing societal norms. It's frustrating to listen to politicians speak and make no statements. It's even more frustrating to watch politicians fold in the presence of the slightest bit of pressure.

Anonymous Trump supporter, *The Atlantic*, August 17, 2015[1]

I'm frustrated beyond belief. I feel like I've been lied to. Nothing's getting better.

Anonymous woman in Frank Luntz's focus group, August 25, 2015[2]

ONE WAY TO DESCRIBE THE 2016 electorate is that it had a historic and dangerous crisis of frustration with government. A November 23, 2015, a Pew survey found that "only 20% would describe government programs as being well-run. And elected officials are held in such low regard that 55% of the public says 'ordinary Americans' would do a better job of solving national problems."[3] In 2014 and 2015, Gallup found that Americans thought that the "most important problem facing this country today" was government—it was the second biggest problem in 2016.[4] Gallup also found that only 33 percent of Americans were "satisfied with the way the US is governed."[5] Frustration with government was linked to political polarization: a June 2016 Pew survey found that 57 percent of Republicans were "frustrated" by Democrats and 58 percent of Democrats were "frustrated" by Republicans.[6] Americans' frustration with their government signaled that 2016 would be a "change election": according to a Real Clear Politics survey on the eve of the election, 62.3 percent of Americans thought that the nation was on the "wrong track."[7] A majority of Americans were frustrated with the direction of the nation, its policies, and its political leaders. Government was seen as the nation's problem, not its solution.

Social psychology research explains that frustration is an energizing emotion. People who experience frustration perceive that they are being blocked from having something that is rightfully theirs, and feeling unjustly blocked, frustrated people want to lash out to get what is owed to them. Because frustration is an energizing emotion, like fear, it can be used in the same way as fear appeals are used to motivate voters. Dangerous demagogues activate people's frustration by directing their followers' attention to their frustration and naming an explicit cause to blame for why they aren't getting what they deserve. Dangerous demagogues offer specific actions for their followers to take to overcome their frustration. Dangerous demagogues make it clear that if their followers take the suggested actions, then their frustrating problems will end.[8] In these ways, dangerous demagogues take advantage of the negative and energizing emotional state of their followers, for their own ends.

America's frustration had left the nation vulnerable to attack. Within this crisis, where Americans believed that government was the biggest issue facing the nation, that the nation was on the wrong track, and that anybody else would do a better job of running the country than current leaders, Trump ran a campaign that was *designed* to increase frustration. As you'll see, Trump's rhetorical strategy sought to take advantage of his followers' frustration and to motivate them to act on his behalf. Trump's *ad baculum* (threats of force or intimidation) threat against Hillary Clinton told his followers that they would never get the justice they deserved unless they voted for Trump. Trump's *paralipsis* ("I'm not saying; I'm just saying") about his relationship with Putin and Russia told his followers that Trump was maybe OK with Russian email hacking, so long as it exposed Hillary Clinton's corruption. Trump's *ad hominem* (attacking the person instead of their argument) attack against Clinton told his followers that Clinton's corruption cheated them out of having the good government they deserved. Trump's reification (treating people as objects) of women told Trump's followers who were frustrated with political correctness and the end of traditional gender roles that women only *really* had value when they were useful to men. Trump's *ad populum* (appealing to the wisdom of the crowd) appeal against the Republican political establishment told his followers that only Trump would end their frustration by fighting for them. And Trump's appeal to American exceptionalism (America's unique status among other nations in the world) told his followers that only he would end their frustration by restoring their rightful place on the social hierarchy. Altogether, Trump took advantage of his followers' frustration: he repeatedly told his followers who to blame for their frustration and how they could act to get what they thought that they deserved. Trump portrayed himself as the one and only hero that could save a frustrated America. He told them that they could act on their frustration by making him president.

CHAPTER 13

"Yeah, 'lock her up' is right. No."

Ad Baculum

Wilkes-Barre, Pennsylvania, October 10, 2016
Favorable: 37.4 percent; Unfavorable: 58.6 percent[1]

"Listen, I was wondering, what are they gonna do about Hillary?" a crowd member identifying himself as a veteran asked at Trump's August 19, 2015, town hall event in Derry, New Hampshire. "What are we gonna do about Hillary?" Trump repeated. "She's got big problems. I don't know." He shrugged and joked, "What's Hillary gonna do about Hillary?" The veteran responded, "That's right. I wanna see that woman in jail—that's where she belongs!" The crowd cheered enthusiastically while Trump smiled and nodded, then shook his head no, while still smiling, then nodded again. "Her and Obama both!" the veteran yelled. "Yeah," said Trump as he nodded, still smiling. "Obama can go with her!" the veteran said over the cheering crowd. "Now I know he's a veteran!" joked Trump, which made the crowd cheer and laugh even more. "She killed four people in Benghazi!" explained the veteran. "Right," said Trump dismissively before moving on with, "OK, one more, go on ahead."[2] The veteran in Trump's town hall was frustrated that Clinton hadn't yet suffered any real consequences for what he believed were her serious crimes. Judging by the crowd's applause, they agreed with the veteran's frustration. "Hillary for Prison" shirts were not yet for sale on the InfoWars website and ubiquitous at Trump rally events, and Trump's rally crowds had not yet chanted "LOCK HER UP!," but their frustration about Hillary Clinton was already apparent just two months into Trump's presidential campaign.[3]

Americans who thought that Clinton had intentionally broken the law when she used a private email account and server as Secretary of State were frustrated that justice had not been done, which was represented by the veteran's insistent question to Trump and the crowd's applause in Derry. The frustration was widespread. Opinion polls like the August 12, 2015, Monmouth University poll found that 82 percent of registered Republicans thought that Clinton's email use as Secretary of State "should be subject to a criminal investigation."[4] An October 19, 2015, *Washington Post*/ABC News poll found that 76 percent of registered Republicans and 51 percent of all registered voters believed that "Clinton broke government regulations in her use of private email."[5] And by July 15, 2016, an AP-GfK poll showed that a whopping 92 percent of all Americans thought that Clinton had either broken the law or showed poor judgment "by using a private email account and server at the State Department" and 39 percent thought that she "did so intentionally."[6] In other words, there was intense and continuous frustration among the American people about Clinton's emails—stoked in no small part by media scrutiny, congressional and FBI investigations, and Trump's political campaign.[7]

Yet Trump's response in Derry and throughout his campaign was mixed. He smiled, he shrugged, he nodded in agreement, he shook his head in disagreement, he made a joke, and he moved on without agreeing that Clinton should be in jail or promising that he would do anything to ensure that she would go to jail. Yet again, while Trump didn't always overtly agree with his rally crowds' *ad baculum* (threats of force or intimidation) threat to "lock up" Hillary Clinton, he certainly took advantage of the rhetorical possibilities inherent in his supporters' frustration. At times, during his campaign, Trump used frustration and *ad baculum* to delegitimize Clinton's campaign. At other times, Trump used frustration and *ad baculum* to threaten Clinton directly, especially when Trump was most threatened. And, at other times, Trump used frustration and *ad baculum* to urge his followers to act by voting for him to "bring justice." In so doing, Trump not only took advantage of preexisting frustration, but he directed it toward specific actions that could help him to gain the presidency. While it was unclear if Trump actually meant his threats or merely used them for rhetorical effect, Trump's use of *ad baculum* had the dire consequence of violating democratic norms.

As early in his campaign as July 25, 2015, Trump attempted to discredit and delegitimize Clinton by claiming that her actions were "criminal" and that she shouldn't be allowed to run for president. "What she did is very criminal," Trump told his rally crowd in Oskaloosa, Iowa, "and it's very serious and it's too bad, it's too bad. And I don't know how a person with that cloud over their head actually can be running for president."[8] The next day, when Jake Tapper asked him about his comments on CNN, he reemphasized that "what she has done is criminal. I don't see how she can run."[9] Four times, Tapper asked Trump to clarify what he thought was "criminal." Trump didn't answer, and Tapper eventually explained to Trump that the ongoing investigation into Clinton's use of a private email server as Secretary of State was a "security" issue rather than a "criminal" issue. Despite Tapper's fact-check, Trump continued to say that Clinton was (or should be) under criminal investigation.

On October 10, 2015, for example, Trump told his rally crowd in Norcross, Georgia, that "she shouldn't be allowed to run. [The crowd cheered and applauded.] No, she shouldn't be. No, she shouldn't be." Then, Trump made a parallel case argument, comparing what Clinton had done to other recent national security cases: "If that were a Republican that did what she did with the emails, they would have been in jail twelve months ago. [The crowd applauded.] They would have been in jail. It's a very unfair system. It is a very, very unfair system," said Trump, attempting to heighten his audience's frustration. "But, I'm telling you, if that were a Republican? It's called 'jail time.' Clink."[10] Trump's parallel case here not only made a direct comparison between Clinton's actions and others who suffered consequences for their actions; it was also embedded within a familiar conspiracy theory of corruption that Trump had told throughout his campaign: Clinton was guilty of a crime, and if she wasn't punished for it, it was only because the conspiracy of corruption protected her. Trump did not complete his parallel case argument, however. He didn't conclude that since the two cases were similar, Clinton should suffer the same consequences for her actions as others would suffer and thus be imprisoned. Trump allowed his audience to arrive at that conclusion themselves. This allowed Trump to walk a fine line between saying that Clinton should be in jail and merely pointing out the hypocrisy of her benefiting from corruption and conspiracy. Trump didn't actually make the *ad baculum* threat to lock up Clinton at his Norcross rally; his careful omission of his argument's conclusion provided him with plausible deniability.

On October 12, 2015, Trump appeared on Fox News' *Hannity*, where he was praised for saying what he had been careful not to say at his Georgia rally two days before: "There's two comments you made this weekend that I think reflect why you're being successful. One, you said Hillary should be in jail," said Hannity, even though Trump hadn't actually said that. Hannity praised Trump because he "said something that very few are willing to say: that you think she shouldn't even be a candidate, that she should be worried about going to jail." Trump responded by once again making his parallel case but not drawing the conclusion: "She shouldn't be a candidate. What she's done is very serious, and everybody else who has done it has either gone to jail or had certain problems like you wouldn't believe."[11] The strategic ambiguity of Trump's *ad baculum* threat allowed him to accept praise from people like Hannity for threatening Clinton and also protected him from accusations by critics that he had violated democratic norms or had authoritarian tendencies.

Trump continued to make his parallel case comparing Clinton to others who'd been punished. He also continued to express his doubts about her legitimacy as a candidate. He did these two things throughout his campaign; it was his default position on the question of whether or not she should be "locked up." Trump also continued to link her "criminal" behavior to the conspiracy of corruption and often explained that Clinton's "greatest achievement" would be staying out of jail for her crimes.[12] When he was asked directly if he would prosecute her, like he was on December 4, 2015, in Raleigh, North Carolina, Trump frequently evaded the question, promising vaguely that "we're going to take a look at it. Very, very strong, OK, look at it."[13] "Taking a look" was an often-used Trump euphemism for "I'm not going to give you a real answer to your question." Trump didn't like to answer questions directly; he didn't like to commit to positions for which he would later be held accountable.

The first time that one of his rally crowds chanted "LOCK HER UP!," it seemed to take Trump somewhat by surprise. Responding to something a crowd member yelled out to him, Trump made a joke about China finding military secrets in Clinton's emails at his February 12, 2016, rally in Tampa, Florida, which caused his rally crowd to roar with laughter and applause. Trump, as was typical of him when his crowd was reacting positively to him, turned away from the podium to give the crowd the chance to enjoy itself. He gave the fans behind him two thumbs-up while the arena continued to cheer and laugh. When he turned back around and attempted to speak again, some members of his rowdy crowd began to chant "LOCK HER UP!" At first, Trump didn't acknowledge the chant. Instead, he began to speak, "You know, you know, with Hillary it's interesting . . . ," but as the crowd continued to chant "LOCK HER UP!," he paused, smiled, and lifted his eyebrows comically, while pointing his index finger at the chanters. As the crowd continued to chant, Trump spoke over them to silence them, "You know what's interesting with Hillary and the emails. . . ."[14] Trump briefly acknowledged, but did not encourage, the chant. Reporters didn't include mention of the chant in their coverage of Trump's rally, and no one chanted "LOCK HER UP!" again until the Republican National Convention in July 2016, where it became the "unofficial slogan" of the convention, according to Michele Gorman of *Newsweek*.[15]

On July 5, 2016, FBI director James Comey made an official announcement that while Clinton had been "extremely careless" in her use of a private email server while Secretary of State, no criminal charges would be filed against her for the misuse of classified information.[16] "The system is rigged," Trump tweeted in response to the FBI's non-indictment: "General Petraeus got in trouble for far less. Very very unfair! As usual, bad judgment."[17] Petraeus pled guilty to mishandling government information and was fined and sentenced to probation in 2015.[18] While Trump once again argued that Clinton's case was just like others that had been prosecuted, Comey had clearly denied Trump's parallel case during his announcement. "In looking back at our investigations into the mishandling or removal of classified information," Comey said, "we cannot find a case that would support bringing criminal charges on these facts." The next day, Trump let loose on Clinton at his rally in Cincinnati, Ohio. As he had previously predicted, the conspiracy of corruption had protected Clinton, and "the only good thing she's ever done is get out of trouble when anybody else would have been in jail by now. That's the only thing that I've ever seen her do that was a great job. I've got to give her credit. I got to give her credit."[19]

It was within this context that the Republican Party faithful arrived in Cleveland, Ohio, for the Republican National Convention. On July 17, 2016, InfoWars flew a "Hillary for Prison" banner from an aircraft circling Cleveland, while "Hillary for Prison" T-shirts sold out across the city.[20] The speeches at the RNC convention seemed to be designed to heighten Republicans' frustration about Clinton. "We do not need a reckless president who believes that *she* is above the law," bellowed General Michael Flynn during his July 18, 2016, RNC speech. As the convention crowd began to chant "LOCK HER UP!," Flynn, who would later plead guilty to making false and misleading statements to the FBI, responded, "'Lock her up' is right!"[21] The next night, New Jersey governor Chris Christie used his speech to "prosecute" Clinton because, as he said, "we've seen this administration refuse to hold her accountable for her dismal record as Secretary of State. So, let's do something fun tonight. Tonight, as a former federal prosecutor, I welcome the opportunity to hold Hillary Rodham Clinton accountable for her performance and her character." The crowd began chanting "LOCK HER UP!" and repeatedly proclaimed Clinton "GUILTY!" when Christie invited it to render a judgment about her record.[22] Christie was pleased with what he heard from the crowd.

Trump was not pleased when the RNC crowd began an extended chant of "LOCK HER UP!" during his Republican nomination acceptance speech on July 21, 2016. "America is far less safe and the world is far less stable than when Obama made the decision to put Hillary Clinton in charge of America's foreign policy," Trump declared, prompting the RNC crowd to chant "LOCK HER UP!" Trump looked on sternly, motioned like an orchestra conductor's caesura for the crowd to be silent, then said, "Let's defeat her in November!" as he held up a finger to emphasize his point.[23] The crowd roared in approval.

The next week at a press conference in Miami, Florida, a reporter asked Trump if he agreed with his crowds chanting "LOCK HER UP!" He said that he didn't, and he wanted more credit from the press than he thought he had been getting for telling the crowd to stop its chant. "I said, 'Don't do that.' Now, I didn't do that for any reason. I really—I didn't like it. And they stopped."[24] Trump didn't like the chant, told the RNC to stop, and it stopped. Frequently that was the way it went. When Trump's rally crowd chanted "LOCK HER UP!," he frequently corrected them by saying something along the lines of "You know what? We're going to do even better. We're going to beat her on November 8th," like Trump told his crowd to enthusiastic applause later that day on July 27, 2016, in Scranton, Pennsylvania.[25] He said the same on August 25, 2016, in Manchester, New Hampshire.[26] And, when the rally crowd interrupted him on October 3, 2016, in Pueblo, Colorado, with chants of "LOCK HER UP!" (twice), he said, "Let's just beat her in November" (twice).[27]

Trump mostly didn't like it when the rally crowds chanted "LOCK HER UP!," except for those times when he did like it. Specifically, Trump took advantage of frustration by using *ad baculum* to threaten Clinton directly at those times when he himself was most threatened. The first time Trump uttered the words "she should be going to jail"—not implied, or hinted, or said that he would "look into it"—was on January 26, 2016, just before the Iowa caucus and just after the *National Review* had published its "Never

Trump" issue, on the same day that Trump refused to attend the Fox News debate moderated by Megyn Kelly. "She should be going to jail," Trump said to the enthusiastic applause of his crowd in Iowa City, Iowa. "I don't know what the hell is going on."[28] He then made his parallel case argument comparing what Clinton did to what Petraeus had done (omitting, of course, that Petraeus did not go to jail but was fined and sentenced to probation).

There were only two other situations in which Trump overtly and openly declared that he thought that Clinton should be imprisoned. The first was in late May and early June 2016, when Federal Judge Gonzalo Curiel released the court documents in the Trump University lawsuit and Clinton called Trump a "fraud" who was "trying to scam America the way he scammed all those people at Trump University."[29] The second was in October 2016 in the aftermath of the release of the 2005 *Access Hollywood* tape in which Trump was caught on a hot mic saying lewd things about women and Clinton tweeted, "This is horrific. We cannot allow this man to become president."[30] Trump's words were most violent toward Clinton in the two situations in which he was most vulnerable to being held accountable for his words and actions.

Clinton called Trump's ideas "dangerously incoherent" and called him "unprepared" and "temperamentally unfit to hold an office that requires knowledge, stability, and immense responsibility" at a campaign event in San Diego, California, on June 2, 2016.[31] Trump responded before his rally crowd in San Jose, California that same day: "Remember I said that I'm a counterpuncher? I am. After what she said about me today in her phony speech—that was a phony speech, that was a Donald Trump hit job—Hillary Clinton has to go to jail. She has to go to jail. She has to go to jail. She's guilty as hell," he roared to the enthusiastic cheers of his crowd.[32]

The next day, Clinton told her crowd in Westminster, California, that Trump University was "a con game that has benefited Donald Trump but hurt so many people, including those who couldn't afford it," and that Trump's attacks on Judge Curiel and her were another attempt to "change the subject, like he does all the time," instead of "facing up to the facts that are coming out." Not only was Trump U "a fraud, from start to finish," she said, but the documents filed in the court case proved that Trump was only "in it for himself, in every way, and that is yet another reason why we can't let him near the White House."[33] In response, Trump said, "Hillary is pathetic and should be in jail for what she did with her emails. She should be in jail. She should be in jail. She should be in jail. She should be in jail for what she did with those emails!" If Trump was a "con man," then Clinton was a "thief" who "should be in jail for what she did to our national security."[34] When Jake Tapper asked Trump about Clinton's criticisms of him two days later on CNN, Trump said, "Here's a woman that should be put in jail for what she did with her emails, and she's commenting on this?"[35] When Clinton increased her criticism of Trump, Trump "counterpunched" by increasing his criticism of her, deploying the rhetorical strategy of *tu quoque* (appeal to hypocrisy) to argue that Clinton had no standing to criticize him because she should be jailed for *her* offenses. Rather than directly respond to Clinton's criticisms, he counterpunched with an *ad baculum* threat.

The second time Trump overtly threatened Clinton with jailtime was on October 9, 2016, during the second presidential debate. The *Washington Post* had published the leaked *Access Hollywood* lewd "hot mic" tape two days before. During the debate, Trump could be seen "looming behind Hillary Clinton like a mob boss," according to the *Washington Post's* Sarah L. Kaufman, which "only reinforced his perception as a schoolyard bully."[36] Not only did Trump's nonverbal behavior—his scowl, his intimidating pacing on the stage, his invasion of Clinton's personal space—appear threatening, but Trump's words matched his nonverbal behavior.[37] During the debate, Clinton explained that Trump "never apologizes to anyone for anything"—including for his attacks on women, Judge Curiel, the Gold Star Khan family, *New York Times* reporter Serge Kovaleski, and Barack Obama—and concluded that "he needs to take responsibility for his actions and his words." In response, Trump threatened, "I'll tell you what. I didn't think I'd say this, but I'm going to say it, and I hate to say it. But if I win, I am going to instruct my attorney general to get a special prosecutor to look into your situation." When Clinton responded that "it's just awfully good that someone with the temperament of Donald Trump is not in charge of the law in our country," Trump interrupted her to sneer "because you would be in jail!"[38]

"This just came out. WikiLeaks—I love WikiLeaks!" Trump told his rally crowd in Wilkes-Barre, Pennsylvania, the next day as he prepared to read to his crowd from bits of the Clinton campaign's stolen emails. "Oh, she's crooked folks. She's as crooked as a three-dollar bill!" When his crowd started chanting "LOCK HER UP!," Trump said, "Yeah, 'lock her up' is right!" Trump then slapped his hand at the crowd as if to say "shame on you" and said, "No." Referring to his debate performance the night before, Trump said, "When I said we are gonna get a special prosecutor to figure this deal out . . .

[The crowd cheered enthusiastically.] I have never been so ashamed of this country as what's gone on with Hillary Clinton and neither have you," he said, appealing to the crowd's sense of frustration.[39] He said he would "investigate the investigation" the next day in Panama City, Florida,[40] and said, "For what she's done, they should lock her up; they should. It's disgraceful," on October 14, 2016, in Greensboro, North Carolina.[41] At his October 15, 2016, rally in Portsmouth, New Hampshire, Trump said, "Hillary Clinton should have been prosecuted and she should be in jail—she should be!" while his rally crowd chanted "LOCK HER UP! LOCK HER UP!"[42] And on Twitter that day, he said, "Hillary Clinton should have been prosecuted and should be in jail. Instead she is running for president in what looks like a rigged election."[43] Feeling threatened, Trump counterpunched with an *ad baculum* threat.

On October 28, 2016, the discovery of a trove of Clinton's emails on a laptop used by Clinton aide Huma Abedin caused FBI director James Comey to send a letter to Congress informing them that the FBI would begin to "review these emails to determine if they contain classified information." Trump told the *New York Times* that he thought that it was "the biggest story since Watergate." "I think this changes everything," he said, optimistically.[44] Trump led off his rally in Manchester, New Hampshire, that day with "a very critical breaking news announcement," which he could barely make over the thunderous chants of "LOCK HER UP!" The FBI, Trump said, was "reopening its case into her criminal and illegal conduct," which it technically wasn't. Instead, the FBI was examining the emails to see if the case should be reopened—and in "reopening" the case, Trump said that the FBI and Department of Justice were going to "right the horrible mistake that they made."[45] Trump called Clinton's email problems the "biggest scandal since Watergate" the next day at his rally in Phoenix, Arizona.[46] Trump told the same thing to his rally crowds in Albuquerque, New Mexico; Grand Rapids, Michigan; Eau Claire, Wisconsin; and Miami, Florida, over the next week.[47] Finally, Trump said repeatedly, someone was *finally* going to do something to hold Clinton accountable for her crimes. With the investigation ongoing and Clinton potentially facing consequences, Trump ceased using his *ad baculum* threat.

On November 6, 2016—just two days before the November 8, 2016, election—Director Comey sent another letter to Congress, informing it that the FBI "reviewed all of the communications that were to or from Hillary Clinton while she was Secretary of State. Based on our review, we have not changed our conclusions that we expressed in July with respect to Secretary

Clinton."[48] As his rally crowd in Sterling Heights, Michigan, chanted "LOCK HER UP!," Trump looked on sternly as he told them that the conspiracy of corruption was still protecting Clinton, who was "the most corrupt person to ever seek the office of the presidency of the United States." Trump's crowd chanted and cheered as Trump stoked their frustration: "Hillary Clinton is guilty, she knows it, the FBI knows it, and the people know it." Then, to the thunderous applause of his crowd, Trump gave his frustrated followers the power to act to end the Clinton conspiracy, to act to finally put an end to the Clinton corruption. "And now it's up to the American people to deliver justice at the ballot box on November 8. It's unbelievable what she gets away with—unbelievable!"[49] As Trump closed out his campaign, he said over and over again that everyone knew that Clinton was guilty and the only way to stop her was for the "American people to deliver justice at the ballot box."[50] While Trump urged his followers to "deliver justice," he did not say he would "lock her up."

Trump used his *ad baculum* strategy to take advantage of preexisting frustration about Hillary Clinton's use of a private email server as Secretary of State and to motivate his followers to act by voting "to deliver justice at the ballot box." Since frustration is an energizing emotion that makes people want to lash out, threats of force help channel existing frustration and direct it at enemies. Trump had successfully taken advantage of the nation's frustration; Clinton's emails represented much more to his frustrated followers than the misuse of government information. Clinton's emails stood for the whole of the Clinton conspiracy of corruption. When the crowd chanted "LOCK HER UP!," they meant it literally, not figuratively. Trump's followers truly believed that Clinton's behavior was criminal and that she belonged in jail.

While Trump took advantage of preexisting frustration, he had a difficult time controlling his crowds. His crowds led him on "LOCK HER UP!," and Trump only occasionally used the threat. Rather than threaten Clinton directly, which carried the appearance of authoritarianism, Trump walked a fine line of leading his audience to the conclusion that he supported "locking her up" without actually saying that he did. Adhering to this fine distinction gave Trump the out of plausible deniability. And yet a frustrated electorate would expect such forceful appeals—anything less would be considered "weak," and so Trump repeatedly abutted the fine line between authoritarianism and plausible deniability. Carefully examining Trump's use of *ad baculum* threats allows us to see that Trump cynically took advantage of what he saw as a line of attack that excited his frustrated rally crowds but that he (mostly) "didn't like it"—except for when he did.

On November 9, 2016, Trump told his supporters gathered to celebrate his election victory that he had just spoken with Clinton and he had "congratulated her and her family on a very, very hard-fought campaign. I mean, she—she fought very hard. Hillary has worked very long and very hard over a long period of time, and we owe her a major debt of gratitude for her service to our country," Trump said to the applause of his crowd. "I mean that very sincerely."[51] On November 13, 2016, Trump explained to *60 Minutes'* Lesley Stahl that he didn't want to put Clinton in jail because "I don't want to hurt them. They're, they're good people. I don't want to hurt them."[52] On November 23, 2016, Trump told the *New York Time's* Maggie Haberman, "I don't want to hurt the Clintons. I really don't. She went through a lot. And suffered greatly in many different ways. And I am not looking to hurt them at all. The campaign was vicious."[53] And as Trump's rowdy victory rally crowd chanted "LOCK HER UP!" on December 10, 2016, in Grand Rapids, Michigan, Trump said, "Nah, nah, forget it" as he slapped his hand toward his rally crowd. "That plays great before the election. Now we do not care, right?"[54]

CHAPTER 14

"Russia, if you're listening . . ."

Paralipsis

Trump National Doral, Miami, Florida, July 27, 2016
Favorable: 36 percent; Unfavorable: 57.1 percent[1]

"Do you think Putin will be going to The Miss Universe Pageant in November in Moscow?," Trump playfully tweeted on June 18, 2013. "If so, will he become my new best friend?"[2] Trump attended the Miss Universe Pageant in Russia that November, but it's unclear if he and Russian president Vladimir Putin became best friends. On November 9, 2013, while in Moscow for the pageant, Trump taped an interview with MSNBC's Thomas Roberts in which he claimed "I do have a relationship" with Putin. "And I can tell you that he's very interested in what we're doing here today," said Trump. "He's probably very interested in what you and I are saying today, and I'm sure he's going to be seeing it in some form, but I do have a relationship with him." Trump also praised Putin as having done "a very brilliant job in terms of what he represents and who he's representing." Putin had "really eaten our president's lunch," Trump added—using the language of a schoolyard bully to reference Putin's tense relationship with then president Barack Obama.[3] The following year, on March 7, 2014, Trump told the Conservative Political Action Conference that he was "in Moscow a few weeks ago. I own the Miss Universe Pageant, and they treated me so great. Putin even sent me a present, a beautiful present, with a beautiful note. I spoke to all of his people."[4] The month after that, Trump spoke at the National Press Club luncheon and told them that he "was in Moscow recently and I spoke indirectly and directly with President Putin, who could not have been nicer, and we had a tremendous success."[5] Trump publicly affirmed that he and Putin had a relationship, spoke indirectly and directly, exchanged beautiful presents and notes, and were cordial toward one another. They were perhaps not "best friends," but in Trump's telling, they were certainly friendly—their relationship was a tremendous success.

As Trump said repeatedly throughout his presidential campaign, he thought that it would be a good thing for him to get along with Putin and for the United States to get along with Russia. Perhaps, if the two nations got along, Trump theorized, then they could join forces together to "knock the hell out of ISIS." As matters then stood, Putin had "no respect" for Obama, which was really embarrassing for the United States, Trump said repeatedly, attempting to heighten Americans' frustrations with Obama's leadership. Trump thought that he could do better. "I was in Moscow two years ago," Trump told Bill O'Reilly on the day he announced his campaign, "and I will tell you, you can get along with those people and get along with them well. You can make deals with those people. I would be willing to bet I would have a great relationship with Putin. I would be able to get along. I think I'd have a good relationship, and it's important for this country to do that."[6]

Trump's opinions about Russia and Putin were at odds with a majority of those held by Americans and citizens around the world. An August 5, 2015, a Pew Global Attitudes survey found that 67 percent of Americans had an unfavorable opinion about Russia and 75 percent had no confidence in Putin's leadership, which was similar to how citizens of other nations viewed Russia and Putin.[7] By October 27, 2016, according to another Pew survey, 73 percent of Americans viewed Russia as an "adversary" or a "serious problem." There were significant partisan differences, however; 30 percent of Trump supporters reported that they thought Russia was "not much of a problem," which was much higher than the 13 percent of Clinton supporters who were unconcerned about Russia.[8]

Despite the nations' deep skepticism about Russia and its leader, Trump continued to praise Putin and continued to argue that it would be a good thing if the United States and Russia got along, befuddling the American political press and eliciting praise from Russian state-sponsored propaganda outlets like RT and Sputnik. Trump relied upon the logic of *paralipsis* ("I'm not saying; I'm just saying") to appeal to his followers' frustrations over Clinton's email server and to signal to Russia that he was receptive to enlisting Russia's help in the search for Clinton's missing emails. The message was received by both his followers and by the Russians.

On July 12, 2015, Trump answered a question at the Freedom Festival from Maria Butina—who pled guilty on December 13, 2018, to "attempting to infiltrate Republican political circles and influence US relations with Russia before and after the 2016 presidential election"—about whether or not he would improve relations with Russia.[9] "I know Putin," Trump said, "and I'll tell you what: we will get along with Putin. Putin has no respect for President Obama. . . . I believe that I would get along very nicely with Putin."[10] Trump made similar claims to Fox News' Janine Pirro on August 23, 2015: "I feel that Putin is somebody I would actually get along with." Trump acknowledged that he got "a lot of heat for that," but he said that he "had a big event in Moscow about two years ago, I think I would have a good relationship. It is ridiculous; he hates Obama. He can't stand him."[11] Since Trump had repeatedly said that he knew Putin and got along well with him, it's no wonder that when Putin was in New York City in September 2015 to attend events at the United Nations that Chuck Todd asked Trump if he had plans to meet with him. "Your outside counsel intimated that you may have a meeting with the Russian president. Do you plan on trying to do that?" asked Todd on the September 20, 2015, *Meet the Press*. "Well," said Trump, "I had heard that he wanted to meet with me. And certainly I am open to it. I would love to do that if he wants to do that. I don't know that it's going to take place. I'm not sure. I know that people have been talking. But we'll see what happens. But certainly, if he wanted to meet, I mean, I'd enjoy doing it."[12] Trump told Bill O'Reilly on September 29, 2015, that he "didn't know anything about him coming to my, my office, but I will tell you that I think in terms of leadership, he's getting an 'A,' and our president is not doing so well."[13]

While he probably didn't get to meet Putin during his trip to New York that month, Trump was pleased that he and Putin both appeared on the September 27, 2015, episode of *60 Minutes*.[14] The day after the episode aired, Trump held a press conference in Trump Tower in which he proudly associated himself with Putin because, as he told reporters, "he was interviewed and I was interviewed last night," which made them sort of the same. But, in comparison, Trump said that he thought Putin's interview was "softer" and that Trump had "a tough interview." Trump conjectured—for a laugh—that perhaps Putin's interview was easier than his because "Putin is a nicer person than I am, OK?"[15] Trump went further than associating himself with Putin on the October 4, 2015, *Fox & Friends* when he explained that Putin "was my co-host on *60 Minutes* the other night and we did the biggest ratings they've had in a long time." Then he said—again, for a laugh—"so I don't know—should I give him the credit or should I take the credit?"[16] Later that month, Trump told the No Labels Convention that he had watched "President Obama last night on television," but Trump panned Obama's performance. "He bombed," Trump said. "They were much nicer to me two weeks ago—don't you agree? I was on with Putin. Do you believe that? Putin and Trump. Nice stablemates, very nice. Putin and Trump."[17] They were a great team, according to Trump. Likewise, during the November 10, 2015, Republican primary debate, Trump said, "I got to know [Putin] very well because we were both on *60 Minutes*. We were stablemates, and we did very well that night."[18]

In all of his references to their mutual appearance on *60 Minutes*, Trump used hyperbole to "anchor" to Putin's status—to connect himself as a leader with Putin as a leader—making it seem like Trump, who had held no political office, held equal status to President Putin as a world leader. Further, Trump continuously contrasted his leadership, toughness, and relationship with Putin with Obama's leadership, toughness, and relationship with Putin. Appealing to his supporters' frustration at American weakness, Trump argued that he would do better than Obama and that doing better would be good for America. Trump's hyperbole caught up with him after he claimed again that he had "got to know" Putin "very well" and that they were "stablemates" on *60 Minutes* at the November 10, 2015, Republican debate. News reports questioned whether this exaggeration could possibly be true. "Trump and Putin appeared on '60 Minutes' together . . . from different continents," wrote Buzzfeed that night, quoting a slew of tweets questioning Trump's hyperbole.[19] Buzzfeed explained that Putin was interviewed in Russia and Trump was interviewed in New York, and that *60 Minutes* doesn't even have a "greenroom," so there was absolutely no truth to Trump's claim that they met and were happy stablemates.

"I need some stuff clarified tonight," Bill O'Reilly said the next night when Trump appeared on his show. "Do you know Putin personally? Do you know him?" "No, I don't," answered Trump. "I was on *60 Minutes* with him four weeks ago. I didn't shoot it at the same time. They did him and then they did me . . . and it was a very successful show. . . . They had us on together. I call us 'stablemates,' but we never met." Forced to admit that he didn't actually know Putin, Trump continued to anchor to Putin's high status by continuing to describe their relationship as "stablemates." The "stablemates" metaphor would indicate that he and Putin were both in the "stable" together—at the same place, at the same time. He and Putin were of the same kind: they were both horses (presumably they were both thoroughbreds) living under the same roof. If Putin was a world leader, then so was Trump.

"Russian president Vladimir Putin offered praise for GOP presidential candidate Donald Trump today, telling ABC News, 'He's a very colorful person. Talented, without any doubt,' and that he believed Trump was 'absolutely the leader in the American presidential race.'" ABC News quoted White House press secretary Josh Earnest saying that Putin's remarks sounded "pretty close" to an endorsement, which he found troubling because it signaled election interference. Ernest said it would be "up to Mr. Trump to decide whether to accept it."[20] Trump decided to accept Putin's endorsement. ABC News followed up their first story that day with another, which added Trump's response. "It is always a great honor to be so nicely complimented by a man so highly respected within his own country and beyond," Trump gushed in a statement. "I have always felt that Russia and the United States should be able to work well with each other towards defeating terrorism and restoring world peace, not to mention trade and all of the other benefits derived from mutual respect."[21] Russia's propaganda network RT praised Trump for accepting Putin's praise. "While the majority of Democrat and Republican candidates have been scoring points by criticizing Russia," wrote RT on December 18, 2015, "Trump has taken a different tone, saying he wants to work with Moscow if elected."[22] RT also praised Trump for repeatedly saying that he liked "that Putin is bombing the hell out of ISIS."[23]

There was some confusion about how to translate what Putin had said in his praise of Trump. As the *Washington Post's* fact-checker noted, "Russian is notoriously complex to translate into English," and there was room for ambiguity in Putin's word choice.[24] "Yarkii" (яркий) was translated by different news organizations as "colorful," "lively," or "flamboyant." RT quoted Putin as saying, "He is a very flamboyant man, very talented, no doubt about that," which lends some credibility to that translation as the official Russian position on Trump: flamboyant, talented.[25] Trump—as hyperbolic as ever when it came to his relationship with Putin—preferred to claim that Putin called him either "brilliant" or a "genius." On the December 18, 2015, *Morning Joe*, Trump used Putin's endorsement to bolster his credibility and brush off concerns that Putin's endorsement was troubling: "When people call you 'brilliant' it's always good, especially when the person heads up Russia."[26] Later that week when Chuck Todd asked Trump, "Why are you so comfortable praising Vladimir Putin?" on *Meet the Press*, Trump replied that "*he* praised me. He called me 'brilliant.' He said very nice things about me. I accept it."[27] Likewise, that day he told George Stephanopoulos, "So, if Putin respects me and if Putin wants to call me 'brilliant' and other things that he said, which were, frankly, very nice, I'll accept that and I'll accept it on the behalf of our country. Because if we get along well with Russia, that's a positive thing, not a negative thing."[28]

As the campaign wore on, Trump continued to use hyperbole when he mentioned Putin's praise, which he did often. He also liked to talk about himself in the third person—like he was marketing a brand—when he recounted Putin's praise. Typically, Trump's rally crowds cheered when Trump invoked Putin's praise—likely cheering for their hero more than cheering for Putin. Trump told his rally crowd in Milford, New Hampshire, on February 2, 2016, that "Putin said 'Donald Trump is a genius and he is the real leader over in that country.'" Trump made his rally crowd laugh when he explained, "They said you should disavow what Putin of Russia said. I said I am not disavowing. He called me a 'genius.' Are you crazy?"[29] Later that month he told his rally crowd in Madison, Alabama, that "Putin was very nice to me. He said, 'Donald Trump is a genius.' He's not getting anything for it, OK? He said, 'Donald Trump is a genius, and Donald Trump is going to be the great leader of the party.' So, he said that. I don't know if he meant it—he probably did. He sees crowds like this. [Trump gestured to his rally crowd.] Why not?"[30] On May 27, 2016, Trump told his rowdy rally crowd in Fresno, California, that Hillary Clinton accused Trump of being "a friend of Putin. Well, actually Putin did call me a 'genius' and he said I am 'the future of the Republican Party.' He's off to a good start, I will say. [The rally crowd cheered.] I will say he's off to a good start—right, folks? And by the way, I am not a friend of Putin. I don't know Putin. I've never met Putin. I respect him; he's a strong leader."[31]

As Trump became the presumptive nominee on May 4, 2016, he quite suddenly decided that he didn't want to talk about his relationship with Putin anymore. Wolf Blitzer asked Trump if he had "ever met" or "ever spoken" with Putin, to which Trump replied, "I don't want to say. But, I think I will have a good relationship with him." Blitzer didn't follow-up to ask Trump why all of a sudden he didn't want to say whether or not he knew Putin, but the next day Fox News' Bret Baier did.[32] "About Russia," began Baier, "you were asked if you've ever spoke to Vladimir Putin and you said 'I don't want to say.'" Trump replied, "Yeah, I have no comment on that. No comment." Baier continued, "But, one of the things people like about you is to answer any question." Trump responded, "Let's assume I did. Perhaps it was personal. You know I don't want to—I don't want to hurt his confidence. But—I know Russia well."[33] The following month CNN's Fareed Zakaria interviewed Putin and asked him about his praise of Trump. Putin replied with a shrug, "I only said he was a bright (colorful) candidate. Do you not find him to be so?"[34]

Trump's relationship with Putin really came under scrutiny after July 22, 2016, when embarrassing emails stolen from the Democratic National Committee were leaked to the public on the eve of the Democratic National Convention.[35] News reports focused both on the salacious content found in the private emails and on who was responsible for the emails being made public.[36] The DNC alleged that Russian hackers had invaded their systems and stolen their data and emails, and that the matter had been turned over to American intelligence agencies.[37] On July 24, 2016, Hillary Clinton's campaign chairman Robby Mook told Jake Tapper on CNN that "experts are telling us that Russian state actors broke into the DNC and stole these e-mails. And other experts are now saying that the Russians are releasing these emails for the purpose of actually helping Donald Trump." When pressed by Tapper to explain how he knew that it was Russia, Mook said that he would "let the experts" sort it out, and he further alleged that the emails were "being released at this time to create maximum damage on Hillary Clinton and to help Donald Trump."[38] Mook's account of who was responsible for the DNC hack was seemingly confirmed in a July 13, 2018, indictment from Special Counsel Robert Mueller alleging that twelve Russian intelligence agency workers conducted the attacks, although that indictment did not state that the email hack was designed to help Trump.[39] Back in 2016 Mook's assertion that Russia hacked the DNC to help Trump caused quite a bit of controversy and led to a seventy-five-minute press conference on July 27, 2016, in which Trump was interrogated repeatedly about his connections to both Russia and Putin.

The first question asked of Trump at his July 27, 2016, press conference was about the Clinton campaign's accusations that Russia had hacked the DNC servers in order to help Trump win the election. "It is just a total deflection, this whole thing with Russia," Trump responded. "By the way they hacked, they probably have her thirty-three thousand emails. I hope they do. They probably have her thirty-three thousand emails she lost and deleted because you would see some beauties there." Trump said that the accusation that Russia had hacked the DNC to help him was "so far-fetched, it is so ridiculous. Honestly, I wish I had that power. I'd love to have that power." Then Trump reversed what he had just said about Russia being responsible for the hack: "If it is Russia, nobody even knows this, it's probably China, or it could be somebody sitting in his bed. But it shows how weak we are; it shows how disrespected we are, so I know nothing about it. It's one of the most far-fetched things I've ever heard." Trump said that Russia did the hacking, but then Trump didn't know that Russia did the hacking.

As the press conference wore on, someone asked Trump about his relationship with Putin. "I never met Putin. I don't know who Putin is," said Trump. "He said one nice thing about me. He said I'm a 'genius.' I said thank you very much to the newspaper, and that was the end of it. I never met Putin." Another reporter asked Trump what he would say to Putin if Russia *had* hacked into the DNC. Trump said that he wasn't "going to tell Putin what to do. Why should I tell Putin what to do?" He said that Putin had already made a statement about it: "He said, 'Don't blame [Russia], essentially, for your incompetence.'" Trump indicated that he accepted Putin's statement and attempted to shift the focus from who had done the hacking to the salacious content of the emails when he told the reporters at the press conference, "It's not even about Russia or China or whoever it is that's doing the hacking. It was about the things that were said in those emails. They were terrible things." When pressed again about his relationship with Putin, Trump sounded a little frustrated when he said, "I have nothing to do with Putin. I've never spoken to him. I don't know anything about him other than he will respect me. He doesn't respect our president. And if it is Russia—which it's probably not, nobody knows who it is—but if it is Russia, it's really bad for a different reason, because it shows how little respect they have for our country, when they would hack into a major party and get everything." Then the look on Trump's face changed, which seemed to indicate that he had a new idea: "But it would be interesting to see . . . I will tell you this. . . ." Trump then stood up straighter, looked directly into the camera, and spoke more clearly. "Russia, if you're listening, I hope you're able to find the thirty thousand e-mails that are missing. I think you will probably be rewarded mightily by our press. [He gestured toward the attendant reporters.] Let's see if that happens. That'll be next."[40]

As Katy Tur described the scene, "a feeling of disbelief filled the room. Here was a presidential hopeful appearing to ask a foreign government to illegally pry into the email server of a private citizen."[41] The *New York Times'* Ashley Parker and Maggie Haberman described it as an "extraordinary moment—in which the Republican nominee basically urged Russia, an adversary, to conduct cyberespionage against a former secretary of state."[42] These takes on Trump's statement were widespread, which caused Trump to make two appearances on Fox News the next day to explain his remark. "I was being obviously—everybody knows—I was being sarcastic when I said it," he told Greta Van Susteren. "Obviously, I was being sarcastic and a lot of people really smiled and laughed. It was said in a sarcastic manner. Obviously. I looked at the cameras; there were tremendous number of press. It was in Florida and everybody sort of chuckled. And what it was, it was being sarcastic."[43] On *Fox & Friends* that day, Brian Kilmeade asked Trump to respond to the Clinton campaign's statement that Trump's request for Russia to "find the thirty thousand emails" was a "national security issue" and that Trump was "calling for a foreign power to commit espionage in the United States for the purpose of somehow changing an election." Trump laughed that off. "You have to be kidding me!" Trump said that he was being "sarcastic." Kilmeade clarified, "Were you being sarcastic?" Trump responded, "Of course I'm being sarcastic."[44]

As a whole, Fox News seemed to accept Trump's explanation. He was just using sarcasm. On July 31, 2016, a panel of contributors agreed with Howard Kurtz when he explained to viewers that "if you listen to Donald Trump's 'Russia, if you're listening,' it sounded sarcastic to my ear, but in the coverage in the *Washington Post* and in the *New York Times* and on CNN, they took it as deadly serious—barely allowing the possibility that he was engaging in sarcasm."[45] As Kurtz noted, it wasn't so "obvious" to everyone that Trump was being sarcastic like he claimed. The *Oxford English Dictionary* tells us that "sarcasm" is "a sharp, bitter, or cutting expression or remark; a bitter gibe or taunt." It derives from the "Greek *sarkazein*, 'to tear flesh.'"[46] Likewise, *Merriam-Webster* describes "sarcasm" as "a sharp and often satirical or ironic utterance designed to cut or give pain." Trump's invitation to Russia to hack Clinton's emails was not sarcasm. It wasn't a biting remark or a bitter gibe. Trump wasn't attacking Russia, attempting verbally to tear its flesh. Trump wasn't being sarcastic technically, but he *was* being ironic. He was saying and not saying. His use of irony allowed him to say two things at once: to both invite Russia to hack and release Clinton's emails and also to not invite Russia to hack and release Clinton's emails. (If it was stated in the form of a *paralipsis*, it would have been, "I'm not saying find her emails; I'm just saying find her emails."). After all, Trump had said earlier in the press conference that "they probably have her thirty-three thousand emails. I hope they do." Andrew Anglin at the neo-Nazi Daily Stormer thought that it was "yet another clever troll by Donald Trump, forcing the spotlight on himself in the middle of the Democrat convention by saying something mildly outrageous in a funny way which draws attention to obvious, simple facts of reality. It is truly incredible that they just keep falling for this." Anglin called Trump's irony "the best thing ever."[47]

It's impossible to say what Trump's intention was, but according to Special Counsel Robert Mueller's June 13, 2018, indictment "on or about" the day of the press conference, Russian intelligence "attempted after hours to spear phish for the first time email accounts at a domain hosted by a third-party provider and used by Clinton's personal office. At or around the same time, they also targeted seventy-six email addresses at the domain for the Clinton Campaign."[48] Russians did not just hack into email systems, however. According to another Mueller indictment, there were two groups of Russians who attempted to influence the 2016 election. Members of the Internet Research Agency (IRA)—"a Russian organization engaged in operations to interfere with elections and political processes"—used social media to distribute Russia propaganda with the "strategic goal to sow discord in the U.S. political system, including the 2016 U.S. presidential election. Defendants posted derogatory information about a number of candidates, and by early to mid-2016, Defendants' operations included supporting the presidential campaign of then-candidate Donald J. Trump ('Trump Campaign') and disparaging Hillary Clinton," according to Mueller's February 16, 2018, indictment.[49] These facts were repeated in the March 2019 *Report on the Investigation into Russian Interference in the 2016 Election*.[50]

According to a January 6, 2017, report from the Office of the Director of National Intelligence, two joint efforts were supported by Russian propaganda outlets RT and Sputnik: (1) *cyberwarfare*, attacking the systems and hardware of an adversary, and (2) *memetic-warfare*, attacking the thoughts, narratives, and emotions of an adversary.[51] "Russia's state-run propaganda machine—comprised of its domestic media apparatus, outlets targeting global audiences such as RT and Sputnik, and a network of quasi-government trolls—contributed to the influence campaign by serving as a platform for Kremlin messaging to Russian and international audiences."[52] Prior to Trump's July 27, 2016, invitation to Russia to find Clinton's emails, RT and Sputnik had written many positive stories about Trump's campaign. For example, on July 7, 2016, Sputnik explained what it called the "Trump Doctrine" as very pro-Russia. According to Sputnik, Trump vowed to work with Russia, draw back NATO, and stop arming Syrian rebels. Sputnik wrote approvingly that "Trump also has a positive view on the Russian government and her people, breaking from his Republican rivals on the debate stage, who all vowed to 'stand up to Putin,' saying instead that he liked the Russian president, saying the two were 'stablemates' on the seminal *60 Minutes* television news show, on which both men appeared for interviews."[53]

When the Clinton campaign fingered the Russians for hacking the DNC emails, Sputnik not only denied the allegation, but it quoted Trump in Russia's defense. On July 26, 2016, Sputnik ran an article criticizing that "America's corporate media have gobbled up the Hillary Clinton campaign's spoon-fed lines that the real story of the WikiLeaks email revelations isn't that they stole a US election, but rather that Putin and Russia are somehow interfering with the election to benefit Trump—despite zero evidence."[54] Sputnik included a July 25, 2016, tweet from Trump: "The new joke in town is that Russia leaked the disastrous DNC e-mails, which should never have been written (stupid), because Putin likes me."[55] That same day, Sputnik included that same Trump tweet in another story mocking "Hillary Clinton's campaign for claiming Russia was behind the damning leak of the US Democratic National Committee's emails in a bid to help Trump into the White House."[56] The next day, RT wrote a story about the Clinton campaign's allegations against Russia, this time quoting three different Trump tweets, including one from July 26, 2016, in which Trump said, "In order to try and deflect the horror and stupidity of the Wikileakes disaster, the Dems said maybe it is Russia dealing with Trump. Crazy!"[57] And it appeared that Russia was indeed listening, because following Trump's July 27, 2016, press conference, RT ran a story mocking the US media: "Beware: the Russians are coming to invade an email near you, and at the invitation of Donald Trump, no less. At least that's how the mainstream media have interpreted the Republican presidential candidate's latest comments." RT again included a Trump tweet in its article: "If Russia or any other country or person has Hillary Clinton's 33,000 illegally deleted emails, perhaps they should share them with the FBI!"[58] Russian propaganda outlets clearly monitored Trump's campaign messages and amplified them when it suited Russian interests.

The July 13, 2018, Mueller indictment alleged that on July 27, 2016—the same day as Trump's press conference—Russian agents sought for the first time to infiltrate the Clinton campaign's emails. They eventually succeeded in hacking into Clinton campaign chairman John Podesta's account. Those emails would be published by WikiLeaks first on October 7, 2016, and then daily for the remainder of the campaign.[59] The timing of the release of the Clinton campaign emails was curious. On that date, two other notable news stories competed for attention with the email release: the release of Trump's leaked *Access Hollywood* "hot mic" tape and a national intelligence warning about Russian election interference.[60] The first mega-story of the day was the release of a joint statement from the Department of Homeland Security and Office of the Director of National Intelligence on Election Security, which warned "that the Russian Government directed the recent compromises of e-mails from US persons and institutions, including from US political orga-nizations." The statement said that the "recent disclosures of alleged hacked e-mails on sites like DCLeaks.com and WikiLeaks and by the Guccifer 2.0 online persona are consistent with the methods and motivations of Russian-directed efforts. These thefts and disclosures are intended to interfere with the US election process." The statement linked the cyberwarfare to the Rus-sian government because "only Russia's senior-most officials could have authorized these activities."[61] Later that day, the *Washington Post* would pub-lish Trump's *Access Hollywood* tape, and about thirty minutes later, WikiLeaks released the first of the Podesta emails.[62]

"Coincidence or conspiracy?" asked an RT headline on October 7, 2016. "US govt officially accuses Russia of hacks during Clinton email dump."[63] RT wanted its readers to think that the US intelligence warning was meant to distract from Clinton's emails. Andrew Anglin at Daily Stormer thought that the release of the *Access Hollywood* tape was meant to "cover these WikiLeaks."[64] Maybe WikiLeaks chose October 7, 2016, to release the Podesta emails merely because it was one month before the election. Maybe the *Washington Post* chose October 7, 2016, to release the *Access Hollywood* tape because that's the first time they had heard of it. (We've not yet learned who leaked it to the *Washington Post*.) Maybe the Department of Homeland Security and Office of the Director of National Intelligence decided that October 7, 2016, was an advisable day to warn the nation of Russian election meddling. In short—despite the coincidence—maybe three independent actors made choices based on their own unique circumstances. While it's unclear if Trump's campaign and WikiLeaks coordinated on the timing of the news events on this day, senior Trump campaign aide Rick Gates and campaign chief executive officer Steve Bannon both testified that the campaign coordinated with Roger Stone, who, in turn, coordinated with Wikileaks.[65] We can see coordination in the way that the Trump campaign, Russian propaganda outlets, and WikiLeaks publicly amplified each other's messages.

The public record shows that Trump's campaign slyly coordinated with Russian cyberwarfare and propaganda outlets similarly to how other American politicians slyly coordinate with supportive political action committees.[66] Federal election law prohibits candidates from directly communicating with political action committees.[67] To get around these restrictions, candidates take advantage of what is called the "safe harbor for publicly available information" rule, which states that political action committees can use any publicly available information about the candidate, including video of the candidate from their websites. For example, if a candidate or elected official posts silent B-roll video (background video) on their website, that video can be harvested and used by political action committees in their supportive advertising without violating the coordination rules. This allows politicians to avoid the Federal Election Commission's rules for campaign coordination by giving them the out of plausible deniability. Skirting around the rules in this way allows campaigns to say, in effect, "We weren't colluding; we were just posting video without any sound of our candidate smiling and signing papers and enjoying his family because we wanted to." Trump's campaign, Russian propaganda outlets, and WikiLeaks mutually put out messages that were harvested, repurposed, and amplified by each other—just like other politicians illicitly coordinate with political action committees. By posting the emails hacked by the Russians, WikiLeaks provided lots of damaging content for Trump to amplify.

On July 23, 2016—just after WikiLeaks published the DNC emails— Trump tweeted, "Leaked e-mails of DNC show plans to destroy Bernie Sanders. Mock his heritage and much more. On-line from Wikileakes, really vicious. RIGGED."[68] WikiLeaks responded helpfully: "That is https:// wikileaks.org/dnc-emails/—everyone can see for themselves."[69] On October 11, 2016, just after WikiLeaks published the first of its Podesta emails, Trump tweeted, "I hope people are looking at the disgraceful behavior of Hillary Clinton as exposed by WikiLeaks. She is unfit to run."[70] The next day,

Trump complained that there was "very little pick-up by the dishonest media of incredible information provided by WikiLeaks. So dishonest! Rigged system!"[71] Trump continued to tweet about the revelations found in WikiLeaks throughout the remainder of the election.[72] Trump also talked about WikiLeaks at every rally, at every presidential debate, and in most interviews from October 10, 2016, until Election Day. ThinkProgress found that Trump mentioned WikiLeaks 164 times in the final month of the election—"more than five times per day."[73] According to their analysis, "Trump encouraged his supporters to read WikiLeaks. He delighted in each new release. He marveled at the damage WikiLeaks was doing to her campaign." WikiLeaks was "a core part of Trump's closing argument against Hillary Clinton." According to the Mueller Report and sworn testimony during the Roger Stone trial, the Trump campaign built its election strategy around WikiLeaks.[74] Circulating WikiLeaks' emails was a winning strategy for Trump: it helped him stoke frustrations that the election was rigged, that the nation was weak, that Clinton was corrupt, that she had benefited from the culture of corruption in Washington, and that the mainstream media was on her side. At Trump's rallies, his followers often began chanting "DRAIN THE SWAMP!" and "LOCK HER UP!" after Trump amplified something from WikiLeaks. "WikiLeaks—I love WikiLeaks," Trump told his October 10, 2016, rally crowd in Ambridge, Pennsylvania. "And I said write a couple of them down. Let's see. During a speech, crooked Hillary Clinton, oh she's crooked, folks. She's crooked as a three-dollar bill. OK, here's one. Just came out."[75]

Throughout the campaign, Trump used irony to say two things at once about his relationship with Putin. First Trump attempted to befriend Putin, then he denied that they were friends. Trump said that he and Putin had talked on many occasions, then he said that he had never talked to Putin, and later he refused to say if they had talked or not, but that we should "assume" that they had talked—and it was "private." Trump used hyperbole to exaggerate his relationship with Putin. Trump anchored to Putin's status, trying to appear to be his equal on the world's political stage. When forced to admit that he didn't know Putin, Trump continued to use the metaphor of them being "stablemates" to indicate that they were similar, two of a kind. Trump called for Russia to find Clinton's emails, then later explained it was "sarcasm," which it technically wasn't. It was irony—saying two things at once—and it was perhaps Trump's attempt to troll the nation into giving him attention during the Democratic National Convention. Finally, Trump amplified the information contained in the WikiLeaks emails and used it as talking points for his criti-cisms of Clinton and to stoke frustration in his followers. Trump did all of this to the exasperation of the political press, who could not seem to pin down Trump's relationship with Putin and Russia.

Special Counsel Robert Mueller's investigation revealed through its many indictments of Russian agents and propagandists that there was a sustained and coordinated attack on the election via both cyberwarfare and memetic warfare. "By their nature," explained the January 6, 2017, National Intelligence report *Assessing Russian Activities and Intentions in Recent US Elections,* "Russian influence campaigns are multifaceted and designed to be deniable because they use a mix of agents of influence, cutouts, front organiza-tions, and false-flag operations." Russian influence campaigns were designed to be deniable, meaning that the intelligence community would likely never be able to prove beyond a reasonable doubt that the campaign existed. Trump's irony worked on the same principle—plausible deniability was central to both. When president-elect Trump was briefed on the intelligence report, he issued a statement declaring that despite the manifest evidence provided to him in the report about Russia's influence campaigns, "there was absolutely no effect on the outcome of the election."[76] Rather, Trump claimed that the Clinton campaign had made up the entire Russian hacking story as an excuse for why she lost the election. This was RT's take on the question as well.[77] On December 23, 2016, Trump tweeted, "Vladimir Putin said today about Hill-ary and Dems: 'In my opinion, it is humiliating. One must be able to lose with dignity.' So true!"[78] RT, of course, wrote a story about Trump approvingly tweeting Putin's comment: "Trump draws flood of criticism for agreeing with Putin that one 'must learn to lose with dignity.'"[79]

CHAPTER 15

"You know the story. It's 'Crooked Hillary.' She's as crooked as they come."

Ad Hominem

Staten Island, New York, April 17, 2016
Favorable 29.4 percent; Unfavorable 64.5 percent[1]

"You know the famous escalator scene?" Trump asked his rally crowd on December 5, 2015, in Manassas, Virginia. "I held my breath," said Trump as he described the "scene" as if it were a movie. "I said to my wife, 'Are you sure I want to be doing this?'" Then Trump exhaled. He summoned his bravery. "I said, 'Let's go.' We went down the escalator."[2] Going down the escalator was a heroic act, according to Trump. "I will tell you, that takes guts," he told his rally crowd on January 25, 2016, in Muscatine, Iowa. "It took guts and certain courage."[3] Trump had a lot of guts, he told his rally crowd in Plymouth, New Hampshire, on February 7, 2016: "It takes guts to run for president. It does. It takes guts. You need a lot of guts, and you need a lot of energy. It is going great, and we love it."[4] Whenever Trump told the story of his campaign, he always emphasized just how brave he had been to run in the first place, represented by his decision to go down that escalator. According to Trump, he was the heroic character in the story of the 2016 presidential election. He loved to tell his rally crowds how brave he had been to run for president. As Trump told the story, his hero's quest for the presidency started with him overcoming his first challenge by bravely announcing his candidacy.

Trump's carefully constructed hero narrative served a central role in his political campaign: it was his main argument for why he was qualified to be president. Trump was heroic because he was successful, he said, and his success in business qualified him to be a successful president and was "just the kind of thinking we need" to make America great again. His hero narrative was designed to appeal to frustrated Americans who were tired of "losing" when they knew that America should be "winning." Trump heroically promised that he would make America win again, and he narrated the story of his campaign as a series of heroic trials, with Trump easily overcoming the many enemy obstacles on his hero's path to victory. With Trump cast as the nation's hero, all opposition to Trump and all criticism of Trump were deemed illegitimate by Trump and his supporters. Since Trump was heroic, he need not even address the criticisms of his enemies; rather, Trump would instead deploy *ad hominem* attacks (attacking the person instead of their argument) to show his fans that his enemies were beneath contempt. Trump's heroic *ad hominem* strategy worked particularly well with the frustrated electorate of 2016 because his followers believed that America was being blocked from something that was legitimately theirs (winning, American greatness). Therefore, attacking Trump's enemies channeled preexisting frustration and directed it at specific targets (Trump's enemies, who were also America's enemies). Trump's hero narrative described him as a heroic demagogue—the people's champion who would fight and defeat corruption—and, in so doing, it helped him paper over difficult truths that Trump preferred not to acknowledge.

According to Trump's hero narrative, taking that escalator in Trump Tower was not only an act of bravery but it represented a heroic rebirth. A corrupted Trump entered the escalator as the "ultimate insider," but as he so frequently recounted, he exited the escalator as the "ultimate outsider"—the people's champion who was qualified to purge the nation of corruption and make America great again. The escalator rebirth gave Trump power because entering the escalator and being reborn to fight corruption not only purified Trump but was his first achievement, his first glory-filled triumph on his hero's quest. Trump's enemies had mistakenly said that he wouldn't run, he recounted. Trump's enemies had mistakenly said that he couldn't run, he crowed. Trump's enemies had mistakenly said that he wouldn't file the necessary forms and release his financial information. But Trump did. He heroically entered the escalator, and he was reborn as the ultimate outsider who would save America by fighting corruption.

When Trump exited the escalator in Trump Tower on "that fateful day," June 16, 2015, he was purified to make his announcement speech and speak the truth. "I talked about illegal immigration," Trump remembered with pride. "Little did I know, I was hitting a nerve that was so incredible. Had I not made that speech and talked about what is happening—and all of a sudden—did I take abuse!" Because Trump told the hard truths that no one wanted to hear about national decline, Trump faced his second hero challenge. "I said, I do not know if I can take this for a year and a half. This is a lot of *incoming*. I had never heard that term with respect to the press. But Rush Limbaugh said, 'I have never seen a man take *incoming* like that.'"[5] Trump's second challenge was to defend his truth from the "incoming" criticisms of those who would not or could not save America.

Because Trump had been purified by the escalator to speak his truth, he would not back down. He fought on. "I am right about it. I know how it works," Trump explained. "You have to be smart and tough. Somebody else would have said, 'I would like to apologize. Is there any way I can apologize?' You cannot do that when you are right. If you are right, you are right. You have to stick with it." Because Trump knew that he was right, he would not back down. The hero suffered. "There is no way a human being can take it for a year. But all of a sudden, people saw that I was right!" And with that, Trump had passed another challenge in his heroic quest to save America. Trump did not apologize, even though there was tremendous pressure for him to do so. In heroically standing his ground, he defeated his enemies. This time his hero credentials were ratified by his followers, who knew that he was right and applauded him for never apologizing.

Trump's enemies were there at his announcement speech in Trump Tower in the form of the media, who were so numerous that it looked like "the Academy Awards," Trump said repeatedly. The media attempted to thwart Trump's heroic quest by circulating the opinions of Trump's enemies as so-called expert pundits. The media pundits represented another challenge in Trump's hero quest. "I get treated very badly by the media," Trump explained in Bluffton, South Carolina, on February 17, 2016. "They have pundits on that are just one after another, negative, negative, negative." Trump thought that the pundits continued to be so negative because he had so often proved them wrong: "They said, 'He'll never run. He'll never run.' Then they look bad, and they don't stop," he said with a shrug. "But it doesn't matter, I guess. Look, we're leading in the polls by a lot. We won New Hampshire in a landslide. It was a landslide victory. Every single group."[6] Winning the New Hampshire primary and leading in the polls had helped Trump vanquish his enemies in the pundit class. They were so bad at stopping Trump that he didn't find them to be worthy adversaries. By March 3, 2016, Trump joked at his rally in Portland, Maine, about how bad the pundits were at assessing Trump. "I watched the pundits," Trump recalled, "and they say, 'Trump, I don't know, we have some great talent running.' I'm trying to figure out where. What is the talent? [The crowd laughed.] I went up and up in the polls, and every time I went up, the pundits said, 'Well he's plateaued.' And I'm very proud of it, because this is not a plateau. This is a movement. We have a movement going on, folks."[7] Trump's movement of frustrated Americans was strong and the pundits were weak—as movement leader, the hero had easily passed another challenge in his quest to become president.

Trump indicated that his movement of frustrated Americans supported him because it knew that their hero was pure. Trump was a hero but also a victim. He had sacrificed so much, he told them repeatedly, and his sacrifices were evidence that he was the noble hero who could save America. "This is a self-funded campaign," Trump explained at a Trump Tower press conference on September 6, 2015. "We have our heart and soul in it. I do not need money, and I do not want money. This will be a campaign like no other, I think. I am not controlled by lobbyists or anybody. I'm controlled by the people of the country, in order to make our country great again."[8] Trump's decision to self-fund his campaign proved that he was uncontrolled and also uncontrollable—here again is where he ran explicitly as a heroic demagogue, arguing repeatedly that he would not be controlled by the lobbyists or a corrupted system.[9] Heroically, Trump promised to be an uncontrollable leader who used his money and power to defend the people from corruption, to make America great again.[10]

By April 17, 2016, Trump had vanquished enough of his Republican primary enemies that he began to look ahead to the last challenge on his quest to become president. That morning Trump tweeted, "Crooked Hillary Clinton is spending a fortune on ads against me. I am the one person she doesn't want to run against. Will be such fun!"[11] Trump's new rival was his and the nation's greatest threat. It was "Crooked Hillary"—the most crooked of all the crooked politicians who were destroying America. She was corruption personified, according to Trump. But the brave hero wasn't scared of his final nemesis. Trump wanted to run against her because he knew that in defeating Crooked Hillary, he would end his presidential hero quest, becoming the nation's hero and making America great again. Defeating her would be fun, he said.

Later that day at his rally on Staten Island, New York, Trump's crowd chanted, "TRUMP! TRUMP! TRUMP!" as he declared, "You know the story. It's 'Crooked Hillary.' She's as crooked as they come, and I'll tell you what, we are gonna beat her badly."[12] Trump's *ad hominem* attack—his nickname for Clinton—was itself "a story," as Trump explained later that day in Poughkeepsie, New York: "She's been crooked from the beginning. And to think that she has a shot at being our president, Crooked Hillary, being our president, Crooked Hillary Clinton."[13] The next day at a rally in Buffalo, New York, Trump once again repeated his *ad hominem* attack: "You have to understand, folks. We haven't even started with Crooked Hillary yet. We have not started the game. . . . You'll hear about the crooked system, Crooked Hillary and the crooked system."[14] Clinton's "crookedness" was Trump's synecdoche (the part that stands for the whole) for why he would defeat his last rival and win his quest for the presidency. She was crooked, and he was pure. He used it relentlessly for the remainder of his campaign. "Finally you came up with a new nickname, 'Crooked Hillary?'" Sean Hannity asked Trump a few days later on April 21, 2016, while a "Crooked Hillary" chyron appeared on-screen. "Well, it's just a name I've been using," Trump explained, "because it's pretty descriptive."[15] He told Bill O'Reilly a few days later, "I call her Crooked Hillary. She is. She is Crooked Hillary."[16] Crookedness was Clinton's essence—her essential characteristic. And Trump was heroically determined to beat her.

"In blunt testimony revealed on Tuesday," reported the *New York Times* on May 31, 2016, "former managers of Trump University, the for-profit school started by Donald J. Trump, portray it as an unscrupulous business that relied on high-pressure sales tactics, employed unqualified instructors, made deceptive claims, and exploited vulnerable students willing to pay tens of thousands for Mr. Trump's insights."[17] Just a few weeks after Trump secured the Republican Party nomination, his carefully constructed hero narrative was threatened by the release of a trove of legal documents related to the federal case against "Trump University," including testimony from Trump, his employees, and "playbooks"—employee manuals—produced by Trump U.[18] The documents alleged that the for-profit Trump U was a marketing scam in which students attended free "real-estate seminars" ("A billionaire is offering you ninety minutes of free advice. No, this isn't a misprint") in rented hotel ballrooms throughout the nation (and in Canada), only to be pressured to spend large sums of money (first $1,495, then $10,000 to $35,000) for more seminars and personalized coaching. According to the legal documents, Trump, who owned a 93 percent share in the company, had promised that experts developed the curriculum, that he had "handpicked" the instructors (who were supposed to be "experienced real-estate investors"), and that he personally oversaw all the details of the school. None of these promises turned out to be true, according to the court documents. The Trump U playbook gave details of the high-pressure sales techniques ("determine who has the most and the least liquid assets," "you must be very aggressive during these conversations in order to push them out of their comfort zone," "money is never a reason for not enrolling in Trump University"); the ways that the seminars played on Trump's reality TV show persona ("cue 'Money, Money, Money' song [The O' Jays] for introduction," students could purchase "apprenticeship support"); and how to set up the seminars for maximum profit.[19]

Trump's final nemesis Hillary Clinton seized on the Trump U court evidence in an attempt to discredit Trump's hero narrative and expose him as "a fraud."[20] In a series of tweets on June 1, 2016, Clinton said that Trump U was "a fraudulent scheme used to prey upon those who could least afford it,"[21] "Trump University's own employees described it as a 'scam,'"[22] and "Trump 'University' was a scam that preyed on families to make money."[23] In a rally in Newark, New Jersey, later that day Clinton directly attacked Trump's hero bona fides. He wasn't a smart and successful businessman, she said, but was instead a serial con artist who had a history of "enriching himself at the expense of hard-working people." Trump University, Clinton explained, "took advantage of vulnerable Americans, encouraging them to max out their credit cards, empty their retirement savings, destroy their financial futures—all while making promises they knew were false from the beginning." To the cheers of her rally crowd, Clinton claimed that the Trump U documents revealed "more evidence that Donald Trump himself is a fraud." And she said that his supposedly heroic presidential campaign was all just a scam: he was "trying to scam America the way that he scammed all those people at Trump U."[24] On June 11, 2016, Clinton's campaign put out a viciously satirical Trump University ad, quoting from news reports and court documents to support its claims and skewering Trump as a con artist. "Donald Trump is world famous for making a fortune from being famous for having a fortune. Now you too can be a source of Trump's wealth with Trump University!" said Clinton's ad. "Don't miss this once in a lifetime chance to give your hard-earned money to an alleged 'billionaire.' Call now!"[25]

Clinton kept up the pressure on Trump. On June 21, 2016, Clinton gave an entire speech dedicated to debunking what Trump had been "promising to do for the economy" that gave example after example of what Clinton described as Trump's "dangerous" and "disastrous" ideas, his history of "filing bankruptcies and skipping his creditors," and how Trump's plans for the economy would cause people to lose their jobs and cause a recession.[26] Above all, Clinton stressed, Trump's economic history proved that "he makes over-the-top promises" and then "disappears when everything falls apart and people get hurt." Clinton thought that the lesson to be drawn from Trump's history is that "those promises you are hearing from him at his campaign rallies—they are the same promises he made to his customers at Trump University. And now, now they are suing him for fraud."[27]

With the release of the Trump U documents and Clinton's stinging attacks, things seemed bleak for the would-be hero, but Trump had been purified to fight corruption, and he wouldn't back down. The hero fought back. The day of Clinton's speech, he announced on Twitter that the next day he'd be giving a speech of his own on "the failed policies and bad judgment of Crooked Hillary Clinton."[28] That night, Trump appeared on Lou Dobbs to explain that crookedness was Clinton's essence: "She is Crooked Hillary. She is Crooked Hillary. She always has been, and nothing is going to change."[29] On June 22, 2016, Trump began his hero's defense by explaining that he had "built an amazing business" and that he was "grateful beyond words to the nation" for his success. Trump said that he was running for president because the nation that he loved needed him. Trump knew that the nation had big problems, but that "we can't solve any of these problems by relying on the politicians who created the problems themselves. The people who rigged the system, the insiders who wrote the rules of the game to keep themselves in power and in the money" would never solve the nation's problems. As an "outsider," Trump was qualified to fix the nation's rigged system. Trump recalled that he "started off in Brooklyn, New York, not so long ago, with a small loan, and built a business that today is worth well over $10 billion." A *Washington Post* fact-check from September 26, 2016, estimated that Trump's father had given him more like $14 million dollars to start his business and keep it afloat.[30] A postelection investigation by the *New York Times* estimated that Trump's dad actually gave him more like $413 million dollars.[31] *Forbes* estimated that Trump's net worth was considerably less than the $10 billion Trump claimed, at around $3 billion dollars, most of which was inherited or earned from branding contracts.[32]

Heroically, Trump promised that he was "running for president to end the unfairness and to put you, the American worker, first." Trump denounced Clinton, who "spent her entire life making money for special interests. And I will tell you, she's made plenty of money for them, and she's been taking plenty of money for herself. Hillary Clinton has perfected the politics of personal profit and even theft. She ran the state department like her own personal hedge fund, doing favors for oppressive regimes and many others, and really many, many others, in exchange for cash, pure and simple, folks." In fact, said Trump, "Hillary Clinton may be the most corrupt person ever to seek the presidency." She was certainly a "world-class liar," he declared.[33] A world-class liar could not be trusted to tell the truth about Trump, so her arguments need not be refuted. She was just Crooked Hillary, telling lies, as a crooked person does.

Did the Trump University documents prove that Trump was a fraud like Clinton claimed? Other politicians had also claimed that Trump was a "con artist"—specifically, Marco Rubio and Michael Bloomberg. Trump was eventually ordered to pay $25 million dollars in restitution to the Trump University students.[34] Did that make Trump a con artist? Trump insisted that he was a "self-made" heroic businessman and had taken great pride in the authenticity of his heroic brand, so perhaps he was a hero after all. Trump explained on the (now defunct) *Trump Blog* on the (now defunct) Trump University website that he had "never planned on becoming a brand name." But, he said, his "wellspring of ideas, my own personal aesthetic, and a variety of circumstances" had combined to create "a great brand name due to my rigorous standards of quality." Trump wrote that his brand was "a promise that whatever bears the name will be elite." In his Trump U advice on "branding strategy," he emphatically explained that the most important thing was "'to thine self be true.' Like a lot of pithy wisdom, Shakespeare said it first, and I second it here—and everywhere else I put the name Trump."[35] The problem with Trump's "true" description of his brand was that it wasn't true—it wasn't even written by him. Shakespeare did indeed say "to thine *own* self be true," but otherwise, Trump's statement about the high quality and authenticity of the Trump brand was written by a Trump University staff writer, not by Trump himself. Adam Eisenstat explained on Vox that he wrote those lines about the high quality and authenticity of the Trump brand when he worked in marketing at Trump U and his job was to be "the voice of Trump."[36] Trump's brand and Trump's hero narrative were both fables—marketing constructs used to sell Trump to frustrated and gullible audiences. Trump's hero narrative—just like his branding—was effective. He used it to paper over the inconvenient truths about Trump U.

Trump deployed well-worn distraction techniques to change the subject from the truths revealed in the Trump University court documents. Trump preferred to talk about whether or not he could receive a fair trial, since the federal judge in the case "is a hater of Donald Trump, a hater. He's a hater. His name is Gonzalo Curiel." Trump caused predictable controversy when he claimed that Judge Curiel, who was an American-born citizen from Indiana, had a name that sounded like he was "Mexican," which was why Trump couldn't get a fair trial.[37] As hero, Trump must prevail. Likewise, Trump chose May 31, 2016—the day that the trove of Trump University documents was made public—to hold a press conference in which he revealed which veterans' groups received donations from him. Trump used the press conference to viciously attack the press—calling one reporter "a sleaze," calling all of the political press "unbelievably dishonest," and berating the press for questioning which veterans' groups had received the money, which, Trump thought, made him "look very bad."[38] Media attention, again predictably, focused more on Trump being forced to make the promised donations to veterans and Trump lashing out at the media than it focused on the documents in the Trump U case.

Ultimately, Trump's marketing of himself as the nation's hero was resilient. Trump's hero narrative protected him along his heroic quest toward the presidency, which is why he constantly invoked it in his argument for why he should be president. Trump used it to argue that Crooked Hillary's corruption was her essence, but that his corruption was in his past. He readily admitted that he had once been "the ultimate insider," but that was the old Trump. The new Trump was the "ultimate outsider," who would heroically defeat corruption. Perhaps counterintuitively, Trump's previous corruption was his strongest argument for why he was the right hero for the moment—he knew all the corrupt tricks, he said. Trump had been cleansed of his previous corruption; he had been purified by the Trump Tower escalator and reborn as a heroic demagogue, the leader of a movement, a champion of the "forgotten men and women of this country." On his hero's quest, Trump continued to tell his hero tale, just as he continued to denounce Crooked Hillary. Trump frequently combined his *ad hominem* attacks against his enemies with heroic appeals steeped in American exceptionalism and *ad populum* appeals to the wisdom of the people. As hero, Trump justly fought the nation's enemies, on behalf of the good and wise people. With less than three weeks left until Election Day, the hero recounted again how he had been purified to save America: "Coming down the escalator, in one day I went from the ultimate insider to, man, have I become the ultimate outsider, right?" His rally crowd roared in response. His campaign had "created a movement the likes of which nobody has seen before in this country." At that moment, someone from his crowd yelled, "You are my hero!," to which Trump responded, "Thank you. You are my hero, let me tell you."[39]

CHAPTER 16

"You've called women you don't like 'fat pigs, dogs, slobs, and disgusting animals.' . . . How will you answer the charge from Hillary Clinton . . . that you are part of the war on women?"

Reification

Cleveland, Ohio, August 6, 2015
Favorable: 26.4 percent; Unfavorable: 61 percent[1]

"You know," Trump said to his rally crowd in Spokane, Washington, on May 7, 2016, just after he had secured enough primary votes to earn the Republican Party nomination,

> [Hillary Clinton] is playing the women's card. By the way, if she didn't play the women's card, she would have no chance—I mean zero—of winning. She's playing the women's card. She's going: "Did you hear that Donald Trump raised his voice while speaking to a woman?" [Trump whined mockingly.] "Oh, I'm sorry [with comically feigned contrition]. I'm sorry." I mean, all of the men, we're petrified to speak to women anymore. We may raise our voice! You know what? [In a serious tone] The women get it better than we do folks, alright? [The audience cheered.] They get it better than we do![2]

Trump's rally crowd roared its agreement with Trump: women like Clinton attempt to control men like Trump by playing the women's card to control men's language. And men were tired of women getting it better than men.

Just before Election Day, a Pew survey found that 60 percent of Americans believed that "Trump has little or no respect for women." News media reported on the survey results as if Trump's perceived disrespect was an unquestionably bad thing, but many Trump supporters actually shared Trump's attitude toward women.[3] In June 2016 political science researchers asked Americans whether or not they agreed with statements such as "most women interpret innocent remarks or acts as being sexist" and "many women are actually seeking special favors, such as hiring policies that favor them over men, under the guise of asking for equality," which the researchers explained are "widely used in social science research on sexism and gender attitudes." They found "that sexism was strongly and significantly correlated with support for Trump, even after accounting for party identification, ideology, authoritarianism, and ethnocentrism."[4] Another set of researchers found that support for Trump was strongly correlated with men's insecurities "about their manhood," or what is sometimes called "fragile masculinity." Researchers tracked online searches for topics such as "erectile dysfunction," "hair loss," "how to get girls," "penis enlargement," "penis size," "steroids," "testosterone," and "Viagra," and "found that support for Trump in the 2016 election was higher in areas that had more searches for [these] topics."[5] Yet another study conducted during the election had voters view an anti-Trump attack ad that "showed women reading statements made by Mr. Trump about women." Voters responded viscerally to Trump's toxic language about women, but men and women did not respond equally: "Trump's unfavorable ratings among women who saw the attack ad went up by 19 points relative to those who did not see it—to a high of 70% unfavorable. Among men, this shift was 1 point."[6] An eighteen-point difference in how men and women evaluated Trump's language about women is noteworthy, to say the least. Trump appealed to frustration, sexism, and fragile masculinity by reifying women (treating people as objects) and successfully turned gender into a wedge issue to activate his followers.

Decades of right-wing propaganda—calling feminists "feminazis" and similar—had persuaded some Americans that "feminism is cancer" in the body politic.[7] A January 2016 *Washington Post*/Kaiser Family Foundation survey found that while 94 percent of respondents agreed "that men and women should be social, political, and economic equals," 55 percent of men said they were either "not a feminist" or were an "anti-feminist." Feminism was seen as unfair to men, by men: 52 percent of the men surveyed agreed that feminism "unfairly blames men for women's challenges."[8] While feminism wasn't popular, most Americans would not say the kinds of things that Trump said about women in public. But some would and did. Men's rights activists—members of the so-called manosphere—saw in Trump a like-minded ally, and they saw Trump's presidential victory as a victory for all men.[9] The manosphere is a collection of websites and discussion boards devoted to "the 'reality' that women run the world without taking responsibility for it, and that their male victims are not permitted to complain," according to an April 14, 2016, *Guardian* article. Like the character Neo in the film *The Matrix*, people who understand the reality presented in the manosphere had "taken the red pill" or had been "red pilled." Neo-Nazi websites like Daily Stormer, men's rights activists like A Voice for Men, Reddit forums like r/TheRedPill (with more than 200,000 subscribers), and right-wing news sites like Breitbart all supported Trump's reification of women during the campaign, cheering him on through his most controversial moments.

"The number one group to suffer from feminism is without doubt White men," wrote Andrew Anglin, May 31, 2016, on Daily Stormer. "Feminists harass and attack boys, deform their minds, force a perverted ideology and value system upon them. They shame and hurt men. They refuse to produce and care for children. They leave men isolated and alienated, painted as the number one enemy of society."[10] Hillary Clinton was the most prominent feminist in America, which caused men's rights advocates to worry that a Clinton presidency would make feminists triumphant in the war against men.[11] They viewed Clinton's campaign as evidence that "misandry [hating men] is mainstream and running for President," according to James Jackson on September 23, 2016, in the popular men's rights website A Voice for Men. "Do we want a President who blatantly hates half of the population?" he asked. Clinton's plan, according to "Roosh" Valizadeh on August 8, 2016, on the website Return of Kings was to "establish a techno-matriarchy where men are second-class citizens." He believed that "all men will be negatively affected under a Hillary presidency in one way or another," but especially "the alt right, alternative media, patriot groups, survivalists, traditionally conservative groups, and anyone else who strongly supports Donald Trump, tradition, or masculinity."[12] Conversely, Trump was seen as the embodiment of "alpha male" masculinity, and men's rights advocates believed that a Trump victory would "restore strength and masculinity as a virtue in America," according to Breitbart's Milo Yiannopoulos on November 4, 2016. "We've had enough nurturing," argued Yiannopoulos. "We've had enough coddling, we've had enough safe spaces: we need to make America hate again. Perhaps that is too strong of a phrase, but I love the pun. If we consider the Cis-Hetero-Patriarchy, or as we used to call it, 'civilization,' masculinity is a tremendous virtue."[13] The dreadful thought of a feminist like Clinton becoming president drove Trump supporters to purchase "anti-Hillary Clinton buttons, T-shirts and bumper stickers" at Trump rallies, "each one more cruel and disgraceful than the last," wrote Chris D'Angelo in the *Huffington Post* on May 3, 2016. He observed that "it appears Donald Trump's misogynistic ways—much like his inciting violence—have rubbed off on his supporters," who could be seen wearing T-shirts that said, "Trump that Bitch" and "Hillary Sucks, but Not Like Monica," in a gleeful celebration of misogyny at Trump rallies.[14]

"One of the things people love about you is you speak your mind and you don't use a politician's filter," Megyn Kelly began in the first question directed to Trump at the first Republican presidential primary debate on August 6, 2015. "However, that is not without its downsides, in particular, when it comes to women. You've called women you don't like 'fat pigs, dogs, slobs, and disgusting animals,'" said Kelly as the debate audience interrupted her with laughter. Kelly tried to resume her question, but Trump stood up straighter, grabbed his microphone, held up his index finger, and with his face contorted in a comedic look of defiance, he interrupted Kelly to clarify, "Only Rosie O'Donnell!," which made the debate audience explode in extended applause and laughter. Trump thanked the audience. Kelly persisted, "For the record, it was well beyond Rosie O'Donnell. . . . Does that sound to you like the temperament of a man we should elect as president, and how will you answer the charge from Hillary Clinton, who is likely to be the Democratic nominee, that you are part of the war on women?" "I think the big problem this country has is being politically correct," Trump said to the thunderous applause of the debate audience. "I've been challenged by so many people, and I don't frankly have time for total political correctness. And frankly, what I say, it's fun, it's kidding. We have a good time. What I say is what I say." He drew boos, whistles, and smatters of applause from the debate audience as he concluded by threatening Kelly: "And honestly, Megyn, if you don't like it, I'm sorry. I've been very nice to you, although I could probably maybe not be, based on the way you have treated me. But I wouldn't do that," said Trump, using *ad baculum* to threaten or intimidate Kelly.[15] He wouldn't do that, he said, but he did do that.[16]

Kelly had used the first question of the Republican Party primary debate to draw the nation's attention to Trump's history of using reifying language against women—his history of using his words to treat women as things ("fat pigs"), not people. The debate audience seemed to agree with Trump that it was fun, kidding, and a good time to call women "disgusting animals" and similar. Trump's immediate response to Kelly's question was to once again use reification—treating Rosie O'Donnell as a punchline, not as a person. The debate audience laughed along with him, but Trump didn't think that Kelly's question about how he talked about women was funny. "The questions to me were not nice," Trump complained to reporters in "spin alley" that night after the debate. "I think Megyn behaved very nasty to me," he said. "They didn't ask those questions of anybody else. So I thought it was an unfair question."[17] Many others seemed to agree with Trump that Kelly had been unfair. "Megyn Kelly's ridiculous question, which was framed to make Trump look as if he was engaged in some made up 'war on women,' specifically sparked a great deal of social media backlash," Andrew Anglin observed on Daily Stormer.[18] That night, Trump used his Twitter account to amplify his complaints against Kelly, gleefully tweeting, "Wow, @megynkelly really bombed tonight. People are going wild on twitter! Funny to watch." Then Trump tweeted or retweeted about the debate thirty-four more times, bolstering his claims to have won the debate and attacking Kelly as "angry," "hostile and unprofessional," "a total failure," "astonishingly biased," "overrated and angry," and a "bimbo" with a "hidden agenda."[19] Trump used his Twitter account to attack Kelly through-out the night until 4:19 in the morning and over the next several days, weeks, and months.

News reports confirmed that Trump had indeed said all of the things about women that Kelly had quoted in her question, but the next morn-ing Trump called into *Good Morning America* to claim, "She came up with words that I didn't recognize. So we'll see what happens. We're going to take a very serious look at it." Kelly's questions were "really unfair," Trump thought, but he was pleased that "when I said the Rosie O'Donnell thing, that got the biggest laugh, applause, et cetera of the evening."[20] Trump was glad that his punchline worked so well and the audience joined him in laughing at O'Donnell's expense. As the debate controversy continued, Trump continued to make controversial remarks about Kelly. That night, Trump called into CNN *Tonight* and told Don Lemon, "I don't have a lot of respect for Megyn Kelly. She came out, reading her script, trying to be tough and sharp. When you meet her you realize she is not very tough or very sharp. She is zippo." Trump didn't have respect for a zippo (a "zero") like Kelly, but at the same time, Trump didn't think that he needed to be more respectful toward her or tone down his attacks against her because "she is able to take care of herself. She is somebody that's pretty tough. I am sure she can take care of herself."[21] As Trump defended himself to Lemon, he continued both to trivialize Kelly's professional qualifications and to frame her as an irrational aggressor—she was at once weak and vicious. Ultimately, Trump said, "I have no respect for her. I don't think she's very good. I think she's highly overrated. . . . She gets out and she starts asking me all sorts of ridiculous questions. You know, you could see there was blood coming out of her eyes, blood coming out of her wherever, but she was, in my opinion, she was—off base."[22]

"I understand you're saying that you did not mean to suggest that Megyn Kelly was having her period?" said Jake Tapper on CNN on August 9, 2015, but "why do you think that there are so many people jumping on you, stating that that is what you were saying? We're not talking about the Women's Studies department at Oberlin," deadpanned Tapper. "We're talking about conservatives. We're talking about [the fact that] Concerned Women for America [issued] a statement saying, quote, 'Every presidential election since 1964 has been carried by women. Women don't like mean, and we certainly don't vote for men or women who we don't trust.' A lot of conservatives are really upset." Trump argued that the controversy about how he talked about women was trivial and that the real issue was about women controlling men's language: "This whole thing with this political correctness in this country is out of control."[23]

"Have you gone too far in your suggestion that she was hormonal in her questions?" John Dickinson asked Trump on *Face the Nation* on August 9, 2015. "John, obviously I never said that," Trump responded. "She was very angry when I interrupted her first question, which I thought was a very unfair question, and I blurted out 'Rosie O'Donnell' and the place went crazy. We had five thousand people in there. They went totally crazy. It really had a big impact on her questioning. I think it angered her." Chuck Todd asked Trump about his "blood coming out of her wherever" comment on that day's *Meet the Press*, pressing Trump about the implications of his words: "You're still making an animalistic or demonic reference, you know, 'with blood coming out of her eyes'—it's still a demeaning comment." Trump responded, "No, she was very angry. I respect people, but Kelly [apparently not 'people'] was very angry because I brought up something that got the loudest applause of the day by far, and it interrupted her question." Trump had revised his history: now Kelly wasn't "trying to be tough and sharp," as he'd told Lemon, but she became "very angry" at being upstaged by Trump. When Todd again pressed Trump to defend his "tendency of disparaging women on looks"—the topic of Kelly's question—Trump defended his actions by explaining that he "was attacked viciously by those people. I don't mean a little bit—I mean viciously. When I'm attacked, I fight back. But I was attacked viciously by those women."[24] Trump thought that since women were so irrational when they criticized him that belittling their looks was justified. "It's very hard for them to attack me on looks because I'm so good looking," Trump said, once again making his behavior into a joke and inviting his audience to laugh along with him.

"Mr. Trump was upset with a question I asked him at the debate last week about his electability," Kelly observed on her Fox News broadcast on August 10, 2015, "specifically comments he has made in the past about women. . . . Apparently, Mr. Trump thought the question I asked was unfair and felt I was attacking him. I felt he was asked a tough but fair question." Kelly vowed to her audience that she would "not apologize for doing good journalism," which provided the frame by which Kelly—as a hated object—could be judged.[25] "Was Kelly's performance 'good journalism'?" asked Trump's future campaign CEO and then Breitbart executive chairman Steve Bannon. Was Kelly a "good journalist"? Or was she a "zippo" or a "bimbo," as Trump had said and retweeted? Bannon argued first that Kelly's questions at the debate weren't good journalism but reflected "the arrogance of power" and "attention-grabbing of the highest order"—twin attacks that mirrored criticisms made about feminists in general.[26] Bannon also drew attention to a press release in which Fox News head Roger Ailes called Kelly "talent" instead of a "journalist," to show that even her employer didn't think she was legitimate.[27]

In response to death threats and harassment, Kelly took a ten-day vacation. When she returned to her job on August 24, 2015, Trump tweeted and retweeted a series of derogatory remarks, including, "The bimbo back in town. I hope not for long."[28] The next day, Fox News released a statement that called Kelly "the very best of American journalism" and advised Trump to apologize: "Trump rarely apologizes; although in this case, he should."[29] Trump refused to apologize: "I totally disagree with the FOX statement. I do not think Megyn Kelly is a quality journalist," Trump replied.[30] Trump's feud with Kelly went on and on, prompting Twitter users to tweet more than eighty thousand hateful messages at Kelly and prompting overt misogyny from men's rights activists like Andrew Anglin. "I hate this bitch so, so much," he wrote on Daily Stormer. "She alone is proof that women should never, under any circumstances, be allowed to leave the kitchen or speak with men who are not their husbands, fathers or brothers." Kelly wasn't doing good journalism, and she certainly wasn't a good journalist. Anglin thought that Kelly was "a feminist whore."[31]

"Megyn Kelly, nice woman, she came up to my office," Trump explained at his rally in Spokane, Washington, on May 7, 2016—the same rally at which he said, "Women get it better than we do!" Trump explained that Kelly was no longer a hated object because, "She came to me. She called me, and I respect her for doing it—and I'm not saying this in any way. I respect her for doing it. I said nothing wrong to her." Trump said he was going to go on Kelly's show soon, since she had apologized to him. "I didn't say anything. These are bad people," Trump said, pointing at the press corps. "They make a big deal out of it." But Trump didn't think that there was anything to make a big deal out of. "They're critical because I speak badly about Rosie O'Donnell? Who the hell wouldn't speak badly about Rosie O'Donnell!" said Trump, once again using O'Donnell as a punchline. His rally crowd roared with laughter while Trump said, "She's terrible. She's terrible!"[32] Megyn Kelly continued to be a hated object until she apologized to Trump, agreeing with him that he "did nothing wrong"; only then did she become a "nice woman," a useful object for which Trump found "respect."

On May 27, 2016, Trump appeared on *Megyn Kelly Presents*, where Kelly began by explaining that during the Republican primary campaign, "it didn't matter what he said or how he said it [because] voters were angry and they liked that he was angry too." Kelly asked Trump if he regretted anything that he had done or said during the campaign. "Yeah, I guess so," replied Trump. "But to look back and say, 'Gee whiz, I wish I didn't do this or that,' I don't think that's good. I don't even think, in a certain way, I don't even think that's healthy." When Kelly pressed him again if he had any regrets, Trump said, "I could have maybe used different language, uh, in a couple of instances, but overall I have to be very happy with the outcome. And I think if I didn't

conduct myself in the way I've done it, I don't think I would have been successful actually." Trump explained to Kelly that he is a "counterpuncher"—
that he was merely responding to other people attacking him, and since it
was a two-way street, his words and actions were justified. Trump believed
that since his tactics were instrumental successes, they were good. Kelly
asked him if he recognized that he had a position of power and responsibility,
and she wondered "whether you will take that responsibility seriously and
change your tone to try to be more unifying and less divisive?" Trump didn't
answer the question. Instead, he said that he was merely "a messenger" for
the "millions and millions of people that have been disenfranchised from this
country." Trump explained that he and his frustrated "fans" have "an unbelievable bond—we have an unbelievable relationship," and sometimes they
might send some "pretty nasty tweets" on Trump's behalf. Kelly asked Trump
why he retweeted them. "You would be amazed at the ones I don't retweet,"
Trump said with a boyish smirk. "Bimbo?" asked Kelly. "Did I say that? Ooh,
OK," Trump said while playfully hanging his head and averting his eyes and
smiling. "Excuse me," he said, and then he looked at Kelly and laughed. Kelly
laughed too.[33]

"Donald Trump has officially finished his conquest of the GOP, having
forced Megyn Kelly to bow down before his Holy Throne," wrote Andrew
Anglin on Daily Stormer in response to Trump's interview with Kelly. "The
establishment has waved a white flag. It's over. We won. Donald Trump will
be the next President of America. We will build the wall. We will deport them
all."[34] Megyn Kelly, the "feminist whore," had capitulated. She invited Trump
on her show, which provided him with the platform to appear charming and
to make jokes about his reification of women. In laughing with Trump about
his use of words like "bimbo" to attack her, Kelly had effectively condoned
his behavior, even while asking whether or not he would change his tone to
be more respectful. Trump agreed that his words had great power, but did
not apologize for anything he had said specifically. Trump defended his
words as justified counterpunching. Since Kelly had "attacked" Trump first
by "unfairly" bringing up Trump's previous reification of women as part of
the "war on women," Trump and his fans could attack her with impunity.
Misogynists like Anglin celebrated Trump's victory over Kelly as a victory for
men and for America.

"Donald Trump bragged in vulgar terms about kissing, groping and
trying to have sex with women during a 2005 conversation caught on a hot

microphone," wrote David Fahrenthold in a blockbuster news story in the October 7, 2016, *Washington Post*.[35] The video showed Trump on a bus talking with *Access Hollywood* host Billy Bush about how he treats women as sexual objects. "I moved on her like a bitch," Trump said about entertainment reporter Nancy O'Dell. "You know, I'm automatically attracted to beautiful— I just start kissing them. It's like a magnet. Just kiss—I don't even wait. And when you're a star, they let you do it. You can do anything. Grab 'em by the pussy. You can do anything."[36] It's unclear whether Trump was the "bitch" or the way that he moved on O'Dell was "bitch-like" or if O'Dell was the "bitch," but all of those interpretations showed Trump treating women as sexual objects rather than as people. On the tape, Trump claimed that he was so attracted to beautiful women that he wouldn't "even wait" sometimes before he started kissing them. He could even "grab 'em by the pussy," he bragged. He could "do anything" he wanted because he was a powerful celebrity. With the release of the *Access Hollywood* tape, Trump once again was confronted with his history of treating woman as objects. This time the controversy was not over whether or not Trump treated women as hated objects, but over whether or not Trump treated women as sexual objects.

"No woman should ever be described in these terms or talked about in this manner. Ever," said then RNC chairman and future Trump chief of staff Reince Priebus. "I am sickened by what I heard today," said Speaker of the House of Representatives Paul Ryan. "Women are to be championed and revered, not objectified. I hope Mr. Trump treats this situation with the seriousness it deserves and works to demonstrate to the country that he has greater respect for women than this clip suggests."[37] Chuck Todd said on NBC News that he thought the controversy over the *Access Hollywood* tape was "unrecoverable" and that Trump's treatment of women may well end the entire Republican Party if he didn't resign from the election.[38] But Trump did not resign from the election.

In response to the controversy, Trump issued two statements on October 7, 2016. In the first, he described what was heard on the tape as "locker-room banter" and attempted to trivialize what he had told Bush about how he treated women by calling it a mere "private conversation that took place many years ago." Trump said that he "apologize[d] if anyone was offended."[39] In the second statement, Trump said, "I said it, I was wrong, and I apologize." But, "let's be honest," said Trump. "We're living in the real world. This is nothing more than a distraction from the important issues we are facing today."[40] In both statements, Trump admitted that the tape accurately reflected what he had said, but he used the apologetic (speech of self-defense) strategy of differentiation ("It's not this; it's that.") to make his statements seem less like sexual violence and more like boyish banter. Trump also used the apologetic strategy of transcendence ("What's important is the bigger picture") to argue that the controversy was merely a distraction and that there were other, more important, issues to discuss than how women should be treated or talked about.

Maggie Haberman described Trump's apology as "a strikingly brief articulation of regret" in the *New York Times* and clarified that despite his seeming apology, his "real message . . . was one of defiance."[41] A defiant Trump ended his apology with an accusation of *tu quoque* (an appeal to hypocrisy or "They do it too."). "I've said some foolish things," said Trump, "but there's a big difference between the words and actions of other people. Bill Clinton has actually abused women, and Hillary has bullied, attacked, and shamed his victims." A defiant Trump refused to withdraw from the election. A defiant Trump brought "three women who have in the past accused former president Bill Clinton of inappropriate sexual behavior" to the October 9, 2016, presidential debate and, using them as props to intimidate Clinton, seated them in the family area in the debate audience.[42] A defiant Trump prowled the debate stage, standing awkwardly close to Clinton and scowling at her in an effort to intimidate her.[43] A defiant Trump once again defended what he had said as mere "locker-room talk" at the debate. A defiant Trump declared several times that he had "great respect for women. Nobody has more." A defiant Trump declared that it was time to "get on to much more important and bigger things."[44]

"Anti-Trump forces in the media, at *The Washington Post* which broke the story, and other outlets, have engineered it into a major scandal," wrote Matthew Boyle in Breitbart. "And the Bushes and anti-Trump Republicans appear at the center of every turn in it."[45] Breitbart readers agreed that the *Access Hollywood* tape was "a big nothingburger, dug up by Hillary's desperate campaign," wrote Eva_Galley in the top comment posted to the story.[46] Another Breitbart reader named Wilson wrote, "They forgot the part about Trump and baby Bush were talking about gold digging bimbo's that throw themselves at rich men. Then they pretend they were talking about all women. Disgusting!"[47] The debate over the *Access Hollywood* tape was a "Pussy-Grabocaust," wrote Andrew Anglin on Daily Stormer, that showed that "Hillary Clinton is a stupid bitch and Trump is STRAIGHT GANGSTA."[48] Anglin thought that the tape showed "Trump talking exactly how normal men talk when they are together with other normal men. To our female readers: yes, all men talk like this when they are alone with each other. Including your husbands and your sons."[49] Anglin loved that the tape showed that Trump was "the world's greatest pussy-grabber," and he believed that the tape wouldn't stop Trump. On Election Day, Anglin expected that Trump would "grab America by the pussy."[50] These comments reflect the perspectives of Trump fans: the *Access Hollywood* story was an irrelevant distraction or part of a conspiracy against Trump. What Trump said on the tape didn't matter anyway, because that's just the way that men talk about women and women deserve it anyway.

As pundits continued to argue that women would choose the next president and women disapproved of the way that Trump treated women, Trump continued to laugh off the accusations, trivialized the issue as "political correctness," attacked the women involved, claimed that he respected women, and justified his language use as "the way men talk" about women in private spaces where men cannot be controlled by women's politically correct language policing. As Trump continued to campaign, he attempted to justify his words and actions as part of his past, rather than his present or future. "I am not proud of everything I have done in life. Who among us is?" asked Trump, attempting to build identification with his October 10, 2016, rally crowd in Ambridge, Pennsylvania. "Is anyone totally proud of every single element?" Then Trump invoked his parents to exonerate him, "If my father and my, my mother were alive today, they would be very, very proud of me. . . . My parents knew what was in my heart."[51] But Trump's parents were not alive to testify about the contents of his heart. On October 18, 2016—ten days after the release of the *Access Hollywood* tape—Trump's wife Melania appeared on Anderson Cooper's 360 on CNN to exonerate him. "I was surprised because that is not the man that I know," said Melania. "And, I wonder if they even knew that the mic was on because they were kind of boy talk, and he was lead on, like, egg on from the host to say dirty and bad stuff."[52] While Melania told Cooper that she had told her husband that the language was "unacceptable," she still condoned what was heard on the tape by explaining that the "boy talk" didn't represent Trump's actual views of women. She argued that her husband was set up to appear to be a misogynist. While Megyn Kelly had helped make Trump's reification of women acceptable in her "feud" with Trump, this time Trump's behavior was excused and exonerated by Trump's wife.

"Donald thinks belittling women makes him bigger," Hillary Clinton explained on October 19, 2016, at the third presidential debate. "He goes after their dignity, their self-worth, and I don't think there is a woman anywhere who doesn't know what that feels like." Trump responded, "Nobody has more respect for women more than I do. Nobody." The debate audience laughed at what seemed obviously false, prompting moderator Chris Wallace to shush them. "Please, everybody," he implored.[53] The debate audience laughed at Trump professing his deep respect for women, but Trump often proclaimed to "promote," "protect," "cherish," and "respect" women.[54] How do we resolve that contradiction? Trump reified women differently than he reified Mexicans or Muslims. Trump's rhetoric made clear that he viewed women as objects with "use value"—they were useful when they helped Trump achieve his goals of appearing to be an alpha male who had everything. So far as they were useful to him (because they were beautiful or sexy or mothers or supporters or hard workers for Trump's brand), then they were precious objects, and he had "great respect" for them. Once they stopped having use value for Trump (because they were not beautiful or sexy or mothers or supporters or hard workers for Trump's brand), then they became hated or despised objects. If a despised object capitulated and provided Trump with use value, then she could be redeemed and once again become a "nice woman."

If Megyn Kelly was correct and Trump's use of reifying language against women could be read as evidence that Trump was a part of the "war on women," then how did he defend his behavior? When anyone questioned Trump about his reifying language, Trump first rejected political correctness as something that real men didn't have time for (echoing the men's rights advocates who called political correctness feminists' tool to suppress men). Second, Trump frequently asserted that he had "great respect for women," that "no one has greater respect for women than me," but when Trump said this, he meant that he had great respect for women who provided him with use value. Third, Trump questioned the competency or motives of the women who mentioned his derogatory use of language: they were so "vicious" and "irrational" and "lightweights," and therefore they were easily dismissed. And, finally, Trump said repeatedly that there were more important issues to discuss than the way that he treated or talked about women. Thus, as Trump claimed repeatedly, all objections to him were reduced to his language use ("She doesn't like my tone," he mocked), which was not only a woman's issue but was part of the plot to destroy America—and so very unimportant. Ulti-mately Trump's defiance meant that his reification was condoned.

Trump spoke for and to the Americans who were frustrated by changing gender dynamics and who blamed feminism and women's rights advocates for the decline of the nation. For example, when asked to name someone in "U. S. society today who represents feminism," most of the January 2016 *Washington Post*/Kaiser Family Foundation survey respondents couldn't name anyone, but 22 percent identified Hillary Clinton as the public figure most associated with feminism.[55] Feminism was unpopular and Hillary Clin-ton represented feminism; voting against Clinton would be a vote against feminism. By Election Day, Pew found that 51 percent of Trump voters said that they were going to vote for him "more as a vote against Clinton" than as a "vote for Trump."[56] The day after the election, Pew reported that "the gender gap in presidential vote preference is among the widest in exit polls dating back to 1972." Fifty-four percent of women voted for Clinton, and 42 percent voted for Trump. Fifty-three percent of men voted for Trump, and 41 percent voted for Clinton.[57]

The day after Trump was inaugurated as the forty-fifth president of the United States, about four million people marched in protest of his election in what researchers said was "likely the largest single-day demonstration in recorded U.S. history."[58] Wearing knitted pink "pussy" hats and carrying signs such as "This pussy grabs back," "The future is female," and "Women's rights are human rights" (and much more), people took to the streets through-out the United States and around the world to express their anger at Trump's reification of women.[59] The *New York Times* described the Women's March as a "counterinauguration." It was "a river of pink hats" stretched out "more than a quarter mile deep" in "what organizers hope could be a sustained campaign of protest in a polarized America, unifying demonstrators around issues like reproductive rights, immigration and civil rights."[60] Men's rights advocates did not see the Women's March in the same way, of course. "Don-ald Trump is the ultimate alpha male. He is an aggressive, hostile conqueror who became ruler of the world through force of will," wrote Andrew Anglin approvingly. "As such, he is the object of sexual fixation of all women on the planet. Hence, hundreds of thousands of women across the globe marching with the demand to have sex with him."[61]

CHAPTER 17

"It is so nice that the shackles have been taken off me and I can now fight for America the way I want to."

Ad Populum

On Twitter, October 11, 2016
Favorable: 36.6 percent; Unfavorable: 58 percent[1]

"The only antidote to decades of ruinous rule by a small handful of elites is a bold infusion of popular will," Trump wrote in an April 14, 2016, *Wall Street Journal* op-ed. "On every major issue affecting this country, the people are right and the governing elite are wrong. The elites are wrong on taxes, on the size of government, on trade, on immigration, on foreign policy. Why should we trust the people who have made every wrong decision to substitute their will for America's will in this presidential election?"[2] Trump's op-ed was full of extreme words—"the only antidote," "ruinous rule," "every major issue"— designed to appeal to a nation frustrated with the "governing elite." Trump's campaign used *ad populum* appeals (appealing to the wisdom of the crowd) to expertly take advantage of preexisting distrust and polarization, turning the nation's frustration into action that would support his campaign against Trump's enemies. Trump used *ad populum* (appealing to the wisdom of the crowd) in three ways: first, he praised his followers as wise and patriotic; second, he praised himself for being so popular with his wise and patriotic followers; and, third, Trump activated his followers to think of themselves as fellow heroes in a movement to defend their shared wise and patriotic values against the corrupt elite. Trump's *ad populum* appeals helped provide him with a "'Teflon'" defense shield by providing a frame by which all actions of the "establishment" could be judged: the establishment was always wrong and Trump's people were always right. Championing the wisdom of the "popular will" against the "governing elite" provided Trump with a lot of leverage when times got tough, like they did in the aftermath of the release of the *Access Hollywood* tape.

"After spending the better part of the 2016 calendar year trying to make the best of their Donald Trump Situation, Republicans began to cut bait in a big way on Saturday," Aaron Blake wrote on October 9, 2016, in the *Washington Post*. "By day's end, more than 30 high-profile Republicans had not only ditched Trump but also said that he had disqualified himself and should step aside for another nominee, thanks to his lewd comments about women on a hot mic in 2005."[3] Trump defiantly refused to withdraw from the race and accused the Republican Party leadership of attempting to sabotage his campaign. "The media and establishment want me out of the race so badly—I WILL NEVER DROP OUT OF THE RACE," Trump tweeted on October 8, 2016, the day after the *Access Hollywood* tape came out. He wouldn't drop out of the race because so doing would abandon his people. "WILL NEVER LET MY SUPPORTERS DOWN! #MAGA," Trump tweeted.[4] Just as Trump had relied previously on his hero narrative and *ad hominem* attacks to defend himself against the evidence that Trump University was a scam, he relied on heroic *ad populum* appeals to defend himself against attacks for the evidence of his history of misogyny. Trump's *ad populum* appeals not only praised his followers for being wiser than the "corrupt political elites" who shunned Trump after the release of the *Access Hollywood* tape, but his *ad populum* appeals helped Trump constitute his followers as fellow heroes—as part of a heroic movement that would defeat the corrupt elite to make America great again. With Trump and his followers constituted as heroes against their shared enemy, seemingly nothing could defeat Trump.

"Everyone involved in the kike media is acting like 'oh my God, this pussy tape, wow, I can't even.' However, most people think it is awesome," wrote Andrew Anglin on Daily Stormer on October 10, 2016. He pointed to an NBC News/Survey Monkey poll released that day showing that "though there has been negative backlash from party elites across the aisle, most Republicans and Republican-leaning likely voters (81 percent) said Trump's 2005 comments make no difference to their vote." Even more astounding—and more exciting to Anglin—the survey found that 6 percent of Republicans and 3 percent of independents said that what they heard on the *Access Hollywood* tape made them *more* likely to vote for Trump.[5] "This fits the eternal rule of memes," explained Anglin. "Every anti-Trump meme automatically becomes a pro-Trump meme."[6] If the eternal rule of memes held, then Trump would find a way to turn elite rejection into a win for him. He did just that by unifying and motivating his followers to act as soldiers in the war against corruption.

At Trump's rally that day in Ambridge, Pennsylvania, Trump certainly tried to prove the "eternal rule" of Trump memes true by using *ad populum* appeals to turn his rally crowd against the party elites. "The last seventy-two hours has framed what this election is all about," Trump explained, framing how his followers should understand events. "It is about the American people fighting back against corrupt politicians that don't care about anything except staying in power and keeping their donors happy," Trump declared to the enthusiastic cheers of his rally crowd. The past seventy-two hours wasn't about whether or not Trump's history of misogyny disqualified him from becoming president; it was about the corruption of the elite. Trump constituted himself as the heroic leader in the fight against corruption. "What I want to say to every American right now is that I accept the mantle of this responsibility for all of us, for all of us," he said solemnly. "I will never stop fighting for you against the Washington establishment that has betrayed each and every one of you," he vowed. "I'm doing this because I just think that it's so damn unfair!" His intense language prompted his rally crowd to cheer enthusiastically for their hero, who promised to defend them from corruption.[7]

On the day that Trump rallied his followers in Ambridge, his enemies continued to plot against him. Speaker of the House of Representatives Paul Ryan explained on his October 10, 2016, weekly conference call with Republican Party members that he would no longer "campaign with or defend Republican presidential nominee Donald Trump through the November election," essentially "breaking up" with Trump.[8] According to news reports, there was considerable "pushback" from some Republicans on the conference call who felt that Ryan was abandoning their base, which still supported Trump. One anonymous lawmaker "who represents a safe Republican district where Trump is popular" explained to the *Washington Post* that his constituents are "just so fed up with Washington, D.C., that all the rest of this stuff is a side point. . . . They're willing to overlook a whole lot to try to take back the country."[9]

Trump acknowledged the breakup with Ryan and the Republican Party leadership the next day with a heroic *ad populum* appeal. "It is so nice that the shackles have been taken off me and I can now fight for America the way I want to," tweeted Trump.[10] "What exactly does that mean?" Bill O'Reilly asked Trump later that night. "Well, we've been having a problem. We have millions and millions of followers, we set records in the primaries, we have a group of people that want to see America be great again," Trump said, using his popularity with his followers as a cudgel. But the Republican Party leadership were "weak and ineffective," and they were "being nasty to the nominee." Trump said that he would "do what I want. Look, I don't want his support. I don't care about his support. What I want to do is I want to win for the *people*."[11] Trump repeated his "shackles" line at a Republican fund-raiser that day in San Antonio, Texas. The *Texas Tribune* reported that Trump said that he "feels more untethered from the Republican establishment than ever" and that "it feels so good."[12] Trump's "shackles" metaphor was unusual for him— he didn't typically speak metaphorically (another noteworthy example was when he called Putin his "stablemate"). Trump used his metaphor to explain that he was a prisoner of the Republican Party; his hands had been tied by the Republican Party leadership. Now freed, he would fight on, and he would do it for the American people, the way that he wanted. Trump didn't like to be controlled or restrained, so his Republican Party shackles had frustrated him. Freedom felt so good.

News reports across the political spectrum framed the controversy between Ryan and Trump as a "war" between the Republican establishment and Trump. Trump was "launching a kamikaze mission," according to CNN.[13] He had "declared war on the Republican establishment" that left party leaders "dealing with another problem: an impulsive and bellicose businessman with an army of loyal supporters willing to exact retribution against elected officials they feel have abandoned them," according to the *Washington Post*.[14] Such framing likely helped Trump with his supporters by reaffirming and amplifying Trump's message that he and his followers had been abandoned by corrupt political elites. That was certainly the take on Daily Stormer, where Hunter Wallace wrote that the "#NeverTrump forces didn't wait to see what voters thought about" the *Access Hollywood* tape, but "seized on the tape as their opportunity to make their move." He thought that for Trump supporters this was "the confirmation of everything they had ever suspected about the Republican Party. It was if the term CUCKSERVATIVE had been etched in granite on the Republican Party's tombstone."[15]

As Trump continued to campaign, he appealed to the innate purity and righteousness of his people, arguing that their movement was correct and that the elites were wrong. "The arrogance of Washington, DC, will come face to face with the righteous American voter. You!" Trump said to the enthusiastic cheers of his October 11, 2016, rally crowd in Panama City, Florida.[16] Trump explained that the corrupt elites were against him and his followers because he was poised to win. The corrupt elites had taken advantage of this trivial "issue" as an excuse to abandon and attack him. Trump knew that his followers were frustrated, but with their support, he would fight on. The *New York Times* published an article on October 12, 2016, in which two more women came forward to tell their stories of Trump sexually assaulting them; Trump brushed it off as more evidence of the elite plot against him and his people.[17] "There is nothing the political establishment will not do—no lie that they won't tell, to hold their prestige and power at your expense," Trump explained to his rally crowd in West Palm Beach, Florida, on October 13, 2016. As Trump defended himself from more "attacks," he described a nation in peril over the elite's treatment of him. Trump believed that the political establishment was so "vicious" toward him because his "campaign represents a true existential threat like they haven't seen before. This is not simply another four-year election. This is a crossroads in the history of our civilization!" Such hyperbolic and apocalyptic language encouraged his followers to choose between the corrupted political elite who abandoned Trump and their hero who vowed to fight for them.

Trump's rally crowd in West Palm Beach booed when Trump mentioned the elite, and cheered or chanted ("TRUMP! TRUMP! TRUMP!" or "USA! USA! USA!") when he mentioned his heroic people and vowed to crush their shared enemies. As Trump finished his speech, he explained that "for them, it is a war. For them, nothing at all is out of bounds. This is a struggle for the survival of our nation—believe me. This will be our last chance to save it, on November 8. Remember that. This election will determine whether we are a free nation, or whether we only have the illusion of democracy." Again, Trump framed the choice between himself and the end of the nation, the end of democracy. It was his followers' last chance. He warned that the corrupt elite "wield control over this nation through means that are very well known. Anyone who challenges their control," as Trump had done, "is deemed a sexist, racist, a xenophobe, and morally deformed. They will attack you, slander you, they will seek to destroy your career and your family," as they had done to Trump. "To destroy everything about you, including your reputation. They will lie, lie, lie, and then again they will do worse than that!" Trump bellowed from the podium as his rally crowd cheered. Such appeals relied on Trump's corruption narrative to inoculate his followers against any damaging news about him—all bad news about Trump would be read within the frame of a ploy by a desperate elite trying to prevent the heroic Trump from saving the nation. Such appeals also relied upon the rhetoric of victimhood: Trump played the victim but also the martyr. He would sacrifice himself for his people and their shared cause.

Despite the corrupt elite's power, Trump believed that the power of his people was stronger. "We will rise above the lies, the smears, the ludicrous slanders from ludicrous and very, very dishonest reporters," Trump said. "We will vote for the country we want. We will vote for the future we want. We will vote for the politics we want," Trump concluded his speech to the thunderous applause of his rally crowd in West Palm Beach. And with that, he had given his followers the power to act on their frustration. His followers would act to defend America and democracy by believing Trump. They would defend America from corruption by voting for Trump.[18] It was their last chance. Democracy was at risk.

In the final few weeks of the campaign, Trump's chances of winning were "approaching zero," wrote the *Washington Post*.[19] Trump relied on his *ad populum* appeals to push back against the consensus view that there was no way that he could win the election. Trump acknowledged that he was in the "fight of his life" against the corrupt establishment, but notably, Trump shifted from a defiant "I will fight" to a more inclusive (and reminiscent of Winston Churchill) "We will fight." For example, in Trump's June 7, 2016, victory speech after he secured enough primary votes to win the Republican Party nomination, he explained that "some people say I'm too much of a fighter," but, said Trump to the applause of his crowd, "if I'm forced to fight for something I really care about, I will never, ever back down." Trump explained that he had "fought for my family, I've fought for my business, I've fought for my employees. And now," vowed Trump, "I'm going to fight for you, the American people. Like nobody has ever fought before. . . . Just remember this—I'm going to be your champion. I'm going to be America's champion.[20] Trump would be his people's hero, fighting the corruption of the establishment elite. Not only did Trump run as a demagogue who fights for his people against the corrupt other parts of the state, but this was his *best argument* for why his followers should act to support him despite the "attacks" against him for his history of misogyny. Trump ran as a heroic demagogue, fighting for his people, and Trump's followers saw him in just that way.

Trump would fight for his people, as their hero, but that wouldn't win Trump the election. Trump needed Trump's people to join the fight too. He needed them to act on their frustration with the corrupt Republican Party elite and the corrupt Clinton globalist conspiracy and the corrupt media. He needed Trump's people to vote for him so that he could be the heroic demagogue who fights for them and saves America. As Trump fought on, he continued to use "I am going to fight" throughout most of October, but then switched to "We will fight." For example, as Trump concluded his October 29, 2016, rally speech in Phoenix, Arizona, he said, "We're asking for the votes of Republicans, Democrats, independents, and first-time voters—and there's going to be a lot of them, believe me." Then collecting all Americans together, he declared, "We're fighting for every citizen who believes that government should serve the people, not the donors and not the special interests. We are fighting to unlock the tremendous potential of every American community and every American family who yearn for a better future—a much better future. With your vote, we are just ten days away from the change you've been waiting for your entire life. I will never let you down." Trump vowed as his rally crowd cheered and clapped, "I promise you that I will never, ever let you down!" Some responded with chants of "BUILD THE WALL!," while others chanted "TRUMP!" and still others chanted "USA!" The crowd continued its asynchronous frenzy of Trump chants while Trump clapped and pointed at crowd members and gave two thumbs up. Trump's rally crowd continued its thunderous cacophony until Trump began again: "We are a divided nation; we will not be divided any longer!"[21] Trump's rally crowd roared its united approval.

"We are going to deliver real change that puts, again, America first," Trump promised his Delaware, Ohio, rally crowd on October 20, 2016. "It's going to be America first!" Trump bellowed as his crowd chanted, "USA! USA! USA!" As the cheers and chants died down, Trump thanked his rally crowd, praising them for their spirit. "Beautiful," he observed. "It's a beautiful thing to see. All over the country. It's a beautiful thing. It's a spirit. It's a movement like they've never seen."[22] Trump liked to describe his presidential campaign not merely as a "campaign" but as a movement. Trump knew that constituting his followers as a "movement" made them sound more powerful than constituting them as a "campaign." A movement implies power and unity, acting together to right a wrong. Calling Trump's followers a "movement" was another *ad populum* appeal, of course, and it helped his followers see themselves as powerful and as a part of something larger than themselves. Trump didn't start calling his campaign a "movement" at the end of the campaign. He'd been doing so since at least August 19, 2015, when Trump told his followers in New Hampshire, "The silent majority is back. We really are in a position that we haven't been in in a long time. The people are speaking. It's an amazing thing. It's like a movement."[23] He continued to invite people to join his "movement," to describe his campaign as "a movement like they've never seen before," and to claim his debate or electoral victories were a win for his "movement" throughout his campaign.[24] As a part of a movement, Trump's followers' lives had a purpose: to restore American greatness. They could end their frustration with America by voting for Trump. Trump's wise crowd understood what was really going on, which was why their frustration was legitimate. In fact, anyone who wasn't a part of Trump's movement was a part of the conspiracy against him and his movement.

As Trump concluded his campaign, he used his *ad populum* appeals to activate the frustrated and motivate them to act on his behalf. "Well, you know what you can do?" Trump asked his rally crowd in Scranton, Pennsylvania, on November 7, 2016. "Go out and vote tomorrow. That is what you can do, OK? That's the only way," he assured the crowd. "If we win, the corrupt politicians and their donors lose. If we lose, the American people lose—big league. This is it, folks. We will never have another opportunity, not in four years, not in eight years. It will be over. With Supreme Court justices, with people pouring into our country. This is it. This is it. Good luck," Trump said over the exuberant cheers of his rally crowd. "They said I set a record. I had crowds—massive crowds. Yes, they said I set the record." As Trump continued to speak, his rally crowd shifted from loud cheering to a frenzied chant: "USA! USA! USA!" "It is time to reject a media and political elite that bled our country dry," said Trump to cheering and chanting. "It's finally time for us to fight for America, to fight for America." "USA! USA! USA!" his crowd chanted. "I'm not a politician," promised Trump. "My only special interest is you!"[25]

CHAPTER 18

"I. Am. Your. Voice!"

American Exceptionalism

Cleveland, Ohio, July 21, 2016
Favorable: 34 percent; Unfavorable: 59.1 percent[1]

"Don't believe anyone who says, 'I alone can fix it,'" Hillary Clinton warned
as she accepted the Democratic Party nomination on July 28, 2016. "Those
were actually Donald Trump's words," she said with a bemused smile as she
described Trump's Republican Party nomination acceptance speech from the
week before. Trump's words were so undemocratic and so un-American that
"they should set off alarm bells for all of us," she said. "He's forgetting every
last one of us. Americans don't say 'I alone can fix it.' We say: 'We'll fix it
together,'" Clinton bellowed as the stadium erupted in cheers. "Remember,"
said Clinton, "our founders fought a revolution and wrote a constitution so
America would never be a nation where one person had all the power. Two
hundred and forty years later, we still put our faith in each other," said Clinton
as cameras showed members of the DNC crowd nodding in agreement with
tears streaming down their faces.[2] Trump had promised to be the authoritarian that our founders had warned us about, explained Clinton, but she
assured the Democratic Party faithful that American democracy was strong
enough to withstand his threat.

Scholars of "democratic erosion" and "democratic backsliding"—
experts in how established democracies around the world and throughout
history have failed—weren't as sure as Clinton that American democracy was
strong enough to withstand what they saw as Trump's attacks on democracy.
The day before the presidential election, Harvard professors of government
Steven Levitsky and Daniel Ziblatt warned that Trump "is an antidemocratic

figure who threatens our country's institutions." They explained that the election would be "a critical test" of the strength of American democracy and warned Republican Party officials that this was their "Churchillian moment." They must "find the political courage to stand up to a popular demagogue and his movement." Their worry, of course, was that if Trump lost the election the next day and refused to concede (as he said he might) and if his followers became violent (as they said they might), then American democracy would be lost to authoritarianism. Democracy hung in the balance, Levitsky and Ziblatt warned.[3] Because Trump won the election, Levitsky and Ziblatt's nightmare scenario did not occur, but even after the election they continued to warn the nation about Trump's dangerous authoritarianism and how leaders like him had historically eroded democratic norms en route to eroding democracy. They saw the same pattern in the United States: "This is not necessarily because Americans have grown more authoritarian (the United States electorate has always had an authoritarian streak)," they wrote on December 16, 2016, "rather it's because the institutional filters that we assumed would protect us from extremists, like the party nomination system and the news media, failed."[4] Trump was uncontrollable. He had taken advantage of Americans' authoritarian streak and used it to overpower the already weakened democratic gatekeepers—the political party apparatus and the news media.

Political scientists and communication experts had noticed that Trump was appealing to America's "authoritarian streak" early in the primary elections. "Trump's strongman rhetoric has activated and energized American authoritarians to his candidacy, providing him with a large and loyal base of supporters," wrote then doctoral candidate Matthew C. MacWilliams on January 27, 2016. His research found that Trump supporters had "an inclination towards authoritarianism," and, more troubling for American democracy, "Trump voters are ready to suspend constitutionally guaranteed rights such as habeas corpus, reject the protection of minority rights, and support the abridgment of religious freedom through the closure of mosques across the US."[5] His research attracted a lot of attention. "I'm not saying they're fascists," MacWilliams explained to the *Washington Post*, "but authoritarians obey."[6]

In March 2016 Vox partnered with authoritarianism researchers and the polling firm Morning Consult to find out just how authoritarian Trump's supporters actually were. "Trump, it turns out, is just the symptom," wrote Amanda Taub. "The rise of American authoritarianism is transforming the

Republican Party and the dynamics of national politics, with profound consequences likely to extend well beyond this election." The Republican Party had an "authoritarian voter" problem that it could not control, even if it had wanted to. The Vox/Morning Consult research found that authoritarian voters tended to support authoritarian leaders "as a response to experiencing certain kinds of threats." If a political candidate could "make people believe that the threats exist," then they could "activate their authoritarianism." Their survey found that "44% of white respondents nationwide scored as 'high' or 'very high' authoritarians." The research found authoritarian voters in both political parties, but found that "more than 65% of people who scored highest on the authoritarianism questions were GOP voters. More than 55% of surveyed Republicans scored as 'high' or 'very high' authoritarians." They asked respondents what made them fearful and found that they "most fear threats that come from abroad," but they also feared internal threats that they viewed as undermining the stability of the social hierarchy. These internal threats could be "in the form of rising diversity" or "any changes, political or economic, that disrupt social hierarchies" or were viewed as threatening authoritarian voters' "status quo as they know it." In response to scary and frustrating instability, authoritarian voters seek "a strong leader who promises to suppress the scary changes, if necessary by force, and to preserve the status quo."[7] If there was a choice to be made between democracy and the stability of the social hierarchy, authoritarian voters were likely to choose stability over democracy.[8]

Over the course of his presidential campaign, Trump told and retold a consistent narrative that would appeal specifically to authoritarian voters: *There are so many scary enemies out there. They are beheading our people, they are invading our nation, they are rapists and murderers. We don't even have a wall to protect us! They are taking our country away, and the corrupt elite are inviting them in. What's worse, the corrupt elite want to take away your guns and leave you defenseless against the invaders and the beheaders and the rapists. They care about the wrong people, but I care about the right people. I will stop the bleeding, the stupid decision-making. I will put you first, I will put America first, I will fight for you—I will never stop fighting for you. I will fix this rigged system, and you will be so proud, you will be so happy. I'll make America great again, like it used to be. America will win again. There will be so much winning that you'll get tired of winning. We're going to say "Merry Christmas" again and end this globalist, feminist, politically correct nightmare.*

Such a narrative would appeal to authoritarian voters who feared external and internal enemies and feared for their place in the social hierarchy. These authoritarian voters would find comfort in a strong authoritarian leader like Trump, who promised to speak the truth, fight corruption, and restore the nation to its former greatness. That authoritarian leader would be their hero, and he would be the apotheosis of American exceptionalism (America's unique status among other nations in the world)—of what once made America great. American exceptionalism itself was threatened by the same forces that threatened authoritarian voters. It's not a coincidence that what once made America "great" also put authoritarian voters at the top of the social hierarchy. Violating democratic norms such as threatening to suspend habeas corpus, revoking immigration laws, restricting protections on religious freedom, refusing to release tax returns, threatening to jail opponents, threatening the press, asserting that the election would be rigged without evidence, and refusing to concede the election—all violations of democratic norms that indicated a dangerous authoritarianism to researchers—would be justified by authoritarian voters as the necessary actions of a strong and heroic authoritarian leader.

Trump's authoritarian narrative told three truths about the relationship between Trump and his followers. First, Trump loved his people (who loved each other and loved him) and his country. As Trump's rally crowd in Tampa, Florida, chanted "USA! USA! USA!" on October 24, 2016, Trump promised them that "the forgotten man and women won't be forgotten anymore. Forgotten men and women: I see you. I hear you. And I will never ever let you down. I promise. We will never let you down."[9] Trump portrayed his authoritarianism as a kind, patriotic paternalism. He positioned himself as a heroic father figure, protecting his people from a scary world that threatened their social stability. His followers were the forgotten men and women—forgotten in the new social hierarchy. But Trump didn't forget them. Trump loved them. Trump saw their suffering. Trump promised to never let them down. "The people in this room love each other, and they protect each other, and that is what we have to do as a country," Trump told his April 16, 2016, rally crowd in Hartford, Connecticut. "I love our loyal people. There are no people like our people."[10] Trump was the hero of his loyal people, who were also heroes. Everyone else was an enemy. "The media and the political elite do not know the pain and the suffering these people are living under," Trump told his rally crowd in Sioux City, Iowa, on November 6, 2016, "but I figured it out a long time ago. That is why I am here. I am with you," he vowed.[11] Throughout his campaign, Trump had promised to love and protect his loyal followers, to right the wrongs, save them from their suffering, and restore their place on the social hierarchy.

Second, Trump would use his powers to crush their shared enemies, which would restore American greatness and authoritarian voters' place in the social hierarchy. "The corrupt political establishment is a machine," Trump explained to his October 13, 2016, rally crowd in West Palm Beach, Florida. "It has no soul." The corrupt establishment had no soul, but it had "unlimited" political resources and "unmatched" media resources. They also had a plot to destroy the nation and, along with it, Trump's followers. "They will allow radical Islamic terrorists to enter our country by the thousands," Trump warned. He told his rally crowd that he would fight "our corrupt political establishment" because it was "the greatest power behind the efforts of radical globalization and the disenfranchisement of working people." Radical globalization brought the dangerous bad people into the country and displaced Trump's good people on the social hierarchy, disenfranchising them from their traditional role in society. But Trump would use his power to stop the corrupt establishment that plotted to destroy the social hierarchy. "I am doing it because this country has given me so much, and I feel so strongly that it is my turn to give back to the country that I love. I am the only one who can fix it," Trump said to the cheers and applause of his rally crowd. "I am doing this for the people and for the movement, and we will take back this country for you, and we will make America great again." Trump portrayed his authoritarianism as legitimate because he would use his power to vanquish his people's and his nation's enemies—both internal and external.

Third, and finally, Trump would break the phony political rules because the system itself was so broken and corrupted that violating the rules was actually *more* democratic than following the rules. Trump didn't like it when protestors infiltrated his loving rallies, for example, and so while free speech was protected by the Constitution, Trump violated democratic norms when he threatened his protestors with physical violence. When repeated protestors interrupted Trump's rally in St. Louis, Missouri, on March 11, 2016, he complained that it was taking too long to remove the protestors because "nobody wants to hurt each other anymore" and so the "protesters, they realize there are no consequences to protesting anymore. There used to be consequences. There are none anymore."[12] Back when social hierarchies were preserved, when America was great, people would hurt the people who stepped out of line like the protestors did at Trump's rallies.[13] But Trump didn't just violate democratic norms by threatening free speech rights.[14] Trump would violate all democratic norms related to the peaceful transfer of power with the election. When Trump was asked if he would "absolutely accept the result of this election" on October 19, 2016, at the third presidential debate, Trump answered, "I will look at it at the time. I'm not looking at anything now. I'll look at it at the time. . . . I'll keep you in suspense."[15] The next day, Trump told his rally crowd in Delaware, Ohio, that he would "totally accept the results of this great and historic presidential election—*if I win*."[16] His rally crowd cheered. By October 27, 2016, Trump told his rally in Toledo, Ohio, "I'm just thinking to myself right now; we should just cancel the election and just give it to Trump, right? What are we even having it for?" The rally crowd roared in approval.[17]

Trump's authoritarian voters showed their loyalty to Trump throughout his campaign by attending his events, contributing to his campaign and buying his campaign merchandise, circulating and amplifying his propaganda, defending him from attacks, and of course, voting for him. Trump's loyal followers could be counted on to remove offending protestors, like they did at Trump's December 4, 2015, rally in Raleigh, North Carolina.[18] Trump's loyal followers agreed with Trump that journalists were the enemy of the people—intimidating, taunting, and jeering at them at Trump's rallies. For a short while, Trump's authoritarian voters even raised their hands and swore an oath to support Trump.[19] "Who likes me in this room?" Trump asked as his crowd in Orlando, Florida, on March 5, 2016, cheered enthusiastically. "Raise your right hand," said Trump. His rally crowd raised their hands. "I do solemnly swear that I will, no matter how I feel, no matter what the conditions, whether there are hurricanes or whatever, will vote on or before the twelfth for Donald J. Trump for president."[20] His crowd did their best to get through that mouthful of a promise before Trump said, "Thank you. Now I know. Don't forget you all raised your hands. You swore. Bad things happen if you don't live up to what you just did!" Trump did the pledge again in Concord, North Carolina, on March 7, 2016. "Should we do the pledge? Should we do the pledge?" Trump asked his rally crowd. "Raise your hand," he said. "I swear I'm going to vote for Donald Trump next week, I swear!"[21] Trump's rally crowd could be seen with their hands raised, gleefully reciting Trump's pledge.

The pledge was pleasing to Trump; he enjoyed having his followers pledge their continued support. And the pledge allowed his followers to see entire rallies full of people vow their support for Trump—a sight that must have been reassuring for authoritarian voters. However, the pictures of Trump and his followers raising their hands and pledging fealty caused quite a bit of concern. Former Anti-Defamation League director Abe Foxman told the *Times of Israel* that the pledge was "a fascist gesture" that was as "offensive, obnoxious and disgusting as anything I thought I would ever witness in the United States of America."[22] Trump stopped asking for a loyalty pledge from his followers, even though he protested that it was all in good fun. "Sometimes we'll do it for fun," Trump said to Matt Lauer on NBC's *Today*. Trump claimed that his rally crowd would "start screaming at me, 'Do the swearing! Do the swearing!' I mean, they're having such a great time," Trump said.[23] Of course, what was fun for Trump and his followers looked like dangerous authoritarianism to others.

According to scholars of democratic erosion, Trump's most dangerous authoritarianism came from his refusal to honor the democratic norms around the peaceful transition of power. Therefore, perhaps the most prominent way that Trump's authoritarian voters demonstrated their loyalty and their willingness to violate democratic norms to elect Trump was in their willingness to stand guard at polling places on Election Day to prevent "election rigging." It all started on July 27, 2016—the day after Hillary Clinton's Democratic Party nomination acceptance speech—when Republican "dirty trickster" and sometime Trump political advisor Roger Stone appeared with Breitbart News' Milo Yiannopoulos for his *Milo Show* to warn Trump that Clinton was planning to use "widespread voter fraud" to steal the election. Stone advised Trump to "begin talking about it constantly." The message to the nation ought to be, "if there's voter fraud, this election will be illegitimate, we will have a constitutional crisis, widespread civil disobedience, and the government will no longer be the government," Stone told Yiannopoulos. Stone warned that there would be "a bloodbath" if Clinton wins. "No, we will not stand for it. We will not stand for it," he insisted. "Trump will go there," Yiannopoulos agreed. "He will go to the places other politicians wont, and he's probably the only person to run for president within the last fifty years who would dare to do this, and might even get away with it. It's remarkable, isn't it, how he's just sort of reinjected reality into politics."[24]

Two days later, conspiracy theorist Alex Jones told his InfoWars audience that Trump was "such a leader, and that's why they're scared of him. He wants to change this country, folks. That's why the whole power structure is going after Donald Trump."[25] Jones also posted an "emergency message to Donald Trump," which, like Stone had done, warned Trump about Clinton's impending election fraud. "It's imperative that the Trump campaign make this one of the central issues: if she steals the primary, then she's going to steal the general election," advised Jones. "I'm asking the American people to support you in standing up to this witch," Jones concluded, speaking directly to Trump through his InfoWars video. "I'm asking the American people to take action and really cause a grassroots brushfire . . . because if you think Hillary's gonna stop with stealing the nomination, if you think she's not going to try to steal the general election, I got a bridge in Brooklyn I want to sell you."[26]

Jones also had Stone on his show on August 1, 2016, where both agreed that Clinton was determined to steal the election from Trump. "If she stole the primary, she's going to try to steal the election," Jones told Stone, "so now Donald Trump really needs to think about what he's going to do, but *we* need to think about what are we going to do to stop Hillary Clinton." Stone, who had already set up a website called "Stop the Steal," agreed and told Jones that he was "convinced that they are looking more and more at the option of stealing it." Stone thought with Russia dropping "truth bombs on her campaign" that she would get even more desperate. Stone said that Trump's message to the nation needed to be that he would "challenge her being sworn in. I will have my people march on Washington and we will block your inauguration," Stone advised. "We're not rolling over," was the message that Trump needed to send, according to both Jones and Stone. Both agreed that the only thing that could prevent Clinton from stealing the election would be an electoral landslide for Trump: "What you can't steal is a landslide—that's been proven," said Jones.[27]

That same day in Columbus, Ohio, Trump told his rally crowd that Bernie Sanders's primary "was rigged. And I'm afraid the election is going to be rigged, I have to be honest. Because I think my side was rigged—if I didn't win by massive landslides. I mean, think of what we won in New York and Indiana, California—78 percent. That's with other people in the race. But think of it," Trump told his rally crowd in Ohio. "I hear more and more that the election on November 8 . . . ," he said, echoing what he had heard over the past three days from Yiannopoulos, Stone, and Jones. (The subject of the speech then changed course and never returned back to the subject of Clinton stealing the election.[28])

"You said at a speech today you're afraid this election is going to be rigged," Sean Hannity said to Trump that night. "Explain."[29] Trump said that he'd "been hearing about it for a long time" and since during the 2012 election "you had precincts where there were practically nobody voting for the Republican" and because "it was rigged, I thought, a little bit for me and we won in landslides. I think it was rigged against Bernie Sanders with his super delegates nonsense," explained Trump. "I'm telling you November 8, we better be careful because that election's going to be rigged, and I hope the Republicans are watching closely, or it's going to be taken away from us."

The next day an InfoWars headline screamed, "TRUMP IS RIGHT: HILLARY STOLE THE NOMINATION AND SHE WILL TRY TO STEAL THE PRESIDENCY" and warned its readers that "the establishment media" were attempting "to characterize Trump's warning that Hillary plans to steal the election as some nebulous conspiracy theory that he has plucked out of thin air." InfoWars knew exactly where Trump got his conspiracy theory and decried mainstream media skepticism as "an insult to objective reality." InfoWars concluded that "Trump's warning . . . is not a conspiracy theory, it's a pinpoint assessment of the most likely scenario."[30] Since Clinton would steal the election, it made sense for Trump to try to prevent it by any means necessary. Within two weeks, Trump's campaign had posted a website to recruit poll watchers to "watch closely" so that the election didn't get "taken away from us," as he had said to Hannity on August 1, 2016.[31] "Hours before the site gained traction Friday night," Politico reported, "Trump said at a rally in Altoona, Pennsylvania, that the only way he would lose in Pennsylvania is 'if cheating goes on. She can't beat what's happening here. The only way they can beat it in my opinion, and I mean this 100 percent, if in certain sections of the state they cheat.'"[32]

"BREAKING" screamed a headline of the *Christian Times* on September 30, 2016, "'Tens of Thousands' of Fraudulent Clinton Votes Found in Ohio Warehouse."[33] After clicking on the headline to read the story, internet users saw a photo of Hillary Clinton looking forlorn with her head in her hand. "They did it once. They'll do it again" was written in red next to Clinton's photo. Beneath her image it read, "We already know that Hillary stole the primary. We can't let her steal the presidency. Join the 'Stop the Steal' team to find out HOW Hillary plans to steal the election and what YOU can do to stop her!"[34] Stop the Steal was Roger Stone's website, active since at least March 2016, that purported to organize Trump supporters to stop election rigging, first during the primary and then during the general election.[35] The *Christian Time*'s lede read, "according to sources, Randall Prince, a Columbus-area electrical worker, was doing a routine check of his companies wiring and electrical systems when he stumbled across approximately one dozen black, sealed ballot boxes filled with thousands of Franklin County votes for Hillary Clinton and other Democrat candidates." Snopes published a fact-check on the article the day it was posted, rating it unequivocally "false."[36] It turned out that the article was written by Cameron Harris, just out of college and hoping to find a break as a political consultant. He had made up the whole website, the story, Randall Prince, and the Clinton ballots, according to what he told the *New York Times* on January 18, 2017, because he wanted to support Trump and also make some money from ad revenue.[37] Harris's *Christian Times* story offering "proof" of election rigging got a lot of attention on social media, but his wasn't the only story that found evidence to support Trump's claims that Clinton would rig the election.

On October 18, 2016, Breitbart highlighted Project Veritas's exposé of voter fraud, announcing that Clinton had a plan to commit voter fraud on a "massive scale."[38] On October 20, 2016, Breitbart exposed the fact that the letters in the third presidential debate set backdrop behind Clinton spelled "Rig it."[39] On October 21, 2016, InfoWars claimed that the public was awakening "to massive fraud."[40] On October 25, 2016, Fox News reported that thousands of dead people were likely on the Indiana voter rolls.[41] On October 26, 2016, Fox News reported that voters in Texas indicated that their votes for Trump were being switched by voting machines.[42] Trump tweeted about it the next day: "A lot of call-ins about vote flipping at the voting booths in Texas. People are not happy. BIG lines. What is going on?"[43] InfoWars made sure its audience knew about the Texas concerns and Trump's tweet.[44] On October 28, 2016, Breitbart reported that charges of voter fraud were filed in Virginia and Florida.[45] And on October 31, 2016, and November 1, 2016, InfoWars alerted its audience that voting machines were being hacked: "George Soros linked voting machine company uses easily rigged software," it reported.[46] And so on. Meanwhile, Trump continued warning his rally crowds about the rigging, like he did on October 17, 2016, at his rally in Green Bay, Wisconsin. "People that have died ten years ago are still voting," Trump told his crowd. "Illegal immigrants are voting!" Then he quoted a Pew study that supposedly supported his assertion that the election would be rigged. Fact-checkers reported that the Pew study did not.[47]

Trump's supporters got the message, according to a story by Dana Milbank in the October 18, 2016, *Washington Post*: "Retiree Gerald Miller, a volunteer at Donald Trump's rally here [shared] Trump's concern that the election may be 'rigged' by the Clinton campaign. 'It is enough to skew the election. They can swing it either way.'" He told Milbank that "Donald Trump is going to holler fraud if he doesn't win. I think we're on the verge of a civil war, a racial war. This could be the spark that sets it off."[48] Many others at Trump's Colorado Springs, Colorado, rally agreed with Miller. Likewise, on October 13, 2016, Trump supporters in Cincinnati, Ohio, told the *Boston Globe*'s Matt Viser and Tracy Jan that they had no doubt that Clinton planned to rig the election. Viser and Jan reported that "anger and hostility were the most overwhelming sentiments" among Trump supporters, along with "a deep sense of frustration, an us-versus-them mentality, and a belief that they are part of an unstoppable and underestimated movement." Even though Trump supporters felt powerful, Viser and Jan reported that they were "worried that Democrats will load up buses of minorities and take them to vote several times in different areas of the city. They've heard rumors that boxes of Clinton votes are already waiting somewhere." A Trump supporter named Jeannine Bell Smith worried that "we're going to have a lot of election fraud. They are having illegals vote. In some states, you don't need voter registration to vote." Another Trump supporter named Steve Webb told Viser and Jan that "Trump said to watch you precincts. I'm going to go, for sure. I'll look for . . . well, it's called racial profiling. Mexicans. Syrians. People who can't speak American. I'm going to go right up behind them. I'll do everything legally. I want to see if they are accountable. I'm not going to do anything illegal. I'm going to make them a little bit nervous."[49]

Trump made a big deal out of the election being rigged throughout the last months of the election. But it turned out that he didn't actually sign up many official poll watchers, even though his loyal followers, like Steve Webb, would have gladly served. A November 3, 2016, Associated Press investigation found that while "Trump regularly warns his crowds to closely watch polling places to prevent Democrats from stealing the election," he had "failed to enlist many to serve as official poll watchers in major population centers." The AP had done "spot-checks" throughout the nation, asking election officials about what the AP had expected would be a surge of Republican poll-watcher registrations. It found that "Democratic monitors will far outnumber Republicans on Election Day," and that there were even fewer Republican poll watchers signed up compared to previous elections. "The Trump team seeks volunteers on his website," wrote the AP, but "it's unclear what the campaign does with its list—voters in Arizona and Virginia who signed up were never contacted." The AP wrote that it was "not clear why there is a discrepancy between Trump's rhetoric urging poll watchers and the lack of signups." Perhaps there was a "failure by the campaign to organize" or perhaps trying to prevent election rigging had never been "a true campaign priority." All the AP could conclude was that "there has been no surge in Trump poll watchers."[50]

"The election is absolutely being rigged by the dishonest and distorted media pushing Crooked Hillary—but also at many polling places—SAD," tweeted Trump on October 16, 2016.[51] The next day, Politico/Morning Consult released a poll that asked Americans, "Donald Trump has said that this election could be 'stolen' from him as a result of widespread voter fraud. Do you agree or disagree with his statement?" Forty-one percent of all registered voters either strongly or somewhat agreed with Trump, and 73 percent of Republicans either strongly or somewhat agreed with Trump.[52] A Pew survey on October 27, 2016, found that 56 percent of registered voters thought that Trump had little or no respect for the "nation's democratic institutions and traditions." The same survey found that only 43 percent of Trump supporters had "a great deal or fair amount of confidence" that the presidential election would be "open and fair." Only 49 percent of Trump supporters agreed that the freedom of the press to criticize political leaders is essential to maintaining a strong democracy and 69 percent of Trump supporters thought it was very important that "people have a right to non-violent protest."[53] Those authoritarian voters who would violate democratic norms to elect Trump won the election, of course. A Morning Consult Election Day exit poll found that "36% of 2016 voters said being a strong leader was the *most* important quality when picking a president"—twice as many as said that a strong leader was most needed in 2012.[54]

Perhaps Hillary Clinton was correct that Trump's Republican Party nomination acceptance speech demonstrated a dangerous authoritarianism. "I will present the facts plainly and honestly," he promised the Republican Party in Cleveland on July 21, 2016. "So if you want to hear the corporate spin, the carefully crafted lies, and the media myths, the Democrats are holding their convention next week. But here, at our convention, there will be no lies,"[55] he vowed as his audience began chanting "USA! USA! USA!" Like Trump had attempted to do throughout his campaign, his speech positioned him as a truth teller. Trump's speech was a dark and horrifying recitation of danger, crime, plots, and corruption. But Trump's supposed "facts" gave fact-checkers a difficult time. The *Washington Post* called Trump's speech "a compendium of doomsday stats that fall apart upon close scrutiny. Numbers are taken out of context, data is manipulated, and sometimes the facts are wrong."[56] Trump's speech wasn't meant for fact-checkers; it was meant to appeal to authoritarian voters.

Throughout the speech, Trump positioned himself as the authoritarian leader who loved his people, would destroy their shared enemies, and would break the phony rules to win. Trump said that he had "visited the laid-off factory workers, and the communities crushed by our horrible and unfair trade deals. These are the forgotten men and women of our country, and they are forgotten, but they will not be forgotten long." Trump signaled to his "forgotten" followers that he understood their fears and frustration at being displaced in the social hierarchy. He saw them like no one else did. Trump lamented that these forgotten people "work hard but no longer have a voice." Trump then pointed directly at the camera while he declared, "I. Am. Your. Voice!" while raising and lowering his finger with each word. The Republican Party convention erupted in wild applause. Trump claimed that he had "joined the political arena so that the powerful can no longer beat up on people that cannot defend themselves." Trump promised he would defend his people by destroying their shared enemies. Trump knew how to do it because he had "seen firsthand how the system is rigged against our citizens," which, he claimed, was "why I alone can fix it." As he ended his speech, Trump explained that Clinton asked her supporters to pledge "I'm with her." Trump said that he chose "to recite a different pledge. My pledge reads: 'I'm with you, the American people.'" As Trump's crowd cheered and chanted "USA! USA! USA!," he said, "I am your voice! I'm with you, and I will fight for you, and I will win for you. We will make America strong again. We will make America proud again. We will make America safe again. And we will make America great again!"[57]

"I am your voice" was ambiguous. Read one way—with an emphasis on "your"—it could mean that Trump would use his voice to speak for the forgotten Americans who could not speak for themselves, that Trump would use his voice to amplify their concerns. Read another way—with an emphasis on "I"—it could mean that Trump would speak for others and their opinions would be silenced. Either way, Trump used his RNC acceptance speech to position himself as an authoritarian leader in order to appeal to authoritarian voters. And Trump's authoritarian appeals worked. "We can't have that lying bitch in the White House," said Judy Wright, a Trump campaign volunteer in Ohio on October 13, 2016. "If Hillary wins, it's rigged," she told the *Boston Globe*'s Matt Viser and Tracy Jan. And if Clinton rigged the election to win, then "our country is not going to be a country anymore. I've heard people talk about a revolution. I've heard people talk about separation of states. I don't even like to think about it," said Wright. "But I don't think this movement is going away. We don't have a voice anymore, and Donald Trump is giving us a voice."[58]

Conclusion

Controlling the Uncontrollable Leader

"For reminding America that demagoguery feeds on despair and that truth is only as powerful as the trust in those who speak it," wrote *Time* editor Nancy Gibbs on December 7, 2016, "for empowering a hidden electorate by mainstreaming its furies and live-streaming its fears, and for framing tomorrow's political culture by demolishing yesterday's, Donald Trump is *Time*'s 2016 Person of the Year."[1] Gibbs clarified that *Time* editors chose the person each year who had the most impact, not necessarily the person who had done the most good. Indeed, previous winners of the distinction included Adolf Hitler in 1938, as well as American presidents like FDR in 1932, 1934, and 1942. Obama had also won the honor in 2008 and 2012 upon his election victories. The 2016 *Time* cover showed Trump seated at a chair in his Trump Tower private residence with a caption that read, "Donald Trump: President of the Divided States of America." Trump thought that it was a "great honor" to be named Person (he preferred "Man") of the Year, but he objected to the "divided states" part.[2] Matt Lauer asked Trump on *Today* whether he thought the *Time* award was meant as a "compliment or a condemnation." Trump of course said that it was a compliment. "When you say, 'divided states of America,' I didn't divide them; they're divided now," Trump explained to Lauer. "I'm not president yet, so I didn't do anything to divide!"[3] It was true that Trump was not yet president, but it was not true that Trump hadn't done anything to divide the nation. Trump's presidential campaign was one of the most divisive in the nation's history.

Trump attacked America's public sphere in 2016. An important part of the story of Trump's presidential campaign is the context within which it succeeded: a nation in crisis. Within a crisis of public trust in which the very viability of democracy was at risk, Trump ran a campaign that was *designed* to increase distrust for government and traditional leadership. Within a crisis of polarization in which Americans believed that they had little common ground with their political opposition, did not share the same values, and that their opposition was an enemy of the state, Trump ran a campaign that was *designed* to increase polarization. Within a crisis of frustration in which Americans believed that government was the biggest issue facing the nation, that the nation was on the wrong track, and that anybody else would do a better job running the country than the current leaders, Trump ran a campaign that was *designed* to increase frustration. Trump's campaign of distrust, polarization, and frustration was designed to take advantage of the rhetorical possibilities inherent in a nation in crisis. Trump's dangerous demagoguery used rhetoric as a weapon—as a "counterpunch"—and in so doing, Trump attacked America's public sphere and its democratic process.

"Ideas are weapons," public policy professor and journalist Max Lerner wrote in 1939—"big sweeping ideas like racism, individualism, Nazism, communism, and democracy are in possession of men. They possess us as evil spirits were once said to have entered into witches and possessed them and made them do their bidding. Under the spell of those ideas a madness seems to sweep over a people, like an engulfing sea that sweeps away the dikes that rationality has painfully and prayerfully built against it over the centuries." Lerner believed that since all "ideas are weapons," we ought to value the autonomy and free will of people so that they could decide what they think for themselves. Lerner distinguished between an "instrumental" and a "manipulative" approach to persuasion: the instrumental approach "recognizes that ideas are used in behalf of a way of life and in the struggles for its achievement. But it is also humanist. It understands that, if democracy is to mean anything, it must have respect for the common man and not use him cynically as a pawn in a political game." Lerner explained that the manipulative approach "sees the common people only as so much material to be used."[4] The difference between these two perspectives is noteworthy here because weaponized rhetoric is despotic: it denies individuals the ability to decide for themselves and treats people as pawns, as a means to an end.

Democracy ought to be the weighing mechanism by which we judge the quality, appropriateness, and value of political campaign rhetoric, because in America—where we consider our government a democracy—whether or not a political candidate or leader's rhetoric promotes and protects democracy is the most fundamental quality in assessing their fitness for office. Trump claimed to be advancing the cause of American democracy by fighting corruption, but his rhetorical strategies actually undermined American democracy.

Because Trump used weaponized rhetoric—because he used rhetoric as force instead of as a method for arriving at truth and decision making—he denied his followers the ability to choose freely. Trump's rhetorical strategies of manipulation, distraction, and obfuscation denied his followers their right to consent to the government under which they live, which made his rhetoric dangerous for democracy itself. Rhetoric that undermines democracy demonstrates a dangerous authoritarianism. How dangerous is Trump? Well, it's hard to tell—largely because it's difficult to discern if Trump is actually an authoritarian or if he is pretending to be an authoritarian for rhetorical effect.

The Dangerous Demagogue and Democracy

Scholars of fascism, authoritarianism, and tyranny have consistently sounded the alarm over Donald Trump's authoritarianism.[5] To demonstrate how dangerous weaponized rhetoric is for democratic governments, we can compare it with Steven Levitsky and Daniel Ziblatt's authoritarian typology in *How Democracies Die*. Levitsky and Ziblatt explained that authoritarian leaders typically erode democracy by doing four things.

First, according to Levitsky and Ziblatt, authoritarians reject or show a weak commitment to the "democratic rules of the game." They give historical examples, such as rejecting or expressing a willingness to violate the Constitution, undermining the legitimacy of elections, and using or endorsing extraconstitutional means to change the government, such as military coups or violent insurrections.[6] Dangerous demagogues likewise use weaponized rhetoric to reject or show a weak commitment to the democratic rules of the game of public deliberation, especially to prevent themselves from being held accountable for their words and actions. Dangerous demagogues attempt to *overwhelm the news cycle* to prevent negative stories from gaining attention by organizing, manipulating, and subverting hashtags on social media; by targeting people for retweets; and by dumping unfavorable news when people are distracted. Dangerous demagogues attempt to *distort reality* by spreading propaganda, conspiracy theory, fake news, and disinformation. Dangerous demagogues attempt to *distort meaning* by taking words out of context, intentionally ignoring contradictory information, and intentionally subverting the dominant meanings of key words or by using dog whistles to appeal to their partisans. Dangerous demagogues attempt to *distort public sentiment* through bots, manipulating algorithms, and computational propaganda.

Dangerous demagogues also use typical rhetorical figures and fallacies such as *paralipsis* and *tu quoque* to say two things at once and accuse their accusers of being hypocrites. In these ways and more, dangerous demagogues weaponize rhetoric. By attempting to overwhelm the news cycle and distort reality, meaning, and public sentiment, dangerous demagogues reject the democratic rules of the game of public deliberation, using these tactics to prevent a critical interrogation of their words and actions—and denying the consent of the governed.

Second, according to Levitsky and Ziblatt, authoritarians "deny the legitimacy of political opponents." They give historical examples, such as describing rivals as subversive or against the constitutional order, claiming that rivals represent an existential threat to the nation or are acting as foreign agents and describing their rivals as criminals who are not qualified to hold office.[7] All of Levitsky and Ziblatt's examples of denying legitimacy are the result of the rhetorical positioning of opposition as illegitimate enemies, which makes this criterion especially relevant for rhetorical analysis. Dangerous demagogues use weaponized rhetoric to deny the legitimacy of political opponents by using *ad hominem* attacks to constitute their opposition as illegitimate and by using reification to constitute their opposition as nonhuman enemy objects who are illegitimate. By using *ad hominem* attacks and reification, dangerous demagogues deny the legitimacy of their opposition, which denies them political standing, makes criticism easier to disregard, and makes it that much more difficult for the opposition to hold them accountable for their words and actions.

Third, according to Levitsky and Ziblatt, authoritarians "tolerate or encourage violence." They give examples such as having ties to armed gangs or militias, sponsoring or encouraging mob attacks, and refusing to condemn or praising political violence conducted in their name or elsewhere in the world.[8] Dangerous demagogues likewise use weaponized rhetoric to conduct violence or to signal that they tolerate or encourage violence. Dangerous demagogues use communication platforms to spread malicious information and spread information maliciously through doxxing, spying, and exposing their opposition to public ridicule, shame, and aggression. Dangerous demagogues organize, encourage, or fail to prevent their supporters from using communication technologies to attack their opposition. They also organize, encourage, or fail to prevent their supporters from physically attacking their opposition. Dangerous demagogues use *ad baculum* threats, *ad populum* appeals, *ad hominem* attacks, reification, and American exceptionalism to polarize citizens and threaten their opposition. In these ways and more, dangerous demagogues weaponize rhetoric by tolerating or encouraging violence.

Fourth, and finally, according to Levitsky and Ziblatt, authoritarians are ready to "curtail the civil liberties of opponents and the media." They give examples such as expanding libel or defamation laws, restricting protest and government criticism, threatening to punish rival parties or media, and praising repressive measures taken by other governments to restrict the civil liberties of opponents and the media.[9] Dangerous demagogues likewise use weaponized rhetoric to curtail civil liberties. Recent examples include jailing, threatening, and undermining journalists; refusing to hold press conferences; lying to reporters and subsequently blaming reporters for carrying false stories; threatening libel; attempting to bankrupt or devalue media companies to force them out of business; speaking only to favorable media organizations; forcing government workers to sign nondisclosure agreements; surveilling citizens by monitoring social media; deploying facial recognition software to track citizens; and using rhetorical appeals such as American exceptionalism, reification, and *ad populum* appeals, *ad baculum* threats, and *ad hominem* attacks against political opposition and the press. In all these ways, dangerous demagogues weaponize rhetoric to restrict the civil liberties of opponents and the media.

Levitsky and Ziblatt warn that violating even one of these four rules would indicate that a potential leader has dangerous authoritarian tendencies. Likewise, we could say the same about any potential leader who weaponizes rhetoric in one of these four ways. Such a person would be a dangerous demagogue who would be difficult to hold accountable to the rule of law once in power. Trump was such a person. He violated these four standards repeatedly throughout his campaign.

Controlling the Dangerous Demagogue

On October 25, 1931, John Dewey gave a radio lecture on the relationship between education and democracy in the age of mass mediated propaganda. "Democracy will be a farce," explained Dewey, "unless individuals are trained to think for themselves, to judge independently, to be critical, to be able to detect subtle propaganda and the motives which inspire it."[10] Dewey assumed that citizen critics could prevent dangerous demagogues from attaining power by using their rationality to assess public discourse—thereby holding leaders accountable for their words and actions. Public speaking, communication, rhetoric, and argumentation scholars have likewise argued that democratic citizenship requires training in critical thinking so that the fallacious techniques of demagogues will not persuade the uninformed electorate. At least one method for controlling the dangerous demagogue's power, therefore, could be for citizens to use critical thinking to analyze the rhetoric of political figures. Since leading the people requires a relationship between the leader and the people, it makes sense that the people have a responsibility to hold their leaders accountable for their words and actions and prevent them from becoming dangerous demagogues.

"What kind of speech training is needed in a democracy?" asked rhetoric scholar William Norwood Brigance in 1952. "The answer is obvious. The kind needed to promote the welfare of a free society." He thought that Americans ought to be held accountable for "speaking the truth," being "intellectually honest," avoiding "reckless assertion," and "lifting the tone of discussion above the level of name calling."[11] Since rhetoric is necessary in any free society (the opposite of rhetoric is not "truth" but violence), how can we tell when political leaders are using rhetoric to manipulate and deceive us against our welfare? Of course, the answer is critical thinking. Critical thinking about rhetoric and argument is not difficult, but it is a skill that needs to be developed. According to argumentation scholars Edward Inch and Kristen Tudor, critical thinking "helps us consider issues and problems systematically and rigorously. It is fundamental to our ability to learn and make sense of the world around us." Using critical thinking, they note, is similar to using the scientific method, but it is used to make sense of everyday news and information.

Argumentation and rhetoric scholars have well-developed analytic tools for identifying and combatting dangerous demagoguery. In competitive debate, simply flagging a statement as a fallacy (objecting to a statement as an *ad hominem* attack, for example) would immediately discount the statement or open up a debate over whether or not the fallacy occurred. Part of why this works is because competitive debate adheres to specific rules: flagging violations of the rules is a part of the game. Real political discourse does not adhere to any rules, and there's no umpire around to enforce them anyway. This means that we all have to be umpires, purging our public sphere of dangerous demagogues and their weaponized rhetoric.

Perhaps the best way to neutralize a dangerous demagogue is also the most democratic way: to let the demagogue's audience in on the demagogue's strategic game so they can decide for themselves what they think about it (as I have done throughout this book). Each of the dangerous demagogue's strategies is a means to an end. Each strategy is a ploy in the game of attracting followers, deflecting criticism, controlling the conversation, and retaining support. Go back and read the descriptions of Trump's rhetorical strategies in this book's introduction and think about how he used those strategies in his campaign, and you'll know how the strategies work and how they can be combated. When we refute a fallacy, we appeal to the force of the better argument over the force of weaponized rhetoric.

This all sounds reasonable, but demagogues try to prevent us from using our good judgment and critical-thinking skills at every turn. Sociologist Sigmund Neumann explained in the 1938 *American Sociological Review* that demagogues primarily seized power through techniques that prevented citizens from using their reason and critical-thinking skills to resist.[12] Totalitarian demagogues merged the techniques of demagoguery with new mass media technology and the newly perfected techniques of propaganda to make themselves ever more dangerous and powerful. According to Neumann, demagogues became dictators, controlling not only the airwaves but what was permitted to be said and what could be considered to be truth: "[T]he demagogue does not recognize controversial attitudes. He declares his adversary a liar, a traitor to the only truth. Dissension is no longer a matter of opinion, but of heresy. The 'party line' wins a sort of mystic holiness. Totalitarian governments and their leaders are 'infallible.' To question their policies is sin. As soon as complete power is obtained, the monopoly over all instrumentalities of communication gives unlimited propaganda possibilities to the totalitarian."[13] What was true in 1938 still holds true today.

Therefore, recognizing that demagogues try to prevent us from thinking critically about their demagoguery, we must learn to think about rhetoric and argument like demagogues do.[14] One way to do that is to understand the rhetorical strategies used by successful demagogues. Rhetorical theorist Kenneth Burke explained in 1939 that Adolf Hitler's rhetoric had a specific kind of "demagogic effectiveness." According to Burke's reading of *Mein Kampf*, Hitler's rhetoric relied upon anti-intellectualism, repetition, spectacle, mass meetings, uniformed guards as authority figures, slogans, symbols, ideology, certainty, polarization, and scapegoating.[15] As Hitler explained in *Mein Kampf*, he based his rhetorical strategies on four principles. First came what modern communication scholars call the *agenda setting* and *framing* functions: Hitler said that he used rhetoric "to attract public attention to certain things, the importance of which can be brought home to the masses only by this means." Hitler said that rhetoric should put "a matter so clearly and forcibly before the minds of the people as to create a general conviction regarding the reality of a certain fact, the necessity of certain things and the just character of something that is essential." Second, Hitler said that rhetoric should "address itself to the broad masses of the people," which meant that its "intellectual level" could not be above "the least intellectual of those to whom it is directed"—it had to be pitched to the "lowest mental common denominator." Third, Hitler said that rhetoric should "appeal to the feelings of the public rather than to their reasoning powers"; it had to "awaken the imagination of the public through an appeal to their feelings, in finding the appropriate psychological form that will arrest the attention and appeal to the hearts of the national masses." And, finally, according to Hitler, rhetoric "must be confined to a few bare essentials and those must be expressed as far as possible in stereotyped formulas. These slogans should be persistently repeated until the very last individual has come to grasp the idea that has been put forward." Hitler's rhetorical strategy centered on agenda setting and framing, simplicity, emotion, and slogans and repetition. Trump used the same rhetorical strategies as Hitler, but he also innovated new tactics that took advantage of new media and propaganda technologies.

Trump is a new kind of demagogue. He is a demagogue of the spectacle—part entertainer, part authoritarian. When French critical theorist Guy Debord described the "society of the spectacle" in 1967, he explained that the term "spectacle" denoted a moment in history when representation had replaced direct experience as our epistemology—as our way of knowing. Whereas human beings used to know things because they experienced them directly (and one's sphere of information and influence was necessarily very small), late-twentieth-century humans had expanded their sphere of information to such an extent that they knew things only because they learned about them from media sources—most, if not all, of our knowledge had become mediated by others. What was worse, this new knowledge was commodified; it was a part of the capitalist system of production and distribution, which meant that it was always only partial knowledge. What was "true" was limited to what would sell.

The spectacle—as mediated experience—was everywhere. It was

ubiquitous. "The spectacle has spread itself to the point where it now perme-
ates all reality," Debord wrote when he updated his description of the spectacle in 1989. Because all knowledge is mediated by the spectacle and because
the spectacle controls the relations between people as well as the methods
that people use to communicate with one another, people "can never free
themselves from the crushing presence of media discourse." Public opinion,
for example, is not what is printed in newspapers and literary journals as the
consensus achieved through the rational-critical debate of a bourgeois public
in coffee houses and salons (as if it ever really was that). But it is the spectacle
of opinion polls created by news organizations as "pseudo-events" for the
purpose of providing news content to audiences: "what the public thinks, or
prefers, is of no importance," explained Debord. "This is what is hidden by
the spectacle of all these opinion polls."

One effect of the spectacle was to collapse history by overwhelming the
public sphere with information, presented as "news," which may or may not
be true, new, or even current. The spectacle's "ceaseless circularity of information, always returning to the same short list of trivialities, passionately proclaimed as major discoveries" actually "organizes ignorance of what is about
to happen and, immediately afterwards, the forgetting of whatever has nonetheless been understood." When information circulates with such frequency
and ubiquity, it is impossible to discern what is important from what is trivial.
Debord believed that ubiquitous information created a smoke screen for hiding crucial information from the public: according to Debord, "[T]he more
important something is, the more it is hidden."

A second effect of the spectacle was to silence opposition, prevent logic
and critical thinking, and inculcate distrust, since without critical thinking
"no one can be sure he is not being tricked or manipulated." The spectacle
"silences anything it finds inconvenient. It isolates all it shows from its context,
its past, its intentions and its consequences. It is thus completely illogical." By
preventing critical thinking, the spectacle turned citizens into "ideologues,"
who demonstrate an "absence of logic, that is to say, loss of the ability immediately to perceive what is significant and what is insignificant or irrelevant,
what is incompatible or what could well be complementary, all that a particular consequence implies and at the same time all that it excludes." Because
there was no information outside of the control of the spectacle, ultimately the
spectators of the spectacle could not escape the spectacle to find information.
The lack of information outside of the spectacle, Debord believed, prevented

spectators from critiquing their government: "[N]ever before has censorship been so perfect. Never before have those who are still led to believe, in a few countries, that they remain free citizens, been less entitled to make their opinions heard, wherever it is a matter of choices affecting their real lives. Never before has it been possible to lie to them so brazenly."

The spectacle's dangerous demagogue uses the power of social media and the tactics of weaponized rhetoric and propaganda to set the agenda, confuse political debate, and marshal supporters to defend the demagogue's positions and overwhelm opposition.[16] Trump is the demagogue of the spectacle—a spectacular demagogue. He plays the spectacle for what it is. He is its creature, its essential qualities. If we put Trump's demagogic rhetorical strategies into a spectacle frame, we ask different questions than if we judge him based on whether or not he is an authoritarian. As a spectacular demagogue, Trump uses strategies that he thinks will make great or compelling TV and dominate the news cycle. He asks: What will attract attention? What will divide people into teams to cheer for (or boo against) the story's main character, Trump? What kinds of plots will distract from other stories? What will drive outrage and engagement?[17] Just like any other brand or app or electronic device, Trump has engineered his demagogic strategies to gain and keep our attention. His "demagogic effectiveness" is thus similar to Hitler's, but also very different. Whereas Hitler's effectiveness was based on totalitarianism and violence, Trump's effectiveness is based on outrage and entertainment.

Trump is the modern-day P. T. Barnum of attracting and keeping our attention, and like Barnum, Trump isn't afraid to use humbug if it suits his strategic goals. We are especially attracted to characters like Trump and Barnum during times of great transition when we feel alienated, things are confusing, and reality can be more easily distorted.[18] Part of the strategy of a showman is to create confusion and distort reality so that audiences are more likely to be misled. The showman's rhetorical strategy is a *legerdemain*—a slight of hand. It's no surprise that on January 10, 2016, Trump told Chuck Todd on *Meet the Press* that he enjoyed being compared to P. T. Barnum. He thought, "We need P. T. Barnum, a little bit, because we have to build up the image of our country."[19] Part of Trump's success was that he dominated the public sphere by saying things so outrageous that we could not look away. Another part of Trump's success was that he dominated the public sphere by saying things so outrageous that we had to respond to him.[20] Trump trolled the nation to win the presidency in 2016.[21]

Ultimately, whether we judge Trump based on the standards of authoritarianism or the spectacle is moot because *both are antidemocratic*. Both rely on compliance-gaining strategies rather than persuasion; both treat people as tools or as pawns; both deny consent and use rhetoric as a strategic means to an end. A political community based on compliance rather than persuasion is oppressive—it's one that none of us want. "How absurd it is to try to change the world by propaganda?" asked Max Horkheimer and Theodor W. Adorno in 1947. "[P]ropaganda makes language an instrument, a lever, a machine. It fixes the condition of men, as they have come to be in under social injustice, by setting them in motion. It counts on being able to count on them. Deep down all men know that through this tool they too will be reduced to a tool as in a factory." Propaganda is but one tactic of the dangerous demagogue, but what is true of propaganda is true for the rest: weaponized rhetoric treats language as an instrument, as a means to an end, and it treats people as tools. Horkheimer and Adorno wrote that propaganda was "misanthropic" because it denied "that policy ought to spring from mutual understanding." Like propaganda, weaponized rhetoric is misanthropic, and it enables dangerous demagogues like Trump to gain compliance and prevent themselves from being held accountable for their words and actions. Weaponized rhetoric treats communication as pure instrumentality, using rhetoric and people as machines. "A community in which the leader and his followers come to terms through propaganda," wrote Horkheimer and Adorno, "is a community of lies."[22]

Over the past several years I've had two phrases in my head. The first is from Eric Hobsbawm, a historian of the era between the two world wars—a time when massive changes in the way we moved, communicated, worked, and organized society, he thought, could best be characterized as "the age of catastrophe." The second is from journalist and public intellectual Max Lerner, writing in 1938 during the age of catastrophe: "[I]t's later than you think," he wrote. Ours is another age of catastrophe, and it might be later than we think too. Lerner's warning deserves to be quoted in full, because it offers us both a stark warning about our present condition and also a way forward:

The political job of our time must be the heroic effort of making our society as safe as possible for the majority principle. . . . When you have made the commonwealth reasonably safe against raids by oligarchies or depredations by individual megalomaniacs; when you have provided the best mechanisms you can contrive for the succession to power, and have hedged both majorities and minorities about with constitutional safeguards of their own devising, then you have done all that the art of politics can ever do. For the rest, insurance against majority tyranny will depend on the health of your economic institutions, the wisdom of your educational processes, the whole ethos and vitality of your culture. If, with all that, the majority within your culture still go berserk and destroy everything of value that the collective life has built up, then scrap the art of government altogether and lock up your libraries.[23]

Part of Trump's rhetorical genius was that he correctly understood one important thing: in 2016 the United States was vulnerable to dangerous demagogues. We were alienated, distrusting, polarized, and frustrated. Trump didn't cause those conditions, but he did take advantage of them. Dangerous demagogues like Trump use rhetoric as a weapon to take advantage of weakened democracies, arguing that only they are the hero who can solve the nation's problems. The way forward is to create and maintain a political community that never reaches crisis levels of alienation—a democracy based upon the majority principle in which people trust one another and their government. Dangerous demagogues like Donald Trump have no power in a properly functioning democracy. This is the political project of our time. We must defend democracy.

Appendix

Chronological List of Trump's Rallies Mentioned In Text

June 16, 2015	New York, NY
July 25, 2015	Oskaloosa, IA
July 27, 2015	Orlando, FL*
August 17, 2015	Columbia, SC*
August 19, 2015	Derry, NH Derry, NH*
August 21, 2015	Mobile, AL
August 25, 2015	Dubuque, IA
August 28, 2015	Norwood, MA
September 12, 2015	Boone, IA
September 15, 2015	Los Angeles, CA
September 30, 2015	Keene, NH
October 3, 2015	Franklin, TN
October 10, 2015	Norcross, GA
November 19, 2015	Newton, IA
November 21, 2015	Birmingham, AL
November 23, 2015	Columbus, OH
November 24, 2015	Myrtle Beach, SC
November 28, 2015	Sarasota, FL

December 1, 2015	Waterville Valley, NH
December 4, 2015	Raleigh, NC
December 5, 2015	Manassas, VA
December 7, 2015	Mount Pleasant, SC
December 21, 2015	Grand Rapids, MI
January 7, 2016	Burlington, VT
January 9, 2016	Clear Lake, IA
January 12, 2016	Cedar Rapids, IA
January 23, 2016	Pella, IA Sioux City, IA
January 24, 2016	Muscatine, IA
January 25, 2016	Farmington, NH Muscatine, IA
January 26, 2016	Iowa City, IA
February 2, 2016	Milford, NH
February 7, 2016	Plymouth, NH
February 12, 2016	Tampa, FL
February 17, 2016	Bluffton, SC Waltersboro, SC
February 22, 2016	Las Vegas, NV
February 28, 2016	Madison, AL
February 29, 2016	Valdosta, GA
March 3, 2016	Portland, ME
March 7, 2016	Concord, NC
March 11, 2016	St. Louis, MO
March 14, 2016	Vienna, OH
March 19, 2016	Tucson, AZ
April 16, 2016	Hartford, CT
April 17, 2016	Staten Island, NY Poughkeepsie, NY
April 18, 2016	Buffalo, NY

April 25, 2016	Wilkes-Barre, PA
May 7, 2016	Lynden, WA Spokane, WA
May 27, 2016	Fresno, CA
June 1, 2016	Newark, NJ[†]
June 2, 2016	San Diego, CA[†] San Jose, CA
June 3, 2016	Westminster, CA[†]
June 15, 2016	Atlanta, GA
July 5, 2016	Cincinnati, OH
July 27, 2016	Scranton, PA
July 29, 2016	Denver, CO
August 1, 2016	Columbus, OH
August 8, 2016	Detroit, MI
August 9, 2016	Wilmington, NC
August 10, 2016	Abingdon, VA
August 12, 2016	Altoona, PA Erie, PA
August 25, 2016	Manchester, NH
October 3, 2016	Pueblo, CO
October 5, 2016	Prescott Valley, AZ
October 10, 2016	Ambridge, PA Wilkes-Barre, PA
October 11, 2016	Panama City, FL
October 13, 2016	West Palm Beach, FL
October 14, 2016	Greensboro, NC
October 15, 2016	Portsmouth, NH
October 17, 2016	Green Bay, WI
October 18, 2016	Colorado Springs, CO
October 20, 2016	Delaware, OH
October 21, 2016	Johnstown, PA

October 22, 2016	Cleveland, OH Gettysburg, PA
October 24, 2016	Tampa, FL
October 27, 2016	Toledo, OH
October 28, 2016	Manchester, NH
October 29, 2016	Phoenix, AZ
October 30, 2016	Albuquerque, NM
October 31, 2016	Grand Rapids, MI
November 1, 2016	Eau Claire, WI
November 2, 2016	Miami, FL
November 6, 2016	Iowa City, IA Sioux City, IA Sterling Heights, MI
November 7, 2016	Scranton, PA
November 8, 2016	New York, NY
December 10, 2016	Grand Rapids, MI

*Jeb Bush rally
†Hillary Clinton rally

Glossary of Rhetorical Terms

American Exceptionalism: The belief that the United States, as a nation, is not only different than other nations but better than other nations; exemplified in Trump's iconic "Make America Great Again" hats.

Apologia: A genre of communication that deals specifically with clearing one's own name or explaining one's motive; a speech of self-defense or image repair.

Argument ad Baculum: Derived from the Latin for "appeal to the stick," arguments *ad baculum* feature a threat of force or intimidation.

Argument ad Hominem: Derived from the Latin for "appeal to the person," arguments *ad hominem* feature an attack against a speaker instead of against their argument.

Argument ad Populum: Derived from the Latin for "appeal to the crowd," arguments *ad populum* feature praise of the audience in order for the speaker to gain credibility and likeability.

Argument ad Verecundiam: Derived from the Latin for "appeal to authority," arguments *ad verecundiam* rest on the testimony of some authority figure as their only evidence ("because I said so," or "because the president said," or "because the Bible says").

Bolstering: The facetious inflation or propping up of a weak or ineffectual idea or plan. Also an apologia strategy of connecting something about yourself with something that the audience already rates highly.

Conspiracy Argument: An argument that draws on the suspected existence of an antagonistic conspiratorial group working against the speaker that can be blamed for the audience's problems.

Constitutive Rhetoric: Similar to framing, constitutive rhetoric calls a person, idea, or object into being, providing a way for that person, idea, or object to be understood.

Context: The interdependent web of circumstances that surround any given person, thought, or event and determine its meaning(s).

Corruption: The intentional destruction of some entity's purity.

Demagogue: As hero: a political leader who defends the rights of the people against corruption. As villain: an uncontrollable political leader who weaponizes rhetoric to gain and maintain power.

Demagoguery: Any techniques used by a demagogue that are characteristic of their being a demagogue (for example, the abuse of language to incite a crowd).

Division: The process of polarizing oneself from a group or individual based on real or perceived differences of interest, ideology, or background.

Eloquence: A term used to describe speech or writing, whose construction is particularly or exceedingly memorable or apt.

Ethos: Drawing on or relating to one's inherent, personal credibility to speak persuasively on a certain subject.

Figure of Speech: Any linguistic construction whose role is to enhance the meaning of its text.

Framing: The process of highlighting one or a few characteristics of a topic in order to effect perception—public or individual—of that person, event, or thing. By deciding how the public sees a person, a framer can decide how the public thinks about a person.

Gaslighting: The intentional act of calling into question another's perceptions of reality; coined in the 1938 play *Gas Light*.

Genre: A class of discursive speech or writing that can be linked by a common style, argument, structure, and/or situation.

Gravitas: With roots that link it to "gravity," *gravitas* refers to the "gravity" of one's speech or presence; a certain importance of person that creates a grandeur of speech.

Hubris: Pride or self-confidence, often in such excess that it leads to the hero's downfall.

Hyperbole: An exaggeration of the truth for dramatic or rhetorical effect.

Identification: The process of linking oneself to a group or individual based on real or perceived commonalities of interest, ideology, or background.

Kairos: Literally translated to "fullness of time," kairos indicates an opportune moment—the perfect time in which to take action.

Logos: One of three means of proof used in rhetoric, generally drawing on an appeal to logic or rationality.

Paralipsis: Literally translated as "to leave to the side," *paralipsis* can now be best understood with the phrase "I'm not saying; I'm just saying." *Paralipsis* involves affirming something in the very act of denying it.

Parrhesia: Loosely translated as "fearless speech," *parrhesia* encompasses the act of telling the full truth, including frankness, truth, danger, criticism, and duty.

Parrhesiastes: Loosely translated from Greek to mean "fearless truth teller," a *parrhesiastes* is one who speaks *parrhesia*.

Pathos: One of three means of proof used in rhetoric, generally drawing on the emotionality of the audience.

Propaganda: The intentional, systematic diffusion of misleading, biased, or false claims via the mass media such that the originating group benefits by the endeavor.

Red Herring: A distraction technique in which one bit of information receives attention that would more reasonably be attributed to a larger scandal or event.

Reification: From the Latin for "thing," reification describes a general "thin-gifying" of people or persons, especially those identified as the speaker's enemies.

Rhetoric: The artful implementation of language, especially figures of speech, in order to communicate one's argument effectively and eloquently. A method of decision-making in the absence of absolute truth.

Sign Arguments: An argument in which one event is considered a clue to or symptom of another event; that the first phenomenon is capable of evoking the second; never indicative of a causal relationship.

Synecdoche: A figure of speech in which a part of an object is substituted for the whole, or vice versa; as in "fifty heads" for "fifty cows."

Tone: Distinct from a speech or speaker's content, tone is identifiable as any element of discourse that illustrates the speaker's attitude toward the subject matter, including diction, delivery, and other rhetorical devices.

Trope: A figure of speech that refers to the figurative sense of a word or phrase; some meaning that is distinct from the usual meaning, as in the trope of American exceptionalism.

Tu Quoque: Latin for "you also." An appeal to hypocrisy used to deny standing in debate. Sometimes referred to as "both siderism"—as in "They do is worse than me, so what's the problem?"

Notes

Preface

1. According to the *New York Times* editorial board on November 24, 2015, "This isn't about shutting off Mr. Trump's bullhorn. His right to spew nonsense is protected by the Constitution, but the public doesn't need to swallow it. History teaches that failing to hold a demagogue to account is a dangerous act. It's no easy task for journalists to interrupt Mr. Trump with the facts, but it's an important one." "Mr. Trump's Applause Lies," *New York Times*, November 24, 2015, https://www.nytimes.com/2015/11/24/opinion/mr-trumps-applause-lies.html.

2. Kenneth Burke, *A Rhetoric of Motives* (Los Angeles: University of California Press, 1969); Kenneth Burke, "The Rhetoric of Hitler's Battle," *The Philosophy of Literary Form: Studies in Symbolic Action* (New York: Vintage Books, 1957), 164–89.

3. Patrick Healy and Maggie Haberman, "95,000 Words, Many of Them Ominous, from Donald Trump's Tongue," *New York Times*, December 6, 2015, https://www.nytimes.com/2015/12/06/us/politics/95000-words-many-of-them-ominous-from-donald-trumps-tongue.html.

4. Jennifer Mercieca, "The Rhetorical Brilliance of Trump the Demagogue," The Conversation, December 11, 2015, https://theconversation.com/the-rhetorical-brilliance-of-trump-the-demagogue-51984.

5. Joe Matthews, "Almost Any Politician in a Democracy Is a Bit of a Demagogue," Zocalo Public Square, June 22, 2016, https://www.zocalopublicsquare.org/2016/06/22/almost-any-politician-in-a-democracy-is-a-bit-of-a-demagogue/events/the-takeaway/.

6. Ann Coulter (@AnnCoulter), "NYT '"His entire campaign is run like a demagogue's," said Jennifer Mercieca, an expert in Amer political discourse @ Texas A&M.' An expert!" Twitter, December 6, 2015, https://twitter.com/AnnCoulter/status/673768238258511873; "Video: Watch Alex Jones Crash Anti-Alex Jones/Trump Event in Austin," InfoWars, September 29, 2018, https://www.infowars.com/video-watch-alex-jones-crash-anti-alex-jones-trump-event-in-austin/?fbclid=IwAR0AGIrv8eKPHyltyiJpPue2boN5TmWBHbyoX0BQThjPEZ4Mt2xKQrVGAZE.

7. Jonathon Tilove, "6 Rhetorical Devices That Have Served Trump Well," Statesman, October 21, 2018, https://www.statesman.com/news/20181021/6-rhetorical-devices-that-have-served-trump-well.

Introduction

1. Ben Terris, "Donald Trump Begins 2016 Bid, Citing His Outsider Status," *Washington Post*, June 16, 2015, https://www.washingtonpost.com/politics/donald-trump-is-now-a-candidate-for-president-of-the-united-states/2015/06/16/5e6d738e-1441-11e5-9ddc-e3353542100c_story.html?postshare=3651434500633671&utm_term=.feb1132f8954.

2. Angelo Carusone, "Donald Trump Hired Paid Actors to Attend Presidential Launch Event," Medium, June 16, 2015, https://medium.com/@GoAngelo/donald-trump-hired-paid-actors-to-attend-presidential-launch-event-7c65e8fadea0#.nzz3nj2f4; Aaron Couch and Emmet McDermott, "Donald Trump Campaign Offered Actors $50 to Cheer for Him at Presidential Announcement," *The Hollywood Reporter*, June 17, 2015, http://www.hollywoodreporter.com/news/donald-trump-campaign-offered-actors-803161; Kieran Corcoran, "Donald Trump Accused of Hiring Actors for $50 Each to Pose as Supporters at Trump Towers Presidential Campaign Launch," *Daily Mail*, June 17, 2015, http://www.dailymail.co.uk/news/article-3128230/Did-Donald-Trump-hire-paid-actors-presidential-campaign-launch-Claims-professionals-extras-brought-pose-supporters.html#ixzz4KSIsBEwc; Rachel Maddow, "GOP's Trump Problem a Monster of Their Own Creation," MSNBC, June 17, 2015, http://www.msnbc.com/rachel-maddow/watch/donald-trump-a-problem-of-gops-own-making-467035203551. According to a Trump campaign press release, "Mr. Trump was joined by his immediate family and stood before thousands of supporters to declare his candidacy for the 2016 GOP Presidential nomination." "Donald J. Trump Declares Candidacy for President of the United States," June 16, 2015, https://www.donaldjtrump.com/press-releases/donald-j.-trump-declares-candidacy-for-president-of-the-united-states. In addition, Trump political adviser Sam Nunberg indicated, "We could have had women in bikinis, elephants and clowns there, for all I care. . . . It would have been the most gloriously disgusting event you've ever seen, as a way to, like, be a complete 'fuck you' to the system." Michael Kruse, "The Escalator Ride That Changed America," Politico, June 14, 2019, https://www.politico.com/magazine/story/2019/06/14/donald-trump-campaign-announcement-tower-escalator-oral-history-227148.

3. "Donald Trump Presidential Announcement Full Speech," YouTube video, 51:14, filmed on June 16, 2015, Posted by Donald J. Trump for President, https://www.youtube.com/watch?v=q_q61B-DyPk; Tobias Salinger, "Rock Legend Neil Young Slams Donald Trump's Use of 'Rockin' in the Free World' for Campaign Announcement," *New York Daily News*, June 17, 2015, http://www.nydailynews.com/entertainment/music/neil-young-slams-donald-trump-song-campaign-article-1.2260711; Lilly Maier, "We Visited Trump Tower, and It Perfectly Epitomizes Its Eccentric, Contradictory Owner," Quartz, March 24, 2016, http://qz.com/646029/we-visited-trump-tower-and-it-perfectly-epitomizes-its-eccentric-contradictory-owner/. Donald Trump is a man who lives on the sixty-eighth floor of a fifty-eight-floor building. The *New York Times* reports that there are actually fifty-eight floors, but Trump requested that the floor numbers be augmented so that the building would

appear to have more floors than the GM Building. Vivian Yee, "Donald Trump's Math Takes His Towers to Greater Heights," *New York Times,* November 1, 2016, http://www.nytimes.com/2016/11/02/nyregion/donald-trump-tower-heights.html?_r=0; Ivanka Trump (@IvankaTrump), "I was honored to introduce my father today as he made a major announcement: http://bit.ly/1LfjFBY #MakeAmericaGreatAgain @realDonaldTrump," Twitter, June 16, 2015, https://twitter.com/IvankaTrump/status/610958193016094720.

4. Hunter Walker, "Donald Trump Got Only 8 Words into His Campaign before We Found a Seriously Questionable Fact," Business Insider, June 16, 2015, http://www.businessinsider.com/problem-with-the-first-8-words-of-donald-trumps-speech-2015-6.

5. Donald J. Trump, "Donald Trump Presidential Campaign Announcement," C-SPAN, recorded June 16, 2015, https://www.c-span.org/video/?326473-1/donald-trump-presidential-campaign-announcement. There is much discrepancy between Trump's estimate of the crowd in attendance and reporters' estimates. Reporter Hunter Walker put the crowd at about three hundred, while Trump's campaign estimated between one thousand and three thousand people. Walker, "Donald Trump Got Only 8 Words into His Campaign before We Found a Seriously Questionable Fact."

6. Alexander Burns, "Donald Trump, Pushing Someone Rich, Offers Himself," *New York Times*, June 15, 2016, http://www.nytimes.com/2015/06/17/us/politics/donald-trump-runs-for-president-this-time-for-real-he-says.html?_r=0.

7. Phillip Bump, "Donald Trump's Spectacular, Unending, Utterly Baffling, Often-Wrong Campaign Launch," *Washington Post*, June 16, 2015, https://www.washingtonpost.com/news/the-fix/wp/2015/06/16/donald-trumps-spectacular-unending-utterly-baffling-often-wrong-campaign-announcement/?utm_term=.6fd8b8097ba1.

8. "Donald Trump may be the man America needs. Having been through four bankruptcies, the ridiculous buffoon with the worst taste since Caligula is uniquely positioned to lead the most indebted organization in the history of the human race." Kevin D. Williamson, "Witless Ape Rides Escalator," *National Review*, June 16, 2015, http://www.nationalreview.com/article/419853/witless-ape-rides-escalator-kevin-d-williamson; Christopher Buckley, "What Would William F. Buckley Have Made of Donald Trump?" *Vanity Fair*, December 5, 2016, http://www.vanityfair.com/news/2016/12/what-would-william-f-buckley-have-made-of-donald-trump.

9. Simon Maloy, "The Puckered Sleazebag Takes the Plunge: Donald Trump Is (Not Officially) Running for President," Salon, June 16, 2015, http://www.salon.com/2015/06/16/the_puckered_sleazebag_takes_the_plunge_donald_trump_is_not_officially_running_for_president/.

10. "8 of the Sleaziest Things Donald Trump Has Said," *Rolling Stone*, June 16, 2015, http://www.rollingstone.com/politics/news/8-of-the-sleaziest-things-donald-trump-has-said-20150616.

11. Phillip Bump, "Donald Trump's Spectacular, Unending, Utterly Baffling, Often-Wrong Campaign Launch," *Washington Post*, June 16, 2015, https://www.washingtonpost.

com/news/the-fix/wp/2015/06/16/donald-trumps-spectacular-unending-utterly-baffling-often-wrong-campaign-announcement/?utm_term=.6fd8b8097ba1; Olivia Nuzzi, "Trump to U.S.: 'I Am Rich,' Hire Me," *Daily Beast*, June 16, 2015, http://www.thedailybeast.com/articles/2015/06/16/trump-to-run-for-president-of-not-china-broken-dreamless-nation.html.

12. Annie Karni and Adam B. Lerner, "Trump Says He's Running for President, Really," Politico, June 16, 2015, http://www.politico.com/story/2015/06/donald-trump-2016-presidential-run-224432; Igor Bobic, "Donald Trump Is Actually Running for President. God Help Us All," *Huffington Post*, June 16, 2015, http://www.huffingtonpost.com/2015/06/16/donald-trump-president_n_7595438.html.

13. Tom McKay, "15 Head-Scratching Quotes from Donald Trump's Presidential Announcement Speech," Mic, June 16, 2015, https://mic.com/articles/120785/best-quotes-from-donald-trumps-2016-presidential-announcement-speech#.4Ukn1Nojd; Craig McCarthy, "11 Controversial Things Donald Trump Said During His Presidential Announcement," NJ.com, June 16, 2015, http://www.nj.com/news/index.ssf/2015/06/11_interesting_things_donald_trump_said_during_his_presidential_announcement.html; Jessica Mendoza, "The Best Lines from Donald Trump's Unusual Presidential Announcement," *Christian Science Monitor*, June 16, 2015, http://www.csmonitor.com/usa/usa-update/2015/0616/the-best-lines-from-donald-trump-s-unusual-presidential-announcement-video; Adam B. Lerner, "The 10 Best Lines from Donald Trump's Announcement Speech," Politico, June 16, 2015, http://www.politico.com/story/2015/06/donald-trump-2016-announcement-10-best-lines-119066; Paula Mejia, "A Roundup of Everyone Donald Trump Upset in His Announcement Speech," *Newsweek*, June 17, 2015, http://www.newsweek.com/round-everyone-donald-trump-upset-his-announcement-speech-344032.

14. Hope Hicks, "Donald J. Trump Declares Candidacy for President of the United States," June 16, 2015, https://www.donaldjtrump.com/press-releases/donald-j.-trump-declares-candidacy-for-president-of-the-united-states.

15. Thomas Novelly (@TomNovelly), "If Donald wins the presidency he'll host another season of celebrity apprentice to fill his cabinet," Twitter, June 16, 2015, https://twitter.com/TomNovelly/status/610830203561099264?ref_src=twsrc%5Etfw.

16. Abby Johnston (@ajohnston12), "Donald Trump sounds like America's drunk conservative uncle. #Trump2016," Twitter, June 16, 2015, https://twitter.com/ajohnston12/status/610827080041783296?ref_src=twsrc%5Etfw.

17. Dan Pfeiffer (@danpfeiffer), "The Trump candidacy is a Veep storyline that would have been discarded for being too absurd even for an HBO comedy," Twitter, June 16, 2015, https://twitter.com/danpfeiffer/status/610827202842660865?ref_src=twsrc%5Etfw.

18. Albert Brooks (@AlbertBrooks), "Donald Trump announces this morning that he will run for president. His hair will announce on Friday," Twitter, June 16, 2015, https://twitter.com/AlbertBrooks/status/610834177223626752?ref_src=twsrc%5Etfw; Dub (@WMsDiary), "if you're old, white, and lost all concept of reality, there isn't a better time to run for the Republican Presidential nomination," Twitter, June 16, 2015, https://twitter.com/WMsDiary/

status/610837020353691649?ref_src=twsrc%5Etfw; Eliot Nelson, "Drunk Guy Next To You At Bar Launches Presidential Campaign," Twitter, June 16, 2015, https://twitter.com/eliotnelson/status/610833080631316481?ref_src=twsrc%5Etfw.

19. Fox Nation (@foxnation), "Editorial: Trump Delivers a Message Republicans Need bit.ly/1J4jtlp #DonaldTrump #Trump2016," Twitter, June 17, 2015, https://twitter.com/foxnation/status/611154696321896448; *New York Post* Editorial Board, "Editorial: Trump Delivers a Message Republicans Need," Fox Nation, June 17, 2015, http://nation.foxnews.com/2015/06/17/editorial-trump-delivers-message-republicans-need.

20. Saltwater Patricia (@muzikgirl11), "I love it. We need someone like him who's not afraid to tell it like it is #MakeAmericaGreatAgain," Twitter, June 16, 2015, https://twitter.com/muzikgirl11/status/610955066787233792.

21. Dawn Carrubba (@DawnCarrubba), "@greta @realDonaldTrump #greta If anyone can #MakeAmericaGreatAgain he can! If given the chance he will do great things for our country!" Twitter, June 16, 2015, https://twitter.com/DawnCarrubba/status/610948460603404288.

22. Peter Enimil (@peter_enimil), "Being a President is like owning a business. You need a way better CEO and who is better than @realDonaldTrump? Lets #MakeAmericaGreatAgain," Twitter, June 16, 2015, https://twitter.com/peter_enimil/status/610953371953045505; Peter Enimil (@peter_enimil), "@realDonaldTrump I will tweet #MAGA #MakeAmericaGreatAgain #DonaldTrump4Prez #Jobs4All #GoodlifeUSA everyday until even after the elections," Twitter, June 16, 2015, https://twitter.com/peter_enimil/status/610951277024014337. In this tweet, Enimil promised to continue to tweet supportive Trump hashtags until "even after the elections." (He didn't.) I asked him why he didn't make good on his promise, and he responded, "Honestly, I could not because I actually left my twitter account unused. Left if for someone to handle it for an event," Twitter, December 12, 2016, https://twitter.com/peter_enimil/status/808391893314928642.

23. Now deleted and unarchived: Proud Boy Nick, https://twitter.com/ProudBoyNick/status/610945602118098944.

24. Now deleted and unarchived: Sarah Carlson, https://twitter.com/sarcarlso/status/610939902595764224.

25. These reports of search interest and comments may very well be inflated by "bots"—computer programs that mimic actual people on social media—and by strategic attempts to game the search interest algorithm. Geoff Earle, "Trump Is Crushing the Social (Media) Scene," *New York Post*, June 17, 2015, http://nypost.com/2015/06/17/trump-is-crushing-the-social-media-scene/. Hope Hicks, "Trump Smashes Social Records Following Presidential Announcement," Democracy in Action, June 17, 2015, http://www.p2016.org/trump/trump061615sp.html.

26. I'm indebted to my political science colleague Joe Ura for this take on the fundamentals: Daniel W. Drezner, "Why Political Science Is Not an Election Casualty," *Washington Post*, November 15, 2016, https://www.washingtonpost.com/posteverything/wp/2016/11/15/

why-political-science-is-not-an-election-casualty/?utm_term=.4d55401685e9.

27. Elspeth Reeve, "Donald Trump Is America's Most Gifted Satirist," The New Republic, June 16, 2015, https://newrepublic.com/article/122047/donald-trump-americas-most-gifted-political-satirist.

28. Michel Foucault, *Fearless Speech* (Cambridge, MA: MIT Press, 2001).

29. Eric Zorn, "Donald Trump? Seriously? Yes, Seriously," *Chicago Tribune,* June 30, 2015, http://www.chicagotribune.com/news/nationworld/ct-donald-trump-republicans-primary-perpect-0701-20150630-column.html.

30. "Lindsey Graham: Trump Is a 'Wrecking Ball,'" CNN video, http://www.cnn.com/videos/politics/2015/07/12/sotu-tapper-lindsey-graham-trump-is-a-wrecking-ball.cnn; Former Texas governor Rick Perry likewise accused Trump of demagoguery calling Trump's tactics a "barking carnival act" and a "toxic mix of demagoguery, mean-spiritedness and nonsense." Abby Livingston, "Perry Rips Trump in Washington Speech," *Texas Tribune,* July 22, 2015, https://www.texastribune.org/2015/07/22/rick-perry-donald-trump-dc/; Referring to an earlier Perry interview, Trump tweeted, "@GovernorPerry just gave a pollster quote on me. He doesn't understand what the word demagoguery means." Donald J. Trump (@realDonaldTrump), Twitter, July 16, 2015, https://twitter.com/realDonaldTrump/status/621783444083884037.

31. Chris Moody, "Donald Trump Gave Out Lindsey Graham's Personal Cell Number to America," CNN, July 22, 2015, http://www.cnn.com/2015/07/21/politics/donald-trump-lindsey-graham-cell-phone/. By August 25, 2015, Trump gleefully tweeted his faux congratu-lations to Graham for his dismal showing in a poll of primary voters in South Carolina: "Con-grats @LindseyGrahamSC. You just got 4 points in your home state of SC—far better than zero nationally. You're only 26 pts behind me." Eugene Scott, "GOP Primary Poll: Donald Trump Leads in South Carolina," CNN, August 25, 2015, http://www.cnn.com/2015/08/25/politics/donald-trump-poll-south-carolina/; Donald J. Trump (@realDonaldTrump), "Con-grats @LindseyGrahamSC. You just got 4 points in your home state of SC—far better than zero nationally. You're only 26 pts behind me," Twitter, August 25, 2015, https://twitter.com/realDonaldTrump/status/636173679093747713. Graham dropped out of the GOP primary on December 21, 2015. Kalie Glueck, "Lindsey Graham Drops Out of Presidential Race," Politico, December 21, 2015, http://www.politico.com/story/2015/12/lindsey-graham-sus-pends-presidential-campaign-217028.

32. M. J. Lee, "Donald Trump: As President, 'I'll Change My Tone,'" CNN Politics, July 23, 2015, http://www.cnn.com/2015/07/22/politics/donald-trump-anderson-cooper/.

33. Vaughn Hillyard, "Cruz Reaffirms Commitment to Trump—If Nominee—Despite 'Demagogery,'" NBC News, March 13, 2016, http://www.nbcnews.com/meet-the-press/cruz-reaffirms-commitment-trump-if-nominee-despite-demagoguery-n537481; Lisa Lerer, "AP Interview: Clinton Says Trump Behaving Like a Demagogue," Associated Press, June 9, 2016, http://bigstory.ap.org/article/633669d8eb1d4648b79777400e1ba5b4/ap-interview-clinton-says-trump-behaving-demagogue; Editorial Board, "Trump Is 'Unfit for

the Presidency,'" *USA Today*, September 29, 2016, http://www.usatoday.com/story/opin-ion/2016/09/29/dont-vote-for-donald-trump-editorial-board-editorials-debates/91295020/; Editorial Board, "Against Donald Trump," *The Atlantic*, November 2016, http://www.theatlantic.com/magazine/archive/2016/11/the-case-for-hillary-clinton-and-against-donald-trump/501161/; Eric DuVall, "LA Times Endorses Hillary Clinton, Calls Trump 'Demagogue,'" UPI, September 23, 2016, http://www.upi.com/top_news/us/2016/09/23/la-times-endorses-hillary-clinton-calls-trump-demagogue/3881474635873/; Editorial Board, "The New Yorker Endorses Hillary Clinton," *New Yorker*, October 31, 2016, http://www.newyorker.com/magazine/2016/10/31/the-new-yorker-endorses-hillary-clinton.

34. "Reporters like to think that logic and reason hold sway, so they believe a dema-gogue can be easily disarmed by exposing his crimes against logic, his pandering to the unin-formed and his manipulative emotionalism. They're entirely wrong. . . . If anything, establish-ment attacks on a demagogue only stiffen the loyalties of his subjects, proving to them that he is telling truth to power. The demagogue's formula, which can vary, tends to simplify all politics and policy to single irrefutable talking points. In Trump's case, he reliably heralds himself as a 'smart' man who can solve problems the 'stupid' people of Washington can't by the pure force of his own will." Jack Shafer, "Donald Trump, American Demagogue," Politico, August 10, 2015, http://www.politico.com/magazine/story/2015/08/dont-write-trumps-obit-yet-121232.

35. "I have thought him a clown—not stupid, but neither funny nor nice. Now I fear he is a demagogue. When a leader (or would-be leader) appeals to emotions and prejudices rather than intellect and reasoning, or spews vitriol rather than hope, and when he (or she) appeals to those who prefer to be led rather than guided, the ground is set for demagoguery." Sydney Williams, "Trump Is a Demagogue," Breitbart News, August 27, 2015, http://www.breitbart.com/big-government/2015/08/27/williams-trump-is-a-demagogue/.

36. This was the first endorsement in *USA Today*'s thirty-four-year history (although they did not actually endorse Trump's Democratic opponent Hillary Clinton). Editorial Board, "Trump Is 'Unfit for The Presidency,'" *USA Today*, September 26, 2016, http://www.usatoday.com/story/opinion/2016/09/29/dont-vote-for-donald-trump-editorial-board-edito-rials-debates/91295020/.

37. Ian Schwartz, "David Brooks: Trump 'The Sort of Demagogue Our Founders Feared Would Upset the American Experiment,'" Real Clear Politics, March 19, 2016, http://www.realclearpolitics.com/video/2016/03/19/david_brooks_trump_the_sort_of_dema-gogue_our_founders_feared_would_upset_the_american_experiment.html.

38. Tom Sykes, "Even Stephen Hawking Can't Explain Donald Trump," *The Daily Beast*, May 31, 2016, http://www.thedailybeast.com/even-stephen-hawking-cant-explain-donald-trump.

39. "That's why anyone who threatens our values, whether fascists or communists or jihadists or homegrown demagogues, will always fail in the end." Barack Obama, "Remarks at the Democratic National Convention," The American Presidency Project, July 27, 2016,

http://www.presidency.ucsb.edu/ws/index.php?pid=118049&st=democratic+national+conv
ention&st1. According to Michael Bloomberg, July 27, 2016, "And we must unite around the
candidate who can defeat a dangerous demagogue." M. J. Lee and Tom LoBianco, "Michael
Bloomberg Endorses Clinton, Calls Trump a 'Dangerous Demagogue,'" CNN, July 28, 2016,
http://www.cnn.com/2016/07/27/politics/michael-bloomberg-dem-convention-speech/.

40. Lisa Lerer, "AP Interview: Clinton Says Trump Behaving Like a Demagogue,"
Associated Press, June 9, 2016, http://bigstory.ap.org/article/633669d8eb1d4648b7977740
0e1ba5b4/ap-interview-clinton-says-trump-behaving-demagogue. German philosopher Leo
Strauss—himself a Jewish refugee from Hitler—dismissed what he called the *argumentum ad
Hitlerum* as a cheap debating trick: "A view is not refuted by the fact that it happens to have
been shared by Hitler." Michael Lind, "Quit Comparing Trump to Hitler!" Politico, March 8,
2016, http://www.politico.com/magazine/story/2016/03/trump-hitler-comparisons-213711;
"Reductio ad Hitlerum," Fallacious, https://www.logicallyfallacious.com/tools/lp/bo/logical-
fallacies/152/reductio-ad-hitlerum. Of course Godwin's law tells us that all internet debates
will eventually end in someone comparing someone to Hitler, but that doesn't mean that we
shouldn't make apt historical comparisons between, say, the rhetorical techniques used by
Hitler and those used by Trump. I asked Mike Godwin to clarify his law, and he assured me
that accurate historical parallel cases do not violate his law. Dr. Jennifer Mercieca (@jenmer-
cieca), "This discussion has made me wonder something: @sfmnemonic does your law mean
that we can't make accurate historical comparisons as a parallel case? I understand the basic
principle about internet arguments, but you weren't suggesting no Nazi comparisons at all,
were you?" reply to @ThatIronFist, Twitter, April 5, 2019, https://twitter.com/jenmercieca/
status/1114156558940811264.

41. Philly Daily News (@PhillyDailyNews), "Today's Daily News, 12/08/15
#DNFrontpage," Twitter, December 8, 2015, https://twitter.com/PhillyDailyNews/
status/674182386423365632?ref_src=twsrc%5Etfw.

42. Meghan Keneally, "Donald Trump Shrugs Off Hitler Comparison," ABC News,
December 8, 2015, http://abcnews.go.com/Politics/donald-trump-shrugs-off-hitler-compari-
son/story?id=35645113; "Stephanopoulos Points Out Trump Is Being 'Compared to Hitler,'
Trump Suggests He Is More Like FDR," originally recorded for *Good Morning America*,
reposted on Media Matters, December 8, 2015, http://mediamatters.org/video/2015/12/08/
stephanopoulos-points-out-trump-is-being-compar/207334.

43. Donald J. Trump (@realDonaldTrump), "@GovernorPerry just gave a pollster quote
on me. He doesn't understand what the word demagoguery means," Twitter, July 16, 2015,://
twitter.com/realDonaldTrump/status/621783444083884037?ref_src=twsrc%5Etfw.

44. With my grateful thanks to Patricia Roberts-Miller, who helped me understand
why "demagoguery" is a noun and not a verb. "demagoguery, n.," *Oxford English Dictionary
Online*, September 2019, https://www.oed.com/view/Entry/49575.

45. For more on constitutive rhetoric, see Jim Jasinski and Jennifer R. Mercieca, "Ana-
lyzing Constitutive Rhetoric," in *The Handbook of Rhetoric and Public Address*, eds. Shawn J.

Parry-Giles and J. Michael Hogan (Oxford: Wiley-Blackwell, 2010).

46. Foucault, *Fearless Speech*, 19.

47. "Donald Trump's File," Politifact, accessed December 27, 2016, http://www. politifact.com/personalities/donald-trump/. According to one reporter, "We used to fact-check everything, every day," another reporter told me, "but it gets hard to keep up." For a writer filing on deadline an hour after a rally ends, there's not enough time to thoroughly fact-check the dozens of fabrications that spilled from the stage. It's also hard to know who the fact-checking is for. At this point, anyone who hates Trump has ample evidence he's a liar. And anyone who loves Trump doesn't care." Seth Stevenson, "A Week on the Trail with the 'Disgusting Reporters' Covering Donald Trump," *Slate*, March 20, 2016, http://www.slate. com/articles/news_and_politics/cover_story/2016/03/on_the_trail_with_donald_trump_s_ disgusting_press_corps.html.

48. Matt Taibbi, "How America Made Donald Trump Unstoppable," *Rolling Stone*, February 24, 2016, http://www.rollingstone.com/politics/news/how-america-made-donald-trump-unstoppable-20160224.

49. Marc Fisher, "Donald Trump, Remade by Reality TV," *Washington Post*, January 27, 2016, http://www.washingtonpost.com/sf/national/2016/01/27/deciders-trump/.

50. Patrick Radden Keefe, "How Mark Burnett Resurrected Donald Trump as an Icon of American Success," *New Yorker*, December 27, 2018, https://www.newyorker.com/ magazine/2019/01/07/how-mark-burnett-resurrected-donald-trump-as-an-icon-of-american-success.

51. Michael Kruse, "The Executive Mr. Trump," *Politico Magazine*, July/August 2016, https://www.politico.com/magazine/story/2016/07/2016-donald-trump-boss-employer-company-hired-fired-employees-workers-management-business-214020.

52. "The key to the video blogs was that I wanted them to not feel professional but feel like your friend's video blog, in a very social media type of way, which meant no lighting, no professional camera, no backdrop. I just wanted them to be real, right from his desk and in your face." Natan Edelsburg, "Exclusive: An Interview with Justin McConney, Trump's Director of Social Media," The Drum, September 22, 2015, http://www.thedrum.com/ news/2015/09/22/exclusive-interview-justin-mcconney-trump-s-director-social-media. Another take on McConney's interview is here: Barbara Nonas, "The Secret Sauce behind Donald Trump's Social Media Success," *Huffington Post*, February 8, 2017, http://www. huffingtonpost.com/advertising-week/the-secret-sauce-behind-d_b_9191280.html; Chris Breikss, "The Power of Social Media: How Trump Haters Help His Marketing Campaign," *Forbes*, August 1, 2016, http://www.forbes.com/sites/forbesagencycouncil/2016/08/01/the-power-of-social-media-how-trump-haters-help-his-marketing-campaign/#23a7730310c0.

53. Scavino reported Trump's social media statistics to Breitbart: "His Facebook page reached more than 21 billion impressions—21,031,446,611 to be exact—from the day Trump launched his campaign until November 22, 2016. There were more than 485 million engagements on his Facebook page during that timeframe, and nearly 50 million 'likes.' On

videos his team posted on Facebook, they have had, Scavino told Breitbart News, more than 1.3 billion views. On Twitter, Trump achieved similar numbers. Scavino told Breitbart News that between June 2015 and November 2016, Trump's Twitter posts have had nearly 9 billion impressions and more than 400 million engagements. Trump's Twitter account now has 16.2 million followers, and his Facebook account has 15.6 million likes. His Instagram account has 4.2 million followers. Between the three, that's 36 million people his personal social media accounts reach." Matthew Boyle, "Under the Hood: How Donald Trump Has Cut around Corporate Media to Reach Millions Directly Online," Breitbart News, November 29, 2016, http://www.breitbart.com/big-government/2016/11/29/exclusive-how-trump-bypasses-corporate-media-reach-millions/.

54. Aristotle, *On Rhetoric: A Theory of Civic Discourse*, ed. George A. Kennedy (New York: Oxford University Press, 1991), 253.

55. Tony Schwartz (@tonyschwartz), "I wrote the Art of the Deal. Donald Trump read it," Twitter, September 16, 2015, https://twitter.com/tonyschwartz/status/644304700884582400.

56. Jane Mayer, "Donald Trump's Ghostwriter Tells All," *New Yorker*, July 25, 2016, http://www.newyorker.com/magazine/2016/07/25/donald-trumps-ghostwriter-tells-all; Mike LaBossiere, "Trump and Truthful Hyperbole," *Talking Philosophy*, December 4, 2015, http://blog.talkingphilosophy.com/?p=9080.

57. "Trump speaks in a direct manner, with simple words and sentences, a style that comes across as authentic and trustworthy." Jeff Hancock, "Trump's Bullsh*t: Why His Supporters Don't Care That He's Lying," CNN, October 17, 2016, http://money.cnn.com/2016/10/17/technology/donald-trump-deception/.

58. Salena Zito, "Taking Trump Seriously, Not Literally," *The Atlantic*, September 23, 2016, http://www.theatlantic.com/politics/archive/2016/09/trump-makes-his-case-in-pittsburgh/501335/.

59. Ryan Skinnell, "What Passes for Truth in the Trump Era: Telling It Like It Isn't," *Faking the News: What Rhetoric Can Teach Us about Donald J. Trump*, ed. Ryan Skinnell (Exeter: Imprint Academic, 2018), 77.

60. Jacques Ranciere, *Hatred of Democracy*, trans. Steve Corcoran (Brooklyn: Verso Books, 2009).

61. Kate Reilly, "Read Hillary Clinton's 'Basket of Deplorables' Remarks about Donald Trump Supporters," *Time*, September 10, 2016, http://time.com/4486502/hillary-clinton-basket-of-deplorables-transcript/.

62. "demagogue, n.," *Oxford English Dictionary* Online, accessed December 2016, http://www.oed.com/view/Entry/49573?rskey=jfJJbc&result=1. The OED also notes that "demagogue" could be used as a verb, but that sense of the word suffers from the dreadful tendency of verbing nouns, which ought to be rejected.

63. Aristotle, *Politics*, trans. H. Rackham (Cambridge, MA: Harvard University Press, 1944); Plato, *Republic*, trans. Paul Shorey (Cambridge, MA: Harvard University Press, 1969).

64. M. I. Finley, "Athenian Demagogues," *Past & Present* 21, no. 1 (April 1962): 3–24.

65. Ernest Barker, trans., *The Politics of Aristotle* (Oxford University Press, 1962), 169, n. 50.

66. Steven Levitsky and Daniel Ziblatt, *How Democracies Die: What History Reveals about Our Future* (London: Viking, 2018), 23–24.

67. Aristotle, *Rhetoric*, trans. J. H. Freese (Cambridge, MA: Harvard University Press, 192).

68. Joshua Gunn, "Donald Trump's Perverse Political Rhetoric," *Faking the News: What Rhetoric Can Teach Us about Donald J. Trump*, ed. Ryan Skinnell (Exeter: Imprint Academic Ltd, 2018), 163;. Joshua Gunn, *Political Perversion: Rhetorical Aberration in the Time of Trumpeteering* (Chicago: University of Chicago Press, 2020).

69. Patricia Roberts-Miller, *Demagoguery and Democracy* (New York: The Experiment, 2017), 33.

70. Jason Stanley, *How Propaganda Works* (Princeton, NJ: Princeton University Press, 2016), 53.

71. As Cicero observed, the most notorious example of someone using rhetoric to deny rhetoric belongs to Plato, who repeatedly had Socrates use rhetoric to deny the value of rhetoric compared to philosophy.

72. "Donald Trump Explains Being a 'Counter-Puncher,'" Fox News video, May 26, 2018, http://video.foxnews.com/v/4914523692001/?#sp=show-clips.

73. Frans H. Van Eemeren and Robert Grootendorst, *Argumentation, Communication, and Fallacies a Pragma-Dialectical Perspective* (New York: Routledge, 2010), 161.

74. Van Eemeren and Grootendorst, *Argumentation, Communication, and Fallacies a Pragma-Dialectical Perspective*, 134.

75. Alexis de Tocqueville, *Democracy in America*, trans. Harvey C. Mansfield and Debra Winthrop (Chicago: University of Chicago Press, 2002), 42.

76. Seymour Martin Lipset, *American Exceptionalism: A Double-Edged Sword* (New York: W. W. Norton, 1993), 26.

77. Jeanne Fahnestock, *Rhetorical Style: The Uses of Language in Persuasion* (Oxford: Oxford University Press, 2012), 119.

78. Van Eemeren and Grootendorst, *Argumentation, Communication, and Fallacies a Pragma-Dialectical Perspective*, 111.

79. Edward Inch and Barbara Warnick, *Critical Thinking and Communication: The Use of Reason in Argument*, 6th ed. (New York: Pearson, 2010), 245.

80. James Jasinski, *Sourcebook on Rhetoric* (Thousand Oaks, CA: SAGE Publications, 2001), 243.

81. Kenneth Burke, "The Rhetoric of Hitler's Battle," *The Philosophy of Literary Form: Studies in Symbolic Action* (New York: Vintage Books, 1957), 225–26. "It was simply stated that we were the masters of the meeting, that consequently we had the authority, and that everyone who would dare to make only so much as one interrupting shout, would mercilessly

be thrown out by the same door by which he had come in. That further we had to reject all responsibility for [the safety of] such a fellow." Adolf Hitler, *Mein Kampf*, trans. Marco Roberto (independently published, 2017).

82. The *Oxford English Dictionary* dates "reification" to 1846 and "objectification" to 1854, and uses the words interchangeably. (Objectification is defined as "To degrade or demote (a person, class of people, etc.) to the status of a mere object; to treat as an object; to reify.")

83. Max Horkheimer and Theodor W. Adorno, *Dialectic of Enlightenment*, ed. Gunzelin Noerr, trans. Edmund Jephcott (Stanford: Stanford University Press, 2002), 191.

84. Axel Honneth, *Reification: A New Look at an Old Idea* (Oxford: Oxford University Press, 2012), 94. According to Herbert Marcuse, "Marx's early writings are the first explicit statement of the process of reification (German Verdinglichung) through which capitalist society makes all personal relations between men take the form of objective relations between things." According to Georg Lukács, "The essence of commodity-structure has often been pointed out. Its basis is that a relation between people takes on the character of a thing and thus acquires a 'phantom objectivity,' an autonomy that seems so strictly rational and all-embracing as to conceal every trace of its fundamental nature: the relation between people." Georg Lukács, *History and Class Consciousness*, trans. Rodney Livingstone (Talgarth, Wales: Merlin Press, 1967), 83.

85. Martha C. Nussbaum, "Objectification," *Philosophy and Public Affairs* 24, no. 4 (1995): 249–91.

86. "I've been saying during this entire campaign that I'm a counterpuncher." "Donald Trump Explains Being a 'Counter-Puncher,'" Fox News video, 06:28, May 26, 2016, http://video.foxnews.com/v/4914523692001/?#sp=show-clips.

Part One: Trump and the Distrusting Electorate

1. Jennifer Mercieca, "When Paranoid Rhetoric and Falsehoods Prevail, Public Trust Crumbles," Zocalo Public Square, March 13, 2017, https://www.zocalopublicsquare.org/2017/03/13/paranoid-rhetoric-falsehoods-prevail-public-trust-crumbles/ideas/nexus/.

2. "Public Trust in Government: 1958–2019," Pew Research Center, April 11, 2019, http://www.people-press.org/2015/11/23/public-trust-in-government-1958-2015/.

3. "Honesty/Ethics in Professions," Gallup, http://www.gallup.com/poll/1654/honesty-ethics-professions.aspx.

4. "Both Parties Have Lost Confidence and Trust in Public's Political Wisdom," Pew Research Center, November 20, 2015, https://www.people-press.org/2015/11/23/beyond-distrust-how-americans-view-their-government/overview-6/.

5. Jürgen Habermas, *Legitimation Crisis* (Boston: Beacon Press, 1975); Aristotle, *Politics*, trans. H. Rackham (Cambridge, MA: Harvard University Press, 1944).

Chapter 1

1. "Trump: Favorable/Unfavorable," Real Clear Politics, http://www.realclearpolitics.com/epolls/other/trump_favorableunfavorable-5493.html#polls.

2. America's News HQ, Fox News, Trump archive video, 1:01, September 12, 2015, https://archive.org/details/foxnewsw_20150912_173700_americas_news_hq/start/1140/end/1200.

3. Robby Soave, "How Political Correctness Caused College Students to Cheer for Trump," Reason.com, February 23, 2016, http://reason.com/blog/2016/02/23/how-political-correctness-caused-college; Robby Soave, "Trump Won Because Leftist Political Correctness Inspired a Terrifying Backlash," Reason.com, November 9, 2016, http://reason.com/blog/2016/11/09/trump-won-because-leftist-political-corr.

4. Krista Jenkins, "Trump Taints America's Views on Political Correctness: Poll Suggests Perceptions of Political Correctness Are Trumped by Trump," Farleigh Dickinson University Public Mind Poll, October 30, 2015, http://view2.fdu.edu/publicmind/2015/151030/.

5. "Deep Dissatisfaction among U.S. Voters, Quinnipiac University Poll Finds; Trump Supporters Want Leader Who Ignores the Rules," Quinnipiac University Poll, April 5, 2016, https://poll.qu.edu/national/release-detail?ReleaseID=2340.

6. A January 27, 2016, Rand survey found that among likely Republican primary voters, the single biggest predictor of whether or not a voter would support Trump was if they agreed that "people like me don't have any say about what the government does." A total of 86.5 percent of those who agreed that people like them had no influence supported Trump, even above other Republicans. Rand concluded that this increased preference for Trump is over and beyond any preferences based on respondent gender, age, race/ethnicity, employment status, educational attainment, household income, attitudes toward Muslims, attitudes toward illegal immigrants, or attitudes toward Hispanics and was not significantly related to preference for any other candidate. Michael Pollard and Joshua Mendelsohn, "Rand Kicks Off 2016 Presidential Election Panel Survey," *The RAND Blog*, January 27, 2016, http://www.rand.org/blog/2016/01/rand-kicks-off-2016-presidential-election-panel-survey.html.

7. Dan Balz, "Donald Trump, America's First Independent President," *Washington Post*, November 19, 2016, https://www.washingtonpost.com/politics/donald-trump-americas-first-independent-president/2016/11/19/b09e1cc6-ade2-11e6-8b45-f8e493f06fcd_story.html?utm_term=.1cea0d2b66dc.

8. Sam Frizell, "Pollster's Legs Wobble after Fawning Donald Trump Focus Group," *Time*, August 25, 2015, http://time.com/4009413/donald-trump-focus-group-frank-luntz/.

9. "Trump Embodies the Rage of the White Middle Class," in "What Do Donald Trump Voters Actually Want?" ed. Conor Friedersdorf, *The Atlantic*, August 17, 2015, http://www.theatlantic.com/politics/archive/2015/08/donald-trump-voters/401408/#Trump%20Embodies%20the%20Rage%20of%20the%20White%20Middle%20Class.

10. "Key Capitol Hill Hearings," C-SPAN, Trump archive video, 11:07, February 22,

2016, https://archive.org/details/cspan_20160223_030000_kcy_capitol_hill_hearings/start/5520/end/5580.

11. "Washington This Week," C-SPAN, Trump archive video, 1:00, August 30, 2015, https://archive.org/details/cspan_20150830_180100_washington_this_week/start/1620/end/1680.

12. "Perhaps the appeal lies elsewhere. Maybe all this electoral chaos has been sown as an excuse to gather in public, under the guise of civil engagement, to say the vile, hateful things that the majority of the country has long shunned. It's not about Mr. Trump; he's just the cover, the cheerleader, not the quarterback. In a perverse way, many Trump supporters want what they criticize: the sense of winning that seems to be the sole preserve of the cultural elite, the ability to set the terms of discussion, the freedom to speak their minds and not face criticism. Whether it's same-sex marriage, the last two presidential elections or the Confederate battle flag (several of which I saw at the rally), they have not won in such a long time." Jared Yates Sexton, "Is the Trump Campaign Just a Giant Safe Space for the Right?" *New York Times*, July 1, 2016, http://www.nytimes.com/2016/07/01/opinion/is-the-trump-campaign-just-a-giant-safe-space-for-the-right.html.

13. "Unfiltered Voices from Donald Trump's Crowds," *New York Times*, August 3, 2016, Erica Berenstein, Nick Corasaniti, and Ashley Parker, 3:11, https://www.nytimes.com/video/us/politics/100000004533191/unfiltered-voices-from-donald-trumps-crowds.html; David M. Halbfinger, "Profanity, Vitriol, Slurs: Why the Times Published Unfiltered Trump Rally Video," *New York Times*, August 5, 2016, http://www.nytimes.com/2016/08/05/insider/profanity-vitriol-slurs-why-the-times-published-unfiltered-trump-rally-video.html?_r=0.

14. Katherine Speller, "Could Trump's Attack on 'Political Correctness' Help the U.S. Discuss Race?" *The Takeaway* from WNYC, October 12, 2016, http://www.wnyc.org/story/could-trumps-attack-political-correctness-help-us-discuss-race/.

15. Moira Weigel, "Political Correctness: How the Right Invented a Phantom Enemy," *The Guardian*, November 30, 2016, https://www.theguardian.com/us-news/2016/nov/30/political-correctness-how-the-right-invented-phantom-enemy-donald-trump?CMP=share_btn_tw.

16. "Annotated Transcript: The Aug. 6 GOP Debate," *Washington Post*, August 6, 2015, https://www.washingtonpost.com/news/post-politics/wp/2015/08/06/annotated-transcript-the-aug-6-gop-debate/?utm_term=.be6b7e30fa86.

17. Donald J. Trump (@realDonaldTrump), "So many 'politically correct' fools in our country. We have to all get back to work and stop wasting time and energy on nonsense!" Twitter, August 8, 2015, https://twitter.com/realdonaldtrump/status/629992743788523520.

18. "This off-the-cuff, unrehearsed style also gives the impression that Trump is speaking for himself and not from a speechwriter's script (a point he explicitly makes), which contributes to what his supporters describe as his 'authentic,' 'trustworthy,' and 'relatable' character—all important qualities to cultivate in a presidential self." Jennifer Sclafani, "The Idiolect of Donald Trump," *Scientific American*, March 25, 2016, https://blogs.scientificamerican.com/mind-guest-blog/the-idiolect-of-donald-trump/.

19. Frank Newport, "American Public Opinion and Immigration," Gallup, July 20, 2015, https://news.gallup.com/opinion/polling-matters/184262/american-public-opinion-immigration.aspx.

20. Martin Pengelly, "'Offensive and Inaccurate': Marco Rubio Rejects Donald Trump's Mexico Remarks," *The Guardian*, July 4, 2015, https://www.theguardian.com/us-news/2015/jul/04/donald-trump-marco-rubio-mexico-immigrants.

21. Mariano Castillo and Brian Stelter, "Rupert Murdoch: Donald Trump 'Wrong' on Immigration," CNN Politics, July 13, 2015, https://www.cnn.com/2015/07/12/politics/rupert-murdoch-trump-tweets/index.html.

22. Michelle Ye Hee Lee, "Donald Trump's False Comments Connecting Mexican Immigrants and Crime," *Washington Post*, July 8, 2015, https://www.washingtonpost.com/news/fact-checker/wp/2015/07/08/donald-trumps-false-comments-connecting-mexican-immigrants-and-crime/?utm_term=.490d8b994195.

23. Rupert Murdoch (@rupertmurdoch), "Mexican immigrants, as with all immigrants, have much lower crime rates than native born. Eg El Paso safest city in U.S. Trump wrong," Twitter, July 12, 2015, https://twitter.com/rupertmurdoch/status/620352927807377408.

24. Jonathon Martin and Alan Rappeport, "Donald Trump Says John McCain Is No War Hero, Setting Off Another Storm," *New York Times*, July 18, 2015, http://www.nytimes.com/2015/07/19/us/politics/trump-belittles-mccains-war-record.html.

25. Evan Osnos, "The Fearful and the Frustrated," *New Yorker*, August 31, 2015, http://www.newyorker.com/magazine/2015/08/31/the-fearful-and-the-frustrated; Jeremy Diamond, "Donald Trump's 4-Hour Swing by the Border," CNN, July 23, 2015, http://www.cnn.com/2015/07/23/politics/donald-trump-border-visit-texas/.

26. The *New York Times* reported that "as he deplaned onto the sweltering tarmac from his private jet emblazoned with his name, protesters and supporters swarmed the fence outside, chanting and screaming in Spanish and English." Trump reportedly waved back and later remarked that "there were a lot of people at the airport, and they were all waving American flags and they were all in favor of Trump and what I'm doing." Nick Corasaniti, "Donald Trump, at Mexican Border, Claims Close Ties to Hispanics," *New York Times*, July 23, 2015, http://www.nytimes.com/2015/07/24/us/politics/donald-trump-at-mexican-border-claims-close-ties-to-hispanics.html.

27. Corasaniti, "Donald Trump, at the Mexican Border," *New York Times*, http://www.nytimes.com/2015/07/24/us/politics/donald-trump-at-mexican-border-claims-close-ties-to-hispanics.html.

28. "An attitude to his listener . . . the tone of his utterance reflects his awareness of this relation, his sense of how he stands towards those he is addressing." I. A. Richards, *Practical Criticism: A Study of Literary Judgment* (London: Kegan Paul, Trench, Trubner & Co. Ltd., 1930), quoted in James Jasinski, *Sourcebook on Rhetoric* (Thousand Oaks, CA: SAGE Publications, 2001), 576.

29. Roderick P. Hart, Jay P. Childers, and Colene J. Lind, *Political Tone: How Readers Talk and Why* (Chicago: University of Chicago Press, 2013), 6.

30. Or, as rhetorical theorist Kenneth Burke wrote in his analysis of the rhetoric that led to World War II, "one need not scrutinize the concept of 'identification' very sharply to see, implied in it at every turn, its ironic counterpart: division." Kenneth Burke, *A Rhetoric of Motives* (Los Angeles: University of California Press, 1969), 23.

31. "Throughout 2014, the three fed Trump strategy memos and political intelligence. 'I listened to thousands of hours of talk radio, and he was getting reports from me,' Nunberg recalled. What those reports said was that the GOP base was frothing over a handful of issues including immigration, Obamacare, and Common Core. While Jeb Bush talked about crossing the border as an 'act of love,' Trump was thinking about how high to build his wall. "We either have borders or we don't," Trump told the faithful who flocked to the annual CPAC conference in 2014. Which is how Trump's scorched-earth strategy coalesced. To break out of the pack, he made what appears to be a deliberate decision to be provocative, even outrageous. "*I'm* the strategist," Trump told me. . . . "If I were totally presidential, I'd be one of the many people who are already out of the race. . . ." You know, there's a difference between being presidential when you're now president of the United States than being presidential when you're running against 17 other people. No one can control him,' said Nunberg. Not even his family." Gabriel Sherman, "Inside Operation Trump, the Most Unorthodox Campaign in Political History," *New York Magazine*, April 3, 2016, http://nymag.com/daily/intel-ligencer/2016/04/inside-the-donald-trump-presidential-campaign.html.

32. Associated Press, "'No More Political Correctness' for Trump Supporters," *PBS NewsHour*, April 10, 2016, http://www.pbs.org/newshour/rundown/no-more-political-correctness-for-trump-supporters/.

33. Donald J. Trump (@realDonaldTrump), "The election is absolutely being rigged by the dishonest and distorted media pushing Crooked Hillary—but also at many polling places—SAD," Twitter, October 16, 2016, https://mobile.twitter.com/realDonaldTrump/status/787699930718695425; Michael Bieksecker, Jill Colvin, and Steve Peoples, "Testy Trump Takes His War with the Press to a New Level," Associated Press, June 1, 2016, http://bigstory.ap.org/article/4257780cdb2245389e04655aff41821b/testy-trump-takes-his-war-press-new-level; Kurt Eichenwald, "How Donald Trump Supporters Attack Journalists," *Newsweek*, October 7, 2016, http://www.newsweek.com/epileptogenic-pepe-video-507417; "Why Campaign Reporters Want You to Watch This Video of Trump Rallies," CNN Media, August 4, 2016, http://money.cnn.com/2016/08/04/media/new-york-times-trump-rally-video/.

34. Tal Kopan, "Marco Rubio Says He's Not 'Proud' of Donald Trump Attacks," CNN Politics, March 9, 2015, http://www.cnn.com/2016/03/09/politics/marco-rubio-not-proud-donald-trump-attack/; Gregory Krieg, "Donald Trump Defends Size of His Penis," CNN Politics, March 4, 2016, http://www.cnn.com/2016/03/03/politics/donald-trump-small-hands-marco-rubio/.

35. "Trump Embodies the Rage of the White Middle Class," in "What Do Donald Trump Voters Actually Want?" ed. Conor Friedersdorf, *The Atlantic*, August 17, 2015, http://

www.theatlantic.com/politics/archive/2015/08/donald-trump-voters/401408/#Trump%20 Embodies%20the%20Rage%20of%20the%20White%20Middle%20Class.

Chapter 2

1. "Trump: Favorable/Unfavorable," Real Clear Politics, http://www.realclearpolitics. com/epolls/other/trump_favorableunfavorable-5493.html#polls.

2. Theodore Schleifer, "Donald Trump on Reporters: 'I Would Never Kill Them,'" CNN Politics, December 21, 2015, http://www.cnn.com/2015/12/21/politics/trump-putin-killing-reporters/. See also Linda Qiu, "Does Vladimir Putin Kill Journalists?" PunditFact, January 4, 2016, http://www.politifact.com/punditfact/article/2016/jan/04/does-vladimir-putin-kill-journalists/.

3. For another example of Trump using ad baculum threats with a paralipsis that shows that he was aware that he was making threats: May 18, 2016, he said, "I will be bringing more libel suits as people–maybe against you folks. I don't want to threaten, but I find that the press is unbelievably dishonest." Donald Trump with Robert O'Harrow, et al., "Washington Post Live Interview with Donald Trump," *Washington Post*, interview, May 18, 2016, https:// www.washingtonpost.com/wp-stat/graphics/politics/trump-archive/docs/donald-trump-interview-with-shawn-boburg-robert-oharrrow-drew-harwell-amy-goldstein-jerry-markon-may-18-2016.pdf.

4. Trevor Timm, "Trump's Many, Many Threats to Sue the Press Since Launching His Campaign," *Columbia Journalism Review*, October 3, 2016, https://www.cjr.org/first_person/donald_trump_lawsuit_new_york_times.php.

5. "You had candidates that got up and insulted you every day. They told everybody that you were liars, that you were making everything up. Those are the things that challenge you when you're at your desk and you're talking about stories with your coworkers. You have to sort of talk through and be like, 'How do we know we're not dismissing something because the thing that got said is, *You're a liar and you make things up and you're trying to throw the election*?'" Ginger Gibson, "Covering Trump: An Oral History of an Unforgettable Campaign," Columbia Journalistic Review, November 22, 2016, https://www.cjr.org/special_report/trump_media_press_journalists.php. "You hear him talk for five minutes and understand that he does not believe in free and independent media. We know how threatening that is, not just to journalists, but to the idea of having accountability and the idea of democratic governance. That's part of what we all react to viscerally." Jacob Weisberg, "Covering Trump: An Oral History of an Unforgettable Campaign," *Columbia Journalistic Review*, November 22, 2016, https://www.cjr.org/special_report/trump_media_press_journalists.php.

6. David A. Fahrenthold and Robert O'Harrow Jr., "Trump: A True Story," *Washington Post*, August 10, 2016, https://www.washingtonpost.com/graphics/politics/2016-election/trump-lies/.

7. Trump was so good for ratings that he could demand that reporters stage their

interviews at Trump Tower or similar Trump venues: "Trump's ability to bring in viewers
to news programs is so powerful he even has a de facto set for his performances. Networks
are acquiescing to his demand that all on-camera sit-downs take place in the marble-walled
atrium of the 58-story Trump Tower on Manhattan's Fifth Avenue, where his corporate office
is located. All of the major TV news outlets have studios a few blocks away. But candidate
Trump takes an elevator from his office down to the front section of a bar that bears his
name. In fact, most of the businesses in the atrium, where tourists shop and take photos of
one another, bear the Trump moniker." Stephen Battaglio, "Donald Trump is Summer's
Biggest TV Hit, and Ratings Gold for Cable News," *Los Angeles Times*, September 2, 2015,
http://www.latimes.com/entertainment/envelope/cotown/la-et-ct-trump-ratings-show-
20150902-story.html.

8. Philip Rucker and Robert Costa, "Trump Tangles with Latino Newsman, Launches
Fresh Attacks on GOP Rivals," *Washington Post*, August 25, 2015, https://www.washington-
post.com/politics/donald-trump-announces-hires-in-key-early-states/2015/08/25/6557056a-
4b60-11e5-902f-39e9219e574b_story.html?utm_term=.43f581075399.

9. The first example I could find of Trump urging his rally crowd to boo the media
was on September 14, 2015, in Dallas. Josh Feldman, "Trump Complains at Rally about
the 'Terrible,' Media 'Distorting' His Crowd Sizes," *MediaITE, September* 25, 2015, http://
www.mediaite.com/online/trump-complains-at-rally-about-the-terrible-media-distorting-
his-crowd-sizes/. Maxwell Tani, "Donald Trump Rages at the Media During 'Massive' Dallas
Rally," *Business Insider*, September 14, 2015, http://www.businessinsider.com/donald-
trump-dallas-rally-crowd-media-2015-9; "Donald Trump Feuds with CNN Reporter,"
CNN video, 4:20, September 24, 2015, https://www.youtube.com/watch?v=f_b2JAHCuVo;
Jonathan Martin, "A Day of Empty Seats and Donald Trump in Full Attack," *New York
Times*, September 23, 2015, https://www.nytimes.com/2015/09/24/us/politics/a-day-of-
empty-seats-and-donald-trump-in-full-attack.html; Ben Schreckinger, "Donald Trump's Size
Fixation," Politico, September 25, 2015, http://www.politico.com/story/2015/09/donald-
trumps-2016-crowd-size-fixation-214093; Becket Adams, "Trump Attacks 'Liar' Reporter
For Noting Small Crowd at Rally," *Washington Examiner,* September 24, 2015, http://www.
washingtonexaminer.com/trump-attacks-liar-reporter-for-noting-small-crowd-at-rally/arti-
cle/2572771; Jennifer Jacobs, "Trump Boots Reporter, Vows to Hold Grudges," *USA Today*,
August 25, 2015, https://www.usatoday.com/story/news/politics/elections/2015/08/25/
trump-boots-reporter-vows-hold-grudges/32369663/. At a rally in Mount Pleasant, South
Carolina, December 7, 2015 (same day as travel ban is announced), Trump calls journalists
"scum" and "dishonest," pointing out NBC's Katy Tur by name for the crowd's derision.
"Presidential Candidate Donald Trump Rally in Mount Pleasant, South Carolina," C-SPAN
video, 57:36, December 7, 2015, https://www.c-span.org/video/?401762-1/presidential-
candidate-donald-trump-rally-mount-pleasant-south-carolina. "Trump asks a crowd in a
high school gym to turn toward the 'sleazebags.' He says they probably will misrepresent
the one empty portion of the bleachers closed for safety concerns as evidence the rally was

poorly attended. 'What sleaze, what sleaze,' he says. 'They're disgusting.'" Rick Hampson, "Donald Trump's Attacks on the News Media: A Not-So-Short History," *USA Today*, March 10, 2016, https://www.usatoday.com/story/news/politics/onpolitics/2016/03/10/donald-trump-versus-the-media/81602878/. Katy Tur (@KatyTurNBC), "Trump trashes press. Crowd jeers. Guy by press 'pen' looks us & screams 'you're a bitch!' Other gentleman gives cameras the double bird," Twitter, February 21, 2016, https://twitter.com/KatyTurNBC/status/701530070381416448.

10. "POLITICO reporter Ben Schreckinger was denied entry to Donald Trump's press conference on Tuesday night, despite having previously been granted credentials by the campaign. The move followed a threat last week from Trump officials to exclude POLITICO reporters from campaign events." Hadas Gold, "Politico Reporter Denied Access to Trump Event," Politico, March 15, 2016, http://www.politico.com/blogs/on-media/2016/03/ben-schreckinger-denied-access-donald-trump-220836. Not too long after Trump's May 31, 2016, press conference his campaign revoked the *Washington Post*'s credentials: "Unhappy with 'incredibly inaccurate coverage,' Donald Trump on Monday announced he would revoke the Washington Post's press credentials." Andrew Rafferty and Alex Seitz-Wald, "Trump Revokes *Washington Post*'s Press Credentials," NBC News, June 13, 2016, http://www. nbcnews.com/politics/2016-election/trump-revokes-washington-post-s-press-credentials-n591586. Trump's campaign explained the matter on Facebook on June 13, 2016: "Based on the incredibly inaccurate coverage and reporting of the record setting Trump campaign, we are hereby revoking the press credentials of the phony and dishonest Washington Post." The post received 172,000 likes, 12,120 shares, and 12,000 comments. The top comment, with 14,000 likes, was from Bryan Schwartz: "Hey ISIS One, two, Trumps comin' for you. Three, four, We are ready for war. Five, six, F*ck politics. Seven, eight, Youve sealed your fate. Nine, ten, America will be great again." The second top comment, with 5,000 likes, was from Kristen Sheldon: "So if you were elected you would have a state-run media, like N. Korea, Iran, & Russia? Will you imprison journalists that dissent like Egypt? Only the news that agrees with you and does your bidding, doesn't sound like freedom of the press. Obama didn't revoke the credentials of Fox News and they are horrifically biased. You are terrifying." Facebook post and comments, June 13, 2016, https://www.facebook.com/DonaldTrump/posts/10157164117925725. John Avlon, editor in chief of the *Daily Beast*, which Trump banned from covering his events in 2015, indicated "[The campaign's] impulse to block principled critics for the vast majority of this campaign shows the candidate's fundamental discomfort with being held accountable." John Avlon, quoted by Paul Farhi, "Trump Lifts Ban That Excluded the *Washington Post* and Other Media," *Washington Post*, September 7, 2018, https://www.washingtonpost.com/lifestyle/style/trump-lifts-ban-that-excluded-the-washington-post-and-other-news-media/2016/09/07/29b11d86-7501-11e6-8149-b8d05321db62_story.html?utm_term=.4f6cb91975c7.

11. "They never responded to a single one of my comment requests for something like five months. My emails were just like 40 unanswered emails to Hope Hicks, his spokesperson.

That was something I never encountered from a professional political campaign in Congress, the Senate, at the presidential level, anywhere. The Trump campaign basically just blacklisted any press they didn't like," Kaczynski, CNN and BuzzFeed, quoted by *Columbia Journalism Review* reporting team, "Accomplices or Antagonists: How the Media Handled the Trump Phenomenon," *The Guardian*, November 22, 2016, https://www.theguardian.com/us-news/2016/nov/22/journalists-media-election-2016-donald-trump. "At his giant rallies, Mr. Trump portrays reporters as irredeemably dishonest. His staff relegates them to fenced-in pens and strictly monitors their movements." Michael Barbaro and Jessica Dimson, "Lights, Camera, Trump," *New York Times*, May 24, 2016, https://www.nytimes.com/interactive/2016/05/25/us/politics/donald-trump-campaign-news-conference.html; "Reporters told me that Trump is incredibly attuned to his coverage in a way that other presidential candidates aren't. The campaign will sometimes single out specific outlets for vindictive treatment. The Des Moines Register, the New York Times, BuzzFeed, and Univision were all denied access to Trump events in the wake of running negative coverage." Seth Stevenson, "A Week on the Trail with the 'Disgusting Reporters' Covering Donald Trump," *Slate*, March 20, 2016, http://www.slate.com/articles/news_and_politics/cover_story/2016/03/on_the_trail_with_donald_trump_s_disgusting_press_corps.html. Elizabeth Preza, "Yes, Trump Will Now Require Press Members Be Escorted to the Bathroom at Rallies," MediaITE, November 25, 2015, http://www.mediaite.com/online/yes-trump-will-now-require-press-members-be-escorted-to-the-bathroom-at-rallies/.

12. Donald J. Trump (@realDonaldTrump), "Boycott @Macys and @Univision. MAKE AMERICA GREAT AGAIN!" Twitter, July 11, 2015, https://twitter.com/realdonaldtrump/status/619835174369398789; "During his four-day boycott of the station, he pumped up the ratings of its rival networks by appearing on their shows and savaging Fox, and escalated his all-out war on Kelly with the crack about her bloody 'wherever.'" Paul Solotaroff, "Trump Seriously: On the Trail with the GOP's Tough Guy," *Rolling Stone*, September 9, 2015, http://www.rollingstone.com/politics/news/trump-seriously-20150909.

13. "Herculean efforts of the *New York Times*, which dedicated 18 journalists to fact-checking the TV debates in real-time, or of NPR, which turned over 30 staffers to a similar endeavor, despite the *Guardian*'s Lyin' Trump column and so much more, some 61 million Americans were unfazed enough by the idea of a serial liar in the Oval Office to vote for him." Ed Pilkington, "Did Trump's Scorched-Earth Tactics Mortally Wound the Media?" *Columbia Journalistic Review,* November 22, 2016, https://www.cjr.org/special_report/trumps_tactics_wound_the_media.php. Brian Ries (@moneyries), "A+ work by chyron writer squeezing in all of the feuds," Twitter, January 16, 2017, https://twitter.com/moneyries/status/821010752722960387; Brendan Nyhan (@BrendanNyan), "Trump-induced news congestion in action," January 16, 2017, comment on Ries, "A+ work," https://twitter.com/BrendanNyhan/status/821011344648445953.

14. Peter Navarro, "Statement on Monopoly Power of New Media Conglomerates," Trump-Pence 2016 media archives, October 23, 2016, https://web.archive.org/

web/20161102024656/https://www.donaldjtrump.com/press-releases/statement-on-monop-
oly-power-of-new-media-conglomerates.

15. "Reporter: Trump Leaked It," CNN video, 06:48, https://www.cnn.com/videos/
tv/2016/05/14/reporter-trump-leaked-own-tape.cnn.

16. "'And believe me, if I become president, oh, do they have problems. They're going
to have such problems. And one of the things I'm going to do, and this is only going to make
it tougher for me, and I've never said this before, but one of the things I'm going to do if I
win—and I hope I do and we're certainly leading—is I'm going to open up our libel laws so
when they write purposely negative and horrible and false articles, we can sue them and win
lots of money,'" Deborah Barfield Berry, "Trump Says He'll 'Open Up' Lebel Laws If He's
Elected," *USA Today*, February 27, 2016, https://www.usatoday.com/story/news/politics/elec-
tions/2016/02/27/trump-says-hell-open-up-libel-laws-if-hes-elected/81042044/.

17. Trump first used the words "fake news" in a tweet on December 10, 2016: Donald
J. Trump (@realDonaldTrump), "Reports by @CNN that I will be working on The Apprentice during my Presidency, even part time, are ridiculous & untrue—FAKE NEWS!" Twitter,
December 10, 2016, https://twitter.com/realdonaldtrump/status/807588632877998081. Of
course, he continued to use the phrase. Haley Britzky, "Everything Trump Has Called 'FAKE
NEWS,'" Axios, July 9, 2017, https://www.axios.com/everything-trump-has-called-fake-
news-1513303959-6603329e-46b5-44ea-b6be-70d0b3bdb0ca.html.

18. According to media ranking company Quant, Trump received a total of $4.96 billion
dollars in free airtime, whereas Hillary Clinton received $3.24 billion: Mary Harris, "A Media
Post-mortem on the 2016 Presidential Election," mediaQuant, November 14, 2016, https://
www.mediaquant.net/2016/11/a-media-post-mortem-on-the-2016-presidential-election/.
Trump received an estimated $2 billion in free media before the Republican Primary was
over, according to the *New York Times*: Nicholas Confessore and Karen Yourish, "$2 Billion
Worth of Free Media for Donald Trump," *New York Times,* March 15, 2016, https://www.
nytimes.com/2016/03/16/upshot/measuring-donald-trumps-mammoth-advantage-in-free-
media.html?_r=0. According to a Shorenstein Center analysis, Trump's media attention
overshadowed the entire election: Thomas E. Patterson, "Pre-primary News Coverage of the
2016 Presidential Race: Trump's Rise, Sanders' Emergence, Clinton's Struggle," Shorenstein Center, June 13, 2016, https://shorensteincenter.org/pre-primary-news-coverage-
2016-trump-clinton-sanders/. According to a *Washington Post* analysis of Google News,
Trump's online mentions dominated the news cycle throughout the campaign: Lazaro Gamio
and Callum Borchers, "A Visual History of Donald Trump Dominating the News Cycle,"
Washington Post, July 21, 2016, https://www.washingtonpost.com/graphics/politics/donald-
trump-vs-hillary-clinton-in-media/?wpisrc=nl_fix&wpmm=1.

19. "When I say he's trying to break the press, I mean the entire system that gives honest
journalism a role in the republic. Trump is running against such basic notions as 'we need
a fact-based debate or there can't be consent of the governed;' 'there's a public record that
cannot just be wiped away;' 'a candidate's position on major issues should be made clear to

the voters;' 'lying cannot become a universal principle in politics without major damage to our democracy.'" Jay Rosen, "Asymmetry between the Major Parties Fries the Circuits of the Mainstream Press," PressThink, September 25, 2016, http://pressthink.org/2016/09/asymmetry-between-the-major-parties-fries-the-circuits-of-the-mainstream-press/.

20. For example, *Morning Joe* did 1,598 stories on Donald Trump from June 14, 2015, to November 8, 2016, while it only did 875 stories about Hillary Rodham Clinton during the same time period. "Donald Trump," Search, MSNBC News, http://www.msnbc.com/search/donald%20trump; "Hillary Clinton," Search, MSNBC News, http://www.msnbc.com/search/hillary%20clinton. "Our ratings have never been better. Revenue from our show has never been higher. The buzz has never been greater," Scarborough, quoted by Emily Jane Fox, "Joe and Mika Defend Themselves against the Haters," *Vanity Fair*, December 15, 2016, https://www.vanityfair.com/news/2016/12/joe-and-mika-defend-themselves-against-the-haters. "*Morning Joe* beat CNN during the first three quarters of this year in the key ratings demographic, the first time it has done so since early 2014, according to MSNBC." Fox, "Joe and Mika Defend Themselves," http://www.vanityfair.com/news/2016/12/joe-and-mika-defend-themselves-against-the-haters. In one instance, a "hot mic" conversation between Mika and Joe and Trump caught them discussing how "tough" the questions would be: "'That's right, nothing too hard, Mika,' Trump interjected. 'OK,' Brzezinski said." Streiff, "Audio: Joe Scarborough and Mika Brzezinski Negotiate with Donald Trump Over 'Hard Questions,'" RedState, February 22, 2016, http://www.redstate.com/streiff/2016/02/22/audio-joe-scarborough-mike-brzezinski-negotiate-donald-trump-hard-questions/. According to Trump's son-in-law Jared Kushner, the Trump campaign negotiated with Sinclair Media Group (owner of 172 local television stations) for more favorable coverage. Josh Dawsey and Hadas Gold, "Kushner: We Struck Deal with Sinclair for Straighter Coverage," Politico, December 16, 2016, http://www.politico.com/story/2016/12/trump-campaign-sinclair-broadcasting-jared-kushner-232764?wpisrc=nl_daily202&wpmm=1; they also required their affiliates to air right-wing content and suppressed news unfavorable to the GOP, like Montana GOP candidate Greg Gianforte's attack on *Guardian* journalist Ben Jacobson. Julia Carrie Wong and Sam Levin, "Republican Candidate Charged with Assault after 'Body-Slamming' *Guardian* Reporter," *Guardian*, May 25, 2017, https://www.theguardian.com/us-news/2017/may/24/greg-gianforte-bodyslams-reporter-ben-jacobs-montana. Once the election was over, Sinclair announced that it planned to buy 42 additional local stations: Syndey Ember, "Sinclair Requires TV Stations to Air Segments That Tilt to the Right," *New York Times*, May 12, 2017, https://www.nytimes.com/2017/05/12/business/media/sinclair-broadcast-komo-conservative-media.html?_r=0.

21. "Perhaps the biggest loser, however, is Donald Trump, who has negative favorability ratings of almost 2–1 in each state, the independent Quinnipiac (KWIN-uh-pe-ack) University Poll finds. The Swing State Poll focuses on key states in the presidential election." "Clinton In Trouble in Colorado, Iowa, Virginia, Quinnipiac University Swing State Poll Finds; Trump's Negatives Are Almost 2–1," Quinnipiac University, July 22, 2015, https://poll.qu.edu/2016-presidential-swing-state-polls/release-detail?releaseid=2261.

22. M. J. Lee, "Donald Trump: As President, 'I'll Change My Tone,'" CNN, July 23, 2015, http://www.cnn.com/2015/07/22/politics/donald-trump-anderson-cooper/.

23. "Trump's objective here is clear, several campaign strategists and political reporters observed: To discredit the people who call attention to his lies, his contradictions, his lack of transparency and the less seemly aspects of his history. 'Why attack media?' asked Michael Barbaro of the *New York Times*. 'So you can keep saying they are "discredited" when tough stories come out. It's deliberate attempt at inoculation.'" Dylan Byers and Jeremy Diamond, "Donald Trump's 'Sleaze' Attack on Reporter Hits New Level of Media Animosity," CNN, May 31, 2016, http://money.cnn.com/2016/05/31/media/donald-trump-reporter-sleaze/.

24. Jennifer R. Mercieca, "The Culture of Honor: How Slaveholders Responded to the Abolitionist Mail Crisis of 1835," *Rhetoric and Public Affairs* 10, no. 1 (2007): 51–76.

25. David A. Fahrenthold, "Trump Said He Raised $6 Million for Veterans. Now His Campaign Says It Was Less," *Washington Post*, May 21, 2016, https://www.washingtonpost.com/politics/trump-said-he-raised-6-million-for-vets-now-his-campaign-says-it-was-less/2016/05/20/871127a8-1d1f-11e6-b6e0-c53b7ef63b45_story.html?utm_term=.da57c6d8c550.

26. "Ernie Ratcliffe, an army veteran who served two tours in Vietnam, drove in from Kansas City for the rally, scoffed when asked for his thoughts on Texas Sen. Ted Cruz's contention that Trump skipped the debate because he was afraid of taunts or difficult questions from the Fox moderators or rival candidates. 'Donald Trump isn't scared of anything. He's not scared of absolutely anything,' said Ratcliffe, who has signed up with his wife to call New Hampshire voters on Trump's behalf next week. 'Donald J. Trump said he was going to do this and he's done it. He's a man of his word.' Ratcliffe said he was convinced that Trump was the only candidate who could clean up the Department of Veterans Affairs and that it would be 'one of the first things he does when he gets into office.' 'He's going to get it squared away,' he said. 'It's not going to take him very long to do it. He's going to put the right people in. He knows how to manage things. He's a very successful businessman. He's going to get it done very quickly and very, very well.' Randal Thom, a former Marine who was among the first admitted to Trump's event, said he loved it that Trump refused to back down. 'When it came out yesterday that he was actually doing this (rally) in less than 24 hours, it was amazing,' Thom said. 'It just shows he has the ability to rally and get things done.' Thom, who raises Alaskan Malamute and Pomalute puppies in Minnesota, and plans to spend Monday in Iowa volunteering for Trump, dismissed Cruz as 'a Canadian-born citizen' and described the Texas senator, as well as the other GOP contenders as 'weak.' 'Trump is a 100% strongman. He's bullet proof,' Thom said. 'People say, "Oh look at his background. Look at the number of wives he's had." You know what? I don't care about that. What I care about is his future.'" Maeve Reston, "Donald Trump Throws a Grand Old Party," CNN, January 29, 2016, http://www.cnn.com/2016/01/28/politics/donald-trump-2016-election-rally-gop-debate/?utm_source=huffingtonpost.com&utm_medium=referral&utm_campaign=pubexchange_article.

27. "In recent weeks, Trump and his campaign repeatedly declined to give new details about how much they have given away. 'Why should I give you records?' Trump said in an

interview with *The Post* this month. 'I don't have to give you records.' Paul Rieckhoff, founder of Iraq and Afghanistan Veterans of America, said Trump's refusal to divulge how much of the money he had distributed raised questions about whether the candidate intended the fundraiser primarily as a public-relations effort for himself. 'That's just shady. Right? No matter how you cut it, that's just shady,' Rieckhoff said. 'If he was going to make it right, a couple of weeks before Memorial Day would be a good time to do it. It behooves him, not just politically but ethically, to come forward and account for this money.' Trump provided no official way for charities to apply for the money. Groups around the country still tried, sending letters and hitting up local veterans-for-Trump leaders." Fahrenthold, "Trump Said He Raised $6 Million for Veterans," https://www.washingtonpost.com/politics/trump-said-he-raised-6-million-for-vets-now-his-campaign-says-it-was-less/2016/05/20/871127a8-1d1f-11e6-b6e0-c53b7ef63b45_story.html?utm_term=.da57c6d8c550.

28. Hunter Walker, "Veterans Hold Trump Tower Protest after Donald Trump's Charity Fundraising Drive Comes Up Short," Yahoo!, May 23, 2016, https://www.yahoo.com/news/veterans-hold-trump-tower-protest-after-donald-trumps-charity-fundraising-drive-comes-up-short-191229776.html; Vets VS Hate, "Today, veterans outside of Trump Tower expressed their solidarity with the Muslim community by opposing Islamophobic rhetoric of presumptive GOP nominee Donald Trump. #VetsVsHate," Facebook, May 31, 2016, https://www.facebook.com/vetsvshate/photos/a.293275041011607.1073741828.243345272671251/296518447353933/?type=3&theater.

29. David A. Fahrenthold, "Four Months after Fundraiser, Trump Says He Gave $1 Million to Veterans Group," *Washington Post*, May 24, 2016, https://www.washingtonpost.com/news/post-politics/wp/2016/05/24/four-months-later-donald-trump-says-he-gave-1-million-to-veterans-group/?utm_term=.ee4eba09883c.

30. "Presidential Candidate Donald Trump News Conference," C-SPAN video, 40:47, May 31, 2016, https://www.c-span.org/video/?410401-1/donald-trump-holds-news-conference-donations-veterans-groups.

31. Jeremy Diamond, "Trump Launches All-Out Attack on the Press," CNN, June 1, 2016, http://www.cnn.com/2016/05/31/politics/donald-trump-veterans-announcement/index.html; "Trump Attacks Media in Fiery News Conference," ABC News, 03:33, http://abcnews.go.com/GMA/video/trump-attacks-media-fiery-news-conference-39521861; Erik Wemple, "Trump's Crazy, Insane, Nonsensical, Bonkers, and Anti-Democratic Press Conference," *Washington Post*, May 31, 2016, https://www.washingtonpost.com/blogs/erik-wemple/wp/2016/05/31/trumps-crazy-insane-nonsensical-bonkers-and-anti-democratic-press-conference/?utm_term=.f65e698984fc.

32. Gabiz (@GabyGabysos), "wimp trump can't handle transparency & accountability questions of public service," May 31, 2016, comment on Donald J. Trump (@realDonaldTrump), "So many veterans groups are beyond happy with all of the money I raised/gave! It was my great honor—they do an amazing job," Twitter, May 31, 2016, https://twitter.com/GabyGabysos/status/737737868160819200.

33. Rush Limbaugh, "The Press Conference Republican Voters Have Wanted to See for Years," *The Rush Limbaugh Show*, May 31, 2016, https://www.rushlimbaugh.com/daily/2016/05/31/the_press_conference_republican_voters_have_wanted_to_see_for_years/.

34. Destiny Storm, "He is right, we were all watching, laughing and cheering Trump on. He owned them!" comment on Jim Hoft, "Rush Limbaugh Praises Trump: The Press Conference Republican Voters Have Wanted to See for Years," Gateway Pundit, May 31, 2016, http://disq.us/p/18qlknw.

35. India Maria, "In watching the entire Presser, there was not one point of Trump's that I did not agree with. The ClintonMedia is scum, and has been for decades. After watching Bush '41, Dole, Dubya, McCain, and Romney cower in fear with each DriveByMedia shenanigan, it is DELIGHTFUL, appropriate, and important to see our next POTUS show courage, leadership, and AMERICAN fighting spirit against the slithering enemy of the AMERICAN people, i.e. the DemocratMedia," comment on Charlie Spierling, "Sleaze! Donald Trump Busts the Press," Breitbart, May 31, 2016, http://disq.us/p/18ql5ri.

36. Donald J. Trump (@realDonaldTrump), "I am getting credit for my press conference today. Crooked Hillary should be admonished for not having a press conference in 179 days," Twitter, May 31, 2016, https://twitter.com/realdonaldtrump/status/737785114239864832?lang=en.

37. Donald J. Trump, *Crippled America: How to Make America Great Again* (New York: Simon & Schuster, 2015), 11. There were allegedly two uncredited ghostwriters for the book. "Donald Trump Had an Uncredited Ghostwriter for His New Book, 'Crippled America: How to Make America Great Again,'" *Daily News*, November 5, 2015, http://www.nydailynews.com/entertainment/gossip/donald-trump-uncredited-ghostwriter-new-book-article-1.2424852.

38. "FNN: FULL Donald Trump Press Conference Before Dubuque, Iowa Rally," Fox 10 Phoenix, YouTube video, 33:06, 29:40, August 25, 2015, https://www.youtube.com/watch?v=Z0_n-LHv6Xs.

39. Trump, *Crippled America*, 10.

40. "'I hear you're not voting for me,' Trump said. 'I just talked to *The New Yorker*—which, by the way, is a failing magazine that no one reads—and I heard you were critical of me.' 'You're running for President,' Schwartz said. 'I disagree with a lot of what you're saying.' 'That's your right, but then you should have just remained silent. I just want to tell you that I think you're very disloyal. Without me, you wouldn't be where you are now. I had a lot of choice of who to have write the book, and I chose you, and I was very generous with you.'" Jane Meyer, "Donald Trump's Ghostwriter Tells All," *New Yorker*, July 25, 2016, http://www.newyorker.com/magazine/2016/07/25/donald-trumps-ghostwriter-tells-all.

41. Donald J. Trump (@realDonaldTrump), "Gee, @meetthepress with @chucktodd was getting terrible ratings then, with me, he set records—I saved his job, but Chuck still not nice!" Twitter, December 6, 2015, https://twitter.com/realdonaldtrump/status/673655438060204032.

42. According to Thomas Patterson, 77 percent of the general election news coverage about Trump was negative: Thomas E. Patterson, "News Coverage of the 2016 General Election: How the Press Failed the Voters," Shorenstein Center, December 7, 2016, https://shorensteincenter.org/news-coverage-2016-general-election/?platform=hootsuite.

43. "Despite the similarly Herculean efforts of *The New York Times*, which dedicated 18 journalists to fact-checking the TV debates in real-time, or of NPR, which turned over 30 staffers to a similar endeavor, despite the *Guardian*'s Lyin' Trump column and so much more, some 61 million Americans were unfazed enough by the idea of a serial liar in the Oval Office to vote for him." Pilkington, "Trump's Scorched-Earth Tactics," https://www.cjr.org/special_report/trumps_tactics_wound_the_media.php.

44. Art Swift, "Americans' Trust in Mass Media Sinks to New Low," Gallup, September 14, 2016, http://www.gallup.com/poll/195542/americans-trust-mass-media-sinks-new-low.aspx.

45. "Donald Trump Campaign Rally in Cleveland, Ohio," C-SPAN video, 1:01:06, October 22, 2016, https://www.c-span.org/video/?417332-1/republican-ticket-campaigns-cleveland-ohio&start=2044.

46. Rosie Gray (@RosieGray), "Friendly interaction outside the press pen. 'Lugen-presse!'" Twitter archive, October 22, 2016, https://web.archive.org/web/20161024212934/https://twitter.com/rosiegray/status/790328143022329856; https://time.com/4544562/donald-trump-supporters-lugenpresse/; Nick Corasaniti, "Partisan Crowds at Trump Rallies Menace and Frighten News Media," *Washington Post*, October 14, 2016, https://www.nytimes.com/2016/10/15/us/politics/trump-media-attacks.html.

Chapter 3

1. "Trump: Favorable/Unfavorable," Real Clear Politics, http://www.realclearpolitics.com/epolls/other/trump_favorableunfavorable-5493.html#polls.

2. Robert Mackey, "Brutal Images of Syrian Boy Drowned Off Turkey Must Be Seen, Activists Say," *New York Times*, September 2, 2015, https://www.nytimes.com/2015/09/03/world/middleeast/brutal-images-of-syrian-boy-drowned-off-turkey-must-be-seen-activists-say.html.

3. Anne Barnard and Karim Shoumali, "Image of Drowned Syrian, Aylan Kurdi, 3, Brings Migrant Crisis into Focus," *New York Times*, September 3, 2015, https://www.nytimes.com/2015/09/04/world/europe/syria-boy-drowning.html?_r=1.

4. Gardiner Harris, David E. Sanger, and David M. Herszenhorn, "Obama Increases Number of Syrian Refugees for U.S. Resettlement to 10,000," *New York Times*, September 10, 2015, https://www.nytimes.com/2015/09/11/world/middleeast/obama-directs-administration-to-accept-10000-syrian-refugees.html.

5. Admin, "Aylan Kurdi's Family Had Free Housing in Turkey, While Father's Story Is Full of Holes," *The Muslim Issue*, September 4, 2015, https://themuslimissue.wordpress.com/2015/09/04/family-of-drowned-toddler-aylan-kurdi-had-been-given-free-housing-in-turkey-while-fathers-story-is-full-of-holes/.

6. Paul Joseph Watson, "The 'Migrant Crisis' Is about Imposing Multiculturalism on the West," Prison Planet, September 7, 2015, https://www.prisonplanet.com/the-migrant-crisis-is-about-imposing-multiculturalism-on-the-west.html.

7. SooperMexican, "Syrian Refugees Chant 'F**k You!' and 'Allah Akbar!' in Hungary," The Right Scoop, September 7, 2015, http://therightscoop.com/syrian-refugees-chant-fk-you-and-allah-akbar-in-hungary/.

8. The Right Scoop charged that "only HALF are actually from Syria, even though the media keeps calling them Syrian refugees. Why the hell are Afghanis sneaking into Europe and calling themselves 'refugees'?!" That same day Breitbart asked and answered "The 5 Awkward Questions They Won't Answer about the Drowned Boy, Syria and Our 'Moral Duty.'" SooperMexican, "United Nations Says 72% of Syrian 'Refugees' Are Men, Only 13% Are Children," The Right Scoop, September 8, 2015, http://therightscoop.com/united-nations-says-72-of-syrian-refugees-are-men-only-13-are-children/; James Delingpole, "The 5 Awkward Questions They Won't Answer about the Drowned By, Syria, and Our 'Moral Duty,'" Breitbart, September 8, 2015, http://www.breitbart.com/london/2015/09/08/the-5-awkward-questions-they-wont-answer-about-the-drowned-boy-syria-and-our-moral-duty/.

9. Rush Limbaugh, "The Caliphate Invades Europe," *The Rush Limbaugh Show*, September 8, 2015, https://www.rushlimbaugh.com/daily/2015/09/08/the_caliphate_invades_europe/.

10. "Although mainstream media coverage of the migrant crisis has focused on happy families and children, footage not broadcast by TV networks shows a different side to some of those crossing into Europe. A video shot just outside Budapest's Keleti railway station shows Muslim migrants chanting 'Allahu Akbar' and 'f**k you' as they engage in running battles with police." Paul Joseph Watson, "Muslim Refugees Chant 'Allahu Akbar,' 'F**k You,' Attack Citizens, Throw Feces," InfoWars, September 8, 2015, https://www.infowars.com/muslim-refugees-chant-allahu-akbar-fk-you-attack-citizens-throw-feces/; "European Migrant Crisis: A Trojan Horse for ISIS Invasion," YouTube, 35:08, September 9, 2015, https://www.youtube.com/watch?v=WU8xKPe5MhA; Callum Borchers, "Alex Jones Should Not Be Taken Seriously, According to Alex Jones's Lawyers," *Washington Post*, April 17, 2017, https://www.washingtonpost.com/news/the-fix/wp/2017/04/17/trump-called-alex-jones-amazing-joness-own-lawyer-calls-him-a-performance-artist/?utm_term=.a00b07f4134e.

11. Emily Arrowood, "*Fox & Friends* Chanting 'Allahu Akbar' Shows Refugees May Be Terrorists," Media Matters for America, September 9, 2015, https://www.mediamatters.org/blog/2015/09/09/fox-amp-friends-suggests-chanting-allahu-akbar/205443. Fox News had been connecting the migrants to potential terrorists repeatedly on its shows since September 2, 2015. Brennan Suen, "Fox News Exploits European Refugee Crisis to Stoke Islamophobic

Fear That Muslim Refugees May Be Terrorists," Media Matters for America, September 10, 2015, https://www.mediamatters.org/research/2015/09/10/fox-news-exploits-european-refugee-crisis-to-st/205472.

12. "So horrible on a humanitarian basis when you see that. It's like incredible what's going on. But, you know, we have so many problems. And the answer is possibly yes, Cokie, possibly yes. But we have so many problems of our own." "Donald Trump Calls in to Morning Joe," MSNBC video, 24:44, September 4, 2015, http://www.msnbc.com/morning-joe/watch/donald-trump-calls-in-to-morning-joe-519432259809.

13. "Trump_Billo_Migrants_Final," clip from *The O'Reilly Factor*, Fox News, reposted on The Right Scoop, 3:14, 0:50–1:41, September 8, 2015, http://therightscoop.com/trump-we-have-to-accept-migrants-here-because-theyre-living-in-hell-in-syria/.

14. John Nolte, "'You Have To': Trump Would Allow Syrian Refugees into America," Breitbart, September 9, 2015, http://www.breitbart.com/big-government/2015/09/09/you-have-to-trump-would-allow-syrian-refugees-into-america/; Jonathon Martin, Jim Rutenberg, and Maggie Haberman, "Donald Trump Appoints Media Firebrand to Run Campaign," *New York Times*, August 17, 2016, https://www.nytimes.com/2016/08/18/us/politics/donald-trump-stephen-bannon-paul-manafort.html?_r=0.

15. Clip from *Hannity*, Fox News, reposted on Media Matters for America, 3:40, https://www.mediamatters.org/embed/clips/2015/09/09/41890/fnc-hannity-20150909-refugees; Joshua Gillin, "Donald Trump: Syrian Refugees Potentially Headed to U.S. Are Mostly Men," Politifact, October 4, 2015, http://www.politifact.com/truth-o-meter/statements/2015/oct/04/donald-trump/donald-trump-syrian-refugees-are-mostly-men/.

16. "That competition to accept refugees would be fine if we knew that the refugees plan on assimilating into Western notions of civilized society, and if we knew that they were indeed victims of radical Muslim atrocities. Unfortunately, we know neither. It is deeply suspicious that major Muslim countries that do not border Syria refuse to take in large numbers of refugees, except for Algeria and Egypt . . . images show a disproportionate number of young males in crowds of refugees. And those images reflect statistical reality: according to the United Nations Human Rights Commission, Mediterranean Sea refugees are overwhelmingly male: just 13 percent are women, and just 15 percent are children. The other 72 percent are men. Compare that population to the refugees in the Middle East from the same conflicts: 49.5 percent male, and 50.5 percent female, with 38.5 percent under the age of 12. Those are wildly different populations." Ben Shapiro, "The Syrian Refugee Wave Hits Europe: Invasion, Immigration, or Both?" Breitbart, September 9, 2015, http://www.breitbart.com/national-security/2015/09/09/the-syrian-refugee-wave-hits-europe-invasion-immigration-or-both/.

17. Jim Tankersley and Scott Clement, "It's Not Just Donald Trump," *Washington Post*, November 24, 2015, https://www.washingtonpost.com/news/wonk/wp/2015/11/24/its-not-just-donald-trump-half-of-republicans-shares-his-views-on-immigrants-and-refugees/?utm_term=.b92e7aa2e8d1.

18. "Presidential Candidate Donald Trump in Keene, New Hampshire," C-SPAN video, 1:00:36, September 30, 2015, https://www.c-span.org/video/?328446-1/donald-trump-campaign-rally-keene-new-hampshire.

19. "But the most striking transformation in the dozen or so feet dividing Africa and the EU is that men, woman and children stop being seen as human." Charlotte McDonald-Gibson, "Refugee Crisis: Far-Right's Rise and Dehumanising of Conflict Victims are Greatest Barriers to Joint European Action," *Independent*, September 8, 2015, http://www.independent.co.uk/news/world/europe/refugee-crisis-far-rights-rise-and-dehumanising-of-conflict-victims-are-greatest-barriers-to-joint-10492109.html.

20. "Speech: Donald Trump in Franklin, TN," Factbase, October 3, 2015, https://factba.se/transcript/donald-trump-speech-franklin-tn-october-3-2015.

21. Politifact also fact-checked this claim: Gillin, "Trump: Refugees Are Mostly Men," Politifact, http://www.politifact.com/truth-o-meter/statements/2015/oct/04/donald-trump/donald-trump-syrian-refugees-are-mostly-men/.

22. Benjamin Bell, "Trump Says He'd 'Sit Back,' 'See What Happens' in Syria as Russia Conducts Airstrikes," ABC News, October 4, 2015, http://abcnews.go.com/thisweek/trump-hed-sit-back-syria-russia-conducts-airstrikes/story?id=34234772.

23. "'This Would Blow the Trojan Horse Away': Trump Warns of ISIS among Syrian Refugees," *Special Report with Bret Baier*, Fox News, 19:50, October 6, 2015, http://insider.foxnews.com/2015/10/06/donald-trump-warns-isis-militants-among-syrian-refugees.

24. "Donald Trump: Refugees Could Be the 'Ultimate Trojan Horse,'" *Hannity*, Fox News, reposted on YouTube, 11:47, November 17, 2015, https://www.youtube.com/watch?v=K9Pr6a_nMU4.

25. "Full Event: Donald Trump Campaign Rally in Newton, IA (11 19 15)," YouTube video, 1:22:05, 20:07–20:35, 21:35–21:45, February 10, 2016, https://www.youtube.com/watch?v=ld-r2pnMH8U.

26. Virgil, "The Trojan Horse: Laocoön's Warning," *The Aeneid Book II*, trans. A. S. Kline, Poetry in Translation, 2012, http://www.poetryintranslation.com/PITBR/Latin/VirgilAeneidII.htm#anchor_Toc536009309.

27. "Trump Rally in Mount Pleasant, South Carolina," C-SPAN, December 7, 2015, https://www.c-span.org/video/?401762-1/presidential-candidate-donald-trump-rally-mount-pleasant-south-carolina.

28. Trump's statement was removed from his website during controversy over his Muslim Ban in 2017: "Donald J. Trump is calling for a total and complete shutdown of Muslims entering the United States until our country's representatives can figure out what is going on. According to Pew Research, among others, there is great hatred towards Americans by large segments of the Muslim population. Most recently, a poll from the Center for Security Policy released data showing '25% of those polled agreed that violence against Americans here in the United States is justified as a part of the global jihad' and 51% of those polled, 'agreed that Muslims in America should have the choice of being governed according to Shariah.'

Shariah authorizes such atrocities as murder against non-believers who won't convert, beheadings and more unthinkable acts that pose great harm to Americans, especially women. Mr. Trump stated, 'Without looking at the various polling data, it is obvious to anybody the hatred is beyond comprehension. Where this hatred comes from and why we will have to determine. Until we are able to determine and understand this problem and the dangerous threat it poses, our country cannot be the victims of horrendous attacks by people that believe only in Jihad, and have no sense of reason or respect for human life. If I win the election for President, we are going to Make America Great Again.'" Donald Trump Campaign Site, "Donald J. Trump Statement on Preventing Muslim Immigration," press release, December 7, 2015, https://web.archive.org/web/20151207230751/https://www.donaldjtrump.com/press-releases/donald-j.-trump-statement-on-preventing-muslim-immigration.

29. "10 Takes on Donald Trump's Muslim Proposal," CNN, December 10, 2015, http://www.cnn.com/2015/12/10/opinions/opinion-roundup-donald-trump/index.html.

30. The Editorial Board, "The Trump Effect, and How It Spreads," *New York Times*, December 10, 2015, https://www.nytimes.com/2015/12/10/opinion/the-trump-effect-and-how-it-spreads.html?action=click&pgtype=Homepage&clickSource=story-heading&module=opinion-c-col-left-region&region=opinion-c-col-left-region&WT.nav=opinion-c-col-left-region&_r=0.

31. *Detroit Free Press* Editorial Board, "We Stand Together. We Are Better Than Bigotry," *Detroit Free Press*, December 9, 2015, http://www.freep.com/story/opinion/editorials/2015/12/08/free-press-editorial-muslims-trump-bigotry-we-stand-together/76974510/.

32. Lisa Hagen, "Poll: Majority of Republicans Support Trump's Muslim Ban," *The Hill*, December 9, 2015, http://thehill.com/blogs/ballot-box/presidential-races/262656-poll-majority-of-republicans-support-trumps-muslim-ban.

33. Scott Clement, "Republicans Embrace Trump's Ban on While Most Others Reject It," *Washington Post*, December 14, 2015, https://www.washingtonpost.com/politics/americans-reject-trumps-muslim-ban-but-republicans-embrace-it/2015/12/14/24f1c1a0-a285-11e5-9c4e-be37f66848bb_story.html?utm_term=.eed48eb8e1c5.

34. Shelley Hepworth et al., "Covering Trump: An Oral History of an Unforgettable Campaign," *Columbia Journalism Review*, November 22, 2016, https://www.cjr.org/special_report/trump_media_press_journalists.php.

Chapter 4

1. "Trump: Favorable/Unfavorable," Real Clear Politics, http://www.realclearpolitics.com/epolls/other/trump_favorableunfavorable-5493.html#polls.

2. Donald J. Trump (@realDonaldTrump), "I didn't suggest a database—a reporter did. We must defeat Islamic terrorism & have surveillance, including a watch list, to protect America," Twitter, November 20, 2015, https://twitter.com/realdonaldtrump/status/667777348029292544.

3. "Donald Trump Rally in Birmingham, AL November 21, 2015," YouTube, 1:10:43, 35:00–37:59, February 10, 2016, https://www.youtube.com/watch?v=akKDHGtMVhI.

4. Maggie Haberman, "Donald Trump Calls for Surveillance of 'Certain Mosques' and a SyrianSyrain Refugee Database," *New York Times*, November 21, 2015, https://www.nytimes.com/2015/11/22/us/politics/donald-trump-syrian-muslims-surveillance.html.

5. Donald Trump and Ben Carson, interview by George Stephanopoulos, "This Week with George Stephanopoulos," ABC News, November 22, 2015, http://abcnews.go.com/Politics/week-transcript-donald-trump-ben-carson/story?id=35336008.

6. Kim LaCapria, "Trump Insists He Witnessed Cheering Muslims on 9/11," Snopes, November 22, 2015, http://www.snopes.com/2015/11/22/donald-trump-cheering-911; David Mikkelson, "Fact Check: Palestinians Dancing in the Street," Snopes, March 9, 2008, http://www.snopes.com/rumors/cnn.asp; David Mikkelson, "Fact Check: Dunkin Donuts 'Celebrating Employees' Rumor," Snopes, April 26, 2008, http://www.snopes.com/rumors/dunkin.asp.

7. Eyder Peralta, "Trump Doubles Down on Claim He Saw Thousands Cheer in N.J. on 9/11," NPR, November 22, 2015, http://www.npr.org/sections/thetwo-way/2015/11/22/457012242/trump-doubles-down-on-claim-he-saw-thousands-cheer-on-9-11.

8. Serge F. Kovaleski and Fredrick Kunkle, "Northern New Jersey Draws Probers' Eyes," *Washington Post*, September 18, 2001, https://www.washingtonpost.com/archive/politics/2001/09/18/northern-new-jersey-draws-probers-eyes/40f82ea4-e015-4d6e-a87e-93aa433fafdc/?tid=a_inl&utm_term=.e3a6906a64c7.

9. Donald J. Trump (@realDonaldTrump), "Via @washingtonpost 9/18/01. I want an apology! Many people have tweeted that I am right! wapo.st/1R1siFz 'In Jersey City, within hours of two jetliners' plowing into the World Trade Center, law enforcement authorities detained and questioned a number of people who were allegedly seen celebrating the attacks and holding tailgate-style parties on rooftops while they watched the devastation on the other side of the river,'" Twitter, November 23, 2015, https://twitter.com/realDonaldTrump/status/668867262456156160?ref_src=twsrc%5Etfw&ref_url=http%3A%2F%2F; LaCapria, "Trump Insists," https://www.snopes.com/news/2015/11/22/donald-trump-cheering-911/; "Donald Trump (2015-11-23) Columbus, Ohio. Full Speech," YouTube, 59:54, 28:25–33:30, December 1, 2015, https://www.youtube.com/watch?v=feJrGAKwN4E.

10. "Trump Columbus, Ohio," 33:45–34:34, https://www.youtube.com/watch?v=feJrGAKwN4E.

11. Glenn Kessler, "Trump's Outrageous Claim That 'Thousands' of New Jersey Muslims Celebrated the 9/11 Attacks," *Washington Post*, November 22, 2015, https://www.washingtonpost.com/news/fact-checker/wp/2015/11/22/donald-trumps-outrageous-claim-that-thousands-of-new-jersey-muslims-celebrated-the-911-attacks/?utm_term=.5d33d5159a17.

12. Corey Lewandowski, interview by Steve Bannon, Breitbart News Daily, republished on Soundcloud from Sirius XM Radio, November 24, 2015, https://soundcloud.com/breitbart/breitbart-news-daily-corey-lewandowski-november-24-2015.

13. "Donald Trump Rally Myrtle Beach South Carolina 11/24/15," YouTube, 1:16:36, November 24, 2015, https://www.youtube.com/watch?v=VNocmPffX4c.

14. Donald J. Trump (@realDonaldTrump), "The failing @nytimes should be focused on good reporting and the papers financial survival and not with constant hits on Donald Trump!" Twitter, November 25, 2015, https://twitter.com/realdonaldtrump/status/669687491100844032; Donald J. Trump (@realDonaldTrump), "The @nytimes is so poorly run and managed that other family members are looking to take over control. With unfunded liabilities-big trouble!" Twitter, November 25, 2015, https://twitter.com/realdonaldtrump/status/669689398112460800; Donald J. Trump (@realDonaldTrump), "The dopes at the @nytimes bought the Boston Globe for $1.3 billion and sold it for $1.00. Their great old headquarters-gave it away! So dumb," Twitter, November 25, 2015, https://twitter.com/realdonaldtrump/status/669690995857080320; Donald J. Trump (@realDonaldTrump), "So, since the people at the @nytimes have made all bad decisions over the last decade, why do people care what they write. Incompetent!" Twitter, November 25, 2015, https://twitter.com/realdonaldtrump/status/669692360465514496; Donald J. Trump (@realDonaldTrump), "The numbers at the @nytimes are so dismal, especially advertising revenue, that big help will be needed fast. A once great institution-SAD!" Twitter, November 25, 2015, https://twitter.com/realdonaldtrump/status/669694813005094912; Donald J. Trump (@realDonaldTrump), "The failing @nytimes should focus on fair and balanced reporting rather than constant hit jobs on me. Yesterday 3 boring articles, today 2!" November 26, 2015, https://twitter.com/realdonaldtrump/status/669995673945808896.

15. Donald J. Trump (@realDonaldTrump), "@CNN has to do better reporting if it wants to keep up with the crowd. So totally one-sided and biased against me that it is becoming boring," Twitter, November 28, 2015, https://twitter.com/realdonaldtrump/status/670815295091683328; Donald J. Trump (@realDonaldTrump), "@wzpd8z: Mr. Trump, Chuck Todd is a moron, all kinds of youtube videos showing muslims celebrating 911. I would show it on your ads," Twitter retweet, November 30, 2015, https://twitter.com/realdonaldtrump/status/671316321443954688; Donald J. Trump (@realDonaldTrump), "Highly untalented Wash Post blogger, Jennifer Rubin, a real dummy, never writes fairly about me. Why does Wash Post have low IQ people?" Twitter, December 1, 2015, https://twitter.com/realdonaldtrump/status/671792600052027393; Donald J. Trump (@realDonaldTrump), "It was recently reported that 3rd rate $ losing @Politico is a foil for the Clintons. Questions given to Clinton in advance. No credibility," Twitter, December 3, 2015, https://twitter.com/realdonaldtrump/status/672498342656634880.

16. Donald J. Trump (@realDonaldTrump), "It Was Recently Reported That 3rd Rate $ Losing @Politico Is a Foil for the Clintons. Questions given to Clinton in Advance. No Credibility," Twitter, December 3, 2015, https://twitter.com/realdonaldtrump/status/672498342656634880.

17. Kovaleski quoted by Erin Durkin, "Reporter Serge Kovaleski, Whom Donald Trump Says He's Never Seen Before, Spent the Day with the Billionaire while Covering His

1989 Airline Launch for the Daily News," *New York Daily News*, November 27, 2015, http://www.nydailynews.com/new-york/reporter-donald-trump-mocked-spent-day-mogul-1989-article-1.2448381?version=meter+at+0&module=meter-Links&pgtype=Blogs&contentId=&mediaId=&referrer=&priority=true&action=click&contentCollection=meter-links-click.

18. Maggie Haberman, "Donald Trump Says His Mocking of *New York Times* Reporter Was Misread," *New York Times*, November 26, 2015, https://www.nytimes.com/2015/11/27/us/politics/donald-trump-says-his-mocking-of-new-york-times-reporter-was-misread.html?_r=0; Jose A. DelReal, "Trump Draws Scornful Rebuke for Mocking Reporter With Disability," *Washington Post*, November 26, 2015, https://www.washingtonpost.com/news/post-politics/wp/2015/11/25/trump-blasted-by-new-york-times-after-mocking-reporter-with-disability/?utm_term=.268a3a7bc629.

19. Selzer & Company, *Bloomberg Politics National Poll*, August 5–8, 2016, http://assets.bwbx.io/documents/users/iqjWHBFdfxIU/rAjnCYJjgvBw/v0; John McCormick, "Clinton Up 6 on Trump in Two-Way Race in Bloomberg National Poll," *Bloomberg*, August 10, 2016, https://www.bloomberg.com/news/articles/2016-08-10/bloomberg-politics-national-poll.

20. Donald J. Trump (@realDonaldTrump), "'@pthebnyc: @realDonaldTrump @Sari_Swensen @nytimes no need to explain, Sir. We've got your back.' Thanks!" Twitter, November 26, 2015, https://twitter.com/realdonaldtrump/status/670073898923384833.

21. Donald J. Trump (@realDonaldTrump), "@DeusVultGeorgia: @MingBlueTeaCup @RickCanton @_Holly_Renee @realDonaldTrump should the reporter's dishonesty be shielded from ridicule?" Twitter, November 27, 2015, https://twitter.com/realdonaldtrump/status/670309883581964288.

22. Donald J. Trump (@realDonaldTrump), "@MargaretCrowth1: @realDonaldTrump So like the media to make something out of nothing. Don't let them sidetrack from the message." Twitter, November 27, 2015, https://twitter.com/realdonaldtrump/status/670356526977179648.

23. "FNN: FULL Donald Trump Rally Waterville Valley, NH," YouTube, 1:10:51, 36:36, December 1, 2015, https://www.youtube.com/watch?v=Cm-0vLdHceY.

24. Quinnipiac University Poll, "Bump for Trump as Carson Fades in Republican Race, Quinnipiac University National Poll Finds; Clinton, Sanders Surge in Matchups with GOP Leaders," December 2, 2015, https://poll.qu.edu/national/release-detail?ReleaseID=2307.

25. Healy and Haberman, "95,000 Words," http://www.nytimes.com/2015/12/06/us/politics/95000-words-many-of-them-ominous-from-donald-trumps-tongue.html?_r=0. I should note that I contributed to the analysis for this story and that I am quoted several times in the article. I realize that this makes my quoting the article to support my analysis here troubling, but I don't see another option. The front-page, above-the-fold Sunday *New York Times* analysis of a week's worth of Trump's words that called them "ominous" and called him a "demagogue" was a significant moment in the public discourse of the 2016 election, particularly within the context of Trump's attacks on the *Times* over the previous two weeks.

The *Times* editorial board had previously printed an editorial on November 24, 2015, calling him a demagogue and comparing him to Joseph McCarthy and George Wallace. Editorial Board, "Mr. Trump's Applause Lies," *New York Times*, November 24, 2015, https://www.nytimes.com/2015/11/24/opinion/mr-trumps-applause-lies.html.

26. Forty-seven percent of GOP voters held pro-deportation and antirefugee positions and, of those, a majority were committed to voting for Trump. "Pro-deportation/anti-refugee voters account for almost three-quarters of Trump's support," according to an ABC/*Washington Post* survey, November 24, 2015: Jim Tankersley and Scott Clement, "It's Not Just Donald Trump: Half of Republicans Share His Views on Immigrants and Refugees," *Washington Post*, November 24, 2015, https://www.washingtonpost.com/news/wonk/wp/2015/11/24/its-not-just-donald-trump-half-of-republicans-shares-his-views-on-immigrants-and-refugees/?utm_term=.b92e7aa2e8d1.

27. "Donald J. Trump today demanded an apology from the failing *New York Times* which accused him (during a major speech before 10,000 people in Myrtle Beach, SC) of mocking a reporter's physical disability when in fact, Mr. Trump does not know anything about the reporter or anything about what the reporter looks like. He was merely mocking the fact that the reporter was trying to pull away from a story that he wrote 14 years ago. Mr. Trump stated, 'Serge Kovaleski must think a lot of himself if he thinks I remember him from decades ago—if I ever met him at all, which I doubt I did. He should stop using his disability to grandstand and get back to reporting for a paper that is rapidly going down the tubes.'" "Donald J. Trump Demands An Apology from New York Times," Trump-Pence campaign site, November 26, 2015, https://web.archive.org/web/20170428151610/; Trump's Twitter account tweeted images of the statement: Donald J. Trump (@realDonaldTrump), Twitter, November 26, 2015, https://twitter.com/realDonaldTrump/status/669980142475845632.

28. "Donald Trump Destroys NY Times at Sarasota Rally 'They Owe Me an Apology,'" YouTube, 14:43, November 28, 2015, https://www.youtube.com/watch?v=Du0M0PS6g8k.

Chapter 5

1. "Trump: Favorable/Unfavorable," Real Clear Politics, http://www.realclearpolitics.com/epolls/other/trump_favorableunfavorable-5493.html#polls.

2. Donald J. Trump (@realDonaldTrump), "@ResisTyr: Mr.Trump . . . BOTH Cruz AND Rubio are ineligible to be POTUS! It's a SLAM DUNK CASE!! Check it! Powderedwigsociety.com/eligibility-of . . ." Twitter, February 20, 2016, https://twitter.com/realDonaldTrump/status/701045567783219201.

3. Thomas Madison, "Video: This Is Why Cruz and Rubio Didn't Attempt to Have a Court Decide Their Eligibility in the Past. They Would Have Been Ruled Ineligible!" Powdered Wig Society, February 12, 2016, http://powderedwigsociety.com/eligibility-of-cruz-and-rubio/. The original source is here: "Natural Born Citizen and Naturalized Citizen Explained," Publius-Huldah's Blog, video, 12:08, February 11, 2016, https://publiushuldah.

wordpress.com/category/natural-born-citizen/. The lawyer is Publius Huldah, "a retired litigation attorney who now lives in Tennessee. Before getting a law degree, she got a degree in philosophy where she specialized in political philosophy and epistemology (theories of knowledge)," Renew America, *Publius Huldah Column*, http://www.renewamerica.com/columns/huldah.

4. Trump also made the attacks at his rallies in Iowa, among other places. According to one CNN report, Trump's attacks did indeed sow doubt about Cruz's eligibility, at least for one of Trump's rally crowd members: "Steve Ziller, a farmer from Belmond, Iowa, said he was 'amazed' to learn that Cruz was born in Canada. 'I really did not know that he was from Canada. So that was new to me. I was not aware of that,' said Ziller, adding that he agrees with Trump that this could raise questions about Cruz's eligibility to be president." M. J. Lee, "In Iowa, Donald Trump Intensifies 'Birther' Attack against Ted Cruz," CNN, January 9, 2016, http://www.cnn.com/2016/01/09/politics/donald-trump-ted-cruz-birther-iowa/index.html.

5. "Trump Rally in Birmingham, AL," 1:10:43, 18:02, https://www.youtube.com/watch?v=akkdhgtmvhi.hgtmvhi.

6. Robert Siegel, "Comic Hero: Why Donald Trump's Candid Rhetoric Resonates with Supporters," *WVTF Virginia Public Radio*, January 19, 2017, http://wvtf.org/post/comic-hero-why-donald-trumps-candid-rhetoric-resonates-supporters.

7. "Trump Connects Cruz's Father to Lee Harvey Oswald," Fox News video, 10:54, May 3, 2016, http://insider.foxnews.com/2016/05/03/watch-trump-calls-out-cruzs-father-old-photo-lee-harvey-oswald.

8. "Lee Harvey Oswald, Ted Cruz Sr. and the Men Who Killed JFK," Reddit, April 14, 2016, https://www.reddit.com/r/conspiracy/comments/4eotqm/lee_harvey_oswald_ted_cruz_sr_and_the_men_who/.

9. MACU, "Was the Father of Presidential Hopeful Cruz Involved in the JFK Assassination? By Wayne Madsen Report," *Milfuegos*, April 7, 2016, http://milfuegos.blogspot.com/2016/04/was-father-of-presidential-hopeful-cruz.html.

10. Wayne Madsen, "Was Cruz's Father Linked to the JFK Assassination?" InfoWars, April 15, 2016, https://www.infowars.com/was-cruzs-father-linked-to-the-jfk-assassination/; Alex Jones, "AJ Show (Full Video Commercial Free) Monday 4/18/16: Wayne Madsen, Lew Rockwell: Election Fraud," YouTube video, 3:03:57, 1:13:00, https://www.youtube.com/watch?v=7EnFIvf36Gs.

11. J. R. Taylor, "Ted Cruz's Father—Caught with JFK Assassin," *National Enquirer*, April 20, 2016, http://www.nationalenquirer.com/celebrity/ted-cruz-scandal-father-jfk-assassination/; Mike Jaccarino et al., "Ted Cruz's Dad Tied to JFK Murder Plot," *National Enquirer*, May 2, 2016, https://archive.org/details/national_enquirer_may_2_2016.

12. Jaccarino et al., "Ted Cruz's Dad," https://archive.org/details/National_Enquirer_May_2_2016.

13. David Mikkelson, "Was Ted Cruz's Father Linked to the JFK Assassination?" Snopes, April 17, 2016, http://www.snopes.com/2016/04/17/

was-ted-cruzs-father-linked-to-the-jfk-assassination/; Louis Jacobson and Linda Qiu, "Donald Trump's Pants on Fire Claim Linking Ted Cruz's Father and JFK Assassination," Politifact, May 3, 2016, http://www.politifact.com/truth-o-meter/statements/2016/may/03/donald-trump/donald-trumps-ridiculous-claim-linking-ted-cruzs-f/; Robert Farley, "Fact Check: Trump Defends Claim on Oswald and Cruz's Father," *USA Today*, July 23, 2016, https://www.usatoday.com/story/news/politics/elections/2016/07/23/fact-check-trump-lee-harvey-oswald-rafael-cruz/87475714/; Robert Farley, "Trump Defends Oswald Claim," FactCheck.org, July 22, 2016, http://www.factcheck.org/2016/07/trump-defends-oswald-claim/.

14. Callum Borchers, "The Very Cozy Relationship between Donald Trump and the *National Enquirer*," *Washington Post*, March 28, 2016, https://www.washingtonpost.com/news/the-fix/wp/2016/03/28/the-very-cozy-relationship-between-donald-trump-and-the-national-enquirer/?utm_term=.fd5dc18c5637; Jeffrey Toobin, "The National Enquirer's Fervor for Trump," *New Yorker*, July 3, 2017, http://www.newyorker.com/magazine/2017/07/03/the-national-enquirers-fervor-for-trump; Sam Reisman, "Okay, *National Enquirer* Literally Linking Ted Cruz to JFK Assassination Now," Mediaite, April 20, 2016, http://www.mediaite.com/online/okay-national-enquirer-literally-linking-ted-cruz-to-jfk-assassination-now/. "In his own words, Presidential hopeful DONALD TRUMP reveals his humble beginning in a blockbuster ENQUIRER exclusive as we launch a blockbuster multipart series written exclusively for our readers by Trump himself." Donald Trump, "Donald Trump the Man Behind the Legend," *National Enquirer*, April 15, 2011, http://www.nationalenquirer.com/celebrity/donald-trump-man-behind-legend/; Gabriel Sherman, "Donald Trump's Alliance with the *National Enquirer*," *New York Magazine*, October 30, 2015, http://nymag.com/daily/intelligencer/2015/10/trumps-alliance-with-the-national-enquirer.html. "During the 2016 presidential election campaign, the tabloid was filled with lurid rumors about Trump's rivals, including assertions that the father of Republican senator Ted Cruz was involved in the assassination of former President John F. Kennedy, which Trump repeated on the campaign trail. Other unsubstantiated stories alleged that Cruz had multiple extramarital affairs, Republican candidate Ben Carson botched operations as a neurosurgeon, and that Hillary Clinton was on her deathbed." Tom Porter, "Trump's Pecker: How the President's Friendship with American Media CEO Gilded Trump's Way to the White House," *Newsweek*, July 1, 2017, http://www.newsweek.com/donald-trump-david-pecker-national-enquirer-630892.

15. Asawin Suebsaeng, "Hannity Encourages Trump's JFK-Cruz Theory," *Daily Beast*, May 3, 2016, http://www.thedailybeast.com/hannity-encourages-trumps-jfk-cruz-theory.

16. Ryan Struyk, "Donald Trump Defends Linking Ted Cruz's Father to JFK Assassin," ABC News, May 4, 2016, http://abcnews.go.com/Politics/donald-trump-apologize-implying-cruz-father-kennedy-assassin/story?id=38865084.

17. "Donald Trump: I'm 'Confident' I Can Unite 'Much' of the GOP," *Today* video, 5:08, May 4, 2016, http://www.today.com/video/donald-trump-i-m-confident-i-can-unite-much-of-the-gop-679094851961.

18. "Donald Trump's Official CNN Interview as Presumptive Nominee (Part 1)," CNN

video, YouTube, 9:41, May 4, 2016, https://www.youtube.com/watch?v=4rj7B0fU1jw.

19. "Ted Cruz's Entire Donald Trump Rant," CNN video, 11:50, May 3, 2016, http://www.cnn.com/videos/politics/2016/05/03/ted-cruz-donald-trump-rant-full-sot.cnn/video/playlists/donald-trump-vs-ted-cruz/.

20. Donald J. Trump (@realDonaldTrump), "Wow, Lyin' Ted Cruz really went wacko today. Made all sorts of crazy charges. Can't function under pressure—not very presidential. Sad!" Twitter, May 3, 2016, https://twitter.com/realdonaldtrump/status/727634574298255361?lang=en.

21. "Did Cruz Drop Out to Cover Up Kennedy Assassination Connection?" YouTube video, The Alex Jones Channel, 12:25, May 4, 2016, https://www.youtube.com/watch?v=BS-HbHfGiec.

22. "Did Cruz Drop Out to Cover Up Kennedy Assassination Connection?" YouTube video, The Alex Jones Channel, 12:25, May 4, 2016, https://www.youtube.com/watch?v=BS-HbHfGiec.

23. "Senator Ted Cruz Declines to Endorse Donald Trump," C-SPAN video, 23:45, July 20, 2016, https://www.c-span.org/video/?c4612566/senator-ted-cruz-declines-endorse-donald-trump.

24. "Senator Ted Cruz Declines to Endorse Donald Trump," C-SPAN video, 23:45, July 20, 2016, https://www.c-span.org/video/?c4612566/senator-ted-cruz-declines-endorse-donald-trump.

25. "Fit to Be President? O'Reilly Debates Krauthammer," Fox News video, YouTube, 11:15, May 3, 2016, https://www.youtube.com/watch?v=0JLzzQHqeeo.

Chapter 6

1. "Trump: Favorable/Unfavorable," Real Clear Politics, http://www.realclearpolitics.com/epolls/other/trump_favorableunfavorable-5493.html#polls.

2. J. Brian Charles, "Transcript of Donald Trump's Economic Policy Speech to Detroit Economic Club," *The Hill*, August 8, 2016, https://thehill.com/blogs/pundits-blog/campaign/290777-transcript-of-donald-trumps-economic-policy-speech-to-detroit.

3. "Change has to come from the outside. Or, we are never going to understand it and I will tell you. I have been on the inside. The day I announced of June 16th of last year, I became the person on the outside. We have to fix our country. The fact that Washington establishment has tried so hard to stop our campaign is only more proof that our campaign represents the kind of change that only arrives once in a lifetime. It is terrible." "Presidential Candidate Donald Trump Rally in St. Augustine, Florida," C-SPAN video, 47:36, October 24, 2016, https://www.c-span.org/video/?417407-1/donald-trump-campaigns-st-augustine-florida.

4. "Americans are warned that they have deviated from the abiding principles of the American Dream; their present suffering is a sign of their infidelity to the past. The

presidential candidate offers to lead the people through repentance back to their fundamental national values and, thereby, restore America to its former greatness. . . . The modern jeremiad both laments America's present condition and celebrates the prospect of its ultimate fulfillment. It glorifies America's special status as man's 'last best hope,' and constantly warns Americans of their failure to live up to that ideal. . . . The jeremiad form is particularly well-suited to the needs of the party that is out of office, for it invites the speaker to attack the incumbent party for failing to adhere to the tenets of the American Dream. . . . Each challenging candidate ultimately asks: 'what made America great?' Posing this question allows the presidential aspirant to identify a single ideal (or a cluster of values) from our past which is missing the present and whose absence accounts for our difficulties." Kurt Ritter, "American Political Rhetoric and the Jeremiad Tradition: Presidential Nomination Acceptance Addresses, 1960–1976," *Central States Speech Journal* 31 (1980): 153–71.

5. "My life has been about victories. I've won a lot. I win a lot. I win—when I do something, I win. And even in sports, I always won. I was always a good athlete. And I always won. In golf, I've won many club championships. Many, many club championships. And I have people that can play golf great, but they can't win under pressure. So I've always won." Donald Trump, Corey Lewandowski, Hope Hicks, and Donald Trump, Jr., interview by Bob Woodward and Bob Costa, *Washington Post*, interview transcript, March 31, 2016, https://www.washingtonpost.com/wp-stat/graphics/politics/trump-archive/docs/donald-trump-interview-with-bob-woodward-and-robert-costa.pdf.

6. Conor Lynch, "Decoding Trump's Meaningless Mantra: Making America Great again for the Sour, Mean, and Delusional," *Salon*, January 21, 2017, http://www.salon.com/2017/01/21/decoding-trumps-meaningless-mantra-making-america-great-again-for-the-sour-mean-and-delusional/; Ellen McGirt, "Why 'Make America Great Again' Is an Offensive Slogan," *Fortune*, October 21, 2016, http://fortune.com/2016/10/21/why-make-america-great-again-is-an-offensive-slogan/; Karen L. Smith, "What 'Make America Great Again' Means," *Psychology Today*, August 27, 2016, https://www.psychologytoday.com/blog/full-living/201608/what-make-america-great-again-means; John Stossel, "Stossel: Why Trump's 'Make America Great Again!' Is a Bad Slogan," Fox News, January 12, 2017, http://www.foxnews.com/opinion/2016/03/23/art-donald-trump.html.

7. *Hannity*, Fox News, Trump archive video, 1:01, May 18, 2016, https://archive.org/details/foxnewsw_20160519_020100_hannity/start/420/end/480.

8. "Transcript: Donald Trump Expounds on His Foreign Policy Views," *New York Times*, March 26, 2016, https://www.nytimes.com/2016/03/27/us/politics/donald-trump-transcript.html.

9. Donald J. Trump, "Remarks to the Detroit Economic Club," August 8, 2016, Gerhard Peters and John T. Woolley, The American Presidency Project, https://www.presidency.ucsb.edu/documents/remarks-the-detroit-economic-club-1.

10. Time Staff, "Here's Trump's Presidential Announcement Speech," *Time*, June 16, 2015, http://time.com/3923128/donald-trump-announcement-speech/.

11. Donald J. Trump, "Remarks to the Detroit Economic Club," August 8, 2016, Gerhard Peters and John T. Woolley, The American Presidency Project, https://www.presidency.ucsb.edu/documents/remarks-the-detroit-economic-club-1.

12. *Donald Trump Holds Rally in Sioux City, Iowa*, C-SPAN, Trump archive video, 1:00, November 6, 2016, https://archive.org/details/CSPAN_20161107_023900_Donald_Trump_Holds_Rally_in_Sioux_City_Iowa/start/1822/end/1882?q=%22America+First%22.

13. Donald J. Trump, "Address Accepting the Presidential Nomination at the Republican National Convention in Cleveland, Ohio," July 21, 2016, Gerhard Peters and John T. Woolley, The American Presidency Project, https://www.presidency.ucsb.edu/documents/address-accepting-the-presidential-nomination-the-republican-national-convention-cleveland.

14. Donald J. Trump, "Remarks at Erie Insurance Arena in Erie, Pennsylvania," August 12, 2016, Gerhard Peters and John T. Woolley, The American Presidency Project, https://www.presidency.ucsb.edu/documents/remarks-erie-insurance-arena-erie-pennsylvania.

15. "Presidential Candidate Donald Trump Rally in St. Augustine, Florida," C-SPAN video, 47:36, October 24, 2016, https://www.c-span.org/video/?417407-1/donald-trump-campaigns-st-augustine-florida.

16. "Donald Trump Campaign Rally in Buffalo, New York," C-SPAN video, 1:02:12, April 18, 2016, https://www.c-span.org/video/?408351-1/donald-trump-campaign-rally-buffalo-new-york.

17. Donald J. Trump, "Make America Great Again," US Patent 4,773,272, registered July 14, 2015, http://tsdr.uspto.gov/documentviewer?caseId=sn85783371&docId=APP20121122072845#docIndex=5&page=1.

18. Karen Tumulty, "How Donald Trump Came Up with 'Make America Great Again,'" *Washington Post*, January 18, 2017, https://www.washingtonpost.com/politics/how-donald-trump-came-up-with-make-america-great-again/2017/01/17/fb6acf5e-dbf7-11e6-ad42-f3375f271c9c_story.html?utm_term=.fb5bb2233af0.

19. Eric Rauchway, "Donald Trump's New Favorite Slogan Was Invented for Nazi Sympathizers," *Washington Post*, June 14, 2016, https://www.washingtonpost.com/posteverything/wp/2016/06/14/donald-trumps-new-favorite-slogan-has-a-nazi-friendly-history/?utm_term=.b318b28ac281; John McNeill, "How Fascist Is Donald Trump? There's Actually a Formula for That," *Washington Post*, October 21, 2016, https://www.washingtonpost.com/posteverything/wp/2016/10/21/how-fascist-is-donald-trump-theres-actually-a-formula-for-that/?utm_term=.bbf15cb9d834.

20. Sam Frizell, "Pollster's Legs Wobble after Fawning Donald Trump Focus Group," *Time*, August 25, 2015, http://time.com/4009413/donald-trump-focus-group-frank-luntz/.

21. Frizell, "Pollster's Legs Wobble," http://time.com/4009413/donald-trump-focus-group-frank-luntz/.

Part Two: Trump and the Polarized Electorate

1. "Political Polarization in the American Public," Pew Research Center, June 12, 2014, http://www.people-press.org/2014/06/12/section-1-growing-ideological-consistency/.

2. Jeffrey M. Jones, "Record-High 77% of Americans Perceive Nation as Divided," Gallup, November 21, 2016, https://news.gallup.com/poll/197828/record-high-americans-perceive-nation-divided.aspx.

3. "Partisanship and Political Animosity in 2016," *Pew Research Center*, June 22, 2016, https://www.people-press.org/2016/06/22/partisanship-and-political-animosity-in-2016/.

4. Jennifer Mercieca, "Can America's Deep Political Divide Be Traced Back to 1832?" *The Conversation*, July 21, 2016, https://theconversation.com/can-americas-deep-political-divide-be-traced-back-to-1832-62474.

5. Terry Smith, "General Trump's Cold Civil War," *Huffington Post*, November 13, 2016, https://www.huffpost.com/entry/general-trumps-cold-civil-war_b_582818d3e4b057e23e31455e.

Chapter 7

1. "Trump: Favorable/Unfavorable," Real Clear Politics, http://www.realclearpolitics.com/epolls/other/trump_favorableunfavorable-5493.html#polls.

2. Trump may have been alerted ahead of the debate that he would be asked this question. See Jane Mayer, "The Making of the Fox News White House," *The New Yorker*, March 4, 2019, https://www.newyorker.com/magazine/2019/03/11/the-making-of-the-fox-news-white-house.

3. Ian Schwartz, "Trump: I Will Not Pledge to Endorse Republican Nominee, Not Run as Independent," Real Clear Politics, August 6, 2015, https://www.realclearpolitics.com/video/2015/08/06/trump_i_will_not_pledge_to_endorse_republican_nominee.html.

4. Michael Grunwald, "The Victory of 'No,'" Politico, December 4, 2016, http://www.politico.com/magazine/story/2016/12/republican-party-obstructionism-victory-trump-214498.

5. Maggie Haberman, "Donald Trump Signs Loyalty Pledge to Republican Party," *New York Times*, September 3, 2015, https://www.nytimes.com/politics/first-draft/2015/09/03/donald-trump-signs-loyalty-pledge-to-republican-party/; Mike Allen, Ben Schreckinger, and Annie Karni, "Trump Calls GOP's Bluff," Politico, September 3, 2015, https://www.politico.com/story/2015/09/trump-will-sign-gop-loyalty-pledge-213302; Donald J. Trump (@realDonaldTrump), "The Pledge #MakeAmericaGreatAgain," Twitter, September 3, 2015, https://twitter.com/realdonaldtrump/status/639517204434800640.

6. Susan Page, "Poll: 68% of Trump's Supporters Would Vote for Him If He Bolts the

GOP," *USA Today*, December 8, 2015, https://www.usatoday.com/story/news/politics/elections/2015/12/08/poll-trump-cruz-rubio-clinton-sanders/76948760/; Donald J. Trump (@realDonaldTrump), "A new poll indicates that 68% of my supporters would vote for me if I departed the GOP & ran as an independent. https://www.facebook.com/DonaldTrump/posts/10156389951165725:0," Twitter, December 8, 2015, https://twitter.com/realDonaldTrump/status/674317248803307520; Jennifer Schmelzle, "Count me as one of them, I'm voting Trump either as a republican, indepdent or as a write in, doesnt matter to me. Screw to worthless GOP," comment on Donald J. Trump, "A new poll indicates that 68% of my supporters would vote for me if I departed the GOP & ran as an independent. http://www.usatoday.com/ . . . /poll-trump-cruz-rubio-c . . . /76948760/," Facebook, December 8, 2015, https://www.facebook.com/DonaldTrump/photos/a.488852220724.393301.153080620724/10156389951165725/?type=3&comment_id=10156389973630725.

7. Jennifer Schmelzle, "Count me as one of them, I'm voting Trump either as a republican, indepdent or as a write in, doesnt matter to me. Screw to worthless GOP," comment on Donald J. Trump, "A new poll indicates that 68% of my supporters would vote for me if I departed the GOP & ran as an independent. http://www.usatoday.com/ . . . /poll-trump-cruz-rubio-c . . . /76948760/," Facebook, December 8, 2015, https://www.facebook.com/DonaldTrump/photos/a.488852220724.393301.153080620724/10156389951165725/?type=3&comment_id=10156389973630725.

8. Rich Lowry, "Inside the 'Against Trump' Issue," Politico, January 23, 2016, https://www.politico.com/magazine/story/2016/01/inside-against-trump-issue-national-review-213556.

9. Callum Borchers, "The Inside Story of National Review's Big Anti-Donald Trump Issue," *Washington Post*, January 22, 2016, https://www.washingtonpost.com/news/the-fix/wp/2016/01/22/the-story-behind-the-national-reviews-big-anti-donald-trump-issue/?utm_term=.d86eae95228a.

10. Dylan Byers, "National Review, Conservative Thinkers Stand against Trump," CNN Politics, January 22, 2016, https://www.cnn.com/2016/01/21/politics/national-review-magazine-opposes-donald-trump/index.html.

11. Fox News, "National Review Disses Donald Trump: Why the Magazine's Plan Won't Work," Fox News, January 22, 2016, http://www.foxnews.com/opinion/2016/01/22/national-review-disses-donald-trump-why-magazines-plan-wont-work.html.

12. Matt Ford, "The National Review Takes on Trump," *The Atlantic*, January 22, 2016, https://www.theatlantic.com/politics/archive/2016/01/national-review/426543/.

13. Jeet Heer, "National Review Fails to Kill Its Monster," *The New Republic*, January 22, 2016, https://newrepublic.com/article/128176/national-review-fails-kill-monster.

14. Floss (@flossbish), "@NRO @freedomtex @realDonaldTrump Shame on you. Think we were mad before, you haven't seen anything yet . . . ," Twitter, January 21, 2016, comment on National Review (@NRO), "Conservatives against @realDonaldTrump is out HERE: bit.ly/1lASj1R," Twitter, January 21, 2016, https://twitter.com/flossbish/

status/690371415376281601; Floss (@flossbish), "@freedomtex @NRO @realDon-
aldTrump Am referring to NR; all this does is push people closer to Trump. We stand with
Trump," Twitter, January 21, 2016, comment on Freedom Tex (@freedomtex), "@flossbish
Are you talking to @NRO or @realDonaldTrump ?" Twitter, January 21, 2016, comment on
previous citation, https://twitter.com/flossbish/status/690372460429058049.

15. Patrick (@CPRxUSA), "@flossbish @freedomtex @nro @realdonaldtrump NRO =
Elitist Cons who are severly out of touch with the real party base," Twitter, January 21, 2016,
comment on Floss (@flossbish), "@NRO @freedomtex @realDonaldTrump Shame on you.
Think we were mad before, you haven't seen anything yet," Twitter, January 21, 2016, https://
twitter.com/CPRxUSA/status/690378476109631489.

16. Donald J. Trump (@realDonaldTrump), "National Review is a failing publication that has lost it's way. It's circulation is way down w its influence being at an
all time low. Sad!" Twitter, January 21, 2016, https://twitter.com/realDonaldTrump/
status/690382564494839809?ref_src=twsrc%5Etfw&ref_url=https%3A%2F%2Fnews.vice.
com%2Farticle%2Fafter-publishing-an-anti-trump-issue-the-national-review-was-dropped-
from-gop-debate; Donald J. Trump (@realDonaldTrump), "Very few people read the
National Review because it only knows how to criticize, but not how to lead," Twitter, January 21, 2016, https://twitter.com/realdonaldtrump/status/690382619213742082; Donald J.
Trump (@realDonaldTrump), "the late, great, William F. Buckley would be ashamed of what
had happened to his prize, the dying National Review!" Twitter, January 21, 2016, https://
twitter.com/realDonaldTrump/status/690382722162913280.

17. "National Review cover: 'Against Trump,'" MSNBC video, 1:06, January 21, 2016,
http://www.msnbc.com/msnbc-quick-cuts/watch/donald-trump-responds-to-national-
review-cover-606451779725; a portion of the Trump quotation about his success in the polls
can be found here: Fox Business News, Fox News, archived video, 1:01, January 22, 2016,
https://archive.org/details/FBC_20160122_100000_FBN_AM/start/1800/end/1860.

18. Donald J. Trump (@realDonaldTrump), "A wonderful article by a writer who truly
gets it. I am for the people and the people are for me. #Trump2016 republicannewswatch.
com/wp/?p=13982," Twitter, January 22, 2016, https://twitter.com/realdonaldtrump/sta-
tus/690732776920743937; Doug Ibendahl, "National Review Just Handed Donald Trump
the Election," *Republican News Watch*, January 22, 2016, http://republicannewswatch.com/
wp/?p=13982; Doug Ibendahl (@DougIbendahl), "Yes was quite an honor to say the least,
and surreal. He tweeted the piece out the night before, but that was only hint I had. Read
it next day in Iowa and then at 2 more rallies. Just glad I could contribute something to the
effort. Thank you for the nice note," Twitter, November 26, 2017, comment on Babs (@
BelBlok), "What an honor to have your post read by @POTUS during a campaign rally in
New Hampshire. Just watched one video, so far. I miss the campaign days, we got to listen to
@realDonaldTrump at his raw best!" Twitter, November 26, 2017, https://twitter.com/Dou-
gIbendahl/status/934861683176112128.

19. Ibendahl's article also appeared in the *Huffington Post* on January 25, 2016.

Ibendahl is listed in his bio there as "a Chicago attorney and former General Counsel of the Illinois Republican Party. Doug was born and raised on the family grain and livestock farm in Southern Illinois before moving to Chicago in 1985. Doug is a graduate of the University of Chicago Graduate School of Business, and the University of Illinois College of Law where he served as Topics Editor of The University of Illinois Law Review." "Doug Ibendahl," *Huffington Post*, https://www.huffingtonpost.com/author/doug-ibendahl; Doug Ibendahl, "National Review Just Handed Donald Trump the Election," *Huffington Post*, January 25, 2016, https://www.huffingtonpost.com/doug-ibendahl/national-review-just-hand_b_9055688.html.

20. "Trump: Sioux City, IA (1/23/16) (Good Audio)," YouTube video, 2:05:55, March 28, 2016, https://www.youtube.com/watch?v=qTS8Y8qqLl4.

21. Jeremy Diamond, "Trump: Establishment Is 'Against Me,'" CNN Politics, January 25, 2016, https://www.cnn.com/2016/01/25/politics/donald-trump-establishment-2016/index.html.

22. A network analysis of internet influence during the 2016 campaign found that the *National Review* did, indeed, lose influence compared to 2012: "First, perhaps the most notable change is the location and prominence of the National Review and the Weekly Standard. In 2012, they were key nodes and well integrated into the right-wing media sphere. Four years later, they were positioned on the center-right and relatively less popular." Rob Faris, Hal Roberts, Bruce Etling, Nikki Bourassa, Ethan Zuckerman, and Yochai Benkler, "Partisanship, Propaganda, and Disinformation: Online Media and the 2016 U.S. Presidential Election," Berkman Klein Center for Internet and Society at Harvard University, August 16, 2017, https://cyber.harvard.edu/publications/2017/08/mediacloud?utm_source=newsletter&utm_medium=email&utm_campaign=newsletter_axiosam&stream=top-stories.

23. "Tantaros: Here's the Counterpunch to Nat'l Review's Anti-Trump Attack," Fox News Insider video, 7:49, January 22, 2016, http://insider.foxnews.com/2016/01/22/tantaros-heres-counterpunch-natl-reviews-anti-trump-attack.

24. "Trump stunned the political world at every turn during the Republican primary, prioritizing large rallies over intimate voter interactions in early voting states and operating with a slim campaign operation. Even as he brings in new staff for the general election, he says his emphasis will continue to be on raucous rallies that put him in front of thousands of voters and generate significant free media coverage." Julie Pace, "AP Interview: Trump Says Big Rallies His Key Campaign Weapon," Associated Press, May 10, 2016, https://apnews.com/ed853e2f84bd42658868a42f997c93fe/ap-interview-donald-trump-says-hes-narrowed-vp-shortlist.

25. "No overview, no excellent radio coverage, no first-rate press or film reports can convey a true-to-life impression of such a meeting or serve the listener or hearer as a substitute. To the contrary, each such report serves only as propaganda for the actual experience itself. It is therefore clear that the mass meeting is generally the strongest form of propaganda that we possess. If we want to trace this phenomenon back to its human origins, we might perhaps say

that in the unity of the crowd each individual receives an uplifted and elevated self-confidence as well as a feeling of power. We find all the strong elements of a people in a mass meeting, while the main weaknesses are kept out." Hitler's propagandist Eugen Hadamovsky, "Chapter 3: Mass Meetings and Powerful Propaganda," *Propaganda and National Power: The Organization of Public Opinion for National Politics* (Oldenburg: Gerhard Stlaling, 1933), http:// research.calvin.edu/german-propaganda-archive/hadamovsky3.htm.

26. Candace Smith and Liz Kreutz, "Hillary Clinton's and Donald Trump's Campaigns by the Numbers," ABC News, November 7, 2016, https://abcnews.go.com/Politics/hillary-clinton-donald-trumps-campaigns-numbers/story?id=43356783; "List of Rallies for the 2016 Donald Trump Presidential Campaign," Wikipedia, last updated February 25, 2019, https://en.wikipedia.org/wiki/List_of_rallies_for_the_Donald_Trump_presidential_campaign,_2016.

27. "Donald Trump Campaign Rally in Muscatine, Iowa," C-SPAN video, 40:55–1:21:54, January 24, 2016, https://www.c-span.org/video/?403595-1/donald-trump-campaign-rally-muscatine-iowa&start=2454.

28. "Donald Trump Campaign in Wilkes-Barre Pennsylvania," C-SPAN, archived video, 1:00, April 26, 2016, https://archive.org/details/CSPAN_20160426_070200_donald_trump_campaign_rally_in_wilkes-barre_pennsylvania/start/2709/end/2769?q=loyal.

29. CNN *Newsroom with Brooke Baldwin*, CNN, archived video, 011:00, August 10, 2016, https://archive.org/details/CNNW_20160810_191500_CNN_newsroom_with_brooke_baldwin/start/1024/end/1084?q=loyal.

30. Kate Reilly, "Read Hillary Clinton's 'Basket of Deplorables' Remarks about Donald Trump Supporters," *Time*, September 10, 2016, http://time.com/4486502/hillary-clinton-basket-of-deplorables-transcript/. I am quoted in this article on Clinton's "basket of deplorables" comment: Amy Chozick, "Hillary Clinton Calls Many Trump Backers 'Deplorables,' and G. O. P. Pounces," *New York Times*, September 10, 2016, https://www.nytimes.com/2016/09/11/us/politics/hillary-clinton-basket-of-deplorables.html.

31. Donald J. Trump (@realDonaldTrump), "Wow, Hillary Clinton was SO INSULTING to my supporter, millions of amazing, hard working people. I think it will cost her at the Polls!" Twitter, September 10, 2016, https://twitter.com/realDonaldTrump/status/774590070355529728.

32. William Cummings, "'Deplorable' and Proud: Some Trump Supporters Embrace the Label," *USA Today*, September 12, 2016, https://www.usatoday.com/story/news/politics/onpolitics/2016/09/12/deplorable-and-proud-some-trump-supporters-embrace-label/90290760/.

33. Hanna Trudo, "Trump Releases New Ad Hitting Clinton for 'Deplorables' Remark," Politico, September 12, 2016, https://www.politico.com/story/2016/09/clinton-deplorables-trump-ad-228018.

Chapter 8

1. "Trump: Favorable/Unfavorable," Real Clear Politics, http://www.realclearpolitics.com/epolls/other/trump_favorableunfavorable-5493.html#polls.

2. Jeb Bush (@JebBush), "Jeb! 2016," Twitter, June 14, 2015, https://twitter.com/JebBush/status/610063493237084160?ref_src=twsrc%5Etfw&ref_url=http%3A%2F%2Fwww.adweek.com%2Fcreativity%2Fjeb-bush-unveiled-his-2016-logo-and-internet-shouted-unkind-things-it-165344%2F. "Milton Glaser, a veteran graphic designer responsible for the iconic 'I heart NY' design of the late 1970s, says the exclamation mark is meant to 'generate a sense of enthusiasm and excitement. Jeb doesn't seem to be a personality who achieves that goal, so you kind of have to invent it for him and indicate that you're enthusiastic.'" Anthony Zurcher, "Just Jeb! Five Things Bush's Logo Tells Us about Him," *BBC*, June 16, 2015, http://www.bbc.com/news/world-us-canada-33104412; Andrew Kaczynski (@KFILE), "Jeb! has used the same logo since 1994," Twitter, June 14, 2015, https://twitter.com/KFILE/status/610096036120539136?ref_src=twsrc%5Etfw&ref_url=http%3A%2F%2Fwww.adweek.com%2Fcreativity%2Fjeb-bush-unveiled-his-2016-logo-and-internet-shouted-unkind-things-it-165344%2F; Elizabeth Stinson, "Typography Is Why Jeb's Logo Is Worse Than a Piece of Crap," *Wired*, June 16, 2015, https://www.wired.com/2015/06/jeb-bush-logo-jeb/; Alfred Maskeroni, "Jeb Bush Unveiled His 2016 Logo, and the Internet shouted Unkind Things at It," *AdWeek*, June 15, 2015, http://www.adweek.com/creativity/jeb-bush-unveiled-his-2016-logo-and-internet-shouted-unkind-things-it-165344/.

3. "Jeb Bush Presidential Campaign Announcement Full Speech (C-SPAN)," C-SPAN video, YouTube, 28:51, June 15, 2015, https://www.youtube.com/watch?v=7w-bnAvrsds.

4. "Trump on Jeb's Candidacy: 'The Last Thing We Need Is Another Bush,'" *Fox & Friends*, Fox News video, 7:23, June 15, 2015, http://insider.foxnews.com/2015/06/15/donald-trump-fox-friends-jeb-bush-last-thing-we-need-another-bush.

5. Zeke J. Miller, "Transcript: Read Full Text of Former Gov. Jeb Bush's Campaign Launch," *Time*, June 15, 2015, http://time.com/3921956/jeb-bush-campaign-launch-transcript/.

6. "Donald Trump Takes Late Night by Storm on 'Jimmy Kimmel Live,'" ABC News, December 17, 2015, https://www.youtube.com/watch?v=28nl-iIFfU

7. Brett LoGiurato, "Trump: Here's the Backstory on 'My Low-Energy' Takedown of Jeb Bush," *Business Insider*, November 19, 2015, http://www.businessinsider.com/donald-trump-jeb-bush-low-energy-2015-11.

8. "Here's Donald Trump's Presidential Announcement Speech," *Time* video, 1:46, June 16, 2015, http://time.com/3923128/donald-trump-announcement-speech/.

9. "Donald Trump: The Country Is Doing Terribly," MSNBC video, 10:04, June 18, 2015, http://www.msnbc.com/morning-joe/watch/donald-trump-the-country-is-doing-terribly-467434563618.

10. Donald J. Trump (@realDonaldTrump), "The highly respected Suffolk

University poll just announced that I am alone in 2nd place in New Hampshire, with Jeb Bust (Bush) in first," Twitter, June 24, 2015, https://twitter.com/realdonaldtrump/status/613681129967747072.

11. "New Hampshire Republican Presidential Primary," Real Clear Politics, https://www.realclearpolitics.com/epolls/2016/president/nh/new_hampshire_republican_presidential_primary-3350.html.

12. Janice Min, "The Donald Trump Conversation: Murdoch, Ailes, NBC and the Rush of Being TV's 'Ratings Machine,'" Hollywood Reporter, August 19, 2015, http://www.hollywoodreporter.com/features/donald-trump-murdoch-ailes-nbc-816131.

13. Chuck Todd and Donald Trump, Meet the Press, NBC, August 16, 2015, https://www.nbcnews.com/meet-the-press/meet-press-transcript-august-16-2015-n412636.

14. Ed O'Keefe, "Jeb Bush on Donald Trump's Immigration Ideas: 'A Plan Needs to Be Grounded in Reality,'" Washington Post, August 17, 2015, https://www.washingtonpost.com/news/post-politics/wp/2015/08/17/jeb-bush-on-donald-trumps-immigration-ideas-a-plan-needs-to-be-grounded-in-reality/?utm_term=.f9b8e3722a43.

15. Olivier Laurent, "Behind Time's Cover Shoot with Donald Trump and an American Bald Eagle," Time, August 20, 2015, http://time.com/4003904/donald-trump-bald-eagle/.

16. Time Staff, "Donald Trump Explains All," Time, August 20, 2015, http://time.com/4003734/donald-trump-interview-transcript/.

17. "Rally in Sioux City," Trump archive video, January 23, 2016, https://archive.org/details/CNNW_20150820_010000_anthony_bourdain_parts_unknown/start/1560/end/1620.

18. Theodore Schleifer, "Town Hall Throw-Down: Trump, Bush Trade Shots," CNN, August 20, 2015, http://www.cnn.com/2015/08/19/politics/donald-trump-mitt-romney-choked-2012/.

19. "Presidential Candidate Donald Trump Rally in Mobile, Alabama," August 21, 2015, C-SPAN, https://www.c-span.org/video/?327751-1/donald-trump-campaign-rally-mobile-alabama.

20. Ian Schwartz, "Trump to Jeb Bush: Not 'An Act of Love' when Illegal Immigrants Rape and Murder," Real Clear Politics, August 25, 2015, https://www.realclearpolitics.com/video/2015/08/25/trump_to_jeb_bush_not_an_act_of_love_when_illegal_immigrants_rape_and_murder.html.

21. Hardball with Chris Matthews, MSNBC, Trump archive video, 11:00, August 25, 2015, https://archive.org/details/MSNBCW_20150825_233700_Hardball_With_Chris_Matthews/start/876/end/936?q=low+energy.

22. "'I'm Not Gonna Say Jeb is Low Energy but He's Pretty Low' Donald Trump at 'Not-a-Fundraiser,'" YouTube video, 21:32, 11:55, August 28, 2015, https://www.youtube.com/watch?v=Eg6twbd4VFY.

23. Jared (@eternaljdg), "When Trump says Jeb is 'low energy' I think he's really saying 'low T,'" Twitter, August 19, 2015, https://twitter.com/eternaljdg/status/634174972995440641.

24. Maggie Haberman (@maggieNYT), "Trump's 'low energy' line about Jeb is a rhetorical knife in the craw that my do lingering damage," Twitter, August 21, 2015, https://twitter.com/maggieNYT/status/634719965267009537. For another example, consider the August 24, 2015, tweet from Time magazine's Zeke Miller (@ZekeJMiller): "Trump is expert at honing in on his rivals' weaknesses. The Jeb 'low energy' attack goes right at a core problem," Twitter, https://twitter.com/ZekeJMiller/status/635779066721902593. For an example of Twitter users merely quoting Trump, consider Roger Simon (@politicoroger), "Trump on CNN: 'He's a very low energy person Jeb Bush. That's OK. Perhaps he'll live a long life. But he's low energy,'" Twitter, August 19, 2015, https://twitter.com/politicoroger/status/634174937855578113.

25. Thomas O. (@tomigoldnet), "'Jeb Bush is a low energy person.'-Donald Trump. Another townhall meeting, another epic take down of the establishment #Jeb2016 #Trump 2016," Twitter, August 19, 2015, https://twitter.com/tomigoldnet/status/634185189296463872.

26. Red821 (@JMJAmen), "@DanScavino @realDonaldTrump Mr. Trump defintely Jeb Bush is a low energy idiot w," Twitter, August 24, 2015, comment on Dan Scavino (@DanScavino), "Who would you rather have negotiating for you? TRUMP or JEB? @realDonaldTrump will #MakeAmericaGreatAgain #Trump2016," Twitter, August 24, 2015, https://twitter.com/JMJAmen/status/635953911246008321.

27. Robert J Stevens (@ganeshpuri89), "Donald Trump just did an impression of a 'low energy' Jeb Bush. Please somebody make a GIF," Twitter, August 25, 2015, https://twitter.com/ganeshpuri89/status/636325715085012992.

28. "Wake up Jeb supporters!" Donald J. Trump, Facebook video, 0:15, September 8, 2015, https://www.facebook.com/DonaldTrump/videos/10156084048215725/; Donald J. Trumprealdonaldtrump (@realdonaldtrump), "Wake up Jeb supporters!" Instagram video, 0:15, September 8, 2015, https://www.instagram.com/p/7YV_u_mhWB/.

29. Adam C. Smith, "Jeb Bush: 'I'm a Joyful Tortoise' in a Long, Acrimonious Race," Miami Herald, July 27, 2015, http://www.miamiherald.com/news/politics-government/election/jeb-bush/article29074546.html.

30. Jeb Bush (@JebBush), "I met a fellow joyful tortoise on my way to the Reagan Library http://postonpolitics.blog.palmbeachpost.com/2015/07/28/jeb-bush-the-joyful-tortoise/," Twitter, August 11, 2015, https://twitter.com/jebbush/status/631194547649818624?lang=en.

31. Ashley Killough, "Jeb Bush, the 'Joyful Tortoise,' Gives Out Tiny Toy Turtles on Trail," CNN Politics, January 6, 2016, http://www.cnn.com/2016/01/06/politics/jeb-bush-turtle-tortoise-joyful/index.html.

32. "Jeb's Got Turtles and Kim's Got Nukes (Maybe)," The Late Show with *Stephen Colbert* clip, YouTube video, 55:27, January 9, 2016, https://www.youtube.com/watch?v=uSASN36T2Zw.

33. Tom LoBianco, "Bush: Trump 'Trying to Insult His Way to the Presidency,'" CNN Politics, September 3, 2015, http://www.cnn.com/2015/09/03/politics/jeb-bush-donald-trump-insults/.

34. Jeremy Diamond, "Jeb Bush Strikes Back at Donald Trump for 'Low-Energy' Attacks," CNN Politics, September 9, 2015, http://www.cnn.com/2015/09/09/politics/jeb-bush-donald-trump-attacks-fighting-back/index.html.

35. Diamond, "Jeb Bush Strikes Back," http://www.cnn.com/2015/09/09/politics/jeb-bush-donald-trump-attacks-fighting-back/index.html.

36. *The Late Show with Stephen Colbert*, CBS, archived video, 11:07, September 8, 2015, https://archive.org/details/kyw_20150909_033500_the_late_show_with_stephen_colbert/start/3180/end/3240.

37. Daniella Diaz, "GOP Candidates Pick Their Secret Service Code Names," CNN Politics, September 17, 2015, http://www.cnn.com/2015/09/17/politics/republican-debate-secret-service-names/.

38. Jonathan Martin, "A Once-Sunny Jeb Bush, Bristling in the Long Shadow of Donald Trump," *New York Times*, September 2, 2015, https://www.nytimes.com/2015/09/03/us/politics/jeb-bush-donald-j-trump-2016-presidential-election.html?smid=tw-nytimes&smtyp=cur.

39. Martin, "Bush Bristling in Trump's Shadow," https://www.nytimes.com/2015/09/03/us/politics/jeb-bush-donald-j-trump-2016-presidential-election.html?_r=0.

40. Justin William Moyer, "Jeb Bush Tweets Trump-Clinton Conspiracy Theory. Here's a Look at the 'Evidence,'" *Washington Post*, December 9, 2015, https://www.washingtonpost.com/news/morning-mix/wp/2015/12/09/jeb-bush-jokes-of-trump-clinton-conspiracy-theory-heres-a-look-at-the-evidence/?utm_term=.3bfd7f734d3a.

41. Ashley Parker, "Jeb Bush Sprints to Escape Donald Trump's 'Low Energy' Label," *New York Times*, December 29, 2015, https://www.nytimes.com/2015/12/30/us/politics/jeb-bush-sprints-to-escape-donald-trumps-low-energy-label.html?_r=0.

42. Brett LoGiurato, "Trump: Here's the Backstory on My 'Low-Energy' Takedown of Jeb Bush," *Business Insider*, November 19, 2015, http://www.businessinsider.com/donald-trump-jeb-bush-low-energy-2015-11.

43. "Donald Trump Takes Late Night by Storm on *Jimmy Kimmel Live*," ABC News, YouTube video, 2:47, December 17, 2015, https://www.youtube.com/watch?v=28nl-iIFfU.

44. Dave Weigel (@daveweigel), "Trump's attack on Jeb! for being 'low-energy' resonates bc a lot of GOP base say their nominees went too easy on Obama in 08 and 12," Twitter, August 28, 2015, https://twitter.com/daveweigel/status/637267515912126464.

45. Frank Luntz (@FrankLuntz), "My #GOPDebate focus group's words to describe Jeb Bush: 'weak,' 'desperate,' and 'whiny.' It's over for him. Sorry," Twitter, December 15, 2015, https://twitter.com/FrankLuntz/status/676965120472387585?ref_src=twsrc%5Etfw&ref_url=https%3A%2F%2Fwww.vox.com%2F2015%2F12%2F16%2F

10274602%2Frepublican-debate-winners-losers; Parker, "Bush Sprints from 'Low Energy' Label," https://www.nytimes.com/2015/12/30/us/politics/jeb-bush-sprints-to-escape-donald-trumps-low-energy-label.html?_r=0.

46. Joe Hackman (@joethehack), "I feel so Jeb Bush, I mean, low energy, today," Twitter, February 27, 2016, https://twitter.com/joethehack/status/703677546999623680.

47. Gabriel Sherman, "Inside Operation Trump, the Most Unorthodox Campaign in Political History," *Daily Intelligencer*, April 3, 2016, http://nymag.com/daily/intelligencer/2016/04/inside-the-donald-trump-presidential-campaign.html.

48. Sherman, "Inside Operation Trump," http://nymag.com/daily/intelligencer/2016/04/inside-the-donald-trump-presidential-campaign.html.

49. Fox News (@FoxNews), "@realDonaldTrump on @marcorubio: 'I call him "Little Marco" . . . He's a very nasty guy.' @FoxNewsSunday," Twitter, February 28, 2016, https://twitter.com/foxnews/status/704020997515509760.

Chapter 9

1. "Trump: Favorable/Unfavorable," Real Clear Politics, http://www.realclearpolitics.com/epolls/other/trump_favorableunfavorable-5493.html#polls.

2. Andrew Anglin, "We Won," Daily Stormer archived post, November 9, 2016, https://web.archive.org/web/20161109110103/http://www.dailystormer.com/we-won/.

3. Kevin MacDonald, "This is an amazing victory. The stars were aligned. . . . Fundamentally, it is a victory of White Americans over the oligarchic, hostile elites what have run this country for decades. Trump accomplished a hostile takeover of the Republican Party and won without the support or with only lukewarm and vacillating support from much of the GOP elite." Occidental Observer, "An Historic, Quite Possibly Revolutionary Victory!" November 9, 2016, https://web.archive.org/web/20161110233749/http://www.theoccidentalobserver.net/2016/11/an-amazing-victory/.

4. Daniel Lombroso and Yoni Appelbaum, "'Hail Trump!': White Nationalists Salute the President-Elect," *The Atlantic*, November 21, 2016, https://www.theatlantic.com/politics/archive/2016/11/richard-spencer-speech-npi/508379.

5. John Daniszewski, "Writing about the 'Alt-Right,'" Associated Press, November 28, 2016, https://blog.ap.org/behind-the-news/writing-about-the-alt-right; "White Nationalist," SPLC Southern Poverty Law Center, https://www.splcenter.org/fighting-hate/extremist-files/ideology/white-nationalist.

6. Daniel Marans, "Hate-Group Watchdog: Trump Has 'White Nationalist Positions,'" *Huffington Post*, August 26, 2015, http://www.huffingtonpost.com/entry/trump-white-nationalist-positions_us_55dde385e4b0a40aa3acfab8?.

7. Andrew Anglin, "A Normie's Guide to the Alt-Right," Daily Stormer archived post, August 31, 2016, https://web.archive.org/web/20161112000734/http://www.dailystormer.com:80/a-normies-guide-to-the-alt-right.

8. "The point is, and as I said it again, he pushes the overton window and normalizes nationalist views like immigration and non-white/immigrant crime. He is getting the common person and low info voters talking about it." Stephen De Grene, post #41 on "#1 Donald Trump thread," Vanguard News Network Forum, July 10, 2015, http://img1.vnnforum.com/showpost.php?p=1874420&postcount=41. "Donald Trump the 'Fair haired boy' who grew up in Jew York. Has consciously chosen to align himself with the Jews in order to achieve Wealth and Power. For that he is a Traitor to the White America not the 'Great White Hope' as many so foolishly believe. Both Eric and Ivanka Trump married Jews. Trump has Jewish grandchildren for God's sake. And he is proud of the fact that his daughter converted to Judaism. On top of all this Trump surrounds himself with Jews both in his campaign and in his business and personal life. Trump going to be the next 'Fuhrer'!? People who believe that are hopelessly deluded you can't be joined with the hip to Jews who are the greatest enemy of the White Race and be pro-White you can't. It doesn't matter that he will build a wall on the border. How will Trump deal with non-White immigration given that Jews use immigration as a way to subvert and enslave White Americans I don't see how Trump the ever loyal Shabbos Goy is going to change the Jewish Status Quo. To undermine and destroy the Aryan Race is written in the DNA of Jews for God sakes! And this man who is joined to the hip with Jews is going to save the White Race! What foolishness and desperation to believe Donald Trump is some closet NAZI!" EricPowers, post #199 on "#1 Donald Trump Thread," Vanguard News Network Forum, December 26, 2015, http://img1.vnnforum.com/showpost.php?p=1966718&postcount=199.

9. Varg, post #1040 on "#1 Donald Trump Thread," Vanguard News Network Forum, March 23, 2016, http://img1.vnnforum.com/showpost.php?p=2015423&postcount=1040.

10. Andrew Anglin, "The Daily Stormer Endorses Donald Trump for President," Daily Stormer archived post, June 28, 2015, https://web.archive.org/web/20170106150337/http://www.dailystormer.com/the-daily-stormer-endorses-donald-trump-for-president/; Andrew Anglin, "Why I Support Donald Trump for President," Daily Stormer archived post, July 12, 2015, https://web.archive.org/web/20150713220312/http://www.dailystormer.com/why-i-support-donald-trump-for-president/.

11. "Kevin MacDonald," Southern Poverty Law Center, https://www.splcenter.org/fighting-hate/extremist-files/individual/kevin-macdonald; Kevin MacDonald, "How It Could Happen: The Candidacy of Donald Trump," *Occidental Observer*, July 10, 2015, http://www.theoccidentalobserver.net/2015/07/how-it-could-happen-the-candidacy-of-donald-trump/.

12. Mr. Curious, "A simple rule of thumb: If the Zionist Media are constantly ridiculing and abusing a White Man, BACK HIM. They are doing it because he threatens the PC feminist /Marxist /Zionist consensus of kosher power to practice White Genocide. God bless you, Donald. Keep up the good work," comment on Kevin MacDonald, "How It Could Happen: The Candidacy of Donald Trump," *Occidental Observer*, July 10, 2015, https://web.archive.org/web/20150726051226/http://www.theoccidentalobserver.net/2015/07/how-it-could-happen-the-candidacy-of-donald-trump/.

13. Andrew Kaczynski, "David Duke Urges His Supporters to Volunteer and Vote for Trump," Buzzfeed, February 25, 2016, https://www.buzzfeed.com/andrewkaczynski/david-duke-urges-his-supporters-to-volunteer-and-vote-for-tr?utm_term=.hxjv7zraq#.jhxbmxd3d.

14. German Lopez, "Donald Trump's Long History of Racism, from the 1970s to 2019," Vox, February 14, 2019, https://www.vox.com/2016/7/25/12270880/donald-trump-racism-history; Michael D'Antonio, "Is Donald Trump Racist? Here's What the Record Shows," *Fortune*, June 7, 2016, http://fortune.com/2016/06/07/donald-trump-racism-quotes/; "Just shows great men have a connection and understanding. And Glorious leader America is also German like Glorious leader eterna." JamesNiveus, post #596 on "The Trump Media Thread," StormFront.org, February 23, 2016, https://www.storm-front.org/forum/t1117558-60/?postcount=596#post13322443; Marina Fang and J. M. Reiger, "This May Be the Most Horrible Thing That Donald Trump Believes," *Huffington Post*, September 9, 2016, https://www.huffingtonpost.com/entry/donald-trump-eugen-ics_us_57ec4cc2e4b024a52d2cc7f9; Pride Isn't Hate, post #180 on "The Trump Media Thread," StormFront.org, December 3, 2015, https://www.stormfront.org/forum/t1117558-18/?postcount=180#post13179309; RickHolland, post #3023 on "#1 Donald Trump Thread," Vanguard News Network Forum, November 9, 2016, http://img1.vnnforum.com/showpost.php?p=2119168&postcount=3023.

15. "The Trump Train has left the station and is running non-stop to total victory over the barbarian hordes of Mexico. Because there is one issue which matters beyond all other issues and that is the invasion of White countries by non-Whites." Andrew Anglin, "Trump Train Running Non-Stop to Total Victory," Daily Stormer archived post, July 13, 2015, https://web.archive.org/web/20150717003624/http://www.dailystormer.com:80/trump-train-running-non-stop-to-total-victory/.

16. Even before he officially announced his campaign, white nationalist forum members approvingly posted about Trump's anti-immigration positions and hoped that he would run for president. On March 10, 2014, anti-immigrant and white nationalist website VDare posted an approving story about Trump's CPAC (Conservative Political Action Conference) speech because he linked together the national debt, boarder insecurity, and American joblessness—"You have a border, you have a country—and if you don't have a border, what do you have? Nothing," said Trump to VDare's approval. Allan Wall, "Trump at CPAC on Immigration and Demographics," VDARE.com archived post, March 10, 2014, https://web.archive.org/web/20170120184721/http://www.vdare.com/posts/trump-at-cpac-on-immigration-and-demographics. "Maybe Trump is an immigration patriot." Matthew Richer, "For Better or Worse, Donald Trump May Be the Only Immigration Patriot Running for President," VDARE.com archived post, April 12, 2015, https://web.archive.org/web/20170106122405/http://www.vdare.com/articles/for-better-or-worse-donald-trump-may-be-the-only-immigration-patriot-running-for-president.

17. Andrew Anglin, "The Don to O'Reilly: Statements on Mexicans 'Totally Accurate,'" Daily Stormer archived post, July 1, 2015, https://web.archive.org/web/20170109030101/

http://www.dailystormer.com/the-don to oreilly-statements-on-mexicans-totally-accurate/; Andrew Anglin, "The Donald on CNN," Daily Stormer archived post, June 29, 2015, https:// web.archive.org/web/20170106150230/http://www.dailystormer.com/the-donald-on-cnn/; "Oy Vey! Mark Potok Says Trump Is a 'White Nationalist,'" Daily Stormer archived post, August 27, 2015, https://web.archive.org/web/20150829230923/http://www.dailystormer. com:80/oy-vey-mark-potok-says-trump-is-a-white-nationalist/; Andrew Anglin, "Trump Refuses to Back Down from Factual Statement about Mexican Rapists," Daily Stormer archived post, June 28, 2015, https://web.archive.org/web/20150629233153/http://www. dailystormer.com:80/trump-refuses-to-back-down-from-factual-statement-about-mexican-rapists/.

18. Donald J. Trump (@realDonaldTrump), "We, as a country, either have borders or we don't. IF WE DON'T HAVE BORDERS, WE DON'T HAVE A COUNTRY!" Twitter, November 12, 2015, https://twitter.com/realdonaldtrump/status/664787273184108545?lang=en.

19. Mark Potok, "The Year in Hate and Extremism," Southern Poverty Law Center, February 15, 2017, https://www.splcenter.org/fighting-hate/intelligence-report/2017/year-hate-and-extremism; Aaron Williams, "Hate Crimes Rose the Day after Trump Was Elected, FBI Data Show," *Washington Post*, March 23, 2018, https://www.washingtonpost.com/news/post-nation/wp/2018/03/23/hate-crimes-rose-the-day-after-trump-was-elected-fbi-data-show/?utm_term=.80d6a0d003c1.

20. Lorenzo Ferrigno, "Donald Trump: Boston Beating Is 'Terrible,'" CNN Politics, August 21, 2015, https://www.cnn.com/2015/08/20/politics/donald-trump-immigration-boston-beating/; Kali Holloway, "10 Hate Crimes Inspired by Donald Trump's Hateful Rhetoric," AlterNet, August 24, 2016, https://www.alternet.org/election-2016/10-hate-crimes-inspired-donald-trumps-hateful-rhetoric; Dennis Romero, "In the Era of Trump, Anti-Latino Hate Crimes Jumped 69% in L.A.," *LA Weekly*, September 29, 2016, http://www. laweekly.com/news/in-the-era-of-trump-anti-latino-hate-crimes-jumped-69-in-la-7443401; Clare Foran, "Donald Trump and the Rise of Anti-Muslim Violence," *The Atlantic*, September 22, 2016, https://www.theatlantic.com/politics/archive/2016/09/trump-muslims-islamophobia-hate-crime/500840/; Justin William Moyer, "Trump Says Fans Are 'Very Passionate' after Hearing One of Them Allegedly Assaulted Hispanic Man," *Washington Post*, August 21, 2015, https://www.washingtonpost.com/news/morning-mix/wp/2015/08/21/trump-says-fans-are-very-passionate-after-hearing-one-of-them-allegedly-assaulted-hispanic-man/?utm_term=.e9348c993029.

21. "Donald Trump: I'm the 'Least Racist' Person on Earth," clip from *The O'Reilly Factor*, Politico video, 0:16, November 24, 2015, https://www.politico.com/video/2015/11/donald-trump-im-the-least-racist-person-on-earth-034643; "Donald Trump: 'I'm the Least Racist Person,'" clip from CNN, YouTube video, 3:12, December 9, 2015, https:// www.youtube.com/watch?v=XRDmWPAtHiA; Marc Fisher, "Donald Trump: 'I Am the Least Racist Person,'" *Washington Post*, June 10, 2016, https://www.washingtonpost.com/

politics/donald-trump-i-am-the-least-racist-person/2016/06/10/eac7874c-2f3a-11e6-9de3-
6e6e7a14000c_story.html?utm_term=.8c4e8c90e167.

22. Dara Lind, "Timeline: Donald Trump Has Been Getting Called Racist Since 1973," Vox, December 9, 2015, https://www.vox.com/2015/8/3/9089495/donald-trump-racist.

23. Andrew Kaczynski and Christopher Massie, "Top Racists and Neo-Nazis Back Donald Trump," BuzzFeed News, August 26, 2015, https://www.buzzfeed.com/andrewkaczynski/meet-the-prominent-white-nationalists-fired-up-to-support-do?utm_term=.glP-v3AKaP#.ebnEqN4od.

24. Scott Bronstein and Drew Griffin, "Trump's Unwelcome Support: White Supremacists," CNN Politics, February 5, 2016, https://www.cnn.com/2016/02/05/politics/donald-trump-white-supremacists-new-hampshire/.

25. Abigail Tracy, "David Duke Missed the Memo that Trump Doesn't Want His Support," *Vanity Fair*, August 29, 2016, https://www.vanityfair.com/news/2016/08/david-duke-donald-trump.

26. "With All Due Respect (08/26/15)," posted by Bloomberg, YouTube video, 22:59, August 26, 2015, https://www.youtube.com/watch?v=UuoZBrK7pRo.

27. Brianna Ehley, "Trump: I Don't Want David Duke's Endorsement," Politico, August 26, 2015, http://www.politico.com/story/2015/08/donald-trump-doesnt-want-david-duke-endorsement-121784.

28. Andrew Anglin, "The Donald Confronted about 'White Supremacist Supporters,'" Daily Stormer archived post, August 27, 2015, https://web.archive.org/web/20150831022715/http://www.dailystormer.com:80/the-donald-confronted-about-white-supremacist-supporters/.

29. Donald J. Trump (@realDonaldTrump), "@SeanSean252: @WayneDupreeShow @Rockprincess818 @CheriJacobus pic.twitter.com/5GUwhhtvyN," Twitter, November 22, 2015, https://twitter.com/realDonaldTrump/status/668520614697820160; the original tweet from SeanSean252 was deleted: https://twitter.com/SeanSean252/status/668516391364890624/photo/1. Media noticed that Trump had retweeted white nationalist content here, but he had retweeted white nationalists at least seven other times: Donald J. Trump (@realDonaldTrump), "@keksec_org: @realDonaldTrump You said it best! #MakeAmericaGreatAgain,'" Twitter, October 4, 2015, https://twitter.com/realdonaldtrump/status/650774060708835328; Donald J. Trump (@realDonaldTrump), "'@keksec_org: @realDonaldTrump I truly believe you are the best #MakeAmericaGreatAgain' Thank you so much!" Twitter, October 7, 2015, https://twitter.com/realdonaldtrump/status/651909287006961664; Donald J. Trump (@realDonaldTrump), "'@keksec_org: The only winner of the #DemDebate is @realDonaldTrump.' This is not a great debate—a little sad!" Twitter, October 13, 2015, https://twitter.com/realdonaldtrump/status/654116860145831936; Donald J. Trump (@realDonaldTrump), "keksec_org: @realDonaldTrump Your performances in every state have been amazing! #MakeAmericaGreatAgain," Twitter, November 3, 2015, https://twitter.com/realdonaldtrump/

status/661555885290967041; Donald J. Trump (@realDonaldTrump), "@keksec_org: @realDonaldTrump Ivanka said it and you said it too, you'll be great for women. #MakeAmericaGreatAgain," Twitter, November 6, 2015, https://twitter.com/realdonaldtrump/status/662559770398838784; Donald J. Trump (@realDonaldTrump), "'keksec_org: @realDonaldTrump I haven't seen anyone carry themselves so Presidential since Reagan. #MakeAmericaGreatAgain' Great!" Twitter, November 7, 2015, https://twitter.com/realdonaldtrump/status/663050817168138241; Donald J. Trump (@realDonaldTrump), "'@NeilTruner_: @realDonaldTrump youtube.com/watch?v=1FJ6WY . . . It's time we take America back! No more puppet presidents! #VoteTrump' So true!" Twitter, January 24, 2016, https://twitter.com/realdonaldtrump/status/691382705217523712.

30. Robert Farley, "Trump Retweets Bogus Crime Graphic," *FactCheck.org*, November 23, 2015, http://www.factcheck.org/2015/11/trump-retweets-bogus-crime-graphic/.

31. "Donald Trump on Confronting ISIS," Fox News video, 07:24, posted November 23, 2015, http://video.foxnews.com/v/4628873335001/donald-trump-on-confronting-isis/?intcmp=hpvid1#sp=show-clips. SeanSean252's profile does not claim any expertise on criminal justice. His bio reads: "Time to put boot on back of the lefty socialists! No meeting in the middle! We are right and they're wrong period!" (https://twitter.com/SeanSean252). According to the website Little Green Footballs, the first Twitter user to post the graphic was a white supremacist named Non Dildo'd Goyim (@CheesedBrit), who posted the image on November 22, 2015: Charles Johnson, "We Found Where Donald Trump's 'Black Crimes' Graphic Came From," Little Green Footballs, November 22, 2015, http://littlegreenfootballs.com/article/45291_we_found_where_donald_trumps_black_crimes_graphic_came_from; Non Dildo'd Goyim (@CheesedBrit), Twitter post, November 21, 2015, https://web.archive.org/web/20151123164359/https://twitter.com/CheesedBrit/status/668282032389230592.

32. "FNN: FULL Donald Trump Press Conference Before Dubuque, Iowa Rally," Fox 10 Phoenix, YouTube video, 33:06, 17:20, August 25, 2015, https://www.youtube.com/watch?v=Z0_n-LHv6Xs.

33. Just Us, post #95 on "Re: Trump Does the Unthinkable and Tweets Crime Statistic Graph Showing Blacks Murder Whites at an Overwhelming Rat," StormFront Forum, November 24, 2015, https://www.stormfront.org/forum/t1131723-10/?postcount=95#post13163396.

34. Ben Kharakh and Dan Primack, "Donald Trump's Social Media Ties to White Supremacists," *Fortune*, May 22, 2016, http://fortune.com/donald-trump-white-supremacist-genocide/.

35. Andrew Anglin, "Happening: Trump Retweet Two More White Genocide Accounts Back-to-Back," Daily Stormer archived post, January 25, 2016, https://web.archive.org/web/20160126000215/http://www.dailystormer.com/happening-trump-retweets-two-more-white-genocide-accounts-back-to-back/. On February 16, 2016, Trump retweeted @WhiteGenocideTM and then deleted it: "Deleted Tweet from Donald J. Trump," ProPublica, "realDonaldTrump (R) (@realDonaldTrump): '@WhiteGenocideTM: @realDonaldTrump

You always have the best crowds #MakeAmericaGreatAgain,' Deleted after 2 minutes at 8:25 PM on 10 Feb 16. It looks like this tweet was not replaced," https://projects.propublica.org/politwoops/tweet/697591556010856448; John Robertson, "Fucking CNN jew Jake Tapper, in his interview with Trump, this Sunday morning, tries to link Trump with White supremacists, and claimed Trump re-tweeted White supremacist comments. Trump claimed he had no knowledge of what Tapper was claiming," post #429 on "#1 Donald Trump Thread," Vanguard News Network Forum, February 21, 2016, http://img1.vnnforum.com/showpost.php?p=1998211&postcount=429; Dan Hadaway, "More Than Half of Trump's Retweets Are White Supremacists Praising Him," post #389 on "#1 Donald Trump Thread," Vanguard News Network Forum, February 5, 2016, http://img1.vnnforum.com/showpost.php?p=1989626&postcount=389.

36. "State of the Union with Jake Tapper," CNN, Trump archive video, 11:01, February 21, 2016, https://archive.org/details/cnnw_20160221_140200_state_of_the_union_with_jake_tapper/start/360/end/420.

37. According to another white supremacist on February 21, 2016, "Fucking CNN jew Jake Tapper, in his interview with Trump, this Sunday morning, tries to link Trump with White supremacists, and claimed Trump re-tweeted White supremacist comments. Trump claimed he had no knowledge of what Tapper was claiming. While it's OK for Hillary to actively solicit blacks, jews and other nonwhites to support her, apparently, it's not permissible to have Whites support Trump. Instead, they are smeared by this fucking low-life, jew, Tapper, as 'supremacists'. Meanwhile, as we know, there are no White supremacists and jews prevent us from having a platform to defend ourselves from their ubiquitous smears. In fact, there are only jew supremacists because only jews are working to subjugate the masses under their rule, while these jews continue to smear Whites who want to stop jews and other nonwhites from destroying all that Whites have created." John Robertson, post #429 on "#1 Donald Trump Thread," Vanguard News Network Forum, February 21, 2016, http://img1.vnnforum.com/showpost.php?p=1998211&postcount=429.

38. Andrew Kaczynski, "David Duke Urges His Supporters to Volunteer and Vote for Trump," BuzzFeed News, February 25, 2016, https://www.buzzfeed.com/andrewkaczynski/david-duke-urges-his-supporters-to-volunteer-and-vote-for-tr?utm_term=.fs1wxLPKk#.cnnpRYjnX; "ADL to Donald Trump: Distance Yourself from White Supremacists and Disavow Their Ideology," Anti-Defamation League, February 25, 2016, https://www.adl.org/news/press-releases/adl-to-donald-trump-distance-yourself-from-white-supremacists-and-disavow-their.

39. "Trump 'Disavows' Former KKK Leader's Support," Reuters, YouTube video, 0:25, February 26, 2016, https://www.youtube.com/watch?v=yseotd_fxWY&feature=youtu.be.

40. Eric Bradner, "Donald Trump Stumbles on David Duke, KKK," CNN Politics, February 29, 2016, http://www.cnn.com/2016/02/28/politics/donald-trump-white-supremacists/.

41. Eun Kyung Kim, "Donald Trump on KKK Non-Answer: A 'Very Bad Earpiece'

Made It Tough to Hear," *Today*, February 29, 2016, https://www.today.com/news/donald-trump-kkk-non-answer-very-bad-earpiece-made-it-t76661.

42. Man of the road, post #486 on "#1 Donald Trump Thread," Vanguard News Network Forum, February 28, 2016, http://img1.vnnforum.com/showpost.php?p=2002045&postcount=486; N. B. Forrest, "And who the FUCK do media kike scum like Tappah think they are, demanding that any even implicitly pro-White candidates 'disavow' open pro-Whites? They sure as hell never demand that juuz or nigs condemn the ADL, the SPLC or the NAACP," post #495 on "#1 Donald Trump Thread," Vanguard News Network Forum, February 28, 2016, http://img1.vnnforum.com/showpost.php?p=2002271&postcount=495.

43. Unermudlich, post #727 on "Re: The Trump Media Thread," Storm-Front Forum, March 4, 2016, https://www.stormfront.org/forum/t1117558-73/?postcount=727#post13343325.

44. notmenomore, post #488 on "#1 Donald Trump Thread," Vanguard News Network Forum, February 28, 2016, http://img1.vnnforum.com/showpost.php?p=2002092&postcount=488.

45. Gidean Resnick, Betsy Woodruff, and Tara Wanda, "David Duke: I Think Trump 'Knows Who I Am'" Daily Beast, accessed April 4, 2019, https://www.thedailybeast.com/david-duke-i-think-trump-knows-who-i-am.

46. 8Man, post #469 on "#1 Donald Trump Thread," Vanguard News Network Forum, February 25, 2016, http://img1.vnnforum.com/showpost.php?p=2000560&postcount=469.

47. Vance Stubbs, post #925 on "#1 Donald Trump Thread," Vanguard News Network Forum, March 20, 2016, http://img1.vnnforum.com/showpost.php?p=2013692&postcount=925.

48. Andrew "weev" Auernheimer, "Why I MAGA," Daily Stormer archived post, May 4, 2016, https://web.archive.org/web/20160506011632/http://www.dailystormer.com/why-i-maga/.

49. Andrew "weev" Auernheimer, "A Brief Experiment in Printing," Storify archived post, March 26, 2016, https://web.archive.org/web/20160326031112/https://storify.com/weev/a-small-experiment-in; Gabrielle Levy, "KKK, White Nationalists Ready to Roll for Trump on Election Day," *U.S. News and World Report*, November 2, 2016, https://www.usnews.com/news/politics/articles/2016-11-02/kkk-white-nationalists-ready-to-roll-for-donald-trump-on-election-day.

50. N. B. Forrest, post #645 on "#1 Donald Trump Thread," Vanguard News Network Forum, March 6, 2016, http://img1.vnnforum.com/showpost.php?p=2006065&postcount=645. Many cheered when the *New York Times* wrote a story about Trump's twitter trolls: Alexander Burns and Maggie Haberman, "To Fight Critics, Donald Trump Aims to Instill Fear in 140-Character Doses," *New York Times*, February 26, 2016, https://www.nytimes.com/2016/02/27/us/politics/donald-trump.html?_r=0.

Craig Cobb, "NYT says Trump's twitter army (some Neo Nazis and WN among them) making mean old pics on twitter and FB against Mr. Trump's enemies! Isn't it a pity? They also say he has "about" ten million twitter followers. Only in the most "rounded" mathematical terms. He hasn't hit 7 million yet," post #637 on "Re: The Trump Media Thread," StormFront Forum, February 27, 2016, https://www.stormfront.org/forum/t1117558-64/?postcount=637#post13329522. On paid-for pro-Trump Twitter ads, see Craig Cobb, post #568 on "Re: The Trump Media Thread," StormFront Forum, February 19, 2016, https://www.stormfront.org/forum/t1117558-57/?postcount=568#post13314514. On organized Twitter posts and hashtags, see "RETWEET these tweets about 'Trump's "Stop White Genocide Wall,"'" StormFront Forum, February 10, 2016, https://www.stormfront.org/forum/t1142896/; "Social Group: Trumpets," StormFront, https://www.stormfront.org/forum/group.php?groupid=599; "Tweeting now: 'Trump's "Stop #WhiteGenocide Wall,"'" Storm-Front Forum, February 5, 2016, https://www.stormfront.org/forum/t1142228/; "Stormfront's Editor and Chief of Staff Jack Boot Offers Encouraging Words," StormFront Forum, February 7, 2016, https://www.stormfront.org/forum/t1142534/.

51. Julia Ioffe, "Melania Trump on Her Rise, Her Family Secrets, and Her True Political Views: 'Nobody Will Ever Know,'" *GQ*, April 27, 2016, https://www.gq.com/story/melania-trump-gq-interview.

52. "The article published in GQ today is yet another example of the dishonest media and their disingenuous reporting. Julia Ioffe, a journalist who is looking to make a name for herself, clearly had an agenda when going after my family. There are numerous inaccuracies in this article including certain statements about my family and claims on personal matters. My parents are private citizens and should not be subject to Ms. Ioffe's unfair scrutiny. Furthermore, the statement surrounding the performance of my skincare collection is completely false. The company in which I was involved with did not honor the contract and did not meet their obligations and as such the courts ruled in my favor. I am hopeful that the media will begin to cover me fairly and be respectful of my family's privacy." Melania Trump, Facebook, April 27, 2016, https://www.facebook.com/MelaniaTrump/posts/10154069359512808.

53. Ioffe is a Russian-born person of Jewish heritage. A lolcow, according to *Urban Dictionary*, is "a person you get extensive laughs from, who doesn't know they are being made fun of. They can often think they are admired for what they are doing, but secretly are being laughed at constantly." "lolcow," *Urban Dictionary*, August 7, 2008, https://www.urban-dictionary.com/define.php?term=lolcow; Andrew Anglin, "Empress Melania Attacked by Filthy Russian Kike Julia Ioffe in GQ!" Daily Stormer archived post, April 28, 2016, https://web.archive.org/web/20160501155443/http://bbs.dailystormer.com:80/t/empress-melania-attacked-by-filthy-russian-kike-julia-ioffe-in-gq/23884.

54. Julia Ioffe (@juliaioffe), "Now I'm getting phone calls from a blocked number that play Hitler's speeches when I pick up. Sad!" Twitter, April 28, 2016, https://twitter.com/juliaioffe/status/725705073389494272; Julia Ioffe (@juliaioffe), "For those among you who appreciate irony: my family arrived in the US (legally) 26 years ago today. We were fleeing anti-Semitism," Twitter, April 28, 2016, https://twitter.com/juliaioffe/

status/725753618830229505; Julia Ioffe (@juliaioffe), "Good morning, from your neighborhood Trump trolls!" Twitter, April 28, 2016, https://twitter.com/juliaioffe/status/725637201372020736; Julia Ioffe (@juliaioffe), "From my inbox. Subject line: 'They know about you!' https://pbs.twimg.com/media/ChJFip4UYAAZ4jw.jpg:large," Twitter, April 28, 2016, https://twitter.com/juliaioffe/status/725718952798613505; Julia Ioffe (@juliaioffe), "@lpolgreen @crampell I should add that this is because the Daily Stormer wrote about my 'attack' on Melania. https://pbs.twimg.com/media/ChImftyWUAE_mgn.jpg:large," Twitter, April 28, 2016, https://twitter.com/juliaioffe/status/725684829141000194; Julia Ioffe (@juliaioffe), "At least they're fluent in 80s pop culture? https://pbs.twimg.com/media/ChH-AYVWgAApPgn.jpg:large," Twitter, April 28, 2016, https://twitter.com/juliaioffe/status/725640300736159745; Julia Ioffe (@juliaioffe), "Finishing the day strong with a call from Aftermath Services, inquiring about that homicide clean up I ordered. #TrumpTrain," Twitter, April 28, 2016, https://twitter.com/juliaioffe/status/725903489126129664. Erik Wemple, "Police Report Reflects the Ugliness of the Trump Era," *Washington Post*, May 9, 2016, https://www.washingtonpost.com/blogs/erik-wemple/wp/2016/05/09/police-report-reflects-the-ugliness-of-the-trump-era/?utm_term=.2dda29cb4d90; Lauren Gambino, "Journalist Who Profiled Melania Trump Hit with Barrage of Antisemeitc Abuse," *The Guardian*, April 28, 2016, https://www.theguardian.com/us-news/2016/apr/28/julia-ioffe-journalist-melania-trump-antisemitic-abuse; Tara Golshan, "Julia Ioffe Profiled Melania Trump. Then She Started Getting Calls from Hitler," Vox, April 30, 2016, https://www.vox.com/2016/4/30/11539078/melania-trump-gq-julia-ioffe-antisemitic-donald-Trump; Brian Stelter, "Reporter Targeted by 'Trump Trolls' Says They Want to 'Silence Criticism,'" CNN Business, May 2, 2016, http://money.cnn.com/2016/05/02/media/julia-ioffe-interview-trump-trolls/index.html?SR=twtsr0504trumpintv.

55. "We see you, Jew. And soon, all of our brothers and sisters will see you just as clearly as we do. We will tell them the truth. We will incite them to rage. We will lead our people out into the streets." Andrew Anglin, "Filthy Kike Julia Ioffe Goes on CNN to Whine about the Stormer Troll Army," Daily Stormer archived post, May 1, 2016, https://web.archive.org/web/20160509012033/http://www.dailystormer.com:80/filthy-kike-julia-ioffe-goes-on-cnn-to-whine-about-the-stormer-troll-army/.

56. *Situation Room with Wolf Blitzer*, CNN, Trump archive video, 1:04, May 4, 2016, https://archive.org/details/CNNW_20160504_212400_Situation_Room_With_Wolf_Blitzer/start/480/end/540; Dan Hadaway, post #1276 on "#1 Donald Trump Thread," Vanguard News Network Forum, May 21, 2016, http://img1.vnnforum.com/showpost.php?p=2043581&postcount=1276.

57. A Daily Stormer commenter, ApolloHermes, wrote, "Wow. In the video at 1:27 he looks directly at the camera whilst saying: 'I don't have a message to the fans' . . . fans. . . . It was as if he were looking us in the eye, addressing us directly!!! It was as if he actually did have a message to the fans. . . . He goes on to say: 'There is nothing more dishonest than the media, and I know it better than anybody, and it's actually gotten to a point where it doesn't even

bother me anymore. It's gotten so ridiculous.' Well Stormers, let me translate the message that Donald Trump said he didn't have for us, yet actually did have for us: 'There is nothing more dishonest than the jews, and I know it better than anybody, and it's actually gotten to a point where (jewish dishonesty) it doesn't even bother me anymore. It's (Jewish lies, have) gotten so ridiculous.' If you had any doubts that Donald Trump is wise to the trickery of the Jew, then there it is, packaged up in that statement," comment on Andrew Anglin, "Glorious Leader Donald Trump Refuses to Denounce Stormer Troll Army," Daily Stormer archived post, May 6, 2016, https://web.archive.org/web/20160506130528/http://www.dailystormer.com/glorious-leader-donald-trump-refuses-to-denounce-stormer-troll-army/.

58. Andrew Anglin, "I Will Not Rage If the Leader Denounces the Troll Army," Daily Stormer archived post, May 7, 2016, https://web.archive.org/web/20160512143300/http://www.dailystormer.com:80/i-will-not-rage-if-the-leader-denounces-the-troll-army.

59. Andrew Anglin, "The Donald Does the Ultimate Evil and Retweets a Hateful Racist," Daily Stormer archived post, October 9, 2015, https://web.archive.org/web/20160116235511/http://www.dailystormer.com:80/the-donald-does-the-ultimate-evil-and-retweets-a-hateful-racist/.

60. Andrew "weev" Auernheimer, "Why I MAGA," Daily Stormer archived post, May 4, 2016, https://web.archive.org/web/20160506011632/http://www.dailystormer.com/why-i-maga/.

Chapter 10

1. "Trump: Favorable/Unfavorable," Real Clear Politics, http://www.realclearpolitics.com/epolls/other/trump_favorableunfavorable-5493.html#polls.

2. "Transcript of Republican Presidential Debate," *New York Times*, January 15, 2016, https://www.nytimes.com/2016/01/15/us/politics/transcript-of-republican-presidential-debate.html.

3. Pew Research Center, "2016, Campaign: Strong Interest, Widespread Dissatisfaction," July 2016, http://assets.pewresearch.org/wp-content/uploads/sites/5/2016/07/07-07-16-Voter-attitudes-release.pdf.

4. Pew Research Center, "Opinions on Gun Policy and the 2016 Campaign," August 2016, 3, http://assets.pewresearch.org/wp-content/uploads/sites/5/2016/08/08-26-16-gun-policy-release.pdf.

5. Time Staff, "Here's Donald Trump's Presidential Announcement Speech," *Time*, June 16, 2015, http://time.com/3923128/donald-trump-announcement-speech/.

6. "Positions: Protecting Our Second Amendment Rights Will Make America Great Again," DonaldJTrump.com archived post, September 19, 2015, https://web.archive.org/web/20150919090024/https://www.donaldjtrump.com/positions/second-amendment-rights.

7. "To grasp the audacity of what Scalia & Co. pulled off, turn to the Second Amendment's text: 'A well regulated Militia, being necessary to the security of a free State, the right

of the people to keep and bear Arms, shall not be infringed.' To find in that wording an individual right to possess a firearm untethered to any militia purpose, the majority performed an epic feat of jurisprudential magic: It made the pesky initial clause about the necessity of a 'well regulated Militia' disappear. Poof! Gone. Scalia treated the clause as merely 'prefatory' and having no real operative effect—a view at odds with history, the fundamental rules of constitutional interpretation, and the settled legal consensus for many decades." Dorothy Samuels, "The Second Amendment Was Never Meant to Protect an Individual's Right to a Gun," *The Nation*, September 23, 2015, https://www.thenation.com/article/how-the-roberts-court-undermined-sensible-gun-control/.

8. "Barbara Walters Presents the 10 Most Fascinating People of 2015," ABC News, Trump archive video, 1:02, December 17, 2015, https://archive.org/details/kgo_20151218_054200_barbara_walters_presents_the_10_most_fascinating_people_of_2015/start/136/end/196?q=second+amendment.

9. "US House of Representatives Special Orders," C-SPAN, Trump archive video, 1:00, December 7, 2015, https://archive.org/details/cspan_20151208_000600_us_house_of_representatives_special_orders/start/2123/end/2183?q=second+amendment.

10. "Donald Trump Campaign Rally in Clear Lake, Iowa," C-SPAN, Trump archive video, 11:00, January 9, 2016, https://archive.org/details/cspan_20160109_221000_donald_trump_campaign_rally_in_clear_lake_iowa/start/1668/end/1728?q=guns.

11. "Key Capitol Hill Hearings," C-SPAN, Trump archive video, 11:03, March 1, 2016, https://archive.org/details/cspan_20160301_102400_key_capitol_hill_hearings/start/2220/end/2280; "Wolf," CNN, Trump archive video, 1:00, June 15, 2016, https://archive.org/details/cnnw_20160615_170100_wolf/start/723/end/783?q=thugs.

12. According to linguist John McWhorter, "The truth is that thug today is a nominally polite way of using the N-word. Many people suspect it, and they are correct. When somebody talks about thugs ruining a place, it is almost impossible today that they are referring to somebody with blond hair. It is a sly way of saying there go those black people ruining things again. And so anybody who wonders whether thug is becoming the new N-word doesn't need to. It's most certainly is." Melissa Block and John McWhorter, "The Racially Charged Meaning Behind the Word 'Thug,'" *All Things Considered*, NPR, April 30, 2015, https://www.npr.org/2015/04/30/403362626/the-racially-charged-meaning-behind-the-word-thug.

13. "Key Capitol Hill Hearings," C-SPAN, Trump archive video, 011:05, March 6, 2016, https://archive.org/details/cspan_20160306_065400_key_capitol_hill_hearings/start/2700/end/2760.

14. "Donald Trump Campaign Rally in Clear Lake, Iowa," C-SPAN, Trump archive video, 1:00, January 9, 2016, https://archive.org/details/cspan_20160109_221000_donald_trump_campaign_rally_in_clear_lake_iowa/start/1668/end/1728?q=guns.

15. "Key Capitol Hill Hearings," C-SPAN, Trump archive video, 1:03, March 1, 2016, https://archive.org/details/cspan_20160301_102400_key_capitol_hill_hearings/start/2220/end/2280.

16. "Kasich Town Hall," MSNBC, Trump archive video, 1:08, March 19, 2016, https://archive.org/details/msnbcw_20160319_190300_kasich_town_hall/start/300/end/360.

17. "Wolf," CNN, Trump archive video, 1:02, June 15, 2016, https://archive.org/details/cnnw_20160615_170100_wolf/start/720/end/780.

18. "US House of Representatives Special Orders," C-SPAN, Trump archive video, 1:00, December 7, 2015, https://archive.org/details/cspan_20151208_000600_us_house_of_representatives_special_orders/start/2123/end/2183?q=second+amendment.

19. "Donald Trump Campaign Rally in Milford New Hampshire," C-SPAN, Trump archive video, 1:00, February 3, 2016, https://archive.org/details/cspan_20160203_092100_donald_trump_campaign_rally_in_milford_new_hampshire/start/236/end/296?q=thugs.

20. Sopan Deb, "Donald Trump's Supreme Court Litmus Test," CBS News, February 17, 2016, https://www.cbsnews.com/news/campaign-2016-donald-trump-supreme-court-litmus-test/.

21. Jeremy Diamond, "Trump Says Clinton Wants to Abolish the 2nd Amendment," CNN Politics, May 7, 2016, https://www.cnn.com/2016/05/07/politics/donald-trump-hillary-clinton-second-amendment/.

22. Eugene Kiely, "Trump Distorts Clinton's Gun Stance," FactCheck.org, May 10, 2016, https://www.factcheck.org/2016/05/trump-distorts-clintons-gun-stance/.

23. Linda Qiu, "Donald Trump Falsely Claims Hillary Clinton 'Wants to Abolish the 2nd Amendment,'" PolitiFact, May 11, 2016, https://www.politifact.com/truth-o-meter/statements/2016/may/11/donald-trump/donald-trump-falsely-claims-hillary-clinton-wants-/.

24. "Key Capitol Hill Hearings," C-SPAN, Trump archive video, 1:00, August 9, 2016, https://archive.org/details/cspan_20160809_230500_key_capitol_hill_hearings/start/2460/end/2520.

25. U.S. Secret Service (@SecretService), "The Secret Service is aware of the comments made earlier this afternoon," Twitter, August 9, 2016, https://twitter.com/SecretService/status/763142627202048000.

26. Nick Corasaniti and Maggie Haberman, "Donald Trump Suggests 'Second Amendment People' Could Act against Hillary Clinton," *New York Times*, August 9, 2016, https://www.nytimes.com/2016/08/10/us/politics/donald-trump-hillary-clinton.html.

27. David Smith, "Donald Trump Hints at Assassination of Hillary Clinton by Gun Rights Supporters," *The Guardian*, August 10, 2016, https://www.theguardian.com/us-news/2016/aug/09/trump-gun-owners-clinton-judges-second-amendment.

28. David S. Cohen, "Trump's Assassination Dog Whistle Was Even Scarier Than You Think," *Rolling Stone*, August 9, 2016, https://www.rollingstone.com/politics/politics-features/trumps-assassination-dog-whistle-was-even-scarier-than-you-think-112138/; David Uberti, "Why Donald Trump Can Kinda, Sorta Say Anything He Wants," *Columbia Journalism Review*, August 10, 2016, https://www.cjr.org/criticism/_trump_second_amendment_speech.php.

29. Tami Luhby and Jim Sciutto, "Secret Service Spoke to Trump Campaign about 2nd

Amendment Comment," CNN Politics, August 11, 2016, https://www.cnn.com/2016/08/10/politics/trump-second-amendment/index.html.

30. Chris Murphy (@ChrisMurphyCT), "Don't treat this as a political misstep. It's an assassination threat, seriously upping the possibility of a national tragedy & crisis," Twitter, August 9, 2016, https://twitter.com/ChrisMurphyCT/status/763106278319198208?ref_src=twsrc%5Etfw.

31. Jason Miller, "Trump Campaign Statement on Dishonest Media," DonaldJTrump.com archived post, August 9, 2016, https://web.archive.org/web/20160810080943/https://www.donaldjtrump.com/press-releases/trump-campaign-statement-on-dishonest-media.

32. "Trump on Hannity," *Fox News Insider*, YouTube video, 1:51, August 9, 2016, https://www.youtube.com/watch?v=5clyv-dkc2e; "Trump Rejects Claims He Advocated Violence against Clinton with '2nd Amendment' Comment," Fox News, August 10, 2016, http://www.foxnews.com/politics/2016/08/10/trump-accused-advocating-violence-against-clinton-with-2nd-amendment-remark.html.

33. David Edwards, "Trump Backer Tells C-SPAN: Second Amendment Remark Means Brace for Armed Revolt, Not Assassination," RawStory, August 10, 2016, https://www.rawstory.com/2016/08/trump-backer-tells-c-span-second-amendment-remark-means-brace-for-armed-revolt-not-assassination/.

34. NRA (@NRA), ".@RealDonaldTrump is right. If @HillaryClinton gets to pick her anti-#2A #SCOTUS judges, there's nothing we can do. #NeverHillary," Twitter, August 9, 2016, https://twitter.com/NRA/status/763110521889402880.

35. Robert Maguire, "Audit Shows NRA Spending Surged $100 Million amidst Pro-Trump Push in 2016," OpenSecrets.org, November 15, 2017, https://www.opensecrets.org/news/2017/11/audit-shows-nra-spending-surged-100-million-amidst-pro-trump-push-in-2016/.

36. "Donald Trump: 2016 NRA-ILA Leadership Forum," NRA, YouTube video, 32:16, May 20, 2016, https://www.youtube.com/watch?v=1iST5oUPNAA.

37. "Hypocrite Hillary Leaves You Defenseless," NRA, YouTube video, 0:30, August 10, 2016, https://www.youtube.com/watch?v=Wxqx5CjfrgE.

38. Sarah Wheaton, "NRA Warns Voters that Clinton Will Leave Them Unprotected," Politico, September 20, 2016, https://www.politico.com/story/2016/09/nra-clinton-leaves-you-unprotected-228410.

Chapter 11

1. "Trump: Favorable/Unfavorable," Real Clear Politics, http://www.realclearpolitics.com/epolls/other/trump_favorableunfavorable-5493.html#polls.

2. David Alire Garcia, "Mexican Government Calls Trump's Comments 'Prejudiced and Absurd,'" Reuters, June 17, 2015, https://www.reuters.com/article/us-usa-election-trump-mexico/mexican-government-calls-trumps-comments-prejudiced-and-absurd-idusk-bn0ox06920150618.

3. "Statement from the Entertainment Division of Univision Communications Inc. on June 25, 2015," Univision, June 25, 2015, https://web.archive.org/web/20150714215444/http://corporate.univision.com/2015/06/statement-from-the-entertainment-division-of-univision-communications-inc-on-june-25-2015; "NBC Statement Regarding Donald Trump," NBC Universal, June 29, 2015, http://www.nbcuniversal.com/press-release/nbc-statement-regarding-donald-trump.

4. Sarah Halzack, "Macy's Parts Ways with Donald Trump," *Washington Post*, July 1, 2015, https://www.washingtonpost.com/news/business/wp/2015/07/01/macys-parts-ways-with-donald-trump/?utm_term=.db30f8d1099f.

5. "State of the Union with Jake Tapper," CNN, Trump archive video, 11:00, June 28, 2015, https://archive.org/details/cnnw_20150628_131400_state_of_the_union_with_jake_tapper/start/312/end/372?q=rapists.

6. Jeffrey M. Jones, "In U.S., 65% Favor Path to Citizenship for Illegal Immigrants," Gallup, August 12, 2015, https://news.gallup.com/poll/184577/favor-path-citizenship-illegal-immigrants.aspx; Gallup's findings were similar to a June 4, 2015, Pew poll finding that 72 percent of Americans believed that "undocumented immigrants living in the United States who meet certain requirements should be allowed to stay legally." Pew likewise found a large partisan gap, with 53 percent of Republicans and 75 percent of Democrats favoring either a path to citizenship or legal permanent residency. "Broad Public Support for Legal Status for Undocumented Immigrants," Pew Research Center, June 4, 2015, http://www.people-press.org/2015/06/04/broad-public-support-for-legal-status-for-undocumented-immigrants/.

7. "Key Capitol Hill Hearings," C-SPAN, Trump archive video, 11:00, March 15, 2016, https://archive.org/details/cspan_20160315_100100_key_capitol_hill_hearings/start/185/end/245?q=we+talk+about+the+wrong+people.

8. Trump memorably used the phrase "bad hombres" twice on October 19, 2016. At a Mesa, Arizona, rally and in the third presidential debate: "Presidential Nominees Debate at the University of Nevada," C-SPAN, Trump archive video, 1:00, October 19, 2016, https://archive.org/details/cspan_20161020_010000_presidential_nominees_debate_at_the_university_of_nevada/start/1370/end/1430?q=bad+hombres.

9. "Votes Want to Build a Wall, Deport Felon Illegal Immigrants," Rasmussen Reports, August 19, 2015, http://www.rasmussenreports.com/public_content/politics/current_events/immigration/august_2015/voters_want_to_build_a_wall_deport_felon_illegal_immigrants.

10. "Donald Trump FULL Press Conference with families of people killed by illegal aliens," YouTube archived post, 51:41, July 10, 2015, https://web.archive.org/web/20170129133350/https://www.youtube.com/watch?v=bsokVoqSOA8&feature=youtu.be.

11. Allison Graves and Neelesh Moorthy, "Who Were the Victims of Illegal Immigrants Named at the RNC?" Politifact, July 21, 2016, https://www.politifact.com/truth-o-meter/article/2016/jul/21/who-were-victims-illegal-immigrants-trump-named-rn/; *Hannity*, Fox News, Trump archive video, 1:00, August 11, 2015, https://archive.org/details/

foxnewsw_20150812_020100_hannity/start/130/end/190?q=animals; *Donald Trump Campaigns in Prescott Valley, Arizona*, C-SPAN, Trump archive video, 1:00, October 5, 2016, https://archive.org/details/cspan2_20161005_043400_donald_trump_campaigns_in_prescott_valley_arizona/start/684/end/744?q=savages.

12. "Presidential Candidate Donald Trump Rally in Springfield, Ohio," C-SPAN video, 42:02, October 27, 2016, https://www.c-span.org/video/?417557-1/donald-trump-campaigns-springfield-ohio; Miriam Valverde, "Trump Leaves Out Context in Claim about Immigrants and Crime," Politifact, November 3, 2016, https://www.politifact.com/truth-o-meter/statements/2016/nov/03/donald-trump/trump-leaves-out-context-claim-about-immigrants-an/.

13. Fox News released a poll of Republican primary voters on June 24, 2015, that had Trump in second place with 11 percent of the vote—just behind presumed Republican nomination front-runner Jeb Bush. He soon surpassed Bush and remained at the top of the polls until he secured the nomination. Dana Blanton, "Fox News Poll: Bush, Trump Score Post-Announcement Bumps," Fox News archived post, June 24, 2015, https://web.archive.org/web/20150624220043/http://www.foxnews.com/politics/2015/06/24/fox-news-poll-bush-trump-score-post-announcement-bumps/.

14. "Donald Trump Campaigns in Prescott Valley, Arizona," C-SPAN, Trump archive video, 1:00, October 5, 2016, https://archive.org/details/cspan2_20161005_043400_donald_trump_campaigns_in_prescott_valley_arizona/start/684/end/744?q=savages.

15. "Key Capitol Hill Hearings," C-SPAN, Trump archive video, 11:03, September 15, 2015, https://archive.org/details/cspan2_20150916_004900_key_capitol_hill_hearings/start/1860/end/1920.

16. "Donald Trump EXPLOSIVE Rally in Columbus, OH 11/23/2015," Donald Trump News, YouTube video, 1:31:24, December 12, 2015, https://www.youtube.com/watch?v=LDda_of-T8g.

17. *Hardball with Chris Matthews*, MSNBC, Trump archive video, 11:00, August 19, 2015, https://archive.org/details/msnbcw_20150820_063000_hardball_with_chris_matthews/start/1607/end/1667?q=trump+wall; "Donald Trump and Mexican President Deliver Join Statement," C-SPAN, Trump archive video, 11:00, August 31, 2016, https://archive.org/details/cspan_20160901_004600_donald_trump_and_mexican_president_deliver_joint_statement/start/213/end/273?q=the+great+wall+of+trump.

18. Ron Nixon and Linda Qiu, "Trump's Evolving Words on the Wall," *New York Times*, January 18, 2018, https://www.nytimes.com/2018/01/18/us/politics/trump-border-wall-immigration.html.

19. Enrique PeNa Nieto (@EPN), "Repito lo que le dije personalmente, Sr. Trump: México jamás pagaría por un muro. [I will repeat what I said personally, Mr. Trump: Mexico will never pay for a wall]," Twitter, September 1, 2016, response to Donald J. Trump (@realDonaldTrump), "Mexico will pay for the wall!" Twitter, September 1, 2016, https://twitter.com/epn/status/771423919978913792?ref_src=twsrc%5etfw%7ctwcamp%5e

tweetembed%7ctwterm%5e771423919978913792&ref_url=https%3a%2f%2fthehill.
com%2fblogs%2fballot-box%2fpresidential-races%2f294155-mexican-president-tweets-to-
trump-mexico-will-never-pay.

20. "Ex-Mexican President to Trump: 'Not Going to Pay for That F****** Wall,'"
ABC News, YouTube video, 00:37, February 26, 2016, https://www.youtube.com/
watch?v=5y6kAwm7uIs.

21. "Trump: 'Who's Gonna Pay for the Wall?' Crowd: 'Mexico!'" MSNBC video, 00:30,
January 7, 2016, https://www.msnbc.com/msnbc-quick-cuts/watch/trump-who-s-gonna-pay-
for-the-wall-crowd-mexico-598086723533.

22. David Neiwert (@DavidNeiwert), "The apotheosis of Trump's eliminationist
rhetoric, however, was his regular reading of the poem 'The Snake,' which depicts a 'silly
woman' who revives a dying viper (immigrants) only to be bitten by it. A classic depictions
of humans as toxic vermin," Twitter, October 31, 2018, https://twitter.com/davidneiwert/
status/1057726360091684864.

23. Eli Rosenberg, "'The Snake': How Trump Appropriated a Radical Black Singer's
Lyrics for Immigration Fearmongering," *Washington Post*, February 24, 2018, https://www.
washingtonpost.com/news/politics/wp/2018/02/24/the-snake-how-trump-appropriated-
a-radical-black-singers-lyrics-for-refugee-fearmongering/?noredirect=on&utm_term=.
f5376571c734.

24. "Speech: Donald Trump in Cedar Falls, IA—January 12, 2016," Factba.se, https://
factba.se/transcript/donald-trump-speech-cedar-falls-ia-january-12-2016.

25. "Key Capitol Hill Hearings," C-SPAN, Trump archive video, 1:00, March 15, 2016,
https://archive.org/details/cspan_20160315_100100_key_capitol_hill_hearings/start/207/
end/267?q=snake.

26. "Key Capitol Hill Hearings," C-SPAN, Trump archive video, 1:00, July 30, 2016,
https://archive.org/details/cspan_20160730_100000_key_capitol_hill_hearings/start/538/
end/598?q=snake.

27. "Key Capitol Hill Hearings," C-SPAN, Trump archive video, 1:00, August 12, 2016,
https://archive.org/details/cspan_20160812_182900_key_capitol_hill_hearings/start/2552/
end/2612?q=pour+into.

28. Deborah Bonello and Erin Siegal McIntyre, "Is Rape the Price to Pay for Migrant
Women Chasing the American Dream?" *Splinter*, September 10, 2014, https://splinternews.
com/is-rape-the-price-to-pay-for-migrant-women-chasing-the-1793842446.

29. *CNN Tonight with Don Lemon*, CNN, Trump archive video, 1:04, July 1, 2015,
https://archive.org/details/cnnw_20150702_020100_cnn_tonight_with_don_lemon/
start/480/end/540.

30. *Meet the Press*, NBC, Trump archive video, 1:00, March 13, 2016, https://archive.
org/details/kntv_20160313_150400_meet_the_press/start/517/end/577?q=rapists.

31. *NOW with Alex Wagner*, MSNBC, Trump archive video, 1:01, July 8, 2015, https://
archive.org/details/msnbcw_20150708_200100_now_with_alex_wagner/start/60/end/120.

32. When his campaign put out its August 16, 2015, Immigration Plan, it included blue underlines where there should have been links to the facts that supported Trump's claims, but those blue underlines were for show; there were no working links, no facts provided to support Trump's claims.

33. NCR Staff, "Read Pope Francis' Speech to the US Bishops," *National Catholic Reporter*, September 23, 2015, https://www.ncronline.org/blogs/ncr-today/read-pope-francis-speech-us-bishops.

34. Pope Francis, "Address of the Holy Father," September 24, 2015, United States Capitol, Washington, DC, transcript, http://w2.vatican.va/content/francesco/en/speeches/2015/september/documents/papa-francesco_20150924_usa-us-congress.html.

35. *New Day*, CNN, Trump archive video, 1:00, September 24, 2015, https://archive.org/details/cnnw_20150924_110100_new_day/start/5/end/65?q=pope.

36. "Trump on the Federal Reserve," Fox Business video, 5:06, February 11, 2016, https://video.foxbusiness.com/v/4750391642001/?#sp=show-clips.

37. Pope Francis, "Homily at U.S.-Mexico Border," February 17, 2016, Ciudad Juárez, transcript, https://ignatiansolidarity.net/blog/2017/02/14/pope-francis-homily-at-u-s-mexico-border-february-17-2016/.

38. Pope Francis, "In-Flight Press Conference of His Holiness Pope Francis from Mexico to Rome," February 17, 2016, transcript, http://w2.vatican.va/content/francesco/en/speeches/2016/february/documents/papa-francesco_20160217_messico-conferenza-stampa.html.

39. "Donald J. Trump Response to the Pope," DonaldJTrump.com archived post, February 18, 2016, https://web.archive.org/web/20160219004407/https://www.donaldjtrump.com/press-releases/donald-j.-trump-response-to-the-pope.

40. Tim Hains, "Trump Responds to Pope Francis: 'He's Got an Awfully Big Wall at the Vatican,'" Real Clear Politics, February 18, 2016, https://www.realclearpolitics.com/video/2016/02/18/trump_responds_to_pope_francis_hes_got_an_awfully_big_wall_at_the_vatican.html.

41. "Presidential Candidate Donald Trump Rally in Las Vegas," C-SPAN video, 1:11:36, February 22, 2016, https://www.c-span.org/video/?405003-1/donald-trump-campaign-rally-las-vegas.

42. *Donald Trump Campaigns in Prescott Valley, Arizona*, C-SPAN, Trump archive video, 1:00, October 5, 2016, https://archive.org/details/cspan2_20161005_043400_donald_trump_campaigns_in_prescott_valley_arizona/start/579/end/639?q=illegal.

Chapter 12

1. "Trump: Favorable/Unfavorable," Real Clear Politics, http://www.realclearpolitics.com/epolls/other/trump_favorableunfavorable-5493.html#polls.

2. *Washington This Week*, C-SPAN, Trump archive video, 1:01, August 30, 2015, https://archive.org/details/cspan_20150830_180100_washington_this_week/start/360/end/420.

3. "Donald Trump Rally Myrtle Beach South Carolina 11/24/15," YouTube, 1:16:36, November 24, 2015, https://www.youtube.com/watch?v=VNocmPffX4c.

4. Glenn Plaskin, "The 1990 Playboy Interview with Donald Trump," *Playboy*, March 1, 1990, https://www.playboy.com/read/playboy-interview-donald-trump-1990.

5. Tim Murphy, "How Donald Trump Became Conspiracy Theorist in Chief," *Mother Jones*, November/December 2016 Issue, http://www.motherjones.com/politics/2016/10/trump-infowars-alex-jones-clinton-conspiracy-theories; Gregory Krieg, "14 of Trump's Most Outrageous 'Birther' Claims—Half from after 2011," CNN, September 16, 2016, http://www.cnn.com/2016/09/09/politics/donald-trump-birther/. "'He doesn't have a birth certificate. He may have one, but there's something on that, maybe religion, maybe it says he is a Muslim,' Trump told Fox News in 2011. 'I don't know. Maybe he doesn't want that.'" Chris Moody and Kristen Holmes, "Donald Trump History of Suggesting Obama Is a Muslim," CNN, September 18, 2015, https://www.cnn.com/2015/09/18/politics/trump-obama-muslim-birther/index.html.

6. Brian Montopoli, "Donald Trump Gets Regular Fox News Spot," *CBS News*, April 1, 2011, https://www.cbsnews.com/news/donald-trump-gets-regular-fox-news-spot/. For example, Trump comments on Obama's 2012 campaign, calling him a two-faced politician who will say anything to get elected: *Fox and Friends*, Fox News, Trump archive video, 1:00, April 2, 2012, https://archive.org/details/foxnewsw_20120402_113500_fox_and_friends.

7. Donald J. Trump (@realDonaldTrump), "The concept of global warming was created by and for the Chinese in order to make the U.S. manufacturing non-competitive," Twitter, November 6, 2012, https://twitter.com/realDonaldTrump/status/265895292191248385?ref_src=twsrc%5Etfw.

8. Brian Tashman, "58 Donald Trump Conspiracy Theories (and Counting!): The Definitive Trump Conspiracy Guide," AlterNet, May 30, 2016, https://www.alternet.org/2016/05/58-donald-trump-conspiracy-theories-and-counting-definitive-trump-conspiracy-guide/.

9. J. Anthony Blair, *Groundwork in the Theory of Argumentation* (Berlin: Springer Science+Business Media, 2012): 14.

10. Blair, *Groundwork in the Theory of Argumentation*, 15.

11. Brian Tashman, "58 Donald Trump Conspiracy Theories (And Counting!): The Definitive Trump Conspiracy Guide," Right Wing Watch, May 27, 2016, http://www.rightwingwatch.org/post/58-donald-trump-conspiracy-theories-and-counting-the-definitive-trump-conspiracy-guide/.

12. Alex Jones, "Part Two: Anger on the Fringes," Anti-Defamation League archived post, March 6, 2016, https://web.archive.org/web/20160306230318/http://archive.adl.org/special_reports/rage-grows-in-America/alex-jones.html; "Rage Grows in America:

Anti-Government Conspiracies," Anti-Defamation League archived post, November 2009, https://web.archive.org/web/20160321034236/http://archive.adl.org/special_reports/rage-grows-in-america/rage-grows-in-america.pdf; Eric Hananoki and Timothy Johnson, "Donald Trump Praises Leading Conspiracy Theorist Alex Jones and His 'Amazing' Reputation," Media Matters, December 2, 2015, https://www.mediamatters.org/blog/2015/12/02/donald-trump-praises-leading-conspiracy-theoris/207181.

13. "Documentary Reveals the 'Dirty Tricks' of One of Trump's Closest Political Advisors," *Fresh Air*, National Public Radio, July 13, 2017, https://www.npr.org/2017/07/13/537023277/documentary-reveals-the-dirty-tricks-of-one-of-trumps-closest-political-advisers; Devlin Barrett, Rosalind S. Helderman, Lori Rozsa, and Manuel Roig-Franzia, "Longtime Trump Advisor Roger Stone Indicted by Special Counsel in Russia Investigation," *Washington Post*, January 25, 2015, https://www.washingtonpost.com/politics/longtime-trump-adviser-roger-stone-indicted-by-special-counsel-in-russia-investigation/2019/01/25/93a4d8fa-2093-11e9-8e21-59a09ff1e2a1_story.html?utm_term=.dd9f89ebb94f; Rachel Weiner, Spencer Hsu, and Matt Zapotosky, "Roger Stone Guilty on All Counts in Federal Trial of Lying to Congress, Witness Tampering," *Washington Post*, November 15, 2019, https://www.washingtonpost.com/local/public-safety/roger-stone-jury-weighs-evidence-and-a-defense-move-to-make-case-about-mueller/2019/11/15/554fff5a-06ff-11ea-8292-c46ee8cb3dce_story.html?wpisrc=al_news__alert-politics--alert-national&wpmk=1.

14. "Two of the major internet tracking companies, Quantcast and Alexa, reported that in January InfoWars had an average of around eight million (Quantcast) or 8.7 million (Alexa) global visitors, who viewed its pages nearly 50 million times. As of Sunday Quantcast ranked its traffic above that of the fact-checking site Politifact.com. Those numbers miss the audiences for his national radio show and his team's videos on YouTube, where the biggest of his 18 channels has 1.2 billion views, and on Facebook, where they draw many millions of views. One, by his editor at large, Paul Joseph Watson, lists 18.1 million views." Jim Rutenberg, "In Trump's Volleys, Echoes of Alex Jones's Conspiracy Theories," *New York Times*, February 19, 2017, https://www.nytimes.com/2017/02/19/business/media/alex-jones-conspiracy-theories-donald-trump.html; "Facebook removed Mr. Jones's pages for violating its policies by 'glorifying violence' and 'using dehumanizing language to describe people who are transgender, Muslims and immigrants.' YouTube terminated Mr. Jones's channel for repeatedly violating its policies, including its prohibition on hate speech. Spotify cited its own prohibition on hate speech as the reason for removing a podcast by Mr. Jones." Elizabeth Williamson, "Alex Jones Urges InfoWars Fans to Fight Back, and Send Money," *New York Times*, August 7, 2018, https://www.nytimes.com/2018/08/07/us/politics/alex-jones-infowars-sandy-hook.html.

15. Fae Jencks, "Caution: Alex Jones Is Using Sheen-Related Media Blitz to Promote His Conspiracy Theories," Media Matters, February 25, 2011, https://www.mediamatters.org/research/2011/02/25/caution-alex-jones-is-using-sheen-related-media/176928.

16. Manuel Roig-Franzia, "How Alex Jones, Conspiracy Theorist Extraordinaire,

Got Donald Trump's Ear," *Washington Post*, November 17, 2016, https://www.washingtonpost.com/lifestyle/style/how-alex-jones-conspiracy-theorist-extraordinaire-got-donald-trumps-ear/2016/11/17/583dc190-ab3e-11e6-8b45-f8e493f06fcd_story.html?utm_term=.c54bec323a00.

17. "InfoWars: Alex Jones Interviews Donald Trump—December 2, 2015," Factba.se, https://factba.se/transcript/donald-trump-interview-new-york-ny-december-2-2015.

18. "11 Times Donald Trump Sounded a Lot Like Alex Jones," Vice News, YouTube video, 3:03, March 10, 2018, https://www.youtube.com/watch?v=MzIOidaeFC0.

19. "Alex Jones: 'It Is Surreal to Talk about Issues Here On Air and Then Word-for-Word Hear Trump Say It Two Days Later,'" Media Matters, August 11, 2016, https://www.mediamatters.org/video/2016/08/11/alex-jones-it-surreal-talk-about-issues-here-air-and-then-word-word-hear-trump-say-it-two-days-later/212339.

20. "Donald J. Trump's Five-Point Plan for Ethics Reform," Trump-Pence archived post, October 17, 2016, https://web.archive.org/web/20161018083847/https://www.donaldjtrump.com/press-releases/donald-j.-trumps-five-point-plan-for-ethics-reform.

21. Scott Shane and Mark Mazzetti, "The Plot to Subvert an Election," *New York Times*, September 20, 2018, https://www.nytimes.com/interactive/2018/09/20/us/politics/russia-interference-election-trump-clinton.html?utm_source=newsletter&utm_medium=email&utm_campaign=newsletter_axiosam&stream=top.

22. "Donald Trump Campaign Event in Green Bay, Wisconsin," C-SPAN video, 1:08:36, October 17, 2016, https://www.c-span.org/video/?417019-1/donald-trump-campaigns-green-bay-wisconsin&start=1437.

23. "Speech: Donald Trump in Colorado Springs, CO—October 18, 2016," Factba.se, https://factba.se/transcript/donald-trump-speech-colorado-springs-co-october-18-2016.

24. "Key Capitol Hill Hearings," C-SPAN, Trump archive video, 1:00, October 20, 2016, https://archive.org/details/cspan_20161020_210000_key_capitol_hill_hearings/start/1088/end/1148?q=swamp.

25. "Discussion Focuses on Same-Sex Marriage and Religious Exemption," C-SPAN, Trump archive video, 1:00, October 29, 2016, https://archive.org/details/cspan_20161029_230100_discussion_focuses_on_same-sex_marriage_and_religious_exemption/start/604/end/664?q=swamp. "And I said that about a week ago, and I didn't like it that much, didn't sound that great, and the whole world picked it up. So it shows you what I know. Crazy. Drain the swamp. We're going to drain the swamp of Washington, we're going to have fun doing it, we're all doing it together. It is funny [cheers and applause], funny how things like that happen. I was listening the other day to a great singer, one of the great legends, and said didn't like it, didn't like it, became one of the greatest hits of all times. Drain the swamp, I didn't like it. Now I love it, right? [laughter]." *Risk and Reward with Deidre Bolton*, Fox Business, Trump archive video, 1:01, October 26, 2016, https://archive.org/details/fbc_20161026_210100_risk_and_reward_with_deidre_bolton/start/1140/end/1200.

26. "Key Capitol Hill Hearings," C-SPAN, Trump archive video, 1:07, October 22,

2016, https://archive.org/details/cspan_20161023_011100_key_capitol_hill_hearings/start/900/end/960.

Part Three: Trump and the Frustrated Electorate

1. Conor Friedersdorf, "What Do Donald Trump Voters Actually Want?" *The Atlantic*, August 17, 2015, http://www.theatlantic.com/politics/archive/2015/08/donald-trump-voters/401408/#trump%20embodies%20the%20rage%20of%20the%20white%20middle%20class.

2. Sam Frizell, "Pollster's Legs Wobble after Fawning Donald Trump Focus Group," *Time*, August 25, 2015, http://time.com/4009413/donald-trump-focus-group-frank-luntz/.

3. "Beyond Distrust: How Americans View Their Government," Pew Research Center, November 23, 2015, https://www.people-press.org/2015/11/23/beyond-distrust-how-americans-view-their-government/.

4. Michael Smith and Lydia Saad, "Economy Top Problem in a Crowded Field," Gallup, December 19, 2016, https://news.gallup.com/poll/200105/economy-top-problem-crowded-field.aspx?g_source=link_newsv9&g_campaign=item_220703&g_medium=copy.

5. Frank Newport, "Seven in 10 Dissatisfied with Way U.S. Is Being Governed," Gallup, September 18, 2017, https://news.gallup.com/poll/219320/seven-dissatisfied-governed.aspx?g_source=Politics&g_medium=newsfeed&g_campaign=tiles.

6. "Partisan and Political Animosity in 2016," Pew Research Center, June 22, 2016, https://www.people-press.org/2016/06/22/partisanship-and-political-animosity-in-2016/.

7. "Direction of Country," Real Clear Politics, https://www.realclearpolitics.com/epolls/other/direction_of_country-902.html.

8. A. Amsel, "Précis of Frustration Theory: An Analysis of Dispositional Learning and Memory," *Psychonomic Bulletin & Review* 1, no. 3 (1994): 280–96; I. J. Roseman, M. S. Spindel, and P. E. Jose, "Appraisals of Emotion-Eliciting Events: Testing a Theory of Discrete Emotions," *Journal of Personality and Social Psychology* 59, no. 5 (1990): 899–915; I. J. Roseman, C. Wiest, and T. S. Swartz, "Phenomenology, Behaviors, and Goals Differentiate Discrete Emotions," *Journal of Personality and Social Psychology* 67, no. 2 (1994): 206–21.

Chapter 13

1. "Trump: Favorable/Unfavorable," Real Clear Politics, http://www.realclearpolitics.com/epolls/other/trump_favorableunfavorable-5493.html#polls.

2. "FULL Event: Donald Trumps First Town Hall Meeting Derry, NH (8 19 15)," Milagro Lesia, YouTube video, 1:35:16, November 9, 2015, https://www.youtube.com/watch?v=3thGIgpuiRQ.

3. "InfoWars Endorses Hillary . . . for Prison 2016," InfoWars, September 2, 2015, https://www.infowars.com/limited-edition-t-shirt-infowars-endorses-hillary-for-prison-2016/.

4. Eric Bradner, "Poll: Most Want Criminal Probe for Clinton Emails," CNN Politics, August 12, 2015, https://www.cnn.com/2015/08/12/politics/poll-hillary-clinton-email-2016/index.html; Michael S. Schmidt, "Hillary Clinton Used Personal Email Account at State Dept., Possibly Breaking Rules," *New York Times*, March 2, 2015, https://www.nytimes.com/2015/03/03/us/politics/hillary-clintons-use-of-private-email-at-state-department-raises-flags.html.

5. "Q: Given what you've heard or read about it, do you think Clinton (stayed within government regulations) in her use of personal e-mail, or do you think she (broke government regulations)?" *Washington Post* poll, September 7–10, 2015, https://www.washingtonpost.com/page/2010-2019/washingtonpost/2015/09/14/national-politics/polling/question_15927.xml?uuid=d2cualqveewedxgcyyuwug.

6. Ken Thomas and Emily Swanson, "AP-GFK Poll: Email Investigation Has Hurt Clinton's Image," Associated Press archived post, July 19, 2016, https://web.archive.org/web/20160720124551/http://hosted.ap.org/dynamic/stories/u/us_ap_poll_campaign_2016_clinton_emails.

7. Duncan J. Watts and David M. Rothschild, "Don't Blame the Election on Fake News. Blame It on the Media," *Columbia Journalism Review*, December 5, 2017, https://www.cjr.org/analysis/fake-news-media-election-trump.php.

8. "Donald Trump Full Speech in Iowa (July 25, 2015)—2016 Presidential Rally Campaign," ™US Presidential Election 2016, 56:11, August 28, 2015, https://www.youtube.com/watch?v=ZWeSdXdI748.

9. "State of the Union," CNN Transcripts, aired July 26, 2015, http://transcripts.cnn.com/transcripts/1507/26/sotu.01.html.

10. "Donald Trump Rally FULL SPEECH—Norcross, GA 10.10.15," News 95.5 and AM 750 WSB, YouTube video, 1:01:21, October 10, 2015, https://www.youtube.com/watch?v=EQXXytNw0Do.

11. *Hannity*, Fox News, Trump archive video, 1:00, October 12, 2015, https://archive.org/details/foxnewsw_20151013_020100_hannity/start/268/end/328?q=jail.

12. For example, November 30, 2015, Macon, Georgia, "greatest achievement"; July 12, 2016, Westfield, Indiana, "greatest achievement"; August 5, 2016, Green Bay, Wisconsin "greatest achievement"; August 9, 2016, Fayetteville, North Carolina, "greatest achievement"; August 11, 2016, Orlando, Florida, "greatest achievement"; September 28, 2016, Council Bluffs, Iowa, "greatest achievement."

13. "Speech: Donald Trump in Raleigh, NC—December 4, 2015," Factba.se, December 4, 2015, https://factba.se/transcript/donald-trump-speech-raleigh-nc-december-4-2015.

14. "Speech: Donald Trump in Tampa, FL—February 12, 2016," Factbase, YouTube video, 55:45, August 31, 2019, https://www.youtube.com/watch?v=WDsZmKO961A.

15. Michael Gorman, "'Lock Her Up!' Hillary Clinton and the Unofficial Slogan of the

2016 Republican National Convention," *Newsweek*, July 20, 2016, https://www.newsweek.com/lock-her-slogan-republicans-hillary-clinton-donald-trump-ted-cruz-482503.

16. It is unclear why Clinton wasn't given the appropriate tools needed to do her job as secretary of state. She and her staff made it very clear that she would need to use her Blackberry for communication, but she was repeatedly denied this setup, which is why she used the private email server. Clinton asked to be provided with the same setup as President Obama but was denied. Mark Landler and Eric Lichtblau, "F.B.I. Director James Comey Recommends No Charges for Hillary Clinton on Email," *New York Times*, July 5, 2016, https://www.nytimes.com/2016/07/06/us/politics/hillary-clinton-fbi-email-comey.html.

17. Donald J. Trump (@realDonaldTrump), "The system is rigged. General Petraeus got in trouble for far less. Very unfair! As usual, bad judgement," Twitter, July 5, 2016, https://twitter.com/realdonaldtrump/status/750352884106223616.

18. Adam Goldman, "Petraeus Pleads Guilty to Mishandling Classified Material, Will Face Probation," *Washington Post*, April 23, 2015, https://www.washingtonpost.com/world/national-security/petraeus-set-to-plead-guilty-to-mishandling-classified-materials/2015/04/22/3e6dbf20-e8f5-11e4-aae1-d642717d8afa_story.html?utm_term=.119ba51c3169.

19. "Key Capitol Hill Hearings," C-SPAN, Trump archive video, 1:00, July 7, 2016, https://archive.org/details/cspan_20160707_064400_key_capitol_hill_hearings/start/490/end/550?q=jail.

20. "Video: 'Hillary for Prison' Banner Flies High over Cleveland, RNC," InfoWars, July 17, 2016, https://www.infowars.com/hillary-for-prison-banner-spotted-in-cleveland/; Peter Schroeder, "'Hillary for Prison' T-Shirt Is Best-Seller in Cleveland," *The Hill*, July 20, 2016, https://thehill.com/homenews/campaign/288540-hillary-for-prison-t-shirt-is-best-seller-in-cleveland.

21. "Michael Flynn Leads 'Lock Her Up' Chant at 2016 RNC," CNN, YouTube video, 2:26, December 1, 2017, https://www.youtube.com/watch?v=tx94428MYcc; *United States of America v. Michael Flynn*, 1:17-cr-00232-RC, Document 4, https://www.justice.gov/file/1015126/download.

22. "Watch Gov. Chris Christie's Full Speech at the 2016 Republican National Convention," PBS NewsHour, YouTube video, 15:11, July 19, 2016, https://www.youtube.com/watch?v=dH5bwvsIB30.

23. Thank you, Liz Case, for teaching me the word *caesura*.

24. "Press Conference: Donald Trump in Doral, FL—July 27, 2016," Factba.se, July 27, 2016, https://factba.se/transcript/donald-trump-press-conference-doral-fl-july-27-2016.

25. "Speech: Donald Trump in Scranton, PA—July 27, 2016," Factba.se, July 27, 2016, https://factba.se/transcript/donald-trump-speech-scranton-pa-july-27-2016.

26. "Speech: Donald Trump Addresses the Republican Jewish Coalition in Las Vegas, Nevada—April 6, 2019," Factba.se, April 6, 2019, https://factba.se/search#let's%2bjust%2bwin; *The Real Story*, Fox News, Trump archive video, 1:03, August 25, 2016, https://archive.org/details/foxnewsw_20160825_181300_the_real_story/start/120/end/180?q=lock+her+up.

27. "Speech: Donald Trump in Pueblo, CO—October 3, 2016," Factba.se, October 3, 2016, https://factba.se/transcript/donald-trump-speech-pueblo-co-october-3-2016.

28. "Speech: Donald Trump in Iowa City, IA—January 26, 2016," Factba.se, January 26, 2016, https://factba.se/transcript/donald-trump-speech-iowa-city-ia-january-26-2016/.

29. "Hillary Clinton Rally in Newark, New Jersey 6/1/2016," LesGrossman News, You-Tube video, 23:27, June 1, 2016, https://www.youtube.com/watch?v=XqDc4MafZnU.

30. David A. Fahrenthold, "Trump Recorded Having Extremely Lewd Conversation about Women in 2005," *Washington Post*, October 8, 2016, https://www.washingtonpost.com/politics/trump-recorded-having-extremely-lewd-conversation-about-women-in-2005/2016/10/07/3b9ce776-8cb4-11e6-bf8a-3d26847eeed4_story.html?postshare=356 1475870579757&utm_term=.65dfa3b7f8d0; Hillary Clinton (@HillaryClinton), "This is horrific. We cannot allow this man to become president. https://twitter.com/Fahrenthold/status/784484724131717124," Twitter, October 7, 2016, https://twitter.com/HillaryClinton/status/784497331647422464.

31. Katie Reilly, "Read Hillary Clinton's Speech on Donald Trump and National Security," *Time*, June 2, 2016, http://time.com/4355797/hillary-clinton-donald-trump-foreign-policy-speech-transcript/.

32. "Speech: Donald Trump in San Jose, CA—June 2, 2016," Factba.se, June 2, 2016, https://factba.se/transcript/donald-trump-speech-san-jose-ca-june-2-2016.

33. "Hillary Clinton Full Speech in Westminster. Trump Has 'Lowered the Bar' Regarding Protests 6/3/2016," LesGrossman News, YouTube video, 12:53, June 3, 2016, https://www.youtube.com/watch?v=yKCWc6z3IYc.

34. "Donald Trump Campaigns in Redding, California," C-SPAN, Trump archive video, 1:00, June 6, 2016, https://archive.org/details/cspan_20160606_051500_donald_trump_campaigns_in_redding_california/start/695/end/755?q=jail.

35. *State of the Union with Jake Tapper*, CNN, Trump archive video, 1:02, June 5, 2016, https://archive.org/details/cnnw_20160605_130100_state_of_the_union_with_jake_tapper/start/720/end/780.

36. Sarah L. Kaufman, "Why Was Trump Lurking Behind Clinton? How Body Language Dominated the Debate," *Washington Post*, October 10, 2016, https://www.washingtonpost.com/news/arts-and-entertainment/wp/2016/10/10/why-was-trump-lurking-behind-clinton-how-body-language-dominated-the-debate/?utm_term=.ea33eb5b63e3.

37. Kevin Uhrmacher and Lazaro Gamio, "What Two Body Language Experts Saw at the Second Presidential Debate," *Washington Post*, October 10, 2016, https://www.washingtonpost.com/graphics/politics/2016-election/second-debate-body-language/?tid=a_inl_manual.

38. "Second Presidential Debate," C-SPAN video, 1:40:06, October 9, 2016, https://www.c-span.org/presidentialDebate/?debate=second.

39. "FULL EVENT: Donald Trump Holds Rally in Wilkes-Barre, PA 10/10/16," Right Side Broadcasting Network, YouTube video, 1:40:43, October 10, 2016, https://www.youtube.com/watch?v=2-Cb9C1N8oE.

40. "Key Capitol Hill Hearings," C-SPAN, Trump archive video, 1:02, October 11, 2016, https://archive.org/details/cspan2_20161012_011500_key_capitol_hill_hearings/start/1020/end/1080.

41. "Speech: Donald Trump—Greensboro, NC—October 14, 2016," Factbase Videos, YouTube video, 39:57, October 23, 2017, https://youtu.be/WtpN7XOgelI.

42. *Washington This Week*, C-SPAN, Trump archive video, 1:00, October 15, 2016, https://archive.org/details/cspan_20161015_144500_washington_this_week/start/5776/end/5836?q=jail.

43. Donald J. Trump (@realDonaldTrump), "Hillary Clinton should have been prosecuted and should be in jail. Instead she is running for president in what looks like a rigged election," Twitter, October 15, 2016, https://twitter.com/realdonaldtrump/status/787267564405653505.

44. Amy Chozick and Patrick Healy, "'This Changes Everything': Donald Trump Exults as Hillary Clinton's Team Scrambles," *New York Times*, October 28, 2016, https://www.nytimes.com/2016/10/29/us/politics/donald-trump-hillary-clinton.html.

45. "Speech: Donald Trump in Manchester, NH—October 28, 2016," Factba.se, October 28, 2016, https://factba.se/transcript/donald-trump-speech-manchester-nh-october-28-2016.

46. "Speech: Donald Trump at the Phoenix Convention Center—October 29, 2016," Factbase Videos, YouTube video, 55:30, October 23, 2017, https://youtu.be/fyCyIAgD8Nc.

47. "Speech: Donald Trump in Grand Rapids, MI—October 31, 2016," Factba.se, October 31, 2016, https://factba.se/transcript/donald-trump-speech-grand-rapids-mi-october-31-2016.

48. "Read the Full Text of James Comey's Letter on the New Clinton Emails," *USA Today*, November 6, 2016, https://www.usatoday.com/story/news/politics/onpolitics/2016/11/06/read-full-text-comeys-letter-new-clinton-emails/93398304/.

49. "Donald Trump Campaign Rally in Sterling Heights, Michigan," C-SPAN video, 41:06, November 6, 2016, https://www.c-span.org/video/?418186-1/donald-trump-campaigns-sterling-heights-michigan.

50. "Speech: Donald Trump in Moon Township, PA—November 6, 2016," Factbase Videos, YouTube video, 28:28, October 23, 2017, https://youtu.be/7ecX1FtlLyI; "Speech: Donald Trump in Leesburg, VA—November 6, 2016," Factbase Videos, YouTube video, 30:26, October 23, 2017, https://youtu.be/m1H2NyzJ0xA; *Public Affairs Events*, C-SPAN, Trump archive video, 1:00, November 7, 2016, https://archive.org/details/cspan_20161107_224300_public_affairs_events/start/826/end/886?q=american+people+to+deliver+justice+at+the+ballot+box; *CNN Newsroom with Brooke Baldwin*, CNN, Trump archive video, 1:00, November 7, 2016, https://archive.org/details/cnnw_20161107_200100_cnn_newsroom_with_brooke_baldwin/start/379/end/439?q=american+people+to+deliver+justice+at+the+ballot+box.

51. "Presidential Candidate Donald Trump Victory Speech," C-SPAN video, 39:06,

November 9, 2016, https://www.c-span.org/video/?418090-1/donald-trump-elected-45th-president-united-states.

52. Lesley Stahl, "President-Elect Trump Speaks to a Divided Country," *60 Minutes*, November 13, 2016, https://www.cbsnews.com/news/60-minutes-donald-trump-family-melania-ivanka-lesley-stahl/.

53. "Donald Trump's New York Times Interview: Full Transcript," *New York Times*, November 23, 2016, https://www.nytimes.com/2016/11/23/us/politics/trump-new-york-times-interview-transcript.html?module=inline.

54. "President-Elect Donald Trump Holds Thank You Rally in Grand Rapids, Michigan," C-SPAN, Trump archive video, 1:01, December 10, 2016, https://archive.org/details/cspan_20161210_110000_president-elect_donald_trump_holds_thank_you_rally_in_grand_rapids_michigan/start/660/end/720.

Chapter 14

1. "Trump: Favorable/Unfavorable," Real Clear Politics, http://www.realclearpolitics.com/epolls/other/trump_favorableunfavorable-5493.html#polls.

2. Donald J. Trump (@realDonaldTrump), "Do you think Putin will be going to The Miss Universe Pageant in November in Moscow—if so, will he become my new best friend?" Twitter, June 18, 2013, https://twitter.com/realDonaldTrump/status/347191326112112640; Philip Bump, "How Well Does Trump Know Putin? A Chronology," *Washington Post*, July 7, 2017, https://www.washingtonpost.com/news/politics/wp/2017/02/07/does-trump-know-putin-a-chronology/?utm_term=.52ef1561f55a.

3. Alferova Yulya (@AlferovaYulyaE), "Right now Mr. Trump @realDonaldTrump interviewed by @ThomasARoberts at new restaurant by @eminoffical #missuniverse," Twitter, November 9, 2013, https://twitter.com/AlferovaYulyaE/status/399110305261043712?ref_src=twsrc%5Etfw%7Ctwcamp%5Etweetembed%7Ctwterm%5E399110305261043712&ref_url=https%3A%2F%2Fthemoscowproject.org%2Fdispatch%2Fthe-moscow-miss-universe-pageant-timeline%2F; "Trump and Putin Tried to Meet in Moscow Three Years Ago: Source," NBC News, July 28, 2016, https://www.nbcnews.com/news/us-news/trump-putin-tried-meet-moscow-three-years-ago-source-n619006.

4. "Key Capitol Hill Hearings," C-SPAN, Trump archive video, 1:06, March 7, 2014, https://archive.org/details/cspan_20140307_052700_key_capitol_hill_hearings/start/480/end/540.

5. "NPC Luncheon with Donald Trump," The National Press Club, YouTube video, 59:44, May 27, 2014, https://www.youtube.com/watch?v=dKkKQmbyECw&feature=youtu.be.

6. *The O'Reilly Factor*, Fox News, Trump archive video, 1:00, June 16, 2015, https://archive.org/details/foxnewsw_20150617_000100_the_oreilly_factor/start/252/end/312?q=putin.

7. Bruce Stokes, "Russia, Putin Held in Low Regard around the World," Pew Research Center, August 5, 2015, https://www.pewglobal.org/2015/08/05/russia-putin-held-in-low-regard-around-the-world/.

8. "Opinions on U. S. International Involvement, Free Trade, ISIS and Syria, Russia and China: As Election Nears, Voters Divided over Democracy and 'Respect,'" Pew Research Center, October 27, 2016, https://www.people-press.org/2016/10/27/7-opinions-on-u-s-international-involvement-free-trade-isis-and-syria-russia-and-china/.

9. Katelyn Polantz, Veronica Stracqualursi, and Marshall Cohen, "Alleged Russian Spy Maria Butina Pleads Guilty to Engaging in Conspiracy against US," CNN Politics, December 13, 2018, https://www.cnn.com/2018/12/13/politics/maria-butina-guilty-plea/index.html.

10. "Trump Answers Question on Russia at FreedomFest 2015," LetsTalkNevada, YouTube video, 02:35, July 12, 2015, https://www.youtube.com/watch?time_continue=7&v=4Fp1TioaLcg.

11. "Fox News Reporting," Trump archive video, 1:00, August 23, 2015, https://archive.org/details/foxnewsw_20150824_040100_fox_news_reporting/start/480/end/540.

12. *Meet the Press*, NBC News, transcript, September 20, 2015, https://www.nbcnews.com/meet-the-press/meet-press-transcript-september-20-2015-n430581.

13. "Trump on Putin: 'If He Wants to Fight ISIS, Let Him Fight ISIS,'" Fox News Insider, YouTube video, 06:54, September 29, 2015, https://www.youtube.com/watch?time_continue=2&v=gdhgmb0iBRo.

14. Scott Pelley, "Trump Gets Down to Business on 60 Minutes," *60 Minutes*, September 27, 2015, https://www.cbsnews.com/news/donald-trump-60-minutes-scott-pelley/.

15. "Key Capitol Hill Hearings," C-SPAN, Trump archive video, 1:06, September 28, 2015, https://archive.org/details/cspan2_20150928_150400_key_capitol_hill_hearings/start/1080/end/1140.

16. *Fox & Friends Sunday*, Fox News, 1:01, October 4, 2015, https://archive.org/details/foxnewsw_20151004_100000_fox_and_friends_sunday/start/9060/end/9120.

17. "No Labels Problem Solver Convention Presidential Candidate Donald Trump . . . ," C-SPAN, Trump archive video, 1:00, October 19, 2015, https://archive.org/details/cspan_20151019_051000_no_labels_problem_solver_convention_presidential_candidate_donald_trump . . . /start/1418/end/1478?q=putin.

18. "Republican Presidential Candidates Debate," Fox Business, Trump archive video, 1:03, November 10, 2015, https://archive.org/details/fbc_20151111_020000_republican_presidential_candidates_debate/start/4920/end/4980.

19. Patrick Reevell, "Russian President Vladimir Putin Praises Donald Trump as 'Talented' and 'Very Colorful,'" ABC News, December 17, 2015, https://abcnews.go.com/International/russian-president-vladimir-putin-praises-donald-trump-talented/story?id=35816611; Christopher Massie, "Trump and Putin Appeared on '60 Minutes' Together. . . from Different Continents," BuzzFeed News, November 10, 2015, https://www.buzzfeednews.com/article/christophermassie/tick-tick-tick-tick.

20. Reevell, "Russian President Vladimir Putin Praises Donald Trump as 'Talented' and 'Very Colorful,'" https://abcnews.go.com/International/russian-president-vladimir-putin-praises-donald-trump-talented/story?id=35816611.

21. John Santucci, "Trump Says 'Great Honor' to Get Compliments from 'Highly Respected' Putin," ABC News, December 17, 2015, https://abcnews.go.com/politics/trump-great-honor-compliments-highly-respected-putin/story?id=35829618.

22. "Trump on Putin's Compliment: 'Great Honor,'" RT World News, December 18, 2015, https://www.rt.com/news/326378-trump-putin-comment-honor/.

23. "Donald Trump Supports Putin 'Bombing the Hell Out of ISIS,'" RT World News, October 5, 22015, https://www.rt.com/usa/317641-trump-syria-putin-isis/; "Putin Says 'Talented' Trump Is 'Absolute Front-Runner,' Welcomes Pledge to Work with Russia," RT World News, December 17, 2015, https://www.rt.com/usa/326328-trump-russia-putin-relations/.

24. Glenn Kessler, "No, Putin Did Not Call Donald Trump 'A Genius,'" *Washington Post*, May 3, 2016, https://www.washingtonpost.com/news/fact-checker/wp/2016/05/03/no-putin-did-not-call-donald-trump-a-genius/?utm_term=.c2c9132ea98b.

25. "Trump on Putin's Compliment: 'Great Honor,'" RT World News, December 18, 2015, https://www.rt.com/news/326378-trump-putin-comment-honor/.

26. *Morning Joe*, MSNBC, Trump archive video, 1:00, December 18, 2015, https://archive.org/details/msnbcw_20151218_122200_morning_joe/start/14/end/74?q=putin.

27. *Meet the Press*, NBC, Trump archive video, 1:00, December 20, 2015, https://archive.org/details/kntv_20151220_160400_meet_the_press/start/197/end/257?q=putin.

28. *This Week with George Stephanopoulos*, ABC News, Trump archive video, 1:00, December 20, 2015, https://archive.org/details/kgo_20151220_160300_this_week_with_george_stephanopoulos/start/219/end/279?q=russia.

29. "Donald Trump Campaign Rally in Milford New Hampshire," C-SPAN, Trump archive video, 1:00, February 2, 2016, https://archive.org/details/cspan_20160203_032000_donald_trump_campaign_rally_in_milford_new_hampshire/start/2290/end/2350?q=putin.

30. *Newsmakers*, C-SPAN, Trump archive video, 1:00, February 28, 2016, https://archive.org/details/cspan_20160228_230100_newsmakers/start/60/end/120.

31. *MSNBC Live*, MSNBC, Trump archive video, 1:00, May 27, 2016, https://archive.org/details/msnbcw_20160527_173700_msnbc_live/start/457/end/517?q=putin.

32. *Situation Room with Wolf Blitzer*, CNN, Trump archive video, 1:00, May 4, 2016, https://archive.org/details/cnnw_20160504_212400_situation_room_with_wolf_blitzer/start/601/end/661?q=putin.

33. *Special Report with Bret Baier*, Fox News, Trump archive video, 00:59, May 5, 2016, https://archive.org/details/foxnewsw_20160505_220100_special_report_with_bret_baier/start/960/end/1020.

34. Joe Sterling, "Putin: We'll Work with Any Candidate U.S. Voters Choose," CNN, June 18, 2016, https://www.cnn.com/2016/06/17/europe/russia-putin/; translation provided by this RT produced and promoted video of the exchange: "Putin Demolishes CNN's Fareed

Zakaria," News Heist, YouTube video, 06:08, December 27, 2016, https://www.youtube. com/watch?v=YyvYjjlVNz4.

35. "Starting on Friday 22 July 2016 at 10:30am EDT, WikiLeaks released over 2 publications 44,053 emails and 17,761 attachments from the top of the US Democratic National Committee—part one of our new Hillary Leaks series. The leaks come from the accounts of seven key figures in the DNC: Communications Director Luis Miranda (10520 emails), National Finance Director Jordon Kaplan (3799 emails), Finance Chief of Staff Scott Comer (3095 emails), Finance Director of Data & Strategic Initiatives Daniel Parrish (1742 emails), Finance Director Allen Zachary (1611 emails), Senior Advisor Andrew Wright (938 emails), and Northern California Finance Director Robert (Erik) Stowe (751 emails). The emails cover the period from January last year until 25 May this year." "Search the DNC Email Database," WikiLeaks, https://wikileaks.org/dnc-emails/.

36. Michael D. Shear and Matthew Rosenberg, "Released Emails Suggest the D.N.C. Derided the Sanders Campaign," *New York Times*, July 22, 2016, https://www.nytimes. com/2016/07/23/us/politics/dnc-emails-sanders-clinton.html; David E. Sanger and Nicole Perlroth, "As Democrats Gather, a Russian Subplot Raises Intrigue," *New York Times*, July 24, 2016, https://www.nytimes.com/2016/07/25/us/politics/donald-trump-russia-emails. html?module=inline; Amy Chozick, "Democrats Allege D.N.C. Hack Is Part of Russian Effort to Elect Donald Trump," *New York Times*, July 25, 2016, https://www.nytimes. com/2016/07/26/us/politics/democrats-allege-dnc-hack-is-part-of-russian-effort-to-elect-donald-trump.html?module=inline; David E. Sanger and Eric Schmitt, "Spy Agency Consensus Grows That Russia Hacked D.N.C.," *New York Times*, July 26, 2016, https://www. nytimes.com/2016/07/27/us/politics/spy-agency-consensus-grows-that-russia-hacked-dnc. html?_r=0; April Glaser, "Here's What We Know about Russia and the DNC Hack," Wired, July 27, 2016, https://www.wired.com/2016/07/heres-know-russia-dnc-hack/; Sam Thielman, "DNC Email Leak: Russian Hackers Cozy Bear and Fancy Bear behind Breach," *The Guardian*, July 26, 2016, https://www.theguardian.com/technology/2016/jul/26/dnc-email-leak-russian-hack-guccifer-2.

37. Russia denied hacking the DNC on June 15, 2016: "'Usually these kinds of leaks take place not because hackers broke in, but, as any professional will tell you, because someone simply forgot the password or set the simple password 123456,' German Klimenko, Putin's top Internet adviser, said in remarks carried by the RIA Novosti state news agency. 'Well, it's always simpler to explain this away as the intrigues of enemies, rather than one's own incompetence.' 'I absolutely rule out the possibility that the government or government agencies were involved in this,' Dmitry Peskov, a spokesman for President Vladimir Putin, told journalists in a curt statement." Andrew Roth, "Russia Denies DNC Hack and Says Maybe Someone 'Forgot the Password,'" *Washington Post*, June 15, 2016, https://www.washington-post.com/news/worldviews/wp/2016/06/15/russias-unusual-response-to-charges-it-hacked-research-on-trump/?utm_term=.5ac3feefb5ae.

38. *State of the Union*, CNN, transcript, July 24, 2016, http://transcripts.cnn.com/transcripts/1607/24/sotu.01.html.

39. According to the indictment, "GRU officers who knowingly and intentionally conspired with each other, and with persons known and unknown to the Grand Jury (collectively the 'Conspirators'), gain unauthorized access (to 'hack') into the computers of U. S. persons and entities involved in the 2016 U. S. presidential election, steal documents from those computers, and stage releases of the stolen documents to interfere with the 2016 U. S. presidential election."

40. "Donald Trump News Conference," C-SPAN video, 57:36, July 27, 2016, https://www.c-span.org/video/?413263-1/donald-trump-urges-russia-find-hillary-clinton-emails-criticizes-record-tpp&start=2046.

41. Katy Tur, "My Crazy Year with Trump," *Marie Claire*, August 10, 2016, https://www.marieclaire.com/politics/a21997/donald-trump-katy-tur/.

42. Ashley Parker and Maggie Haberman, "Donald Trump Calls Comments about Russia and Clinton Emails 'Sarcastic,'" *New York Times*, July 28, 2016, https://www.nytimes.com/2016/07/29/us/politics/donald-trump-russia-obama-putin.html.

43. *On the Record with Greta Van Susteren*, Fox News video, 1:02, July 28, 2016, https://archive.org/details/foxnewsw_20160728_230000_on_the_record_with_greta_van_susteren/start/240/end/300.

44. "Kilmeade Hits the Campaign Trail with Donald Trump," Fox News, YouTube video, 07:34, July 28, 2016, https://www.youtube.com/watch?v=o8RmipdIVSg.

45. "Media's Trump Treason Charge," Fox News video, 04:59, July 31, 2016, https://video.foxnews.com/v/5066133687001/#sp=show-clips.

46. "Sarcasm, n.," *Oxford English Dictionary* Online, accessed April 15, 2019, http://www.oed.com/view/Entry/170938?.

47. Andrew Anglin, "TOP KEK: Trump Calls on Russia to Release Hillary's Deleted Emails!" Daily Stormer, July 28, 2016, https://dailystormer.name/top-kek-trump-calls-on-russia-to-release-hillarys-deleted-emails/.

48. *United States of America v. Viktor Borisovich, et al.*, accessed July 13, 2018, https://int.nyt.com/data/documenthelper/80-netyksho-et-al-indictment/ba0521c1eef869deecbe/optimized/full.pdf?action=click&module=intentional&pgtype=article.

49. According to Mueller's indictment, by February 10, 2016, the IRA had determined "to post content that focused on 'politics in the USA' and to 'use any opportunity to criticize Hillary and the rest (except Sanders and Trump—we support them).'" *United States of America v. Internet Research Agency LLC a/k/a Mediasintez LLC a/k/a Glavset LLC a/k/a Mixinfo LLC a/k/a Azimut LLC a/k/a Novinfo LLF, et al.*, filed February 16, 2018, https://www.justice.gov/file/1035477/download.

50. "Report on the Investigation into Russian Interference in the 2016 Presidential Election," April 18, 2019, https://www.documentcloud.org/documents/5955118-the-mueller-report.html.

51. Kathleen Hall Jamieson, *Cyberwar: How Russian Hackers and Trolls Helped Elect a President: What We Don't, Can't, and Do Know* (New York: Oxford University Press, 2018).

52. "Background to 'Assessing Russian Activities and Intentions in Recent US

Elections': The Analytic Process and Cyber Incident Attribution," Office of the Director of National Intelligence, January 6, 2017, https://www.dni.gov/files/documents/ica_2017_01. pdf.

53. "Trump Doctrine: Work with Russia, Draw Back NATO, Stop Arming Syrian Rebels," Sputnik News, July 16, 2017, https://sputniknews.com/politics/201607161043135284-trump-syria-nato-daesh-putin/.

54. "US Media Hides Real Scandal, Says 'Trump a Manchurain Candidate for Putin,'" Sputnik News, July 26, 2016, https://sputniknews.com/politics/201607261043649971-dnc-hillary-wikileaks-putin-trump/.

55. Donald J. Trump (@realDonaldTrump), "The new joke in town is that Russia leaked the disastrous DNC e-mails, which should never have been written (stupid), because Putin likes me," Twitter, July 25, 2016, https://twitter.com/realDonaldTrump/status/757538729170964481.

56. "Trump Retorts Claims Russia Orchestrated New DNC Leaks as 'New Joke in Town,'" Sputnik News, July 25, 2016, https://sputniknews.com/us/201607251043594580-trump-leaks-russia/.

57. "Democrats Trying to 'Deflect Horror and Stupidity of WikiLeaks Disaster'—Trump," RT World News, July 27, 2016, https://www.rt.com/usa/353500-trump-wikileaks-russia-dnc/; Donald J. Trump (@realDonaldTrump), "In order to try and deflect the horror and stupidity of the Wikileakes disaster, the Dems said maybe it is Russia dealing with Trump. Crazy!" Twitter, July 26, 2016, https://twitter.com/realDonaldTrump/status/758071264128806912.

58. Donald J. Trump (@realDonaldTrump), "If Russia or any other country or person has Hillary Clinton's 33,000 illegally deleted emails, perhaps they should share them with the FBI!" Twitter, July 27, 2016, https://twitter.com/realDonaldTrump/status/758335147183788032.

59. "The Podesta Emails," WikiLeaks, https://wikileaks.org/podesta-emails/.

60. Yahoo News Staff, "64 Hours in October: How One Weekend Blew Up the Rules of American Politics," *Huffington Post*, October 6, 2017, https://www.huffpost.com/entry/yahoo-64-hours-october-american-politics_n_59d7c567e4b072637c43dd1c.

61. "Joint Statement from the Department of Homeland Security and Office of the Director of National Intelligence on Election Security," *Homeland Security*, October 7, 2016, https://www.dhs.gov/news/2016/10/07/joint-statement-department-homeland-security-and-office-director-national.

62. WikiLeaks (@wikileaks), "RELEASE: The Podesta Emails #HillaryClinton #Podesta #imWithHer wikileaks.org/Podesta-emails," Twitter, October 7, 2016, https://twitter.com/wikileaks/status/784491543868665856?ref_src=twsrc%5Etfw%7Ctwcamp%5Etweetembed%7Ctwterm%5E784491543868665856&ref_url=https%3A%2F%2Fwww.huffpost.com%2Fentry%2Fyahoo-64-hours-october-american-politics_n_59d7c567e4b072637c43dd1c.

63. "Coincidence or Conspiracy? US Govt Officially Accuses Russia of Hacks during Clinton Email Dump," RT World News, October 7, 2016, https://www.rt.com/usa/361996-clinton-emails-wikileaks-hacking-accusations/.

64. "This latest 'bombshell'—dropped to coincide with a WikiLeaks drop showing Hillary Clinton to be even more corrupt than we had previously supposed—is so gay. . . . The good news is, I think this was the big drop. They had to use it to cover these WikiLeaks." Andrew Anglin, "Stupid Goyim Shocked That Trump Talks Like a Normal Person," Daily Stormer, October 8, 2016, https://dailystormer.name/stupid-goyim-shocked-that-trump-talks-like-a-normal-person/.

65. "According to direct testimony and dozens of email and text messages introduced over the last week, the Trump campaign got its first heads up about Julian Assange's ability to upend U.S. politics as far back as April 2016. . . . Additionally, a wider cast of Trump aides participated in WikiLeaks strategy sessions than previously known as they mapped out an attack plan to take advantage of the hacked Democratic emails. Trump son-in-law Jared Kushner, campaign chairman Paul Manafort, campaign CEO Steve Bannon and senior adviser Stephen Miller were all part of those broader discussions about how to best turn the WikiLeaks surprises into political gold." Darren Samuelsohn and Josh Gerstein, "What Roger Stone's Trial Revealed about Donald Trump and WikiLeaks," Politico, November 12, 2019, https://www.politico.com/news/2019/11/12/roger-stone-trial-donald-trump-wikileaks-070368. At the time of this writing, the House of Representatives was investigating whether Trump lied in his responses during the Mueller investigation. "Mr. Trump wrote that he was 'not aware during the campaign of any communications' between 'any one I understood to be a representative of WikiLeaks' and people associated with his campaign. Mr. Stone was convicted last week of lying to congressional investigators about his efforts to reach out to WikiLeaks and his discussions with the campaign. 'I do not recall discussing WikiLeaks with him,' Mr. Trump also wrote of Mr. Stone, 'nor do I recall being aware of Mr. Stone having discussed WikiLeaks with individuals associated with my campaign.' But the publicly available portions of the Mueller report suggest that evidence exists to the contrary. Several Trump aides, including Michael D. Cohen and Rick Gates, testified that they heard Mr. Trump discussing coming WikiLeaks releases over the phone. And in October 2016 Stephen K. Bannon, the campaign chairman, wrote in an email that Mr. Stone had told the campaign 'about potential future releases of damaging material' by WikiLeaks shortly before it began publishing more hacked emails." Charlie Savage, "Impeachment Investigators Exploring Whether Trump Lied to Mueller," *New York Times*, November 18, 2019, https://www.nytimes.com/2019/11/18/us/politics/trump-mueller-impeachment.html.

66. Ashley Parker, "Viral Video Turns Senator Into a Silent Comedy Star," *New York Times*, March 16, 2014, https://www.nytimes.com/2014/03/17/us/politics/mcconnelling-video-turns-senator-into-a-silent-comedy-star.html; Benny Johnson, "This Is the Weirdest New Thing in Modern Politics," BuzzFeed News, May 9, 2014, https://www.buzzfeednews.com/article/bennyjohnson/this-is-the-weirdest-new-thing-in-modern-politics.

67. "Coordinated Communications," FEC.gov, https://www.fec.gov/help-candidates-and-committees/candidate-taking-receipts/coordinated-communications/.

68. Donald J. Trump (@realDonaldTrump), "Leaked e-mails of DNC show plans to destroy Bernie Sanders. Mock his heritage and much more. On-line from Wikileakes, really vicious. RIGGED," Twitter, July 23, 2016, https://twitter.com/realDonaldTrump/status/756804886038192128.

69. WikiLeaks (@wikileaks), "That is wikileaks.org/dnc-emails/—everyone can see for themselves," Twitter, July 23, 2016, reply to Donald J. Trump (@realDonaldTrump), "Leaked e-mails of DNC show plans to destroy Bernie Sanders. Mock his heritage and much more. On-line from Wikileakes, really vicious. RIGGED," Twitter, July 23, 2016, https://twitter.com/wikileaks/status/756852586645426176.

70. Donald J. Trump (@realDonaldTrump), "I hope people are looking at the disgraceful behavior of Hillary Clinton as exposed by WikiLeaks. She is unfit to run," Twitter, October 11, 2016, https://twitter.com/realDonaldTrump/status/785898532645502980.

71. Donald J. Trump (@realDonaldTrump), "Very little pick-up by the dishonest media of incredible information provided by WikiLeaks. So dishonest! Rigged system!" Twitter, October 12, 2016, https://twitter.com/realDonaldTrump/status/786201435486781440.

72. Donald J. Trump (@realDonaldTrump), "WikiLeaks proves even the Clinton campaign knew Crooked mishandled classified info, but no one gets charged? RIGGED! https://t.co/FgGxDsS0a1," Twitter, October 17, 2016, https://twitter.com/realDonaldTrump/status/788031447932215300; Donald J. Trump (@realDonaldTrump), "Hillary's Aides Urged Her to Take Foreign Lobbyist Donation and Deal With Attacks: https://t.co/o2qvr1myIZ," Twitter, October 18, 2016, https://twitter.com/realDonaldTrump/status/788440948275421184; Donald J. Trump (@realDonaldTrump), "WikiLeaks reveals Clinton camp's work with 'VERY friendly and malleable reporters' #DrainTheSwamp #CrookedHillary https://t.co/bcYLslrxi0," Twitter, October 18, 2016, https://twitter.com/realDonaldTrump/status/789598795315150853; Donald J. Trump (@realDonaldTrump), "'WikiLeaks Drip-Drop Releases Prove One Thing: There's No Nov. 8 Deadline on Clinton's Dishonesty and Scandals' https://t.co/MfRy3Nvd4F," Twitter, October 27, 2016, https://twitter.com/realDonaldTrump/status/791642669256769536; Donald J. Trump (@realDonaldTrump), "WikiLeaks emails reveal Podesta urging Clinton camp to 'dump' emails. Time to #DrainTheSwamp! https://t.co/P3ajiACiXK," Twitter, November 1, 2016, https://twitter.com/realDonaldTrump/status/793572802729086976.

73. Judd Legum, "Trump Mentioned WikiLeaks 164 Times in Last Month of Election, Now Claims It Didn't Impact One Voter," ThinkProgress, January 8, 2017, https://thinkprogress.org/trump-mentioned-wikileaks-164-times-in-last-month-of-election-now-claims-it-didnt-impact-one-40aa62ea5002/.

74. Ben Popken, Brandy Zadrozny, and Ben Collins, "Trump Campaign Planned for WikiLeaks Dump, Tried to Acquire Clinton Emails, Mueller Report Finds," NBC News, April 18, 2019, https://www.nbcnews.com/politics/donald-trump/

trump-campaign-planned-wikileaks-dump-tried-acquire-clinton-emails-mueller-n996081.

75. "Speech: Donald Trump in Ambridge, PA—October 10, 2016," Factba.se, https://factba.se/transcript/donald-trump-speech-ambridge-pa-october-10-2016.

76. "Donald Trump's Statement after Intelligence Briefing on Hacking," *New York Times*, January 6, 2017, https://www.nytimes.com/2017/01/06/us/politics/donald-trump-statement-hack-intelligence-briefing.html.

77. "Democrats Trying to 'Deflect Horror and Stupidity of WikiLeaks Disaster'—Trump," RT World News, July 27, 2016, https://www.rt.com/usa/353500-trump-wikileaks-russia-dnc/; "Kremlin: Idea of Russia's Involvement in US Democratic Party Mail Hack is 'Absurd,'" RT World News, July 26, 2016, https://www.rt.com/news/353360-russians-kremlin-dnc-hacking/; "Clinton Campaign Blames Russian Hackers as Assange Promises More Leaks," RT World News, October 8, 2016, https://www.rt.com/op-ed/362032-clinton-dnc-leak-russia/; "Coincidence or Conspiracy? US Govt Officially Accuses Russia of Hacks during Clinton Email Dump," RT World News, October 7, 2016, https://www.rt.com/usa/361996-clinton-emails-wikileaks-hacking-accusations/.

78. Donald J. Trump (@realDonaldTrump), "Vladimir Putin said today about Hillary and Dems: 'In my opinion, it is humiliating. One must be able to lose with dignity.' So true!" Twitter, December 23, 2016, https://twitter.com/realDonaldTrump/status/812450976670121985.

79. "Trump Draws Flood of Criticism for Agreeing with Putin That One 'Must Learn to Lose with Dignity,'" RT World News, December 24, 2016, https://www.rt.com/viral/371561-trump-agrees-putin-tweet/.

Chapter 15

1. "Trump: Favorable/Unfavorable," Real Clear Politics, http://www.realclearpolitics.com/epolls/other/trump_favorableunfavorable-5493.html#polls.

2. "Donald Trump Campaign Rally in Manassas, Virginia," C-SPAN, Trump archive video, 1:00, December 5, 2015, https://archive.org/details/cspan_20151206_034500_donald_trump_campaign_rally_in_manassas_virginia/start/3096/end/3156?q=escalator.

3. "Donald Trump Campaign in Muscatine, Iowa," C-SPAN, Trump archive video, 1:00, January 25, 2016, https://archive.org/details/cspan_20160125_083500_donald_trump_campaign_rally_in_muscatine_iowa/start/121/end/181?q=escalator.

4. "Donald Trump Campaign Rally in Plymouth, New Hampshire," C-SPAN, Trump archive video, 1:00, February 7, 2016, https://archive.org/details/cspan_20160207_181700_donald_trump_campaign_rally_in_plymouth_new_hampshire/start/2455/end/2515?q=escalator.

5. "Donald Trump Campaign Rally in Manassas, Virginia," C-SPAN, Trump archive video, 1:00, December 5, 2015, https://archive.org/details/cspan_20151206_

034500_donald_trump_campaign_rally_in_manassas_virginia/start/3096/end/3156?q
=escalator.

6. "The Place for Politics 2016," MSNBC, Trump archive video, 1:00, February 17, 2016, https://archive.org/details/msnbcw_20160217_152000_the_place_for_politics_2016/start/331/end/391?q=pundits.

7. "Donald Trump Response to Mitt Romney," C-SPAN, Trump archive video, 1:00, March 3, 2016, https://archive.org/details/cspan_20160304_012400_donald_trump_response_to_mitt_romney/start/278/end/338?q=escalator.

8. *Washington This Week*, C-SPAN, Trump archive video, 1:00, September 6, 2015, https://archive.org/details/cspan_20150906_213300_washington_this_week/start/1349/end/1409?q=hero.

9. Dave Levinthal, "Actions, Not Words, Tell Trump's Political Money Story," *The Center for Public Integrity*, January 19, 2018, https://www.publicintegrity.org/2018/01/19/21480/actions-not-words-tell-trumps-political-money-story.

10. According to the Center for Public Integrity, Trump spent about sixty-six million dollars of his own money on his campaign, which was roughly 20 percent of all money spent. According to a report from Politico, Trump funneled about thirteen million dollars in campaign money back to his own businesses during the campaign. If these numbers are correct, then Trump paid about fifty-three million dollars to become president. Dave Levinthal, "Actions, Not Words, Tell Trump's Political Money Story," *The Center for Public Integrity*, published January 19, 2018, updated January 20, 2018, https://www.publicintegrity.org/2018/01/19/21480/actions-not-words-tell-trumps-political-money-story; Kenneth P. Vogel, "Trump's Campaign Paid His Businesses Millions over Course of Campaign," Politico, February 1, 2017, https://www.politico.com/story/2017/02/trump-campaign-paid-trump-business-234489.

11. Donald J. Trump (@realDonaldTrump), "Crooked Hillary Clinton is spending a fortune on ads against me. I am the one person she doesn't want to run against. Will be such fun!" Twitter, April 17, 2016, https://twitter.com/realdonaldtrump/status/721695114943442946.

12. "Speech: Donald Trump in Richmond County, NY—April 17, 2016," Factba.se, April 17, 2016, https://factba.se/transcript/donald-trump-speech-richmond-county-ny-april-17-2016.

13. "Speech: Donald Trump in Poughkeepsie, NY—April 17, 2016," Factba.se, April 17, 2016, https://factba.se/transcript/donald-trump-speech-poughkeepsie-ny-april-17-2016.

14. "Donald Trump Campaign Rally in Buffalo New York," C-SPAN, Trump archive video, 1:00, April 19, 2016, https://archive.org/details/cspan_20160419_100500_donald_trump_campaign_rally_in_buffalo_new_york/start/686/end/746?q=crooked+hillary.

15. *Hannity*, Fox News, Trump archive video, 1:00, April 21, 2016, https://archive.org/details/foxnewsw_20160422_050300_hannity/start/540/end/600.

16. *The O'Reilly Factor*, Fox News, Trump archive video, 1:00, April 28, 2016,

https://archive.org/details/foxnewsw_20160429_000400_the_oreilly_factor/start/937/
end/997?q=crooked+hillary.

17. Michael Barbaro and Steve Eder, "Former Trump University Workers Call the
School a 'Lie' and a 'Scheme' in Testimony," *New York Times*, May 31, 2016, https://www.
nytimes.com/2016/06/01/us/politics/donald-trump-university.html.

18. *The Washington Post* successfully sued to have the Trump University documents
released: "Documents Released in Class Action Lawsuit Filed against Trump University,"
Washington Post, https://www.washingtonpost.com/apps/g/page/politics/documents-
released-in-class-action-lawsuit-filed-against-trump-university/2041/?tid=a_inl_manual.

19. "Trump University 'Playbook' Released in Class Action Lawsuit Filed against
Trump University," *Washington Post*, https://www.washingtonpost.com/apps/g/page/politics/
trump-university-playbook-released-in-class-action-lawsuit-filed-against-trump-univer-
sity/2042/.

20. "Clinton on Trump: 'He Is Trying to Scam America the Way He Scammed All
Those People at Trump U,'" NJ.com, YouTube video, 1:28, June 1, 2016, https://www.
youtube.com/watch?v=uViXOtAiDP0.

21. Hillary Clinton (@HillaryClinton), "Trump University was a fraudulent scheme
used to prey upon those who could least afford it. nyti.ms/1TXAqZh," Twitter, June
1, 2016, https://twitter.com/HillaryClinton/status/738006865100087297?ref_src=t
wsrc%5Etfw%7Ctwcamp%5Etweetembed%7Ctwterm%5E738006865100087297&
ref_url=https%3A%2F%2Fwww.politico.com%2Fstory%2F2016%2F06%2Fhillary-clinton-
trump-con-man-223776.

22. Hillary Clinton (@HillaryClinton), "Trump University's own employees described
it as a 'scam.' wapo.st/1WXQPz3," Twitter, June 1, 2016, https://twitter.com/HillaryClinton/
status/738011007256137729?ref_src=twsrc%5Etfw%7Ctwcamp%5Etweetembed%7Ctwter
m%5E738011007256137729&ref_url=https%3A%2F%2Fwww.politico.com%2Fstory%2F
2016%2F06%2Fhillary-clinton-trump-con-man-223776.

23. Hillary Clinton (@HillaryClinton), "New documents confirm Trump 'University'
was a scam that preyed on families to make money. Caution—may cause nausea. https://www.
nytimes.com/2016/06/01/us/politics/donald-trump-university.html," Twitter, June 1, 2016,
https://twitter.com/HillaryClinton/status/738033823464710144.

24. "Clinton on Trump: 'He Is Trying to Scam America the Way He Scammed All
Those People at Trump U,'" NJ.com, YouTube video, 1:28, June 1, 2016, https://www.
youtube.com/watch?v=uViXOtAiDP0.

25. Hillary Clinton (@HillaryClinton), "Trump University: Pad Donald's pock-
ets and put your own finances at risk—all for the low price of $35,000!" Twitter, June
11, 2016, https://twitter.com/HillaryClinton/status/741694471000072192?ref_src
=twsrc%5Etfw%7Ctwcamp%5Etweetembed%7Ctwterm%5E74169447100007219
2&ref_url=https%3A%2F%2Fthehill.com%2Fblogs%2Fballot-box%2Fpresidential-
races%2F283150-clinton-campaign-releases-parody-ad-for-trump-university.

26. "Presidential Candidate Hillary Clinton Economic Remarks in Columbus, Ohio," C-SPAN video, 46:24, June 21, 2016, https://www.c-span.org/video/?411393-1/hillary-clinton-delivers-remarks-economy&start=2013.

27. "Presidential Candidate Hillary Clinton Economic Remarks in Columbus, Ohio," C-SPAN video, 46:24, June 21, 2016, https://www.c-span.org/video/?411393-1/hillary-clinton-delivers-remarks-economy&start=2013.

28. Donald J. Trump (@realDonaldTrump), "I will be making a big speech tomorrow to discuss the failed policies and bad judgement of Crooked Hillary Clinton," Twitter, June 21, 2016, https://twitter.com/realdonaldtrump/status/745260520282951681.

29. *Lou Dobbs Tonight*, Fox Business, Trump archive video, 1:00, June 21, 2016, https://archive.org/details/fbc_20160621_231300_lou_dobbs_tonight/start/466/end/526?q=hillary+clinton.

30. Glenn Kessler, "Fact Check: How Much Help Did Trump's Father Give His Son?" *Washington Post*, September 26, 2016, https://www.washingtonpost.com/politics/2016/live-updates/general-election/real-time-fact-checking-and-analysis-of-the-first-presidential-debate/fact-check-how-much-help-did-trumps-father-give-his-son/?utm_term=.49c1d9d3486e.

31. David Barstow, Susanne Craig, and Russ Buettner, "Special Investigation: Trump Engaged in Suspect Tax Schemes as He Reaped Riches from His Father," *New York Times*, October 2, 2018, https://www.nytimes.com/interactive/2018/10/02/us/politics/donald-trump-tax-schemes-fred-trump.html.

32. "The Definitive Net Worth of Donald Trump," *Forbes*, September 2019, https://www.forbes.com/donald-trump/#32d9c5572899.

33. "Politics and Public Policy Today," C-SPAN, Trump archive video, 1:00, June 22, 2016, https://archive.org/details/cspan3_20160622_193500_politics_and_public_policy_today/start/124/end/184?q=hillary+clinton; "Friday Wrap-Up: Top 50 Facts about Hillary Clinton from Trump 'Stakes of the Election' Address," DonaldJTrump.com, https://assets.donaldjtrump.com/ClintonFacts.pdf.

34. Rubio called him a "con artist": "Donald Trump, Ted Cruz, and Marco Rubio Weigh in Ahead of Super Tuesday," Fox News archived post, interview transcript, February 28, 2016, https://web.archive.org/web/20160229094257/https://www.foxnews.com/tran-script/2016/02/28/donald-trump-ted-cruz-and-marco-rubio-weigh-in-ahead-super-tuesday/. Bloomberg indicated at the Democratic National Convention, "Trump says he wants to run the nation like he's run his business. God help us. I'm a New Yorker, and I know a con when I see one." Dan Primack, "Michael Bloomberg Calls Donald Trump a Con Man," *Fortune*, July 28, 2016, http://fortune.com/2016/07/27/michael-bloomberg-donald-trump-con-man/; Josh Hafner, "Judge Finalizes $25 Million Trump University Settlement for Students of 'Sham University,'" *USA Today*, April 10, 2018, https://www.usatoday.com/story/news/politics/onpolitics/2018/04/10/trump-university-settlement-judge-finalized/502387002/.

35. Donald J. Trump, "On Being a Brand: What's in a Name?" *Trump University Blog* archived post, June 28, 2005, https://web.archive.org/web/20060507011939/http://

donaldtrump.trumpuniversity.com/default.asp?item=93497; Adam Eisenstat, "I Was a Donald Trump Ghostwriter. Here's What I Learned about the Donald—and His Fans," Vox, February 10, 2016, http://www.vox.com/2016/1/29/10862134/donald-trump-university.

36. Adam Eisenstat, "I Was a Donald Trump Ghostwriter. Here's What I Learned about the Donald—and His Fans," Vox, February 10, 2016, http://www.vox.com/2016/1/29/10862134/donald-trump-university.

37. Katie Reilly, "Donald Trump Rails against Judge in Trump University Case," *Time*, May 28, 2016, http://time.com/4351376/donald-trump-university-lawsuit-gonzalo-curiel/.

38. "Documents Released in Class Action Lawsuit Filed against Trump University," *Washington Post*, May 31, 2016, https://www.washingtonpost.com/apps/g/page/politics/documents-released-in-class-action-lawsuit-filed-against-trump-university/2041/; David A. Fahrenthold, "Four Months after Fundraiser, Trump Says He Gave $1 Million to Veterans Group," *Washington Post*, May 24, 2016, https://www.washingtonpost.com/news/post-politics/wp/2016/05/24/four-months-later-donald-trump-says-he-gave-1-million-to-veterans-group/?utm_term=.6893fc4341f8; Maggie Haberman and Ashley Parker, "Donald Trump Lashes Out at Media While Detailing Gifts to Veterans," *New York Times*, May 31, 2016, https://www.nytimes.com/2016/06/01/us/politics/donald-trump-veterans-affairs-donation.html.

39. *Washington This Week*, C-SPAN, Trump archive video, 1:02, October 22, 2016, https://archive.org/details/cspan_20161022_231000_washington_this_week/start/3120/end/3180.

Chapter 16

1. "Trump: Favorable/Unfavorable," Real Clear Politics, http://www.realclearpolitics.com/epolls/other/trump_favorableunfavorable-5493.html#polls.

2. "Donald Trump Spokane Rally Speech May 7, 2016," KHQ6, YouTube video, 59:59, May 7, 2016, https://www.youtube.com/watch?v=4BVZG1aumc4.

3. Jocelyn Kiley, "Majorities of Women, Men Say Trump Has Little or No Respect for Women," Pew Research Center, November 4, 2016, http://www.pewresearch.org/fact-tank/2016/11/04/trump-respect-for-women/.

4. "In June 2016, we conducted a nationally representative survey of 700 U.S. citizens. They were asked whether they agreed with statements such as 'Most women interpret innocent remarks or acts as being sexist' and 'Many women are actually seeking special favors, such as hiring policies that favor them over men, under the guise of asking for equality.' An index based on these statements is widely used in social science research on sexism and gender attitudes. We found that sexism was strongly and significantly correlated with support for Trump, even after accounting for party identification, ideology, authoritarianism and ethnocentrism. In fact, the impact of sexism was equivalent to the impact of ethnocentrism

and much larger than the impact of authoritarianism." Carly Wayne, Nicholas Valentino, and Marzia Oceno, "How Sexism Drives Support for Donald Trump," *Washington Post*, October 23, 2016, https://www.washingtonpost.com/news/monkey-cage/wp/2016/10/23/how-sexism-drives-support-for-donald-trump/?utm_term=.40884b9c7802.

5. Eric Knowles and Sarah DiMuccio, "How Donald Trump Appeals to Men Secretly Insecure about Their Manhood," *Washington Post*, November 29, 2018, https://www.washingtonpost.com/news/monkey-cage/wp/2018/11/29/how-donald-trump-appeals-to-men-secretly-insecure-about-their-manhood/?utm_term=.fc700e903236.

6. Lynn Vavreck, "Insults and Ads: How Gender Hurts Trump but Doesn't Lift Clinton," *New York Times*, April 30, 2016, https://www.nytimes.com/2016/05/01/upshot/insults-and-ads-how-gender-hurts-trump-but-doesnt-lift-clinton.html?_r=0.

7. Rush Limbaugh, "How Feminazis Confused Gender Roles," *The Rush Limbaugh Show*, transcript, July 17, 2017, https://www.rushlimbaugh.com/daily/2017/07/17/how-feminazis-confused-gender-roles/; Milo Yiannopoulos, "Full Text: Milo on How Feminism Hurts Men and Women," Breitbart, October 7, 2016, https://www.breitbart.com/social-justice/2016/10/07/full-text-milo-feminism-auburn/.

8. *The Washington Post* and the Kaiser Family Foundation, "Feminism Survey," January 2016, http://files.kff.org/attachment/topline-methodology-washington-post-kaiser-family-foundation-feminism-survey.

9. David Futrelle, "Surviving the Trumpocalypse," We Hunted the Mammoth, November 11, 2016, http://www.wehuntedthemammoth.com/2016/11/11/surviving-the-trumpocalypse/comment-page-4/.

10. Andrew Anglin, "The number one group to suffer from feminism is without doubt White men. Feminists harass and attack boys, deform their minds, force a perverted ideology and value system on them. They shame and hurt men. They refuse to produce and care for children. They leave men isolated and alienated, painted as the number one enemy of society." Andrew Anglin, "Men Who Support Women's Suffrage Are De Facto Supporters of Gang-Rape," Daily Stormer archived post, May 31, 2016, https://archive.is/OvY2I#selection-605.0-605.335.

11. *The Washington Post* and the Kaiser Family Foundation, "Feminism Survey," January 2016, http://files.kff.org/attachment/topline-methodology-washington-post-kaiser-family-foundation-feminism-survey.

12. "Obama was the 'race' president, and look how badly he has damaged race relations in only eight years. Hillary will be the 'gender' president. The future we have in store should be absolutely clear to you if she happens to defeat Trump. Not only will she move to establish a techno-matriarchy where men are second-class citizens to any female, but she will ensure that no movement or organization will be able to challenge her or her establishment cronies ever again. This isn't a trivial matter of getting banned from a web site like Twitter or Youtube—many of you will be forced to escape the country for no other reason than you happening to be a man who found himself on the wrong side of the establishment. Many men

say that Trump is controlled opposition. The evidence to that has been wholly uncompelling based on the genuine establishment attacks he's received, but even if he's lying about *all* of his policies, including building a wall, the one guarantee we can make about him is that he won't attack men. There's absolutely nothing in his candidacy or behavior in the past 40 years of his life that suggests it. If Trump happens to win and does attack us, I will proudly wear egg on my face, with the depressing realization that our last hope for some semblance of normality has been destroyed and the dark age will be brutal for us all." Roosh Valizadeh, "If Donald Trump Doesn't Win, We're Screwed," Return of Kings archived post, August 8, 2016, https://archive.is/5etVq#selection-603.0-619.225.

13. Milo Yiannopoulos, "FULL TEXT: Milo at the Ohio State University in Dangerous Faggot Pre-Election Extravaganza," Breitbart, November 4, 2016, https://www.breitbart.com/social-justice/2016/11/04/full-text-milo-ohio-state-university-donald-trumps-tough/.

14. Chris D'Angelo, "Trump Supports Are Peddling Disgustingly Sexist Anti-Hillary Clinton Swag," *Huffington Post*, May 3, 2016, https://www.huffingtonpost.com/entry/deplorable-anti-clinton-merch-at-trump-rallies_us_572836e1e4b016f378936c22.

15. "First Republican Primary Debate—Main Stage—August 6 2015 on Fox News," US Presidential Debates, YouTube video, 1:55:17, April 15, 2016, https://www.youtube.com/watch?v=2rU4W3yfd58.

16. Two years into Trump's presidency, Jane Mayer reported on the mutually beneficial relationship between Trump and Fox News, including that according to "a pair of Fox insiders and a source close to Trump" that then Fox News president Roger Ailes had "informed the Trump campaign about Kelly's question. Two of those sources say that they know of the tipoff from a purported eyewitness." If Mayer's reporting is true, then the whole Trump-Kelly feud was political theater designed to exploit the nation's frustration over gender issues. Jane Mayer, "The Making of the Fox News White House," *New Yorker*, March 4, 2019, https://www.newyorker.com/magazine/2019/03/11/the-making-of-the-fox-news-white-house.

17. "Here's What Happens When Donald Trump Walks into a Debate Spin Room," ABC News, 03:47, August 7, 2015, https://abcnews.go.com/Politics/video/donald-trump-walks-debate-spin-room-32942132.

18. Daily Slave, "Fox News Lost Credibility with White Conservatives after Attempting to Holocause Trump," Daily Stormer, August 9, 2015, https://dailystormer.name/fox-news-lost-massive-amounts-of-credibility-with-white-conservatives-after-attempting-to-holocaust-trump/.

19. Donald J. Trump (@realDonaldTrump), "@ElvisFever: @megynkelly @FoxNews Out to get you with baited questions. She was angry at you. Very hostile and unprofessional," Twitter, August 7, 2015, https://twitter.com/realdonaldtrump/status/629582600571592704; Donald J. Trump (@realDonaldTrump), "@GotMade: @realDonaldTrump Great Job!!! Winning the debate last night will take over half the field out, @FoxNews was not fair to Trump," Twitter, August 7, 2015, https://twitter.com/realdonaldtrump/status/629582396346757120; Donald J. Trump (@realDonaldTrump), "@TIME poll: @

realDonaldTrump winner of last night's debate by wide margin,. 45% v, 12% @RealBenCarson, 10% @JohnKasich, http://time.com/3988073/republican-debate-fox-first-gop/?xid=tcoshare," Twitter, August 7, 2015, https://twitter.com/realdonaldtrump/status/629581720602451968; Donald J. Trump (@realDonaldTrump), "@CaptTimScrim: Dear @megynkelly, your attempted hatchet job on @realDonaldTrump was unbecoming & a total failure. @FoxNews," Twitter, August 7, 2015, https://twitter.com/realdonaldtrump/status/629579550113054720; Donald J. Trump (@realDonaldTrump), "@StefanVersac: @megynkelly @ChrisStirewalt @ChrisChristie @realDonaldTrump Rosie O'Donnell was the best answer of that whole debate," Twitter, August 7, 2015, https://twitter.com/realdonaldtrump/status/629579101930717184; Donald J. Trump (@realDonaldTrump), "@Southern_Anon63: I am a stone cold down to the bone democrat. But I will be voting @realDonaldTrump on Election Day," Twitter, August 7, 2015, https://twitter.com/realdonaldtrump/status/629578878307147776; Donald J. Trump (@realDonaldTrump), "@joshuapantoja: @megynkelly @FrankLuntz @realDonaldTrump you tried to attack Trump, he took it and smiled. Trump will be the next president," Twitter, August 7, 2015, https://twitter.com/realdonaldtrump/status/629578564388700160; Donald J. Trump (@realDonaldTrump), "@Domenclature: TIME POLL: @RealDonaldTrump wins the first #Republicanpresidentialdebate by Wild Margin http://ti.me/1IRqVp2 #Politics," Twitter, August 7, 2015, https://twitter.com/realdonaldtrump/status/629577707827949568; Donald J. Trump (@realDonaldTrump), "@Sulli1963: @AnnCoulter final four-Trump, Cruz, Waler, Carson wild card Fiorina," Twitter, August 7, 2015, https://twitter.com/realdonaldtrump/status/629568286062190592; Donald J. Trump (@realDonaldTrump), "@italy2320: @Reid2962 @FoxNews @megynkelly Tell me what I can do to help you. She really has made me want to never watch fox again," Twitter, August 7, 2015, https://twitter.com/realdonaldtrump/status/629567328829710336; Donald J. Trump (@realDonaldTrump), "@678b4612a62641f: @realDonaldTrump @Reid2962 @FoxNews @megynkelly my vote remains for trump!" Twitter, August 7, 2015, https://twitter.com/realdonaldtrump/status/629565459256487936; Donald J. Trump (@realDonaldTrump), "@Mannamalistic: I'm s lifelong liberal and have come to fucking love @realDonaldTrump. He speaks the truth!" Twitter, August 7, 2015, https://twitter.com/realdonaldtrump/status/629565360858103808; Donald J. Trump (@realDonaldTrump), "@Diplomt: @realDonaldTrump is in a greater position w/ 52% to 12% @Drudge_Report even after @MegynKelly & @BretBaier tried to take him out," Twitter, August 7, 2015, https://twitter.com/realdonaldtrump/status/629564889498001408; Donald J. Trump (@realDonaldTrump), "@stinger_inc: @realDonaldTrump @megynkelly's behaviour at the #GOPDebate was astonishingly biased," Twitter, August 7, 2015, https://twitter.com/realdonaldtrump/status/629564465613275136; Donald J. Trump (@realDonaldTrump), "@BrianCraigShow: @realDonaldTrump your rocked & won BIG TIME!!!! Make America Great Again Mr. Trump," Twitter, August 7, 2015, https://twitter.com/realdonaldtrump/status/629564198603911168; Donald J. Trump (@realDonaldTrump), "@agcaddauan: @realDonaldTrump @DRUDGE_REPORT Megyn could have done a far better job*," Twitter, August 7, 2015, https://twitter.com/realdonaldtrump/status/629563913848377344; Donald J. Trump (@realDonaldTrump), "@Diplomtc_Immnty: @realDonaldTrump They tried to take you out & your poll numbers skyrocketed. Voters matter, not @FoxNews moderators," Twitter, August 7, 2015, https://twitter.com/realdonaldtrump/status/629563335051202560; Donald J. Trump (@realDonaldTrump), "@Reid2962: @realDonaldTrump @FoxNews I expected better from @megynkelly, wondering what is her hidden agenda," Twitter, August 7, 2015, https://twitter.com/realdonaldtrump/status/629562617548378112; Donald J. Trump (@realDonaldTrump), "@Resi_Diederich: @PlatinumRosie @realDonaldTrump @FoxNews @megynkelly is that all you've got??? Haha," Twitter, August 7, 2015, https://twitter.com/realdonaldtrump/status/629562357044412416; Donald J. Trump (@realDonaldTrump), "@JetRanger69: @realDonaldTrump @FoxNews @megynkelly @BretBaier WAS A DISASTER ALSO," Twitter, August 7, 2015, https://twitter.com/realdonaldtrump/status/629562265323372544; Donald J. Trump (@realDonaldTrump), "@Lking2fly: I gotta have @realDonaldTrump in the White House that'd be such a game changer," Twitter, August 7, 2015, https://twitter.com/realdonaldtrump/status/629562171891052545; Donald J. Trump (@realDonaldTrump), "@11phenomenon: Despite the hype, @realDonaldTrump wins the debate by a wide margin. http://t.co/2KRx2TBETS," Twitter, August 7, 2015, https://twitter.com/realdonaldtrump/status/629562135471910912; Donald J. Trump (@realDonaldTrump), "I really enjoyed the debate tonight even though the @FoxNews trio, especially @megynkelly, was not very good or professional!" Twitter, August 7, 2015, https://twitter.com/realdonaldtrump/status/629561051982495744; Donald J. Trump (@realDonaldTrump), "@FrankLuntz, your so-called 'focus groups' are a total joke. Don't come to my office looking for business again. You are a clown!" Twitter, August 7, 2015, https://twitter.com/realdonaldtrump/status/629558921779412992; Donald J. Trump (@realDonaldTrump), "Wow, @megynkelly really bombed tonight. People are going wild on twitter! Funny to watch," Twitter, August 7, 2015, https://twitter.com/realdonaldtrump/status/629557762427604992; Donald J. Trump (@realDonaldTrump), "@FrankLuntz I won every poll of the debate tonight by massive margins @DRUDGE_REPORT & @TIME so where did you find that dumb panel," Twitter, August 7, 2015, https://twitter.com/realdonaldtrump/status/629556966835265536; Donald J. Trump (@realDonaldTrump), "@FrankLuntz: I'm getting a lot of @MegynKelly hatemail tonight. #GOPDebate She is totally overrated and angry. She really bombed tonite," Twitter, August 7, 2015, https://twitter.com/realdonaldtrump/status/629555367362605056; Donald J. Trump (@realDonaldTrump), "@FrankLuntz is a low class slob who came to my office looking for consulting work and I had zero interest. Now he picks anti-Trump panels!" Twitter, August 7, 2015, https://twitter.com/realdonaldtrump/status/629554738766479360; Donald J. Trump (@realDonaldTrump), "@timjcam: @megynkelly @FrankLuntz @realDonaldTrump Fox viewers give low marks to bimbo @MegynKelly will consider other programs!" Twitter, August 7, 2015, https://twitter.com/realdonaldtrump/status/629553612839124992; Donald J. Trump (@

realDonaldTrump), "@RubenMMoreno: @realDonaldTrump The biggest loser in the debate was @megynkelly. You can't out trump Donald Trump. You will lose!" Twitter, August 7, 2015, https://twitter.com/realdonaldtrump/status/629553442944602112; Donald J. Trump (@realDonaldTrump), "@ept_rudyru: @DRUDGE_REPORT Excellent job! @realDonaldTrump You are real & everyone saw that 2nite! #MakeAmericaGreatAgain #SilentMajority," Twitter, August 7, 2015, https://twitter.com/realdonaldtrump/status/629553260681142272; Donald J. Trump (@realDonaldTrump), "Wow! What a great honor from @DRUDGE_REPORT http://t.co/fokcASBVuN," Twitter, August 7, 2015, https://twitter.com/realdonaldtrump/status/629548582199291904; Donald J. Trump (@realDonaldTrump), "@FoxNews: @realDonaldTrump: 'When you have $18–$19 trillion in debt, they need someone like me to straighten it out' http://t.co/hTUJ35ja0Q," Twitter, August 6, 2015, https://twitter.com/realdonaldtrump/status/629520356487864320; Donald J. Trump (@realDonaldTrump), "Thank you @TIME readers- a great honor! http://t.co/2KRx2TBETS," Twitter, August 6, 2015, https://twitter.com/realdonaldtrump/status/629518315711500288; Donald J. Trump (@realDonaldTrump), "#MakeAmericaGreatAgain #GOPdebate http://t.co/SNrr9YZmou," Twitter, August 6, 2015, https://twitter.com/realdonaldtrump/status/629512519174918145; Donald J. Trump (@realDonaldTrump), "Wow! What a great honor from @DRUDGE_REPORT http://t.co/fokcASBVuN," Twitter, August 6, 2015, https://twitter.com/realdonaldtrump/status/629509392468209664.

20. "Donald Trump Slams Megyn Kelly on Twitter over Rosie O'Donnell Comments," ABC 6, August 7, 2015, https://6abc.com/politics/trump-slams-megyn-kelly-over-rosie-odonnell-comments/909946/.

21. *CNN Tonight with Don Lemon*, CNN, Trump archive video, 1:00, August 7, 2015, https://archive.org/details/cnnw_20150808_010100_cnn_tonight_with_don_lemon/start/0/end/60.

22. *CNN Tonight with Don Lemon*, CNN, Trump archive video, 1:00, August 7, 2015, https://archive.org/details/CNNW_20150808_010100_CNN_Tonight_With_Don_Lemon/start/0/end/60.

23. "Donald Trump vs. Megyn Kelly: 'I Did Nothing Wrong' (Full CNN Interview)," CNN, YouTube video, 9:24, August 9, 2015, https://www.youtube.com/watch?v=hpm5GT7ZOTc.

24. *Meet the Press*, NBC, Trump archive video, 1:00, August 9, 2015, https://archive.org/details/wcau_20150809_143300_meet_the_press/start/13/end/73?q=megyn+kelly.

25. Fox News, "Megyn Kelly Addresses the Donald Trump Debate Controversy on 'The Kelly File,'" Fox News, published August 10, 2015, updated January 24, 2017, https://www.foxnews.com/transcript/megyn-kelly-addresses-the-donald-trump-debate-controversy-on-the-kelly-file.

26. Stephen K. Bannon and Alexander Marlow, "The Arrogance of Power: Megyn Kelly's 'Good Journalism,'" Breitbart, August 11, 2015, https://www.breitbart.com/the-media/2015/08/11/the-arrogance-of-power-megyn-kellys-good-journalism/.

27. Breitbart News, "Fox Shock: Network Calls Megyn Kelly 'Talent,' Not 'Journalist,'" Breitbart, August 14, 2015, https://www.breitbart.com/the-media/2015/08/14/fox-shock-network-calls-megyn-kelly-talent-not-journalist/.

28. Donald J. Trump (@realDonaldTrump), "@mstanish53: @realDonaldTrump @ megynkelly The bimbo is back in town. I hope not for long," Twitter, August 24, 2015, https://twitter.com/realDonaldTrump/status/635995703182016513.

29. Tom McCarthy, "Fox Chief Asks Trump to Apologize for 'Verbal Assaults' on Megyn Kelly," *The Guardian*, August 25, 2015, https://www.theguardian.com/us-news/2015/aug/25/fox-chief-donald-trump-verbal-assaults-megyn-kelly.

30. Hadas Gold, "Roger Ailes: Donald Trump Should Never Apologize to Megyn Kelly," Politico, August 25, 2015, https://www.politico.com/blogs/media/2015/08/roger-ailes-donald-trump-should-apologize-to-megyn-kelly-212934.

31. Andrew Anglin, "Megyn Kelly BTFO by Newt: 'You Are Fascinated with Sex,'" Daily Stormer, October 26, 2016, https://dailystormer.name/megyn-sic-kelly-btfo-by-newt-you-are-fascinated-with-sex/.

32. "Donald Trump Spokane Rally Speech May 7, 2016," KHQ6, YouTube video, 59:59, May 7, 2016, https://www.youtube.com/watch?v=4BVZG1aumc4.

33. *Megyn Kelly Presents*, Fox News, Trump archive video, 1:02, May 27, 2016, https://archive.org/details/foxnewsw_20160528_040000_megyn_kelly_presents/start/480/end/540.

34. Andrew Anglin, "The Megyn Kelly Interview with Donald Trump," Daily Stormer, May 18, 2016, https://dailystormer.name/the-megyn-sic-kelly-interview-with-donald-trump/.

35. David A. Fahrenthold, "Trump Recorded Having Extremely Lewd Conversation about Women in 2005," *Washington Post*, October 8, 2016, https://www.washingtonpost.com/politics/trump-recorded-having-extremely-lewd-conversation-about-women-in-2005/2016/10/07/3b9ce776-8cb4-11e6-bf8a-3d26847eeed4_story.html?utm_term=.35922496532f.

36. "Transcript: Donald Trump's Taped Comments about Women," *New York Times*, October 8, 2016, https://www.nytimes.com/2016/10/08/us/donald-trump-tape-transcript.html.

37. Zeke J. Miller, "Donald Trump's Lewd Comments Send Republicans Reeling," *Time*, October 8, 2016, http://time.com/4523757/donald-trump-women-comments-lewd/.

38. "Chuck Todd: Trump's Comments about Women in 2005 Are 'Unrecoverable,'" NBC News video, 4:07, October 8, 2016, https://www.nbcnews.com/video/chuck-todd-trump-s-comments-about-women-in-2005-are-unrecoverable-781857859898.

39. David A. Fahrenthold, "Trump Recorded Having Extremely Lewd Conversation about Women in 2005," *Washington Post*, October 8, 2016, https://www.washingtonpost.com/politics/trump-recorded-having-extremely-lewd-conversation-about-women-in-2005/2016/10/07/3b9ce776-8cb4-11e6-bf8a-3d26847eeed4_story.html?utm_term=.5ead911bd306.

40. "All Business: The Essential Donald Trump," CNN, Trump archive video, 1:01, October 7, 2016, https://archive.org/details/

cnnw_20161008_040000_all_business_the_essential_donald_trump/start/480/end/540.

41. Maggie Haberman, "Donald Trump's Apology That Wasn't," *New York Times*, October 8, 2016, https://www.nytimes.com/2016/10/08/us/politics/donald-trump-apology.html.

42. Daniella Diaz and Jeff Zeleny, "Trump Appears with Bill Clinton Accusers before Debate," CNN Politics, October 10, 2016, https://www.cnn.com/2016/10/09/politics/donald-trump-juanita-broaddrick-paula-jones-facebook-live-2016-election/index.html.

43. "Clinton: 'My Skin Crawled' in Trump Debate," BBC video, 1:35, August 23, 2017, https://www.bbc.com/news/av/world-us-canada-41028024/hillary-clinton-my-skin-crawled-in-trump-debate.

44. "Presidential Nominees Debate at Washington University," C-SPAN, Trump archive video, 1:00, October 9, 2016, https://archive.org/details/cspan_20161010_010000_presidential_nominees_debate_at_washington_university/start/711/end/771?q=women.

45. Matthew Boyle, "Anti-Trump Republicans Rush to Express Outrage over Trump Video with George H. W. Bush's Nephew," Breitbart, October 8, 2016, https://www.breitbart.com/politics/2016/10/08/anti-trump-republicans-rush-express-outrage-trump-video-george-h-w-bushs-nephew/.

46. Eva_Galley, "This is a big nothingburger, dug up by Hillary's desperate campaign," comment on "WaPo: Donald Trump, Billy Bush Caught on Tape in 'Extremely Lewd Conversation about Women,'" Breitbart, October 7, 2016, http://disq.us/p/1clotts.

47. Wilson, "They forgot the part about Trump and baby Bush were talking about gold digging bimbo's that throw themselves at rich men. Then they pretend they were talking about all women. Disgusting!" comment on Matthew Boyle, "Anti-Trump Republicans Rush to Express Outrage over Trump Video with George H. W. Bush's Nephew," Breitbart, October 8, 2016, http://disq.us/p/1cmgydn.

48. Andrew Anglin, "Billy Bush Fired over Pussy-Grabocaust," Daily Stormer, October 10, 2016, https://dailystormer.name/billy-bush-fired-over-pussy-grabocaust/; Andrew Anglin, "Awesome Pussy Tape Won-Over Millions of Democrats," Daily Stormer, October 13, 2016, https://dailystormer.name/awesome-pussy-tape-won-over-millions-of-democrats/.

49. Andrew Anglin, "Stupid Goyim Shocked that Trump Talks Like a Normal Person," Daily Stormer, October 8, 2016, https://dailystormer.name/stupid-goyim-shocked-that-trump-talks-like-a-normal-person/.

50. Andrew Anglin, "Grimy Scumbucket Paul Ryan Encourages Congressmen to Attack TOP PUSSY-GRABBER," Daily Stormer, October 10, 2016, https://dailystormer.name/grimy-scumbucket-paul-ryan-encourages-congressmen-to-attack-top-pussy-grabber/; Andrew Anglin, "Last Day: Time to Grab America by the Pussy," Daily Stormer, November 7, 2016, https://dailystormer.name/last-day-time-to-grab-america-by-the-pussy/.

51. "Donald Trump Campaigns in Ambridge, Pennsylvania," C-SPAN, Trump archive video, 1:00, October 10, 2016, https://archive.org/details/cspan2_20161011_022500_donald_trump_campaigns_in_ambridge_pennsylvania/start/1840/end/1900?q=women.

52. *Anderson Cooper 360*, CNN, Trump archive video, 1:00, October 17, 2016, https://archive.org/details/cnnw_20161018_000300_anderson_cooper_360/start/26/end/86?q=women.

53. *PBS News Hour Debates 2016: A Special Report*, PBS, Trump archive video, 0:24, October 19, 2016, https://archive.org/details/kqed_20161020_010000_pbs_newshour_debates_2016_a_special_report/start/3274.2/end/3298.5?q=women.

54. Aaron Blake, "21 Times Donald Trump Has Assured Us He Respects Women," *Washington Post*, March 8, 2017, https://www.washingtonpost.com/news/the-fix/wp/2017/03/08/21-times-donald-trump-has-assured-us-he-respects-women/?utm_term=.16ff66dd5aaf.

55. *The Washington Post* and the Kaiser Family Foundation, "Feminism Survey," January 2016, http://files.kff.org/attachment/topline-methodology-washington-post-kaiser-family-foundation-feminism-survey.

56. Pew Research Center, "Most Clinton Backers Say Their Vote Is 'For' Her Rather Than 'Against' Trump," October 27, 2016, figure 2_1, http://www.people-press.org/2016/10/27/2-factors-underlying-voter-preferences-positive-and-negative-voting/2_1-6/.

57. Alec Tyson and Shiva Maniam, "Behind Trump's Victory: Divisions by Race, Gender, and Education," Pew Research Center, November 9, 2016, http://www.pewresearch.org/fact-tank/2016/11/09/behind-trumps-victory-divisions-by-race-gender-education/.

58. Erica Chenoweth and Jeremy Pressman, "This Is What We Learned by Counting the Women's Marches," *Washington Post*, February 7, 2017, https://www.washingtonpost.com/news/monkey-cage/wp/2017/02/07/this-is-what-we-learned-by-counting-the-womens-marches/?utm_term=.5a80eb559cef.

59. Art of the March, image archive, http://artofthemarch.boston/container/archive; "Signs from 2017 Women's Marches," *Huffington Post*, image 18 of 23, https://www.huffingtonpost.com/entry/89-badass-feminist-signs-from-the-womens-march-on-washington_us_5883ea28e4b070d8cad310cd?slideshow=true#gallery/5883c3a0e4b096b4a2323f77/17.

60. Anemona Hartocollis and Yamiche Alcindor, "Women's March Highlights as Huge Crowds Protest Trump: 'We're Not Going Away,'" *New York Times*, January 21, 2017, https://www.nytimes.com/2017/01/21/us/womens-march.html.

61. "Donald Trump is the ultimate alpha male. He is an aggressive, hostile conqueror who became ruler of the world through force of will. As such, he is the object of sexual fixation of all women on the planet. Hence, hundreds of thousands of women across the globe marching with the demand to have sex with him." Andrew Anglin, "Half a Million Pussies March on Washington Demanding President Trump Grab Them," Daily Stormer archived post, January 22, 2017, https://archive.is/G3tLt#selection-717.0-723.101.

Chapter 17

1. "Trump: Favorable/Unfavorable," Real Clear Politics, http://www.realclearpolitics.com/epolls/other/trump_favorableunfavorable-5493.html#polls.

2. Donald J. Trump, "Let Me Ask America a Question," *Wall Street Journal*, April 14, 2016, https://www.wsj.com/articles/let-me-ask-america-a-question-1460675882.

3. Aaron Blake, "The GOP Exodus from Donald Trump Couldn't Have Come at a Worse Time," *Washington Post*, October 9, 2016, https://www.washingtonpost.com/news/the-fix/wp/2016/10/09/the-gop-exodus-from-donald-trump-couldnt-have-come-at-a-worse-time/?utm_term=.eb624ffad34c.

4. Donald J. Trump (@realDonaldTrump), "The media and establishment want me out of the race so badly—I WILL NEVER DROP OUT OF THE RACE, WILL NEVER LET MY SUPPORTERS DOWN! #MAGA," Twitter, October 8, 2016, https://twitter.com/real-DonaldTrump/status/784840992734064641.

5. Hannah Hartig, John Lapinski, and Stephanie Psyllos, "Poll: More Voters Say Trump Doesn't Respect Women after Lewd Tape Surfaces," NBC News, October 10, 2016, https://www.nbcnews.com/storyline/data-points/poll-more-voters-say-trump-doesn-t-respect-women-after-n663296.

6. Andrew Anglin, "Billy Bush Fired over Pussy-Grabocaust," Daily Stormer, October 10, 2016, https://dailystormer.name/billy-bush-fired-over-pussy-grabocaust/; Andrew Anglin, "Awesome Pussy Tape Won-Over Millions of Democrats," Daily Stormer, October 13, 2016, https://dailystormer.name/awesome-pussy-tape-won-over-millions-of-democrats/.

7. "Donald Trump Campaigns in Ambridge, Pennsylvania," C-SPAN, Trump archive video, 01:07, October 10, 2016, https://archive.org/details/cspan2_20161011_022500_donald_trump_campaigns_in_ambridge_pennsylvania/start/2160/end/2220.

8. Amber Phillips, "Paul Ryan Just Officially Broke Up with Donald Trump," *Washington Post*, October 10, 2016, https://www.washingtonpost.com/news/the-fix/wp/2016/10/10/paul-ryan-just-officially-broke-up-with-donald-trump/?utm_term=.cf2f916a63cf; Kelsey Snell, Juliet Eilperin, and Mike DeBonis, "Paul Ryan Won't Defend or Campaign for Trump Ahead of Election," *Washington Post*, October 10, 2016, https://www.washingtonpost.com/news/powerpost/wp/2016/10/10/paul-ryan-wont-defend-or-campaign-for-trump-ahead-of-election/?utm_term=.3abbbe13c36a.

9. Snell, Eilperin, and DeBonis, "Ryan Won't Defend or Campaign for Trump," https://www.washingtonpost.com/news/powerpost/wp/2016/10/10/paul-ryan-wont-defend-or-campaign-for-trump-ahead-of-election/?utm_term=.3abbbe13c36a.

10. Donald J. Trump (@realDonaldTrump), "It is so nice that the shackles have been taken off me and I can now fight for America the way I want to," Twitter, October 11, 2016, https://twitter.com/realdonaldtrump/status/785842546878578688?lang=en.

11. "Bill O'Reilly Donald Trump FULL Interview October 11 2016 Fox News," YouTube video, 16:04, October 15, 2016, https://www.youtube.com/watch?v=PUktOX4MhqE; Caitlin MacNeal, "WATCH: Trump Goes On Tirade about 'Shackles' Paul Ryan, John McCain," *Talking Points Memo*, October 12, 2016, https://talkingpointsmemo.com/livewire/trump-shackles-ryan-mccain-o-reilly.

12. Patrick Svitek, "In San Antonio, Trump Attacks Ryan for 'Total Disloyalty,'" *Texas*

Tribune, October 11, 2016, https://www.texastribune.org/2016/10/11/san-antonio-fund-raiser-trump-vents-over-gop-leader/.

13. Stephen Collinson, Eugene Scott, and Eric Bradner, "Donald Trump: 'The Shackles Have Been Taken Off Me,'" CNN Politics, October 11, 2016, https://www.cnn.com/2016/10/11/politics/donald-trump-paul-ryan-tweets/.

14. Sean Sullivan, Robert Costa, and Dan Balz, "Trump Declares War on GOP, Says 'The Shackles Have Been Taken Off,'" *Washington Post*, October 11, 2016, https://www.washingtonpost.com/politics/trump-declares-war-on-the-republican-party-four-weeks-before-election-day/2016/10/11/93b21dc4-8fc9-11e6-9c52-0b10449e33c4_story.html?utm_term=.c5f9c3ef5255.

15. Hunter Wallace, "#NeverTrump Has Destroyed the Republican Party," Daily Stormer, October 11, 2016, https://dailystormer.name/nevertrump-has-destroyed-the-republican-party.

16. "Presidential Candidate Donald Trump Rally in Panama City, Florida," C-SPAN video, 1:06:14, October 11, 2016, https://www.c-span.org/video/?416754-1/donald-trump-campaigns-panama-city-florida.

17. Megan Twohey and Michael Barbaro, "Two Women Say Donald Trump Touched Them Inappropriately," *New York Times*, October 12, 2016, https://www.nytimes.com/2016/10/13/us/politics/donald-trump-women.html; Megan Twohey and Michael Barbaro, "Crossing the Line: How Donald Trump Behaved with Women in Private," *New York Times*, May 14, 2016, https://www.nytimes.com/2016/05/15/us/politics/donald-trump-women.html?module=inline.

18. "Donald Trump Campaigns in West Palm Beach, Florida," C-SPAN, Trump archive video, 1:00, October 13, 2016, https://archive.org/details/cspan_20161014_004100_donald_trump_campaigns_in_west_palm_beach_florida/start/907/end/967?q=women; "Transcript: Donald Trump's Speech Responding to Assault Accusations," NPR, October 13, 2016, https://www.npr.org/2016/10/13/497857068/transcript-donald-trumps-speech-responding-to-assault-accusations.

19. Chris Cillizza and Aaron Blake, "Donald Trump's Chances of Winning Are Approaching Zero," *The Washington Post*, October 24, 2016, https://www.washingtonpost.com/news/the-fix/wp/2016/10/24/donald-trumps-chances-of-winning-are-approaching-zero/?utm_term=.5620c054a807.

20. "The Place for Politics 2016," MSNBC, Trump archive video, 1:00, June 7, 2016, https://archive.org/details/msnbcw_20160608_010700_the_place_for_politics_2016/start/244/end/304?q=fight+for+the+american+people.

21. *Citizen Trump with Chris Matthews*, MSNBC, Trump archive video, 1:00, October 29, 2016, https://archive.org/details/msnbcw_20161029_230000_citizen_trump_with_chris_matthews/start/3312/end/3372?q=fight+for+the+american+people.

22. "Key Capitol Hill Hearings," C-SPAN, Trump archive video, 1:01, October 20, 2016, https://archive.org/details/cspan_20161020_210000_key_capitol_hill_hearings/start/60/end/120.

23. "This Is a Movement," TV News Archive, accessed April 15, 2019, https://archive.org/details/tv?q=this+is+a+movement&and%5B%5D=collection%3A%22trumparchive%22&sort=publicdate.

24. Donald J. Trump (@realDonaldTrump), "Join the MOVEMENT! Donald-JTrump.com," Twitter, October 4, 2016, https://twitter.com/realdonaldtrump/status/783452759462850560; Donald J. Trump (@realDonaldTrump), "This is more than a campaign—it is a movement. #MakeAmericaGreatAgain SIGN UP TODAY & WE WILL WIN!" Twitter, September 22, 2016, https://twitter.com/realdonaldtrump/status/779127602988650498; Donald J. Trump (@realDonaldTrump), "Such a great honor. Final debate polls are in—and the MOVEMENT wins! #AmericaFirst #MAGA #ImWithYou DonaldJTrump.com," Twitter, September 27, 2016, https://twitter.com/realdonaldtrump/status/780796008854876160; Donald J. Trump (@realDonaldTrump), "We need your vote. Go to the POLLS! Let's continue this MOVEMENT! Find you poll location: vote.gop #ElectionDay #VoteTrump," Twitter, November 8, 2016, https://twitter.com/realdonaldtrump/status/796050609254395905.

25. *Public Affairs Events*, C-SPAN, Trump archive video, 1:00, November 7, 2016, https://archive.org/details/cspan_20161107_224300_public_affairs_events/start/262/end/322?q=crowd.

Chapter 18

1. "Trump: Favorable/Unfavorable," Real Clear Politics, http://www.realclearpolitics.com/epolls/other/trump_favorableunfavorable-5493.html#polls.

2. Politico Staff, "Full Text: Hillary Clinton's DNC Speech," Politico, July 28, 2016, https://www.politico.com/story/2016/07/full-text-hillary-clintons-dnc-speech-226410.

3. Steven Levisky and Daniel Ziblatt, "Democracy's Fate My Hang in the Balance Even If Donald Trump Loses," Vox, November 7, 2016, https://www.vox.com/polyarchy/2016/11/7/13547642/democracy-fate-trump-loss.

4. Steven Levitsky and Daniel Ziblatt, "Is Donald Trump a Threat to Democracy?" *New York Times*, December 16, 2016, https://www.nytimes.com/2016/12/16/opinion/sunday/is-donald-trump-a-threat-to-democracy.html.

5. Matthew C. MacWilliams, "Donald Trump Is Attracting Authoritarian Primary Voters, and It May Help Him to Gain the Nomination," *United States Politics and Policy*, January 27, 2016, https://blogs.lse.ac.uk/usappblog/2016/01/27/donald-trump-is-attracting-authoritarian-primary-voters-and-it-may-help-him-to-gain-the-nomination/.

6. Max Ehrenfreund, "A Strange but Accurate Predictor of Whether Someone Supports Donald Trump," *Washington Post*, February 1, 2016, https://www.washingtonpost.com/news/wonk/wp/2016/02/01/how-your-parenting-style-predicts-whether-you-support-donald-trump/?utm_term=.b4d75dc7d0a7.

7. Amanda Taub, "The Rise of American Authoritarianism," Vox, May 1, 2016, https://www.vox.com/2016/3/1/11127424/trump-authoritarianism.

8. I discuss the history of America choosing stability over democracy in my book *Founding Fictions*.

9. "Donald Trump Campaigns in Tampa, Florida," C-SPAN, Trump archive video, 1:00, October 24, 2016, https://archive.org/details/cspan_20161025_012500_donald_trump_campaigns_in_tampa_florida/start/1362/end/1422?q=fight+for+the+american+people.

10. "Donald Trump Campaign Rally in Hartford, Connecticut," C-SPAN, Trump archive video, 1:00, April 16, 2016, https://archive.org/details/cspan_20160416_172800_donald_trump_campaign_rally_in_hartford_connecticut/start/938/end/998?q=crowd.

11. "Donald Trump Holds Rally in Sioux City, Iowa," C-SPAN, Trump archive video, 1:00, November 6, 2016, https://archive.org/details/cspan_20161107_023900_donald_trump_holds_rally_in_sioux_city_iowa/start/745/end/805?q=fight+for+the+american+people.

12. "Donald Trump Inciting Violence at Rally in St. Louis: March 11, 2016," Jeffrey Guterman, YouTube video, 12:48, March 12, 2016, https://www.youtube.com/watch?v=PCZEAcSsx7w; Nick Gass, "Trump: 'There Used to Be Consequences,'" Politico, March 11, 2016, https://www.politico.com/blogs/2016-gop-primary-live-updates-and-results/2016/03/trump-defends-protest-violence-220638.

13. Trump had made similar threats: "If you see someone getting ready to throw a tomato, knock the crap out of them, would you? Seriously. Knock the hell out of them. I promise you I will pay for the legal fees. I promise," Trump told his rally crowd in Cedar Rapids, Iowa, on February 1, 2016. "I'd like to punch him in the face, I'll tell you," Trump told his Las Vegas rally about a protestor on February 22, 2016; "in the good old days, they'd rip him out of that seat so fast," Trump said about another protestor in Oklahoma City, Oklahoma, on February 26, 2016. *Fox News Sunday with Chris Wallace*, Fox, Trump archive video, 1:00, March 13, 2016, https://archive.org/details/wtxf_20160313_130200_fox_news_sunday_with_chris_wallace/start/198/end/258?q=i+will+pay+for+the+legal+fees.

14. Trump told his rally in Mount Pleasant, South Carolina, on December 7, 2015, that "we have to talk to them closing up that internet. People say, 'freedom of speech,' 'freedom of speech.' We have a lot of foolish people. We have to do something with the internet because [terrorists] are recruiting by the thousands." "US House of Representatives Special Orders," C-SPAN, Trump archive video, 1:00, December 7, 2015, https://archive.org/details/cspan_20151208_000600_us_house_of_representatives_special_orders/start/2246/end/2306?q=close+the+internet.

15. "Open Discussion on Fitness to be President," C-SPAN video, 14:00, October 19, 2016, https://www.c-span.org/video/?c4626113/open-discussion-fitness-president.

16. "Key Capitol Hill Hearings," C-SPAN, Trump archive video, 1:05, October 20, 2016, https://archive.org/details/cspan_20161020_210000_key_capitol_hill_hearings/start/1080/end/1140.

17. "Speech: Donald Trump in Toledo, OH—October 27, 2016," Factba.se, October 27, 2016, https://factba.se/search#we%2Bshould%2Bcancel%2Bthe%2Belection.

18. Nick Corasaniti, "At Donald Trump Rally in North Carolina, the Protestors Just Keep Coming," *New York Times*, December 5, 2015, https://www.nytimes.com/politics/first-draft/2015/12/05/at-donald-trump-rally-in-north-carolina-the-protesters-just-keep-coming/; "Speech: Donald Trump in Raleigh, NC—December 4, 2015," Factba.se, December 4, 2015, https://factba.se/transcript/donald-trump-speech-raleigh-nc-december-4-2015.

19. At a January 7, 2016, Burlington, Vermont, rally, the Trump campaign reportedly gave out 20,000 free tickets for a 1,400 capacity theater. The campaign would only admit those who swore their loyalty to Trump at the door. "Trump Enforces 'Loyalty Oath' at Vermont Rally, Ejects Any Who Don't Comply," NBC News, January 8, 2016, https://www.nbcnews.com/video/trump-enforces-loyalty-oath-at-vermont-rally-ejects-any-who-dont-comply-598299203674; Brad Evans, "Donald Trump's Campaign Issues 20,000 Tickets for 1,400 Rally Seats," NBC News, January 6, 2016, http://www.mynbc5.com/article/donald-trump-s-campaign-issues-20-000-tickets-for-1-400-rally-seats/3326004.

20. "WATCH: Donald Trump Demand a Loyalty Pledge from an Audience of . . .," Daily Motion video, 00:57, March 5, 2016, http://www.dailymotion.com/video/x5puhfq.

21. Jesse Byrnes, "Trump Doubles Down on Voter Loyalty Pledge," *The Hill*, March 7, 2016, http://thehill.com/blogs/ballot-box/presidential-races/272047-trump-again-asks-supporters-to-pledge-support.

22. Eliza Collins, "Ex-ADL Director: Trump Pledge 'Is A Fascist Gesture,'" Politico, March 7, 2016, https://www.politico.com/blogs/2016-gop-primary-live-updates-and-results/2016/03/adl-donald-trump-fascist-gesture-220364.

23. Nick Gass, "Trump Defends Loyalty Oaths: 'We're Having Such A Great Time,'" Politico, March 8, 2016, https://www.politico.com/blogs/2016-gop-primary-live-updates-and-results/2016/03/donald-trump-loyalty-oaths-220416.

24. Charlie Nash, "Roger Stone on the Milo Show: How Trump Can Fight Voter Fraud," Breitbart, July 29, 2016, https://www.breitbart.com/social-justice/2016/07/29/roger-stone-milo-show-trump-can-fight-voter-fraud/; "The Milo Show Teaser: Roger Stone on How Trump Can Stop Voter Fraud," MILO, YouTube video, 04:05, July 29, 2016, https://www.youtube.com/watch?v=1bPR846gO8U.

25. "Hillary Clinton Is Losing Her Secret Plans Revealed," Prison Planet video, July 31, 2016, http://tv.infowars.com/index/display/id/7419.

26. "Message to Donald Trump," Bing.com video, 05:27, August 1, 2016, https://www.bing.com/videos/search?q=an+emergency+message+to+donald+trump&&view=detail&mid=8aab71120009b2abdd628aab71120009b2abdd62&&form=vdrvrv.

27. "Hillary Clinton Is Losing Her Secret Plans Revealed," Prison Planet video, July 31, 2016, http://tv.infowars.com/index/display/id/7419; Paul Joseph Watson and Alex Jones "Crooked Hillary Will Try to Steal the Election from Trump," InfoWars, August 1, 2016, https://www.infowars.com/crooked-hillary-will-try-to-steal-the-election-from-trump/;

"Hillary Clinton Is Losing Her Secret Plans Revealed," Prison Planet video, July 31, 2016, http://tv.infowars.com/index/display/id/7419.

28. "Speech: Donald Trump in Columbus, OH—August 1, 2016," Factba.se, https://factba.se/transcript/donald-trump-speech-columbus-oh-august-1-2016; Robert Farley, "Trump's Faulty 'Rigged' Reasoning," FactCheck.org, August 2, 2016, https://www.factcheck.org/2016/08/trumps-faulty-rigged-reasoning/.

29. *Hannity*, Fox, Trump archive video, 00:29, August 1, 2016, https://archive.org/details/foxnewsw_20160802_020100_hannity/start/1260/end/1320.

30. Paul Joseph Watson and Alex Jones, "Trump Is Right: Hillary Stole the Nomination and She Will Try to Steal the Presidency," InfoWars, August 2, 2016, https://www.infowars.com/trump-is-right-hillary-stole-the-nomination-and-she-will-try-to-steal-the-presidency/.

31. "Help Me Stop Crooked Hillary from Rigging This Election!" Trump-Pence archived post, August 12, 2016, https://web.archive.org/web/20160812193331/https://www.donaldjtrump.com/lp/volunteer-to-be-a-trump-election-observer; "Trump Ballot Security Project," *Committee to Restore America's Greatness*, archived post, March 10, 2016, https://web.archive.org/web/20160310155755/https://stopthesteal.org/.

32. Rebecca Morin, "Trump Campaign Launches Drive to Recruit 'Election Observers,'" Politico, August 13, 2016, https://www.politico.com/story/2016/08/donald-trump-election-observers-226981.

33. Scott Shane, "From Headline to Photograph, a Fake News Masterpiece," *New York Times*, January 18, 2017, https://www.nytimes.com/2017/01/18/us/fake-news-hillary-clinton-cameron-harris.html.

34. admin1, "BREAKING: 'Tens of Thousands' of Fraudulent Clinton Votes Found in Ohio Warehouse," *Christian Times Newspaper* archived post, September 30, 2016, https://web.archive.org/web/20161001064328/http://christiantimesnewspaper.com/breaking-tens-of-thousands-of-fraudulent-clinton-votes-found-in-ohio-warehouse/.

35. "Trump Ballot Security Project," Committee to Restore America's Greatness archived post, March 10, 2016, https://web.archive.org/web/20160310155755/https://stopthesteal.org/.

36. Dan Evon, "Tens of Thousands of Fraudulent Clinton Votes Found in Ohio Warehouse," Snopes, September 30, 2016, https://www.snopes.com/fact-check/clinton-votes-found-in-warehouse/.

37. Shane, "From Headline to Photograph," https://www.nytimes.com/2017/01/18/us/fake-news-hillary-clinton-cameron-harris.html.

38. Rebecca Mansour, "'How to Commit Voter Fraud on a Massive Scale': Part II of Project Veritas Investigation into Clinton Network," Breitbart, October 18, 2016, https://www.breitbart.com/politics/2016/10/18/commit-voter-fraud-massive-scale-part-ii-project-veritas-investigation-clinton-network/.

39. Katherine Rodriguez, "Letters behind Clinton Spell Out 'Rig It' in Debate," Breitbart, October 20, 2016, https://www.breitbart.com/politics/2016/10/20/letters-behind-clinton-spell-rig-debate/.

40. "Breaking! Public Awakens to Massive Election Fraud," InfoWars, October 21, 2016, https://www.infowars.com/breaking-public-awakens-to-massive-election-fraud/.

41. Associated Press, "Thousands of Dead People Likely on Indiana Voter Rolls, Analysts Say," Fox News, October 25, 2016, https://www.foxnews.com/politics/thousands-of-dead-people-likely-on-indiana-voter-rolls-analysts-say.

42. Adam Shaw, "Texas Voters Claim Machines Switching Their Votes," Fox News, October 26, 2016, https://www.foxnews.com/politics/texas-voters-claim-machines-switching-their-votes.

43. Donald J. Trump (@realDonaldTrump), "A lot of call-ins about vote flipping at the voting booths in Texas. People are not happy. BIG lines. What is going on?" Twitter, October 27, 2016, https://twitter.com/realdonaldtrump/status/791625798792974336.

44. "Donald Trump Warns of 'Vote Flipping' on Machines," InfoWars video, October 29, 2016, https://www.infowars.com/donald-trump-warns-of-vote-flipping-on-machines/.

45. Warner Todd Huston, "Three New Charges of Vote Fraud Filed in Florida and Virginia," Breitbart, October 28, 2016, https://www.breitbart.com/politics/2016/10/28/vote-fraud-virginia-florida/.

46. "How America's Elections Are Hacked, Missing Link Discovered," InfoWars, October 31, 2016, https://www.infowars.com/how-americas-elections-are-hacked/; "Here's How Voting Machines Are Hacked," InfoWars, November 1, 2016, https://www.infowars.com/heres-how-voting-machines-are-hacked/.

47. Philip Bump, "No, 1.8 Million Dead People, Aren't Going to Vote in November," *Washington Post*, October 18, 2016, https://www.washingtonpost.com/news/the-fix/wp/2016/10/18/no-1-8-million-dead-people-arent-going-to-vote-in-november/?utm_term=.513545678f85&wprss=rss_the-fix.

48. Dana Milbank, "Trump Supporters Are Talking about Civil War. Could a Loss Provide the Spark?" *Washington Post*, October 18, 2016, https://www.washingtonpost.com/opinions/trump-supporters-are-talking-about-civil-war-could-a-loss-provide-the-spark/2016/10/18/f5ce081a-9573-11e6-bb29-bf2701dbe0a3_story.html?utm_term=.c91e7a7bdf68&wpisrc=nl_most-draw5&wpmm=1.

49. Matt Viser and Tracy Jan, "Warnings of Conspiracy Stoke Anger among Trump Faithful," *Boston Globe*, October 15, 2016, https://www.bostonglobe.com/news/politics/2016/10/15/donald-trump-warnings-conspiracy-rig-election-are-stoking-anger-among-his-followers/LcCY6e0QOcfH8VdeK9UdsM/story.html.

50. "Trump Tells Backers to 'Watch the Polls' but Few Republicans Sign Up to Be Poll Watchers," *Chicago Tribune*, November 3, 2016, https://webcache.googleusercontent.com/search?q=cache:whkbP1sMfHAJ:https://www.chicagotribune.com/news/nationworld/politics/ct-trump-election-poll-watchers-20161103-story.html+&cd=3&hl=en&ct=clnk&gl=us.

51. Donald J. Trump (@realDonaldTrump), "The election is absolutely being rigged by the dishonest and distorted media pushing Crooked Hillary—but also as many polling

places—SAD," Twitter, October 16, 2016, https://twitter.com/realDonaldTrump/status/787699930718695425.

52. "Crosstabulation Results," *Morning Consult*, October 13–15, 2016, https://morningconsult.com/wp-content/uploads/2016/10/politicomccrosstabs10.17.pdf.

53. "As Election Nears, Voters Divided over Democracy and 'Respect,'" Pew Research Center, October 27, 2016, http://www.people-press.org/2016/10/27/as-election-nears-voters-divided-over-democracy-and-respect/.

54. Cameron Easley, "Voters Want a Strong Leader More Than Anything Else, Exit Poll Shows," *Morning Consult*, November 8, 2016, https://morningconsult.com/2016/11/08/voters-want-strong-leader-anything-else-exit-poll-shows/.

55. "Full Text: Donald Trump 2016 RNC Draft Speech Transcript," Politico, July 21, 2016, http://www.politico.com/story/2016/07/full-transcript-donald-trump-nomination-acceptance-speech-at-rnc-225974.

56. Glenn Kessler and Michelle Ye Hee Lee, "Fact-Checking Donald Trump's Acceptance Speech at the 2016 RNC," *Washington Post*, July 22, 2016, https://www.washingtonpost.com/news/fact-checker/wp/2016/07/22/fact-checking-donald-trumps-acceptance-speech-at-the-2016-rnc/?utm_term=.d6199f9769ce.

57. "Donald Trump 2016 Acceptance Speech," C-SPAN, Trump archive video, 1:00, July 23, 2016, https://archive.org/details/cspan_20160723_140200_donald_trump_2016_acceptance_speech/start/4536/end/4596?q=we+will+fight; Brad Plumer, "Full Transcript of Donald Trump's Acceptance Speech at the RNC," Vox, July 22, 2016, https://www.vox.com/2016/7/21/12253426/donald-trump-acceptance-speech-transcript-republican-nomination-transcript.

58. Matt Viser and Tracy Jan, "Warnings of Conspiracy Stoke Anger among Trump Faithful," *Boston Globe*, October 15, 2016, https://www.bostonglobe.com/news/politics/2016/10/15/donald-trump-warnings-conspiracy-rig-election-are-stoking-anger-among-his-followers/LcCY6e0QOcfH8VdeK9UdsM/story.html.

Conclusion

1. Nancy Gibbs, "The Choice," *Time*, http://time.com/time-person-of-the-year-2016-donald-trump-choice/?iid=toc.

2. Donald J. Trump (@realDonaldTrump), "Thank you to Time Magazine and Financial Times for naming me 'Person of the Year'—a great honor!" Twitter, December 15, 2016, https://twitter.com/realdonaldtrump/status/809384826193276928.

3. Eun Kyung Kim, "TIME Person of the Year for 2016 Is President-Elect Donald Trump," *Today*, December 7, 2016, https://www.today.com/news/president-elect-donald-trump-time-person-year-2016-t105684. Trump thought that once he became president, he'd be able to unite the nation, and he told Lauer that he thought "putting 'divided' is snarky." In

2017 *Time* named "the silence breakers"—people who had spoken out against sexual harassment as part of the #MeToo movement. Trump tweeted in response, "Time Magazine called to say that I was PROBABLY going to be named 'Man (Person) of the Year,' like last year, but I would have to agree to an interview and a major photoshoot. I said probably is no good and took a pass. Thanks anyway!" Donald J. Trump (@realDonaldTrump), Twitter, November 24, 2017, https://twitter.com/realDonaldTrump/status/934189999045693441.

4. Max Lerner, *Ideas Are Weapons: The History and Uses of Ideas* (New York: Viking Press, 1939), p. 10.

5. Jason Stanley. *How Fascism Works: The Politics of Us and Them* (New York: Random House, 2018); Timothy Snyder, *On Tyranny: Twenty Lessons from the Twentieth Century* (New York: Tim Duggan Books, 2017).

6. Steven Levitsky and Daniel Ziblatt, *How Democracies Die: What History Reveals about Our Future* (London: Viking, 2018), 23.

7. Levitsky and Ziblatt, *How Democracies Die*, 23.

8. Levitsky and Ziblatt, *How Democracies Die*, 24.

9. Levitsky and Ziblatt, *How Democracies Die*, 24.

10. Levitsky and Ziblatt, *How Democracies Die*, 98.

11. William Norwood Brigance, "Demagogues, 'Good' People, and Teachers of Speech," *The Speech Teacher* 1, no. 3 (September 1952), https://doi.org/10.1080/03634525209376553.

12. Sigmund Neumann, "The Rule of the Demagogue," *American Sociological Review*, 3, no. 4 (August 1938): 487–98, 492.

13. Sigmund Neumann explained this in the 1938 *American Sociological Review*, 497.

14. With sincere apologies to Rosa Eberly, who knows that we ought not to think this way at all and that metaphors matter. See her *Citizen Critics: Literary Public Spheres* (University of Illinois Press, 2002).

15. Kenneth Burke, "The Rhetoric of Hitler's Battle," *The Philosophy of Literary Form: Studies in Symbolic Action* (New York: Vintage Books, 1957), 225–26.

16. Jennifer Mercieca, "Ignoring the President," from *Columns to Characters* (College Station: Texas A&M University Press, 2017), 206–230.

17. James Poniewozik, *Audience of One: Donald Trump, Television, and the Fracturing of America* (New York: Liveright Publishing, 2019).

18. Jennifer Mercieca, "The Greatest Story Ever Told about Hyperbole, Humbug, and P. T. Barnum!" *Zocalo Public Square*, October 27, 2017, https://www.zocalopublicsquare.org/2017/10/27/greatest-story-ever-told-hyperbole-humbug-p-t-barnum/ideas/essay/.

19. *Meet the Press*, NBC video, 17:19, January 10, 2016, https://archive.org/details/KNTV_20160110_160000_Meet_the_Press/start/203/end/1242?q=barnum.

20. Jeffrey M. Berry and Sarah Sobieraj, *The Outrage Industry: Political Opinion Media and the New Incivility* (Oxford: Oxford University Press, 2016).

21. "Trolling," Know Your Meme, accessed April 15, 2019, https://knowyourmeme. com/memes/cultures/trolling; Evita March, "'Don't Feed the Trolls' Really Is Good Advice— Here's the Evidence," *The Conversation*, October 6, 2016, https://theconversation.com/dont-feed-the-trolls-really-is-good-advice-heres-the-evidence-63657.

22. Max Horkheimer and Theodor W. Adorno, *Dialectic of Enlightenment*, ed. Gunze-lin Noerr, trans. Edmund Jephcott (Stanford: Stanford University Press, 2002).

23. Max Lerner, *It's Later Than You Think: The Need for Militant Democracy* (New York: Viking Press, 1939), 109–12.

Index